A Special Issue of
Cognitive Neuropsychology

The Multiple Functions of Sensory-Motor Representations

Edited by

Raffaella I. Rumiati
Scuola Internazionale Superiore di Studi Avanzati (SISSA), Trieste, Italy

and

Alfonso Caramazza
Harvard University, Cambridge, MA, USA

Routledge
Taylor & Francis Group
LONDON AND NEW YORK

First published 2005 by Psychology Press Ltd

Published 2018 by Routledge
2 Park Square, Milton Park, Abingdon, Oxon, OX14 4RN
52 Vanderbilt Avenue, New York, NY 10017

First issued in paperback 2018

Routledge is an imprint of the Taylor & Francis Group, an informa business

British Library Cataloguing in Publication Data
A catalogue record for this book is available from the British Library

This book is also a special issue of the journal *Cognitive Neuropsychology* and forms Issues 3 and 4 of Volume 22 (2005).

Cover by Hybert Design, Waltham St Lawrence, Berkshire, UK
Typeset by Techset Composition Limited, Salisbury, Wiltshire, UK

ISBN 13: 978-1-138-87801-3 (pbk)
ISBN 13: 978-1-84169-971-4 (hbk)
ISSN 0272–4987

COGNITIVE NEUROPSYCHOLOGY

Volume 22 Issue 3/4 May–June 2005

Special issue: The multiple functions of sensory-motor representations

Guest editors: Raffaella I. Rumiati and Alfonso Caramazza

Contents

COGNITIVE NEUROPSYCHOLOGY, 2005, 22 (3/4), 259–261

THE MULTIPLE FUNCTIONS OF SENSORY-MOTOR REPRESENTATIONS: AN INTRODUCTION

Raffaella Ida Rumiati
Scuola Internazionale Superiore di Studi Avanzati (SISSA), Trieste, Italy
Alfonso Caramazza
Harvard University, Cambridge, MA, USA

The papers in this issue consider the role of sensory-motor processes and their neural structures in higher cognitive functions such as visual and motor imagery, iconic memory, temporal judgement, mental rotation, and the representation of object and action concepts. The papers draw on a range of methodologies, from computational modelling to behavioural studies of brain-damaged subjects, to fMRI, TMS, and ERP studies with normal subjects, and they present various theoretical perspectives. What unites them is the explicit effort to understand how sensory-motor processes might be integrated into cognitive theory.

Damage to a particular area of the brain can result in complex deficits involving different types of cognitive domains. For example, damage to Broca's area has been variously associated with deficits in syntactic processing, morphological processing, selecting among potential responses, short-term memory, procedural memory, sequencing, spoken and written word production, verb and preposition semantics, and motor imitation among others. It is hard to imagine what common cognitive mechanism might underlie this varied set of processes.

Even more dramatic differences are found in the neuroimaging literature, where it is routinely reported that the same brain area is activated by radically different tasks, which supposedly implicate distinct cognitive operations and mechanisms. For example, Price and Friston (2005 this issue) note that the left posterior lateral fusiform (PLF) area has been implicated in reading, picture categorisation, repetition priming of words and pictures, colour naming, categorisation of Heider-Simmel stimuli, tactile object recognition, and semantic and phonological decisions on auditory words. This situation seems to undermine the classical view of a one-to-one mapping between cognitive mechanism and brain region and has stimulated anew the old debate between localisationist and non-localisationist theories of the functional organisation of the brain. However, the putative many-cognitive-processes-to-one-brain-region result has also encouraged a different type of theorising from the classical view of cognition, which was based primarily on behavioural studies with normal subjects. New approaches emphasise a different way of carving cognition at its joints. For example, Price and Friston (2005 this issue) argue for the development of new theories of cognitive processing that explicitly incorporate the noted variability in brain-cognition mapping. In the case of the left PLF it could be proposed that its function is some sort of sensory-motor integration and that it participates in a network that gives specificity to this general function. The idea that a network approach is the best way to proceed for

Correspondence should be addressed to Alfonso Caramazza, Department of Psychology, William James Hall, Harvard University, 33 Kirkland Street, Cambridge, MA, USA (Email: caramazz@fas.harvard.edu).

understanding brain-function relations is also the argument developed from a computational perspective by Treves (2005 this issue) and experimentally by Manjaly, Marshall, Stephan, Gurd, Zilles, and Fink (2005 this issue). Similarly, Alexander, Cowey and Walsh (2005 this issue) suggest a role of the parietal cortex in time perception as part of a larger network including motor and supplementary motor areas, prefrontal cortex, and the cerebellum. And, Keysers, Xiao, Földiák, and Perrett (2005 this issue) present evidence implicating the superior temporal sulcus as part of a network involved in iconic memory.

The observation that an area whose putative function is one type (e.g., motor) is also activated (or implicated) in the processing of a different cognitive function (e.g., visual recognition) has stimulated debate on another long-standing issue: the role of motor processes in perception and cognition. Perhaps the best known case of a motor theory of perception is the one proposed by Liberman and colleagues (Liberman, Cooper, Shankweiler, & Studdert-Kennedy, 1967) for speech perception. In recent years, the general issue of a motor basis for certain cognitive processes has regained prominence in the context of "simulationist" theories of cognition, stimulated in part by the discovery of mirror neurons (for a review of the empirical evidence, see Rizzolatti, Fogassi, & Gallese, 2001). Theories of this type assume that perceptual and conceptual processing is dependent on the reactivation of sensory-motor information.

A number of the papers in this issue articulate "simulationist-type" theories of cognitive processes on the basis of results showing activation of sensory-motor areas in the context of cognitive tasks. For example, Kosslyn (2005 this issue) points to the activation of primary visual cortex during imagery tasks to argue for a direct role of low-level visual processes in imagery. Tomasino, Borroni, Isaja, and Rumiati (2005 this issue) point to the disruptive influence of TMS applied to area M1 on mental rotation of hand stimuli to argue for a role of motor processes in a visual-cognitive task. Analogous arguments are made for the role of sensory-motor processes in cognitive operations in the papers by van Schie, Wijers, Mars, Benjamins, and Stowe (2005 this issue), Tsakiris and Haggard (2005 this issue), Farnè, Bonifazi, and Làdavas (2005 this issue), and Bekkering, Brass, Woschina, and Jacobs (2005 this issue), while Sebanz, Knoblich, Stumpf, and Prinz (2005 this issue)—though recognising the important role of sensory-motor processes—do not seem to be committed to a simulationist approach to higher cognitive processing.

Finally, Gallese and Lakoff (2005 this issue) propose the boldest simulationist theory of cognition yet. They argue that all conceptual knowledge is "embodied" and that therefore sensory-motor representations are at the core of all cognitive operations. However, Mahon and Caramazza (2005 this issue) discuss neuropsychological evidence showing that the recognition of actions and understanding of objects do not depend necessarily on the ability to produce object-associated actions. The implication of this analysis is that the precise role of the interaction between motor processes and the understanding of actions and objects is in need of further clarification.

REFERENCES

Alexander, I., Cowey, A., & Walsh, V. (2005). The right parietal cortex and time perception: Back to Critchley and the Zeitraffer phenomenon. *Cognitive Neuropsychology*, *22*, 306–315.

Bekkering, H., Brass, M., Woschina, S., & Jacobs, A. M. (2005). Goal-directed imitation in patients with ideomotor apraxia. *Cognitive Neuropsychology*, *22*, 419–432.

Farnè, A., Bonifazi, S., & Làdavas, E. (2005). The role played by tool-use and tool-length on the plastic elongation of peri-hand space: A single case study. *Cognitive Neuropsychology*, *22*, 408–418.

Gallese, V., & Lakoff, G. (2005). The brain's concepts: The role of the sensory-motor system in conceptual knowledge. *Cognitive Neuropsychology*, *22*, 455–479.

Keysers, C., Xiao, D.-K., Földiák, P., & Perrett, D. I. (2005). Out of sight but not out of mind: The neuropsychology of iconic memory in the superior temporal sulcus. *Cognitive Neuropsychology*, *22*, 316–332.

Kosslyn, S. M. (2005). Mental images and the brain. *Cognitive Neuropsychology*, *22*, 333–347.

Liberman, A. M., Cooper, F. S., Shankweiler, D. P., & Studdert-Kennedy, M. (1967). Perception of the speech code. *Psychological Review*, *74*, 431–461.

Mahon, B. Z., & Caramazza, A. (2005). The orchestration of the sensory-motor systems: Clues from neuropsychology. *Cognitive Neuropsychology*, *22*, 480–494.

Manjaly, Z. M., Marshall, J. C., Stephan, K. E., Gurd, J. M., Zilles, K., & Fink, G. R. (2005). Context-dependent interactions of left posterior inferior frontal gyrus in a local visual search task unrelated to language. *Cognitive Neuropsychology*, *22*, 292–305.

Price, C. J., & Friston, K. J. (2005). Functional ontologies for cognition: The systematic definition of structure and function. *Cognitive Neuropsychology*, *22*, 262–275.

Rizzolatti, G., Fogassi, L., & Gallese, V. (2001). Neurophysiological mechanisms underlying the understanding and imitation of action. *Nature Review Neuroscience*, *2*, 661–670.

Sebanz, N., Knoblich, G., Stumpf, L., & Prinz, W. (2005). Far from action-blind: Representations of others' actions in individuals with autism. *Cognitive Neuropsychology*, *22*, 433–454.

Tomasino, B., Borroni, P., Isaja, A., & Rumiati, R. I. (2005). The role of the primary motor cortex in mental rotation: A TMS study. *Cognitive Neuropsychology*, *22*, 348–363.

Treves, A. (2005). Frontal latching networks: A possible neural basis for infinite recursion. *Cognitive Neuropsychology*, *22*, 276–291.

Tsakiris, M., & Haggard, P. (2005). Experimenting with the acting self. *Cognitive Neuropsychology*, *22*, 387–407.

van Schie, H. T., Wijers, A. A., Mars, R. B., Benjamins, J. S., & Stowe, L. A. (2005). Processing of visual semantic information to concrete words: Temporal dynamics and neural mechanisms indicated by event-related brain potentials. *Cognitive Neuropsychology*, *22*, 364–386.

COGNITIVE NEUROPSYCHOLOGY, 2005, 22 (3/4), 262–275

FUNCTIONAL ONTOLOGIES FOR COGNITION: THE SYSTEMATIC DEFINITION OF STRUCTURE AND FUNCTION

Cathy J. Price and Karl J. Friston
Institute of Neurology, London, UK

Cognitive scientists have traditionally specified the functional components of cognitive skills on the basis of behavioural studies of normal and neurologically impaired subjects. The results of functional imaging studies are challenging these classical models because there is a high degree of overlap among the neural systems activated by tasks that share no cognitive components. This suggests that a given neuronal structure can perform multiple functions that depend on the areas with which it interacts. However, there will be a limited range of functions that an area can perform given that its anatomical (intrinsic and extrinsic) connectivity is fixed. Assigning labels that encompass the operations that each area performs should enable a task to be re-described in terms of the functions of the areas activated. In other words, function should predict the structure and conversely structure should predict function. These systematic descriptions are referred to as ontologies. We argue that a systematic ontology for cognition would facilitate the integration of cognitive and anatomical models and organise the cognitive components of diverse tasks into a single framework. These points are illustrated with cognitive and anatomical models of reading and object recognition.

INTRODUCTION

Functional neuroimaging is now widely used to identify the neural correlates of cognitive processes. In initial applications of this technique, the experimental design and interpretation of the results were based on cognitive models that have been established on the basis of a long history of behavioural experiments with normal and neurologically impaired subjects. The simplest interpretation of functional neuroimaging data would be a one-to-one mapping between a cognitive process and an anatomical region. However, the brain clearly does not and cannot operate in this fashion, not least because the number of hypothesised cognitive processes exceeds the number of brain regions supporting them. Functional neuroimaging data preclude a one-to-one mapping in two ways. First, attempts to manipulate a "single" cognitive process (e.g., semantics) often elicit a distributed pattern of activation over many areas (i.e., a one-to-many mapping from function to structure). Second, the same brain region, or set of regions, may be activated by tasks with different cognitive processes (i.e., a many-to-one mapping). In short, there is a many-to-many mapping between cognitive functions and anatomical regions, with a range of cognitive processes emerging from different patterns of activation among a limited number of brain regions (McIntosh, 2000; Mesulam, 1990).

Correspondence should be addressed to Dr Cathy Price, Wellcome Department of Imaging Neuroscience, Institute of Neurology, 12 Queen Square, London WC1N 3BG, UK (Email: c.price@fil.ion.ucl.ac.uk).

As results from functional neuroimaging studies accumulate, the overlap among the neural systems engaged by different tasks is becoming more apparent. In some cases, it might be possible to ascribe a region with a functional label that describes a process common to all the tasks that activate it. The overlap in activations, however, does not generally correspond to the overlap in the cognitive processes hypothesised from behavioural studies. Consequently, we are left with a situation where the functional components of a given task could have two sets of labels: a "cognitive set" that is specified on the basis of behavioural dissociations, and an "anatomical set" that is specified on the basis of the regions that respond to the task. What we need is a systematic definition of structure–function relations whereby structures predict functions and functions predict structures. These systematic descriptions are called ontologies (Lan, Montelione, & Gerstein, 2003). In brief, we will suggest that the advent of functional neuroimaging speaks to a neurobiologicaly informed ontology that is constrained and "boot-strapped" by our increasing knowledge of functional anatomy. Ontologies for cognition will not only unify structure–function relationships, but will also provide a single theoretical framework to describe the functional components of diverse tasks.

The aims of this paper are to demonstrate how the same area can be engaged in more than one function/task and to discuss different levels of description for functional anatomy. Claims that an anatomical area can have multiple functions depend on the precision with which functional imaging techniques can locate and distinguish neuronal responses. Therefore, the first section addresses some of the methodological issues that attend assigning responses to specific neuronal populations. The following section considers different levels of structure–function relationships and the last section discusses some guiding principles for developing ontologies for cognition. We conclude that the hierarchical mapping between any functional ontology and anatomy should be recapitulated by hierarchical patterns of activation evoked by higher level functions. Critically, this recapitulation can, in principle, be used to constrain and guide the construction of cognitive ontologies.

METHODOLOGICAL ISSUES

In this section we review two methodological issues that need to be considered before concluding that an area has an underlying function that accounts for all observed activations. The first is the precision with which functional neuroimaging techniques can locate an area or disambiguate responses of neuronal populations. The second relates to the application of cognitive models to functional imaging studies.

Resolving neuronal populations with functional imaging

Resolving the responses of neuronal populations depends on how accurately the neuroimaging technique can localise activation (i.e., the spatial precision). For example, activation within a prespecified area may be (1) in spatially proximate but functionally independent neuronal populations; or (2) expressed by the same, or highly interconnected, neuronal populations. Spatial precision is not the same as spatial resolution. Spatial resolution reflects the spread of activation underlying the peak and it is well recognised that the intrinsic resolution of fMRI is much higher (<1 mm) than that of PET (>6 mm)—although the final resolution will depend on the spatial smoothing applied to the data. In contrast, the spatial precision (the accuracy of locating the peak) of PET and fMRI are very similar. For a single subject analysis, spatial precision is usually in the order of 2 mm for PET (Mintun, Fox, & Raichle, 1989) and 1–6 mm for fMRI depending on the voxel size (activations within the same voxel cannot be spatially resolved). Individual differences in neuroanatomy, however, mean that spatial precision is greatly reduced when data from several subjects are pooled (as in most functional imaging studies). Thus, two different areas might be resolved, in terms of peak response, when data analysis proceeds at the individual subject level, but not when data are pooled over subjects. For example, Kim, Relkin, Lee, and Hirsh (1997) found that, in subjects who learnt a second language late in life, different regions within Broca's area were activated for the first and second language relative to a baseline condition. The relative position of the first and second language areas, however, varied over subjects in both the caudal-rostral and ventral-dorsal dimensions. In other words, in some subjects the region for the first language lay anterior to that for the second language whereas in others the region for the first language lay posterior to that for the second language. The first and second language areas could therefore only be distinguished when activation was considered at the individual subject level. If data had been pooled over subjects, then the same area might have been identified for both languages.

The ability to distinguish two sources of activation can be further improved by using "neuronal adaptation techniques." This approach is based on the well-characterised effects of stimulus repetition on neuronal and behavioural responses (Henson & Rugg, 2003). In functional imaging experiments, neuronal adaptation is expressed as a response decrease to a target stimulus when the target is preceded (primed) with an identical stimulus (Grill-Spector, Kushnir, Edelman, Avidan, Itzchak, & Malach, 1999). The degree of adaptation depends on the nature of the response and the similarity of the prime to the target. For instance, if neuronal responses to objects are viewpoint dependent, then neuronal adaptation will be greater when the prime is in the same view as the target than when the prime is in a different view. In contrast, if the responses in a region are viewpoint independent, then neuronal adaptation will be the same irrespective of whether the prime and target are in the same or different views. The point here is that neuronal adaptation can be used to distinguish different neuronal populations, even if they are spatially overlapping (i.e., in the same area). Thus, if the same neuronal population responded to pictures of objects and their written names, then neuronal adaptation within modality (word followed by word) would be similar to adaptation between modality (word followed by picture). In contrast, if words and pictures were processed in the same area but in different neuronal populations, then neuronal adaptation within modality would be greater than adaptation between modality. In other words, differential effects of adaptation could distinguish word and picture responses even if the direct comparison of word and object activation did not reveal a difference.

In summary, asserting that different functions activate the same area depends critically on the precision with which activation is located. For PET and fMRI, spatial precision can be improved by examining data at the individual subject level and using designs that harness neuronal adaptation to isolate functional populations.

Cognitive models for behavioural and functional imaging studies

Mapping function to anatomy depends on a clear understanding of the cognitive processes that are being tapped by the experimental paradigm. Cognitive models for behavioural experiments usually only specify the cognitive components that are necessary for a particular task. Functional imaging, in contrast, detects activation that may be incidental to task requirements—i.e., evoked by a stimulus even when it is not necessary for the task. For example, a traditional cognitive model for naming pictures of tools might include: visual processes, object perception, semantic processing, phonological retrieval, and articulation. Semantic processing might also be segregated into perceptual and functional knowledge, where functional knowledge includes the type of actions that are used for tools. Traditional cognitive models do not, however, usually include "motor processing for hand movements" as this is not necessary for naming the tools, but if "motor processing for hand movements" was implicitly activated in response to seeing a tool, then brain areas involved in preparation of hand movements might be activated automatically. Interpretation of the activations solely on the basis of the cognitive model would be forced to attribute the "hand areas" with a cognitive process that was in the model (e.g., phonological processing). The fallacy of this interpretation could only be disclosed in the context of a fuller understanding of the functional anatomy underlying different types of motor processing. The point here is that it might be easy to ascribe a brain area a given function, but the validity of the functional label depends on the validity and scope of the cognitive model applied. This, in turn, depends on whether the model includes cognitive processes that are both necessary for the task and invoked incidentally. Furthermore, even if the cognitive model is fully specified, inferring that an area is involved in a function of interest is not the same as inferring that the area is specific to that function. To infer functional specificity requires a demonstration that an area is activated only by tasks that engage its function and no others.

LEVELS OF STRUCTURE–FUNCTION DESCRIPTIONS

The main aim of this paper is to consider whether a brain region can have more than one function. The answer can be either *yes* or *no* because it depends on the definition of a function and the level at which the structure–function relationship is described. In the following, we consider two questions that are posed to investigate structure–function relationships: (1) What are the neural correlates of a cognitive function? and (2) What is the function that best explains the responses of a brain region? To illustrate these approaches, we consider the paradigms that activate an area in the left posterior lateral fusiform (PLF).

Most functional imaging studies of cognitive function aim to find the neural correlates of a cognitive operation rather than trying to find a function that best predicts regional responses. Consequently, since most experimenters focus on one type of cognitive task, different investigators assign different labels to the same area. For example, studies of reading refer to a left posterior lateral fusiform region as the "visual word form area—VWFA" (Cohen et al., 2000). Studies of category-specific object processing refer to the same area as being sensitive to the visual attributes of animals (Martin & Chao, 2001); and Amedi and colleagues (Amedi, Jacobson, Hendler, Malach, & Zohary, 2002) call this area "the lateral occipital tactile-visual region" (LOtv). Thus, this area appears to have more than one function. Is this because there are two or more different areas in close proximity? Or is there one function that can account for all activations and, if so, how should this area be labelled? To address these questions, we need to compare the exact location of the activations. How close are the activations in the left lateral fusiform for words and objects, are they really the same, or is there a consistent relationship? In order to address these questions, we need to change the focus of the question from "What are the neural correlates of a cognitive operation?" to "What is the function associated with activation of a brain region?" To answer the latter question, we need to examine the range of conditions under which an area responds.

Table 1 reports the coordinates from a collection of studies that have all reported activation in the left posterior lateral fusiform. Part (a) shows the inter-study and inter-subject variability in the activations reported for reading. Part (b) includes studies when subjects are asked to name or make actions to pictures of real and nonsense objects. Part (c) illustrates similar effects of neuronal adaptation for repetition priming of written words and pictures of objects. Part (d) illustrates that activation is not limited to the presence of visual form but is also observed when subjects name colours relative to saying "OK" to the same stimuli; and for simple shapes that move interactively relative to random movements of the same shapes. Part (e) illustrates that responses are not dependent on visual input because activation has also been reported in studies of tactile processing when subjects were not able to see the stimulus. Likewise, part (f) includes studies that have shown left posterior lateral fusiform activation in response to semantic or phonological decisions on auditory words. Examination of the activation foci for this range of paradigms reveals that the variability between these studies is no greater than the variability between reading activations for individual subjects (see part a). Thus, there is no evidence that the activations for any of these paradigms come from distinct neuronal populations. This would require analysis of individual subjects performing a range of different tasks (see previous section).

If the same left lateral fusiform area is involved in many different functions, what is its appropriate label? Labels such as "visual word form area" are not particularly useful because they only indicate that the area is involved in the function but

Table 1. *Activations reported in left posterior lateral fusiform area*[a]

Reference		*Activation > Baseline*	*Coordinates*	*Voxel size*
		(a) Reading written words		
Cohen et al., 2000			−42, −57, −6	3 mm
Cohen et al., 2000			−43, −54, −12	3 mm
Cohen et al., 2002:	Sub. 1	View words > chequerboards	−42, −60, −15	5 mm
	Sub. 2	View words > chequerboards	−42, −63, −21	5 mm
	Sub. 3	View words > chequerboards	−51, −63, −12	5 mm
	Sub. 4	View words > chequerboards	−36, −48, −18	5 mm
	Sub. 5	View words > chequerboards	−36, −54, −18	5 mm
	Sub. 6	View words > chequerboards	−48, −57, −9	5 mm
	Sub. 7	View words > chequerboards	−42, −51, −15	5 mm
	Mean	**View words > chequerboards**	**−42, −57, −15**	5 mm
Brunswick et al., 1998		Reading aloud > Rest	−42, −56, −16	3 mm
		(b) Objects and nonobjects		
Bookheimer et al., 1995		Picture naming > View random lines	−42, −58, −20	3 mm
Murtha et al., 1999		Picture naming > View plus signs	−44, −59, −21	5 mm
Moore and Price, 1999		Picture naming > Say OK—same stimuli	−42, −54, −14	3 mm
Moore and Price, 1999		Picture naming > Reading object names	−42, −60, −14	3 mm
Chao et al., 1999		View pictures of animals > tools	−40, −59, −10	5 mm
VanTurennout et al., 2000		View nonobjects > Visual noise	−38, −56, −20	5 mm
Phillips et al., 2002		Action dec. to objects > Nonobjects	−40, −58, −12	3 mm
Phillips et al., 2002		Actions dec. > Size dec. to nonobjects	−46, −56, −14	3 mm
		(c) Visual priming		
Van Turennout et al., 2000		Picture name: Unprimed > primed	−44, −54, −12	5 mm
Dehaene et al., 2001		Words sem. dec.: Unprimed > primed	−44, −52, −20	5 mm
		(d) Other visual discrimination		
Price et al., 1996		Colour patches: Name > say "OK"	−42, −54, −14	3 mm
Castelli et al., 2002		Moving shapes: Interactive > random	−46, −60, −10	3 mm
		(e) Tactile words/objects (no visual input)		
Buchel et al., 1998		Feature dec. braille words > nonwords	−46, −56, −14	3 mm
Amedi et al., 2002		Sem. dec. Objects > textures	−47, −62, −10	5 mm
		(f) Auditory words (no visual input)		
Booth et al., 2002a, 2002b		Rhyming dec. words > pitch dec.—noise	−45, −60, −18	4 mm
Thompson-Schill et al., 1999		Sem. dec. object names > reversed words	−41, −53, −11	5 mm
Mellet et al., 1998		Imagine object > rest	−48, −60, −14	–

[a] Coordinates according to Talairach and Tournoux (1988).

this is not the same as identifying the role the area plays in that function. Therefore, task-specific labels of this sort can not predict the cause of activation in other tasks. For example, why is left posterior fusiform activation observed when subjects are required to make action decisions in response to pictures of unfamiliar objects relative to perceptual judgments on the same stimuli (Phillips, Humphreys, Noppeney, & Price, 2002; Price & Devlin, 2003)? After all, action decisions in response to nonobjects do not require visual word form, animal, or object representations. To explain why we see activation in this region during action decisions, we need an alternative functional label with predictive validity that generalises beyond the cognitive domain studied. In other words, given that the same area is also activated by reading and object recognition, it would be preferable to use a functional label that explains activation in other contexts (see Table 1). In short, the most useful functional labels are those that explain and predict how an area responds in different contexts.

What functional label would explain the causal basis of left posterior lateral fusiform activation? Figure 1 summarises the conditions under which this area responds. Responses are strongest when a motor response (name or action) is retrieved from sensory cues; and this effect is observed irrespective of stimulus modality. In other words, it appears to function as a sensorimotor integration area. This does not exclude the possibility that there are other sensorimotor areas that integrate different types of inputs and outputs. Nor does it exclude the possibility that within the left posterior lateral fusiform, there are different neuronal populations that integrate different types of information. For example, there may be different neuronal populations for integrating visual objects with the corresponding hand movements (Phillips et al., 2002), and for integrating tactile inputs with speech output (Buchel, Price, & Friston, 1998). On the other hand it is also possible that the same neuronal populations integrate both visual and tactile information with either hand or mouth responses. In this case, the type of sensorimotor integration would depend on which regions were sending signals to the posterior lateral fusiform. For example, when visual–hand responses are required, there might be bottom-up inputs for visual cortex and top-down inputs from the motor regions for the hand. In contrast, when tactile–speech responses are required, there might be bottom-up inputs from parietal cortex, and top-down inputs from articulation regions.

If the left posterior lateral fusiform area is a sensorimotor area, some may wonder where the visual word form area is. The answer is that there is no evidence for a brain area that is specifically dedicated to visual word form processing. Instead, visual word form processing is likely to result from

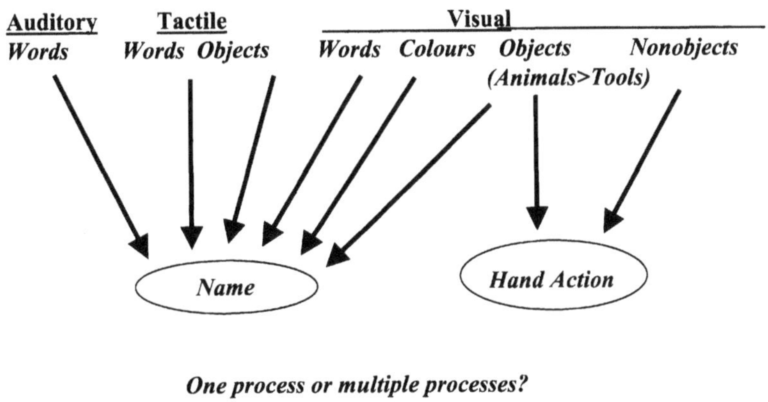

Figure 1. *Examples of some of the conditions that activate the left posterior lateral fusiform. The top row corresponds to stimulus type. The bottom row corresponds to task. The arrows represent some of the stimulus-response computations that activate the left posterior lateral fusiform.*

the pattern of activation in multiple regions that each serve many different functions. For example, the left posterior lateral fusiform area plays a role in visual word form processing when the stimuli are words, the task is reading, and there is coactivation in occipital, temporal, and frontal areas. In contrast, the same area plays a role in action retrieval when the stimuli are novel objects, the task is manipulation, and there is coactivation in occipital parietal and motor regions. Thus, at one level of the description, the area has multiple functions that are determined by the regions that it coactivates with, whereas at another level, the area can be assigned a single function—to integrate sensory cues with motor output.

To help clarify the importance of interactions with other areas, consider the structure–function relationships that might be used to describe the role of the forefinger. At one level, the forefinger can be attributed multiple and diverse functions including "piano playing," "typing," "scratching," "pinching," "feeding." At a second level, these functions could be classified so as to distinguish them from those that the forefinger cannot perform—such as "digestion," "thinking," or "walking." The functions of the forefinger could, for example, be categorised as "interactions between body and environment" or "hand actions." At a third level of description, however, the forefinger can only do one thing—"bend" and "straighten." Its role in other tasks is therefore entirely dependent on what the other fingers and thumbs are doing and what environmental context they are in—scratching requires only one finger whereas pinching requires the opposition of the finger and thumb. Likewise, the function of a neuron or neuronal population depends on its interactions with other neurons. At one level of description, a neuron can only do one thing—fire. The firing will stimulate activation in a fixed set of output regions. Therefore, there will be a limited range of functions that an area can perform. However, at another level of description, the consequence of the firing will depend on which neuronal populations (input regions) caused the firing, and which neuronal populations send concurrent signals to the output regions. In this sense, a neuron participates in multiple functions. Likewise, the type of sensorimotor integration provided by the left posterior lateral fusiform area will depend on the inputs to this region (visual, auditory, tactile) and the task (naming, hand action) being performed.

In summary, structure–function relationships can be described at multiple levels. Each level may be appropriate in a different context. Nevertheless, we argue that it is more useful to label a region with a function that explains all patterns of activation. As an example, we have described the range of tasks that the posterior lateral fusiform is engaged by, and proposed that the common denominator is a role in sensorimotor integration. Understandably, a sensorimotor integration label may not be particularly attractive to cognitive psychologists as it does not correspond to any of the components hypothesised to be involved in reading or object processing. Nevertheless, it does provide a prediction about the conditions under which the left posterior lateral fusiform area responds. In this sense the sensorimotor label is more useful than task-specific labels.

Attempts to find functional labels that explain the cause of activation focuses our questions about functional attribution on what the area is important or necessary for. Furthermore, it calls into question our understanding of the cognitive components involved in a task. For example, we have argued that appreciating the range of tasks that elicit left lateral fusiform activation forces us to re-evaluate the cognitive model of reading. In some cases, this might require the inclusion of cognitive components that were not there previously (e.g., a region/component specialised for sensory-motor integration). In other cases, it might require that a cognitive component was replaced or removed. For example, there does not appear to be an area that is specialised for orthography or visual word forms—instead, visual word form processing may arise from the interactions among early visual and later reading stages. Finding the range of attributes or dimensions that determine responses in a given area will clearly require an enormous amount of empirical study and cannot be covered by a handful of language studies predicated on traditional cognitive models. In the long term, however, a new ontology of this sort will enable cognitive and anatomical models to converge and be built in a mutually consistent way.

WHAT ARE THE GUIDING PRINCIPLES FOR FUNCTIONAL ONTOLOGIES

In this section we consider the nature of structure–function and function–structure mappings and how they can be established empirically. Although it may seem an odd place to start, we will introduce ontologies though their use in proteomics. There are many homologies between functional genomics and functional anatomy and the problems faced in both these fields. After the successes of genome sequencing the focus of molecular and cell biology has "shifted from DNA to RNA and proteins and the main challenge for bio-informatics is to integrate the ever growing amount of data to fully ascribe the biological role of proteins, cells, and ultimately organisms" (Lan et al., 2003). This calls for the development of ontologies that conceptualise and represent key information on proteins that can scale to the genomic level and be sufficiently standardised to support data mining. By analogy, cognitive neuroscience aims to ascribe the cognitive role of cortical areas and neuronal structures. Indeed, current excitement about databasing, and related neuroinformatic challenges in imaging neuroscience, reflects the need to organise and relate information from cognitive science, functional neuroimaging, and neuropsychology, (http://www.fmridc.org). The development of ontologies in structural genomics and functional proteomics is somewhat more advanced than in cognitive neuroscience (e.g., the hierarchical representations adopted by Structural Classification of Proteins Database [SCOP]; http://scop.mrclmb.cam.ac.uk/scop, Hubbard, Alley, Brenner, Murzin, & Chothia, 1999, and the Gene Ontology [GO], Ashburner et al., 2000). Figure 2 shows a simplified functional ontology based on SCOP. Note that the hierarchy indicates the functions at a particular level of description, but does not encode the order or mechanisms that might be implemented. A putative functional ontology for cognitive function is provided, by analogy, below (this and the following ontologies are just schematics and should not be taken too seriously). In proteomics the construction of ontologies is informed by reference to structure, biological function, genetic encoding and protein-protein interactions. What are the guiding principles for ontologies of cognitive function?

We will adopt the common sense position that the construction of cognitive ontologies should integrate structural and functional information. In other words, the functional ontology should "rationalise" structure-function relationships, such that a given function predicts the brain structures engaged and the architecture of the ontology is predicted by neuronal infrastructure. Again we can take our lead from proteomics, in which protein–protein interactions can inform hierarchical ontologies of function. In terms of cognitive anatomy, it is the functional interactions (i.e., the effective connectivity) rather than the structural anatomical connections themselves that are important for the ontology. These functional interactions are usually inferred by coactivation in different brain regions. The key insight afforded by this observation is that relationships between activations should be reflected in the cognitive ontology. For example, if two areas do not coactivate then they should not be hierarchically linked in the ontology. In contrast, coactivation among all hierarchically subordinate areas should be observed if the functional ontology is properly specified. This principle is illustrated in Figure 3. If the functional ontology is properly specified, then a task that engages process 2 should engage all the cortical areas in its hierarchically subordinate processes (i.e., BA39, V5, V3, and V1). This perspective affords a way of assessing how "good" an ontology is. A good ontology will correctly predict activation patterns over all levels of task analysis. A poorly constructed ontology will give prediction errors that can be assessed empirically and used to refine the ontology (see below). Before returning to the single word reading example of the previous section we will consider briefly the nature of structure–function mappings.

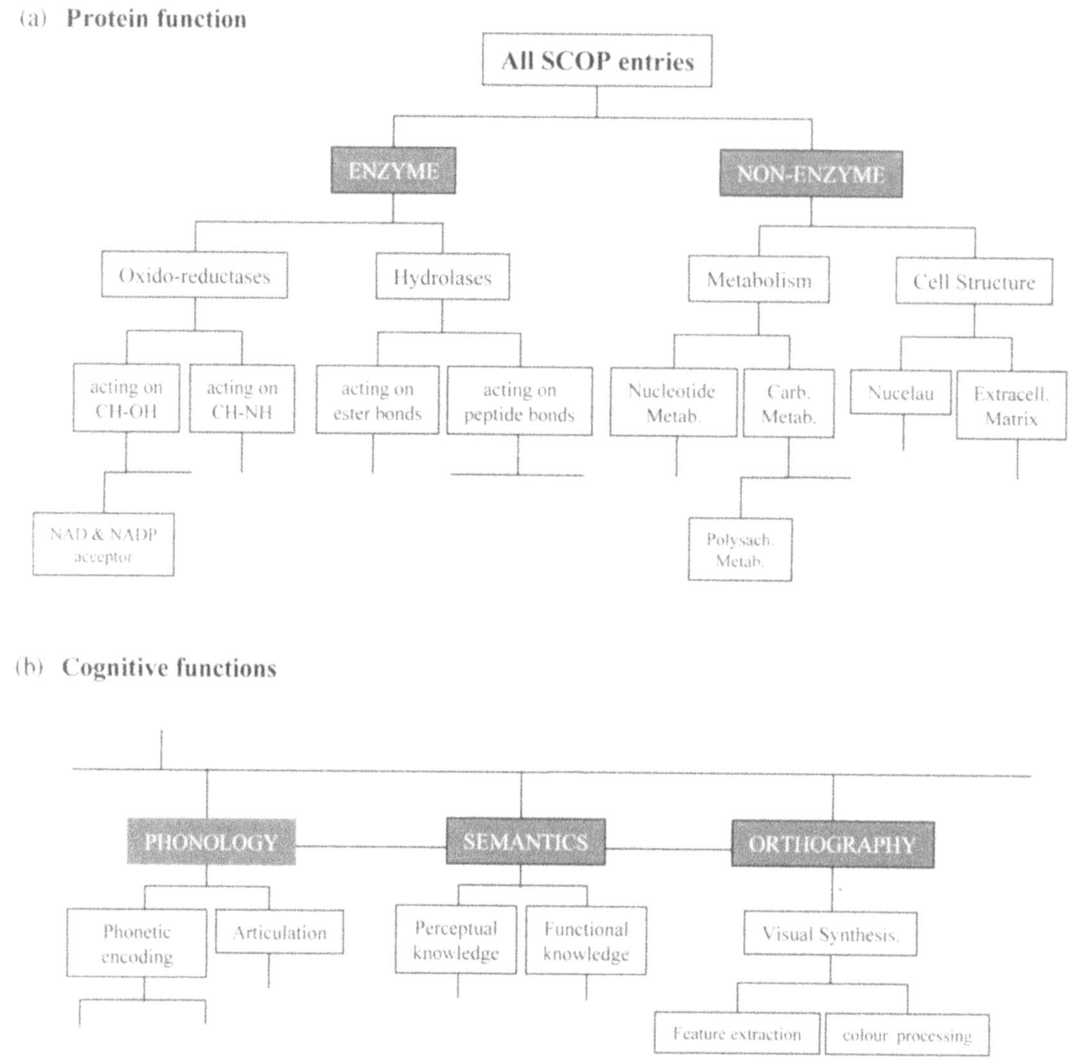

Figure 2. *Functional ontologies for Genes and Cognition. (a) A simplified ontology based on SCOP. (b) A putative functional ontology for cognitive function.*

Figure 3 (opposite). *Structure–function mappings. (a) A putative functional ontology illustrating the integration of cognitive processes and anatomical region. The grey arrows from cognitive process to brain region indicate the areas that might be engaged by each process. The dotted arrows from brain region to cognitive process indicate where performance might be impaired following damage. BA = Brodmann area. V = Visual area. STS = superior temporal sulcus. IT = Inferior temporal. (b) If the ontology above is correct, then a particular sub-process should activate its associated areas. In the right hand example, process 2 engages V1, V3, V5 (subprocess 2b), and BA39 (all highlighted black).*

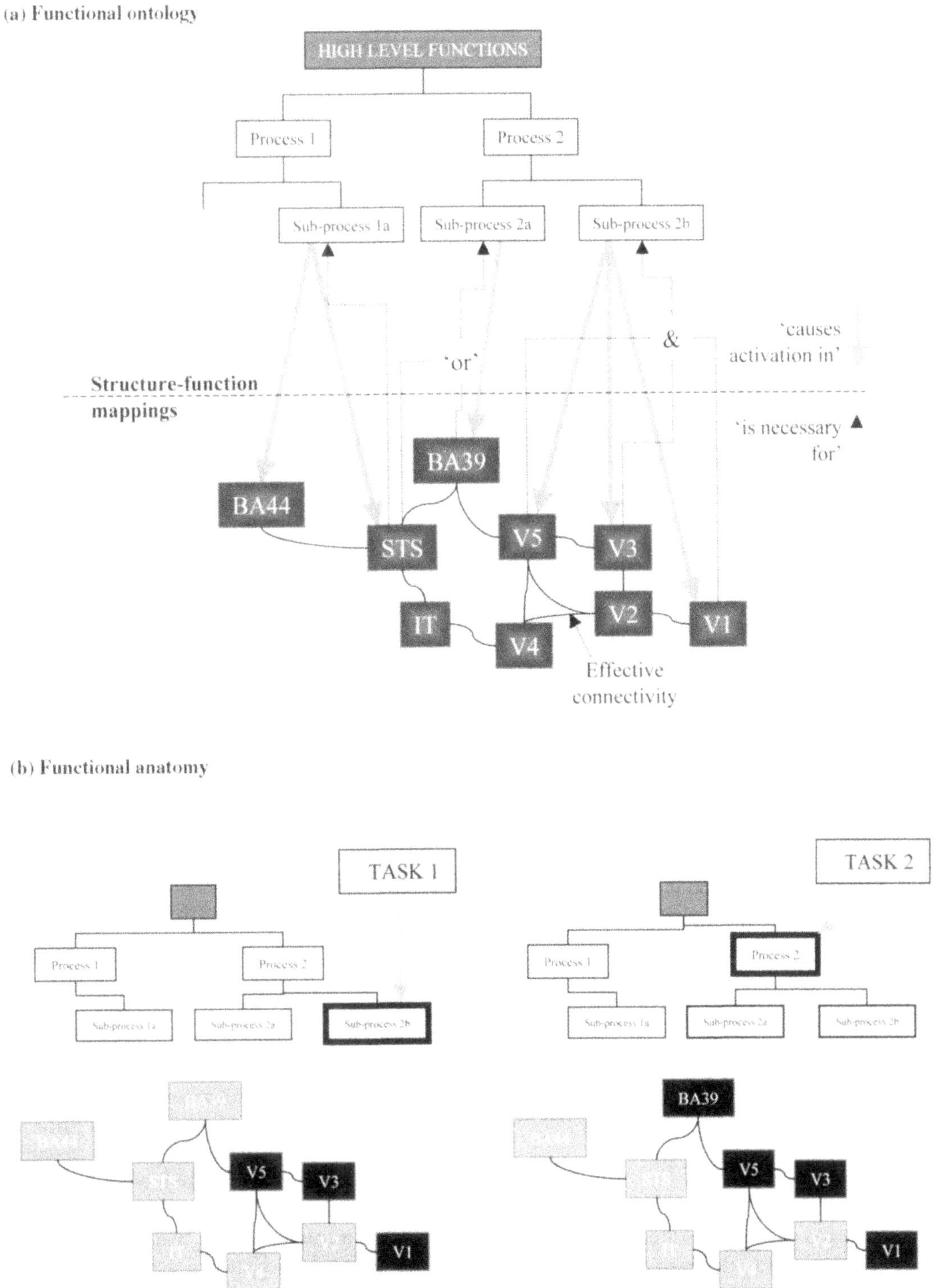
(a) Functional ontology
HIGH LEVEL FUNCTIONS
Process 1
Process 2
Sub-process 1a
Sub-process 2a
Sub-process 2b
'or'
&
'causes activation in'
Structure-function mappings
'is necessary for'
BA39
BA44
STS
V5
V3
IT
V2
V1
V4
Effective connectivity
(b) Functional anatomy
TASK 1
TASK 2
Process 1
Process 2
V5
V3
V1
BA39

Structure–function mappings

Clearly the construction of functional ontologies that are constrained by functional anatomy (see Figure 3) rests upon the definition of a structure–function mapping. These mappings are central to the cognitive neuroscience endeavour and require careful definition. A simple way to classify mapping is in terms of operational characterisation: There are a number of important concepts embedded in the schematic of Figure 3(a), which we will now describe briefly. First, the mappings from structure to function and function to structure are not symmetrical. These directed mappings correspond to the two most commonly employed ways of measuring structure–function dependencies: Namely, lesion studies that assess the functional deficit following structural damage and functional imaging studies that manipulate function and measure evoked responses (activations) in brain structures. These two approaches can be summarised as *is necessary for* (dotted arrows) and *causes activation in* (thick grey arrows). The first (structure–function) mapping is investigated by neuropsychology and, more recently, transient lesions using TMS (transmagnetic stimulation). The second (function–structure) mapping is used by functional neuroimaging and is usually taken to identify the set of regions that are sufficient for a particular function. For example, in the figure, BA39 is sufficient for subprocess 2a but it is not necessary because STS can also support this function if BA39 is damaged (Price & Friston, 2002). Notice that in Figure 3, the structure–function mapping can be one-to-many and many-to-one, in other words divergent and convergent. The many-to-one aspect represents a degenerate mapping and the one-to-many reflects a simple form of pluripotentiality. Together these constitute the complicated many-to-many function–structure relationships referred to in the introduction.

Single-word reading revisited

In Figure 4a and 4b we contrast conventional and revised ontologies for the results presented in Table 1. The problem with the ontology in Figure 4a is that it is not informed about the underlying functional anatomy, namely more than one function engages the same cortical region. Although, given the task, one could predict that the left posterior lateral fusiform would activate, it would be very difficult to predict the task a subject was engaged in, knowing only that the left posterior lateral fusiform was activated. In contradistinction, an integrated ontology (Figure 4b) allows one to predict that all tasks activate the left posterior lateral fusiform and furthermore that activation of this area means the subject is explicitly categorising a precept (e.g., for integrating sensory information with the requisite response). As above, this example is only schematic. Clearly, designating the left posterior lateral fusiform as a visual word form area, although tenable from the point of view of cognitive models of reading, does not do justice to a more integrated and holistic ontology.

Rules for "good" ontologies

We will conclude with some ideas about constructing "good" ontologies. Clearly, a good ontology should:

1. Have a hierarchical structure that predicts the coactivation of anatomical regions, where sets of coactivated regions should have demonstrable (effective) connections.
2. Enable cognitive processing to be predicted given any distribution of activations, based on which area, or set of areas, is necessary for that processing.

These criteria emphasise that function should be predicted from anatomical activation and conversely that anatomical activation should predict function. This can be embodied operationally in a cost function that reflects the prediction error in going from function to structure and back again. For example, such a cost function could be defined for a particular task in the following way. Identify all the cognitive processes involved in the task and compute the areas activated given the function–structure mapping. Using the structure–function mapping, identify all the processes for which the activated areas are necessary. The discrepancy between these processes, and those comprising the task, constitutes that cost

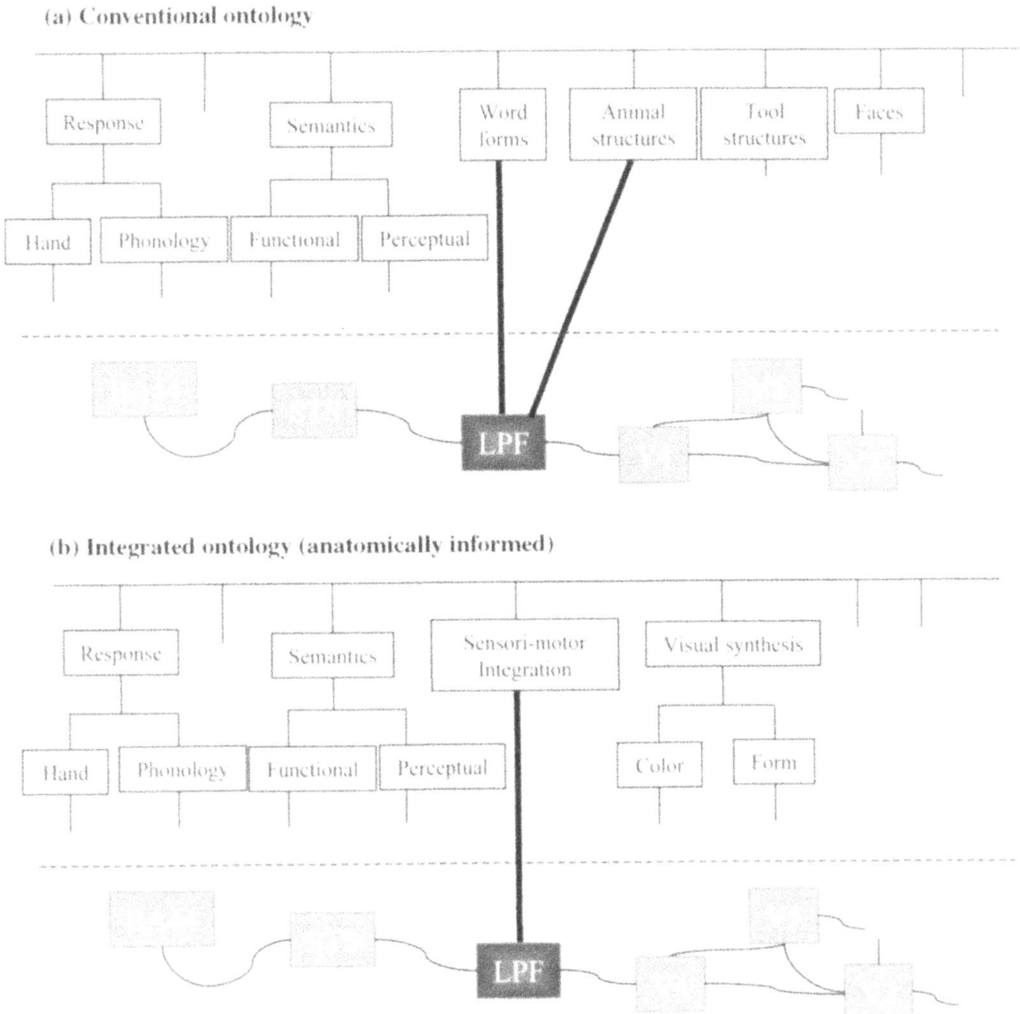

Figure 4. *Conventional and revised ontologies. (a) A conventional ontology that is not formed by the underlying functional anatomy. Here, more than one function can engage the same cortical region. (b) An integrated ontology where functional labels are constrained by the anatomical response. Here, activation in an area predicts the process that is engaged.*

function for that task. A good ontology will minimise this cost function over all tasks. Similar devices have been used in computational anatomy to define the hierarchical organisation of visual cortices using only anatomical connectivity information (e.g., Young & Scannell, 2000).

Note that this strategy relies on knowing which areas activate, given a particular set of processes (determined by neuroimaging) and which regions are necessary for each process (determined by the lesion-deficit model). This approach to cognitive ontology therefore rests upon an integration of neuroimaging and neuropsychological techniques, a pleasing point on which to end.

PrEview proof published online 20 December 2004

REFERENCES

Amedi, A., Jacobson, G., Hendler, T., Malach, R., & Zohary, E. (2002). Convergence of visual and tactile shape processing in the human lateral occipital complex. *Cerebral Cortex, 12,* 1202–1212.

Ashburner, M., Bail, C. A., Blake, J. A., Botstein, D., Butler, H., Cherry, J. M., Davis, A. P., Dolinski, K., Dwight, S. S., Eppig, J. T., Harris, M. A., Hill, D. P., Issel-Taryer, L., Kasarskis, A., Lewis, S., Matese, J. C., Richardson, J. E., Ringwald, M., Rubin, G. M., & Sherlock, G. (2000) Gene ontology: Tool for the unification of biology. *Nature Genetics, 25,* 25–29.

Bookheimer, S. Y., Zeffiro, T. A., Blaxton, T., Gaillard, W., & Theodore, W. (1995). Regional cerebral blood flow during object naming and word reading. *Human Brain Mapping, 3,* 93–106.

Booth, J. R., Burman, D. D., Meyer, J. R., Gitelman, D. R., Parrish, T. B., & Mesulam, M. M. (2002a). Functional anatomy of intra- and cross-modal lexical tasks. *NeuroImage, 16,* 7–22.

Booth, J. R., Burman, D. D., Meyer, J. R., Gitelman, D. R., Parrish, T. B., & Mesulam, M. M. (2002b). Modlaity independence of word comprehension. *Human Brain Mapping, 16,* 251–261.

Brunswick, N., McCrory, E., Price, C. J., Frith, C. D., & Frith, U. (1999). Explicit and implicit processing of words and pseudowords by adult developmental dyslexics—A search for Wernicke's Wortschatz? *Brain, 122,* 1901–1917.

Buchel, C., Price, C., & Friston, K. (1998). A multimodal language region in the ventral visual pathway. *Nature, 394,* 274–277.

Castelli, F., Frith, C., Happé, F., & Frith, U. (2002). Autism, Asperger syndrome and brain mechanisms for the attribution of mental states to animated shapes. *Brain, 125,* 1839–1849.

Chao, L., Haxby, J. V., & Martin, A. (1999). Attribute-based neural substrates in temporal cortex for perceiving and knowing about objects. *Nature Neuroscience, 2,* 913–919.

Chao, L., Weisberg, J., & Martin, A. (2002). Experience dependent modulation of category-related cortical activity. *Cerebral Cortex, 12,* 545–551.

Cohen, L., Dehaene, S., Naccache, L., Lehericy, S., Dehaene-Lambertz, G., Henaff, M., & Michel, F. (2000). The visual word form area: Spatial and temporal characterization of an initial stage of reading in normal subjects and posterior split-brain patients. *Brain, 123,* 291–307.

Cohen, L., Lehericy, S., Chochon, F., Lemer, C., Rivard, S., & Dehaene, S. (2002). Language-specific tuning of visual cortex? Functional properties of the visual word form area. *Brain, 125,* 1054–1069.

Dehaene, S., Le Clec'H, G., Poline, J. B., Bihan, D. L., & Cohen, L. (2002). The visual word form area: A prelexical representation of visual words in the left fusiform gyrus. *NeuroReport, 13,* 321–325.

Dehaene, S., Naccache, L., Cohen, L., Bihan, D. L., Mangin, J. F., Poline, J. B., & Riviere, D. (2001). Cerebral mechannisms of word masking and unconscious repetition priming. *Nature Neuroscience, 4,* 752–758.

Fiez, J. A., & Petersen, S. E. (1998). Neuro-imaging studies of word reading. *Proceedings of the National Academy of Sciences, USA, 95,* 914–921.

Grill-Spector, K., Kushnir, T., Edelman, S., Avidan, G., Itzchak, Y., & Malach, R. (1999). Differential processing of objects under various viewing conditions in the human lateral occipital cortex. *Neuron, 24,* 187–203.

Henson, R. N., & Rugg, M. D. (2003). Neural response suppression, haemodynamic repetition effects, and behavioural priming. *Neuropsychologia, 41,* 263–270.

Hubbard, T. J., Alley, B., Brenner, S. E., Murzin, A. G., & Chothia, C. (1999). SCOP: A structural classification of proteins database. *Nucleic Acids Research, 27,* 254–256.

Kim, K. H., Relkin, N. R., Lee, K. M., & Hirsch, J. (1997). Distinct cortical areas associated with native and second languages. *Nature, 388,* 171–174.

Lan, N., Montelione, G. T., & Gerstein, M. (2003). Ontologies for proteomics: Towards a systematic definition of structure and function that scales to the genome level. *Current Opinion in Chemical Biology, 7,* 44–54.

Martin, A., & Chao, L. L. (2001). Semantic memory and the brain: Structure and processes. *Current Opinions in Neurobiology, 11,* 194–201.

McIntosh, A. R. (2000). Towards a network theory of cognition. *Neural Networks, 13,* 861–876.

Mellet, E., Tzourio, N., Denis, M., & Mazoyer, B. (1998). Cortical anatomy of mental imagery of concrete nouns based on their dictionary definition. *NeuroReport, 9,* 803–808.

Mesulam, M. M. (1990). Large scale neurocognitive networks and distributed processing for attention, language and memory. *Annals of Neurology, 28,* 597–613.

Mintun, M. A., Fox P. T., & Raichle, M. E. (1989). A highly accurate method of localizing regions of neuronal activation in the human brain with positron emission tomography. *Journal of Cerebral Blood Flow Metabolism, 9,* 96–103.

Moore, C. J., & Price, C. J. (1999). Three distinct ventral occipitotemporal regions for reading and object naming. *NeuroImage, 10,* 181–192.

Murtha, S., Chertkow, H., Beauregard, M., & Evans, A. (1999). The neural substrate of picture naming. *Journal of Cognitive Neuroscience, 11,* 399–423.

Patterson, K., & Shewell, C. (1987). Speak and spell: Dissociations and word class effects. In M. Coltheart, G. Sartori, & R. Job (Eds.), *The cognitive neuropsychology of language* (pp. 273–294). London: Lawrence Erlbaum Associates Ltd.

Phillips, J. A., Humphreys, G. W., Noppeney, U., & Price, C. J. (2002). The neural substrates of action retrieval: An examination of semantic and visual routes to action. *Visual Cognition, 9,* 662–684.

Polk, T. A., & Farah, M. J. (2002). Functional MRI evidence for an abstract, not perceptual, word-form area. *Journal of Experimental Psychology: General, 131,* 65–72.

Price, C. J. (2000). The anatomy of language: Contributions from fuctional neuroimaging. *Journal of Anatomy, 197,* 335–359.

Price, C. J., & Devlin, J. T. (2003). The myth of the visual word form area. *NeuroImage, 19,* 473–481.

Price, C. J., & Friston, K. J. (2002). Degeneracy and cognitive anatomy. *Trends in Cognitive Science, 6,* 416–201.

Price, C. J., Moore, C. J., Humphreys, G. W., Frackowiak, R. S. J., & Friston, K. J. (1996). The neural regions sustaining object recognition and naming. *Proceedings of the Royal Society of London Series B—Biological Sciences, 263,* 1501–1507.

Seidenberg, M., & McClelland, J. (1989). A distributed, developmental model of word recognition and naming. *Psychological Review, 96,* 523–568.

Talairach, J., & Tournoux, P. (1988). *Co-planar stereotaxic atlas of the human brain.* Stuttgart, Germany: Thieme.

Thompson-Schill, S. L., Aguirre, G. K., D'Esposito, M., & Farah, M. J. (1999). A neural basis for category and modality specificity of semantic knowledge. *Neuropsychologia, 37,* 671–676.

Vandenberghe, R., Price, C. J., Wise, R., Josephs, O., & Frackowiak, R. S. J. (1996). Functional anatomy of a common semantic system for words and pictures. *Nature, 383,* 254–256.

Van Turennout, M., Ellmore, T., & Martin, A. (2000). Long lasting cortical plasticity in the object naming system. *Nature Neuroscience, 3,* 1329–1334.

Young, M. P., & Scannell, J. W. (2000). Brain structure–function relationships: Advances from neuroinformatics. *Philosophical Transactions of the Royal Society of London Series B—Biological Sciences, 355,* 3–6.

COGNITIVE NEUROPSYCHOLOGY, 2005, 22 (3/4), 276–291

FRONTAL LATCHING NETWORKS: A POSSIBLE NEURAL BASIS FOR INFINITE RECURSION

Alessandro Treves
SISSA, Trieste, Italy, and NTNU, Trondheim, Norway

Understanding the neural basis of higher cognitive functions, such as those involved in language, requires a shift from mere localisation to an analysis of network operation. A recent proposal points at infinite recursion as the core of several higher functions, and thus challenges cortical network theorists to describe network behaviour that could subserve infinite recursion. I propose here that a capacity for infinite recursion may be associated with the natural adaptive dynamics of large semantic associative networks, once their connectivity becomes sufficiently extensive to support structured transition probabilities between global network states. The crucial development endowing a semantic system with a nonrandom dynamics would thus be an increase in connectivity, perhaps to be identified with the dramatic increase in spine numbers recently observed in the basal dendrites of pyramidal cells in Old World monkey and particularly in human frontal cortex.

MULTIPLE BRAIN AREAS, ONE OPERATING MODE?

Cognitive neuropsychology, based as it has been on the analysis of the effects of brain lesions and now on functional imaging, has had a methodological bias towards *localisation*, towards establishing what belongs where on the surface of the cortex. A posteriori, such a bias has been justified by the purely philosophical notion of the modularity of mind (Fodor, 1983), augmented by the wishful thinking that the brain be as modular as philosophers claim the mind to be. Now that the methodological challenge has been largely met, the localisation approach offers diminishing intellectual returns, and the best functional imaging experts are veering away from it, and are increasingly searching for new tools (see, e.g., Price & Friston, 2002) useful in analysing the *mechanisms* and the *network interactions* at the basis of the processing of information by the brain, and in particular by the cerebral cortex. The quest for the neural basis of cognitive phenomena begins to focus, rather than on localisation, on such network mechanisms, as in the global workspace model proposed for effortful tasks (Dehaene, Kerszberg, & Changeaux, 1998).

A cornerstone of the search for cortical network mechanisms is the observation, old but often neglected, that each small patch of neocortex is basically wired up in the same way. This holds across areas as well as across mammalian species,

Correspondence should be addressed to Alessandro Treves, SISSA, Cognitive Neuroscience sector, via Beirut 4, 34014 Trieste, Italy (Email: ale@sissa.it).

I am indebted to Edvard and May-Britt Moser for providing the continuous enlightenment of a northern 'midsommer' night, when this paper was first drafted; to Daniele Amati and Yasser Roudi for several stimulating discussions, which helped improve it; and to anonymous reviewers for their constructive comments, in particular the suggestion to include a mathematical appendix.

with relatively minor differentiations and specialisations that do not alter substantially the basic neocortical local network (DeFelipe, Alonso-Nanclares, & Arellano, 2002; Douglas & Martin, 1991; Rockel, Hiorns, & Powell, 1980) nor the basic overall cortical plan (Krubitzer, 1995; Young, Scannell, Burns, & Blakemore, 1994). It holds even in areas implicated in language functions in humans, areas that are still suspected by some to conceal "uniquely human" neural traits (Marcus, Vouloumanos, & Sag, 2003). The fundamental organising principle of neocortical microcircuitry, which distinguishes it from older cortical forms, is lamination, i.e., the differentiation among layers of neurons. In evolution, lamination may have emerged as contributing a specific advantage in sensory processing (Allman, 1990), a hypothesis that I have considered at the network level (Treves, 2003). Thus the origin of lamination may have to be seen in the restricted context of its functional role in the sensory cortex of early mammals, in contrast with the rich variety of cognitive functions seemingly carried out by most of the human cortex. Yet, lamination is still there, throughout the vast expanse of the human cortex, albeit with varying degrees of saliency (Rempel-Clower & Barbas, 2000) and, more importantly, no subsequent clear organising principle has emerged at the microcircuit level. The possibility that this one advanced principle that informs sensory cortex may have been retained in "association" cortex by a sort of genetic inertia, without being replaced by novel, more powerful, and area-specific principles, has wide implications. It suggests that the local network mechanisms subserving the rich variety of cognitive functions are always essentially the same, and functional differentiation corresponds solely, in a first approximation, to differences in the long-range connections of different cortical areas. The local "transaction," or elementary cortical network operation, is likely to be roughly the same everywhere (Lorente de Nó, 1938), in sensory cortex as in association cortex.

Further, the long-range connections, denoted as the A system by Braitenberg (1978), in contrast with the B system of local connections that do not leave the gray matter, do indeed follow a specific wiring plan, which—when compared to simple mammalian species—is similar but more complex in elaborated species such as ours. However, these connections do not seem to differ in ways other than in their overall wiring diagram: Their layers of origin and termination, their synaptic mechanisms, their plasticity, their modulation by different neurotransmitters, all follow the same set of basic rules across cortical areas and across mammalian species.

One is led, therefore, to speculate that an understanding of the cortical operations underlying cognitive functions requires two main steps. First, the local network transaction has to be captured by a functional description, abstract enough to apply independently of areas and modalities yet accurate enough at the network level to be useful as a building block for system-level analyses. Second, global network operations have to be reduced to the combination of multiple instances of the universal local transaction, implemented along the wiring diagram relevant to each cognitive function.

INFINITE RECURSION AND ITS AMBIGUITIES

Are there clues about the nature of such global network operations that come from purely cognitive analyses? In a recent review, Marc Hauser, Noam Chomsky, and Tecumseh Fitch (2002) reevaluate the requirements for the faculty of language. They state that language in the broad sense requires an adequate sensory-motor system and an adequate conceptual-intentional system, which, however, are both unlikely to be uniquely human attributes. They further propose that what may be uniquely human is a third necessary component of the faculty of language, that is, a computational mechanism for *recursion*. Such a mechanism would provide the capacity to generate an infinite range of expressions from a finite set of elements. They also speculate that a capacity for infinite recursion may have evolved for reasons other than language, such as number processing, navigation, or social relations. In a related analysis, Daniele Amati (personal communication) wonders what could be a component that distinguishes uniquely human cognitive abilities, which he calls "H" capacities, from the "1-H" capacities shared with other species; and he identifies this component with an ability for producing arbitrarily long sequences that, at an abstract level, obey certain rules. This implies an ability to process cognitive states remote from those directly elicited by sensory inputs, and to generate such states recursively, i.e., a notion very close to the Chomskian one of infinite recursion in language, as manifested in a generative grammar. Thus a computational mechanism for infinite recursion may be utilised in other "H" capacities, for example (as proposed by Amati), in the production of music (see Hauser & McDermott, 2003, and other articles in the same issue), in the formulation of strategies by managers and politicians, and so on.

Recursion, referred to as the generation of infinite sequences of elements drawn from a finite alphabet, is an abstract and very loose notion. Computationally, at the most pedestrian level, it might simply mean that the transitions from one element to the next follow certain rules instead of being effectively random. A mathematical formulation of a grammar can be reduced, in fact, to the study of a system with certain forbidden transitions among its elements (see, e.g., Namikawa & Hashimoto, 2004, and references therein). What the elements are, how they may be represented in the brain, and how restrictive the rules they have to adhere to are, remain to be clarified. Linguistically, and in other cognitive domains, recursion is often implied to mean something less pedestrian, like an embedding of clauses one inside the other in syntax, or the nesting of *do*-loops in Fortran codes. Recursion in this more sophisticated sense tends to be *domain-specific*, however, and it is not necessarily *infinite*. An approach to explain infinite recursion mechanistically, in general, while taking into account domain-specific connotations, is therefore likely to be ill-directed. More promising appears an almost opposite, nearly bottom-up approach, that considers the generic, pedestrian meaning of recursion, assumes the quality of its being infinite as critical, and focuses on the universal cortical transaction at the local network level.

A MEMORY-BASED ANALYSIS OF THE WORLD

In one of his ambitious and difficult papers discussing the organisation of the brain, David Marr (1970) proposed to regard the cerebral cortex in terms of its ability to decode the outside world using memory of previous experiences. In their 1991 book, Braitenberg and Schüz summarised a series of insightful observations on the quantitative anatomy of the cortex, concluding that in general terms it operates as an associative memory machine. Over the last 15 years the interpretation of local cortical networks as attractor networks performing memory computations (Amit, 1995) has diffused across the neuroscience community, leading to increased attention to the role of recurrent collateral processing even in early vision (Ringach, Hawken, & Shapley, 2003) and in brain slices examined *in vitro* (Cossart, Aronov, & Yuste, 2003; Shu, Hasenstaub, & McCormick, 2003). Memory computations take different forms (Rolls & Treves, 1998), including self-organised recoding useful for categorisation, pattern association (or *directed memory* in the terminology of Marr, 1971), and autoassociation or *free memory*. Common to all is the use of neurons as simple devices summating multiple inputs, of representations distributed over the activity of many neurons, and of associative plasticity mechanisms at their synaptic connections. With such minimal and neurally plausible ingredients, memory operations at the single neuron level can be depicted as simple *analogue* operations on vectors of synaptic weights and on vectors of firing rates. These analogue computations, widely accepted as the neural basis of memory in cortical networks, are seemingly far removed from the *symbolic* computations often subsumed as the logical basis of language and other higher cognitive faculties. Yet, apparent differences notwithstanding, analogue computations at the single neuron level can implement symbolic computations at the local network level.

The crucial element for this to occur is the discrete nature of local network attractors. The discreteness of local attractors can provide the error-correction capability and the robustness to noise that are often associated with the processing of discrete symbols.

In most simple models, local attractors are viewed as final states reached by a relaxation type of dynamics, that is, they coincide with the distribution of firing rates across neurons, which the local network would tend to reach in the absence of new perturbing inputs. This is, however, not necessarily the case. In his proposal of the notion of "synfire chains" (1982), Moshe Abeles has envisioned inherently dynamical attractors, in which the identity of neurons firing in each attractor changes rapidly with time, along chains of links, each comprised of simultaneously firing neurons. The attractive nature of a chain expresses itself both in the convergence towards one of the sequences of links that are stored in memory, and in the progressive synchronisation of the units comprising each link (Bienenstock, 1995; Hertz & Prugel-Bennet, 1996). Distinct sequences and distinct links within a sequence can share a number of participating units, and if this number does not exceed a value that can in principle be calculated, each chain continues to operate as a dynamical attractor. Further, distinct sequences can share the very same link or set of links, provided the activation of a link depends on previous links extending sufficiently into the past as to disambiguate each sequence. Although the original synfire chain model may be oversimplified, theoretically this notion has the merit of unleashing the computational capabilities of attractors, with their analogue-to-symbolic transformation, into the temporal dimension. If provisions are made for the composition of individual chains, and for "switch" links with multiple possible outcomes, synfire chains can implement the structure of transition probabilities of a grammar. It has indeed been noted how synfire chains, or objects of a similar nature, could be at the basis of language (e.g., Pulvermuller, 2002); interestingly, the concept derives from the experimental observation of neural activity recorded in the *frontal* cortex of monkeys (Abeles, Bergman, Margalit, & Vaadia, 1993). In contrast, the "static" notion of fixed-point attractors finds its most salient experimental inspiration in data recorded in the *temporal* lobe (Miyashita & Chang, 1988). While the details of the synfire chain model will not be considered further in this paper, the model offers a suggestion as to the significance, along the temporal dimension, of possible quantitative differences in the organisation and in the dynamics of temporal and frontal cortices.

In the temporal cortex, if a local static attractor may be taken to correspond to a feature represented over a limited patch of cortex, a global attractor extending over many patches may be taken to correspond to an item from semantic memory (Devlin, Gonnerman, Andersen, & Seidenberg, 1998; Farah & McClelland, 1991). In the past we have analysed quantitatively simple multimodular associative memory networks, to check whether they could serve as models of semantic memory. In line with the distinction between the A and B systems of connections among pyramidal cells (Braitenberg, 1978), we considered models in which each module, including N units, is densely connected through associatively modifiable weights (in fact each pair of units in the same module are pre- and post-synaptic to each other, so the number of local connections per unit C_B equals $N-1$), while different modules are sparsely connected (each unit receives C_A connections, coming from other units widely distributed over M modules). Anatomical evidence suggests that C_B and C_A are large numbers of similar magnitude, e.g., of order 10^4 in primates (Abeles, 1991). N determines the number of *local* attractor states, denoted here as S, which analytical studies show scales up with the number of local connections per units, i.e., is proportional to C_B. In a first study of a multimodular network, we concluded that the number P of *global* attractor states cannot be much larger than S for the system to retrieve each memory item correctly. Analytical results show that if P is much larger than S, random combinations of local attractors, which do not correspond to any stored global pattern of activity, prevail as fixed points over the meaningful, stored combinations, which the C_A long-range connections per unit try to enforce (O'Kane & Treves, 1992). Thus a simple-minded multimodular network could not serve as an effective semantic memory, since it would be limited to storing a very low number of items, of the same order as that of local attractor states. In a subsequent study, we identified two modifications to the first model we had considered, which increase its storage capacity beyond such a limited value (Fulvi Mari & Treves, 1998). The first modification is a long-range connectivity that is not uniformly sparse across modules, but is concentrated between a module and a subset of other modules that strongly interact with it. The second modification is to consider global activity patterns, or semantic memory items, that are not defined across all modules, but only over a subset, different for each pattern, which tends to include strongly interacting modules. With these combined modifications, the storage capacity, as measured by P, can increase well beyond the local capacity S, although its exact value is difficult to calculate, and depends on the details of the model. The tentative conclusion of the second study, therefore, was that a viable model of semantic memory based on a collection of interacting local associative networks should include (1) nonuniformly distributed long-range connections and (2) activity patterns distributed over a sparse fraction of the modules (Fulvi Mari & Treves, 1998).

The analyses above refer to the operation of semantic memory retrieval, which has to be initiated by an input that conveys a partial cue. In the temporal cortex, the so-called stimulus specific delay activity, which is observed for up to a few seconds following the offset of the stimulus, is typically weak and disrupted by successively intervening stimuli (see Brunel, 2003). In the frontal cortex, similar delay activity can instead be quite strong and persist in the face of intervening stimuli (Freedman, Reisenhuber, Poggio, & Miller, 2003), reflecting the overall weaker influence that sensory inputs to the cortex have on frontal networks, compared to that on networks of the temporal lobe (as modelled by Renart, Parga, & Rolls, 1999). It becomes pertinent to ask, then, especially in the case of frontal cortex, what type of dynamics may follow semantic memory retrieval: What happens to a network comprised of multiple associative modules, once it has been activated by a cue and it has retrieved a given semantic memory? In the following, I propose that what can happen depends critically on the number of semantic memories stored, that is, on the number of global attractor states. While allowing for a special contribution of the frontal cortex to temporal integration, due to its position in the overall cortical plan (Fuster, 2002), and while broadly compatible with the declarative/procedural model of Ullman (2001), my proposal focuses on a network mechanism that is not restricted to frontal cortex, but that in human frontal cortex may have found a novel expression because of a purely quantitative feature: the abundance of its connections.

HYPOTHESIS

Stating the hypothesis requires considering one additional ingredient, which, however, in the cortex comes for free, so to speak. This is a passive mechanism for moving a local network out of an attracting state, after some time. A combination of firing rate adaptation in pyramidal cells, short-term depression at excitatory synapses (Tsodyks & Markram, 1997), and slow rebound inhibition would produce such an effect, and in different proportions would tend exclusively to inactivate the local network or also to favour its transition to a different attractor state, or even to enable flip-flop switching between pairs of states, as in binocular rivalry (Laing & Chow, 2002). Globally, under certain conditions the collection of modules will move continuously from global attractor to global attractor or, more precisely, it will hop from state to state, given the discrete nature of the attractor states. It may rapidly pass through intermediate states, but in a well-behaving semantic system mixture states are unstable (see Roudi & Treves, 2003, for a simplified model) and the trajectory, in the absence of new inputs, will essentially include periods close to attracting states, which would be fixed points except for the adaptation/inhibition mechanism, and rapid transitions between them. The system *latches* between attractors. We now focus on whether such transitions will continue to occur one after the other in the absence of inputs and, if they occur, on the degree to which they follow rules, or are effectively random. When relatively few global attractors exist, in the high-dimensional space in which they live (in which each module represents a component), the attractors will tend to be orthogonal, or approximately equally distant from each other. This is a statistical tendency that follows simply from the high dimensionality of the space, without special assumptions. In such a regime, transitions will be nearly random, if they occur at all. This is because as the system moves out of the previous global attractor none of the other attractors will be strongly engaged to take over; small fluctuations in the instantaneous condition of the system may favour a particular hopping among many essentially equiprobable ones, or else selective activity in the system may simply die out. When more global patterns exist, they populate more densely their high dimensional space, and at some point each pattern will have a subset of other patterns that are closer to it, or more similar, than the rest. In such a regime, transitions between states will tend to be structured, and the dynamics will appear to follow certain rules, i.e., a grammar. The critical density of global attractor states at which structured transitions begin to prevail depends markedly on how patterns are generated, and one has to make more concrete assumptions in order to proceed with more quantitative arguments. It is not fully clear at this stage whether the transition between the two regimes takes the sudden character of a phase transition, akin perhaps to a percolation transition (Hammersley, 1983). In general, however, it should remain valid that such critical density does not depend much on the long-range connectivity: It is determined mainly by the number of modules and by the number of their local attractors, not by how extensive their connections are. The storage capacity for semantic memory, instead, does depend on the connectivity. My hypothesis, then, is that a connectivity increase may increase the storage capacity of a frontal semantic multimodular network until it can store enough patterns such that, when left without inputs, it can follow structured dynamics, which express a sort of transition rules. This hypothesis can be formulated in more detail by considering a concrete model, amenable to computer simulations.

Before discussing the concrete model, it is tempting to speculate freely on the relation, within this framework, between the universal grammar, posited to underlie all human languages, and the grammar constraining each particular language, characterised by its choice of parameters (see, e.g., Baker, 2002). The universal grammar should reflect the associative nature of the semantic network, largely embodied in a time-independent matrix of similarities between global attractors, but also endowed with the restricted extent of time arrows characteristic of any action semantics (Zanini, Rumiati, & Shallice, 2002). Such time arrows, or directed associations in Marr's terms, can be realised by simple and biologically plausible mechanisms, e.g., by spike-timing dependent synaptic plasticity. The same mechanisms can operate, when learning a specific language, to resolve the residual temporal order ambiguities left by the fact that action semantics does not specify all the temporal relations necessary to produce (one-dimensional) speech. Thus, in this interpretation, language parameters are set (arbitrarily, from a formal point of view, that is according to one's mother tongue) when funnelling the more loosely time-constrained action semantics into the strict order of sequential discourse. Also parameters that seemingly do not reflect simple temporal order, like the polysynthesis parameter, might be indirect by-products of such a funnelling effort.

A SIMPLE POTTS MODEL

A Potts spin is a variable that can take several (say, S) values, all equally "distant" to each other. If $S = 3$, for example, the three states can be represented as the vertices of an equilateral triangle, if $S = 4$, as those of an equilateral triangular pyramid, and for general S as the vertices of an $S-1$ simplex (a hyperpyramid in $S-1$ dimensional space). As such, Potts spins are ideally suited to represent the generic attractor states of a local network, which operates more effectively, in a sense, the more its attractor states are equally distant from each other (this applies to networks storing discrete attractors, not continuous ones such as orientation columns, see, e.g., Sompolinsky & Shapley, 1997). A system comprised of many local associative networks can then be mapped onto a network of Potts spins, one for each module. This allows one to neglect the local network operation and to concentrate on the global dynamics, guided by the long-range connections, which remain the only connectivity present in the reduced Potts system.

Potts models of associative networks were introduced 15 years ago by Ido Kanter, who has shown that in a fully connected network of Potts spins one can store, with the analogue of the "Hebbian" plasticity rule used in the Hopfield (1982) model, up to a critical number P_c of patterns. His numerical results for $S = 3, 4, 5$, and 9 are remarkably well fitted by the formula

$$P_c \cong 0.138\ MS\ (S - 1)/2, \qquad (1)$$

a result that neatly extends the analogue result for the Hopfield model, which can be regarded as a Potts model for $S = 2$. As noted by Kanter, this critical storage load scales up with the number of Potts states squared because, effectively, a connection weight between a pair of Potts units is comprised of $S(S - 1)/2$ independently tunable synaptic variables. When the network is loaded close to its memory capacity, each such variable ends up storing up to a fraction of a bit, as in the Hopfield model (Kanter, 1988). A more detailed analysis of the large S limit (sketched in Appendix A, the full calculation to be reported elsewhere) shows that in fact in this limit P_c scales, more precisely, as

$$P_c \cong MS^2/\log(kS). \qquad (2)$$

In Kanter (1988) the attenuation with log(S) was overlooked, probably because numerically k turns out to be very large, of order 10^6, and the term log(k) overshadows the term log(S) in the denominator.

To apply a Potts model to our multimodular semantic network, one needs to consider at least two extensions of the Kanter model. The first is incomplete connectivity between the Potts units. As for the analogue extensions of the Hopfield model (see Derrida, Gardner, & Zippelius, 1987; Domany, Kinzel, & Meir, 1989; Treves & Rolls, 1991), the formula for the storage capacity is modified in that the number of connections each unit receives, denoted as c_M (as Potts units represent cortical modules), replaces M, the number of modules, and the numerical prefactor becomes much larger (due to less reverberation of the noise along closed loops). The second extension is that if the S Potts states are to represent local attractor states, there should be at least one additional state, not symmetrical to the others, to represent a local network that is not active, or that has not reached one of its specific attractor states. Adding this additional "0" state is analogue to considering $0-1$ spin extensions of the Hopfield model with sparse coding (Buhmann, Divko, & Schulten, 1989; Tsodyks & Feigel'man, 1988). Such an extension of the Potts model has been considered by Bollé and colleagues (Bollé, Cools, Dupont, & Huyghebaer, 1993; Bollé, Dupont, & Van Mourik, 1991), but without optimal threshold setting. Let us denote with a the average fraction of modules actively participating in the representation of a global pattern (i.e., not in the "0" state). It is possible to show (the calculation will be published in a technical report), that with optimal threshold setting a Potts model with sparse coding and dilute connectivity can store a number of global attractors up to the critical value

$$P_c \approx c_M S^2/a, \qquad (3)$$

where $a \leq 1$ indicates sparse coding, the number of local states is taken to be $S \geq 1$, and the logarithmic attenuation is neglected in the formula for the sake of simplicity. This result holds for a not too small, and in the analytically treatable situation in which the global patterns of activity to be stored are independent and spatially uncorrelated. Formally, this latter condition means that each Potts unit can be regarded as taking, in each of the P global attractors, a randomly chosen value among the S ones representing local attractor states (each chosen with probability a/S) or else can be in the nonspecific "0" state with probability $1-a$.

In more realistic models of semantic storage, global attractor states cannot be assumed to be independent of one another and spatially uncorrelated. Correlations among patterns can drastically reduce the storage capacity of an autoassociative network. However, I hypothesise that in some models with correlations, one of which is described in Appendix B and is adopted in the simulations sketched below, storage capacity is indeed drastically reduced, but essentially by a prefactor dependent on the correlations, preserving the general dependence of P_c on the connectivity per unit, c_M—a linear dependence—and on the number S of local attractors—roughly, a quadratic dependence.

Before discussing the implications of the storage capacity of the Potts model, it is useful to clarify how its connectivity parameters could be mapped onto those of an underlying multimodular network model. In the "reduced" Potts model, each unit receives c_M connections from other units, for a total of c_M S (S − 1)/2 independently variable weights per unit. A storage capacity of

$$P_c \approx c_M S^2/[a \log(kS)] \quad (4)$$

patterns, each of which contains about

$$i_{patt} \approx M\, a \log_2(S) \quad (5)$$

bits of information, implies that the total information that can be stored in the reduced network is of order

$$I_{tot} \approx M\, c_M S^2, \quad (6)$$

that is, of order one bit per synaptic variable. In the full multimodular network, including N units per module, each unit would receive C_A single-variable weights from units in other modules. Note that one can further take S, the number of local attractors to be of order the number C_B of short-range (local) connections per unit in the underlying model, that is of order N. If also the full network, like the reduced network, can store of the order of one bit per synaptic variable, in this case it would amount even counting long-range connections only, to

$$I_{tot} \approx M\, N\, C_A \approx M\, C_B\, C_A. \quad (7)$$

This implies that the bound on the number of global patterns, or semantic items, should scale up as

$$P_c \approx C_A C_B/[a \log(kS)], \quad (8)$$

that is, not only should it increase with sparser modular coding (the *a* factor), but it should also scale up with the *product* of the number of long- and short-range connections per unit in the underlying model, not with their *sum*. This is a possibility left open in the Fulvi Mari and Treves calculation, which should be verified by further analysis and simulation. From a quantitative point of view, it would resurrect the idea (Braitenberg, 1978; Braitenberg & Schüz, 1991) that multimodular cortical networks can serve as efficient semantic memory storage devices, raising their capacity from several thousands to several millions of items.

SCHEME OF THE SIMULATIONS

I have simulated memory retrieval by a network of Potts units, in which global activity patterns to be stored as memory items were generated by an algorithm that could be parametrically varied from producing independent to highly correlated patterns. This was obtained, in a manner sketched in Appendix B and to be described in detail elsewhere, by using a series of underlying *factors*, each affecting a subset of the Potts units, to generate each pattern. When very many factors are of roughly equal importance, the patterns they generate tend to be spatially uncorrelated. When instead the importance of each factor in the series, or the fraction of total variance it accounts for, decreases exponentially, then each pattern becomes spatially correlated with a subset of the others, those sharing the main factor that influences them, and positively correlated with a fraction 1/S of this subset. In this scheme, the number of memory items significantly overlapping with one recently retrieved, and which can be the target of a nonrandom transition, scales up as P/S, and does not depend on c_M. By contrast, the storage capacity for retrieval, although severely reduced by correlations, should still scale as $P_c \approx c_M\, S^2/a$. This

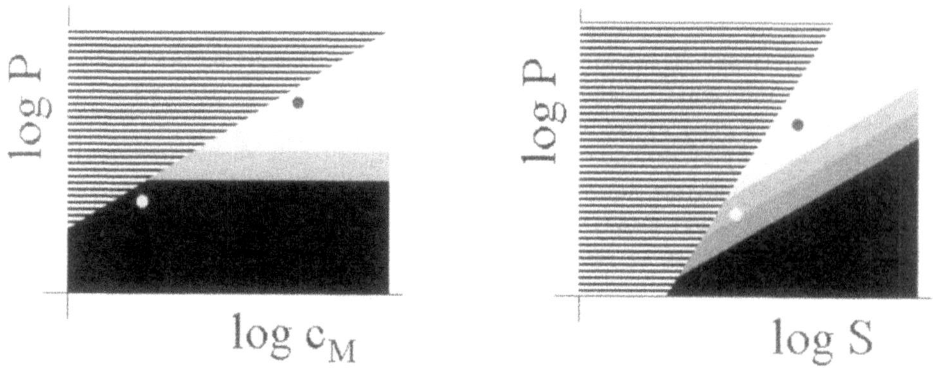

Figure 1. *Hypothetical useful ranges for the number of global attractors, on bilogarithmic diagrams. In the striped area above the critical line, which is linear in the connectivity between modules, c_M (left)—and almost quadratic in the number of local attractors, S (right)—semantic retrieval is not possible, because P is above the maximum storage load. Below the critical line, I propose that there is a (dark) region of low P values where long sequences of structured transitions are not possible. This region extends up to P values that are independent of c_M and proportional (in the multifactor model) to S. The allowed region for both semantic retrieval and infinite recursion, therefore, is close to the upper right corner of both the P−c_M and the P−S plane (uniform light area). The transition from dark to light should be sudden in a system with large S and c_M (akin to a percolation phase transition).*

leads to the two diagrams in Figure 1, which indicate that conjoint semantic retrieval and structured transitions should be possible only above critical values for c_M and S. Translated into the language of an underlying multimodular network, the expectation is that there should be critical values for both the short and the long-range connectivity, C_A and C_B, beyond which a model that follows this factorial scheme would be capable of both semantic retrieval and infinite recursion.

Whereas simulating the full multimodular network is a long-term project, the reduced Potts model requires only manageable CPU times and memory loads and can easily be simulated on a standard PC. Figure 2 shows a sample of the types of network dynamics that emerge in the simulation of the reduced Potts model.

When adaptation is turned off, typically the network remains in the retrieved attractor indefinitely. When adaptation is on, it gradually decreases the overlap between current network activity and the retrieved attractor. During this decay phase, other attractors see their overlaps increase. If one of them becomes sufficiently strong to pass an effective threshold (around .5 in the simulations), it manages to attract the entire network, and rapidly it reaches values close to 1, before decaying away in its turn. This transition can be repeated several times (Figure 2b), reminiscent of the series of transitions seen in monkey frontal cortex (Abeles et al., 1995). The crucial ingredient for an indefinite repetition, and thus for infinite recursion to occur, is that any activated global pattern must have at least one "neighbour" that can reach an overlap above threshold before its predecessor has decayed away. Although this is a dynamic phenomenon, it is closely related to the (static) matrix of similarities among stored patterns. The more significantly correlated global patterns exist to the one currently activated, the more likely is latching to proceed. For it to proceed indefinitely, each of the patterns activated in sequence must be able to activate the next, and this is more likely to occur when the density of patterns is higher, as posited in Figure 1. To check more quantitatively the expectation expressed in Figure 1, I have run extensive simulations in which I have varied c_M, S, and the storage load P systematically, and kept other parameters constant.

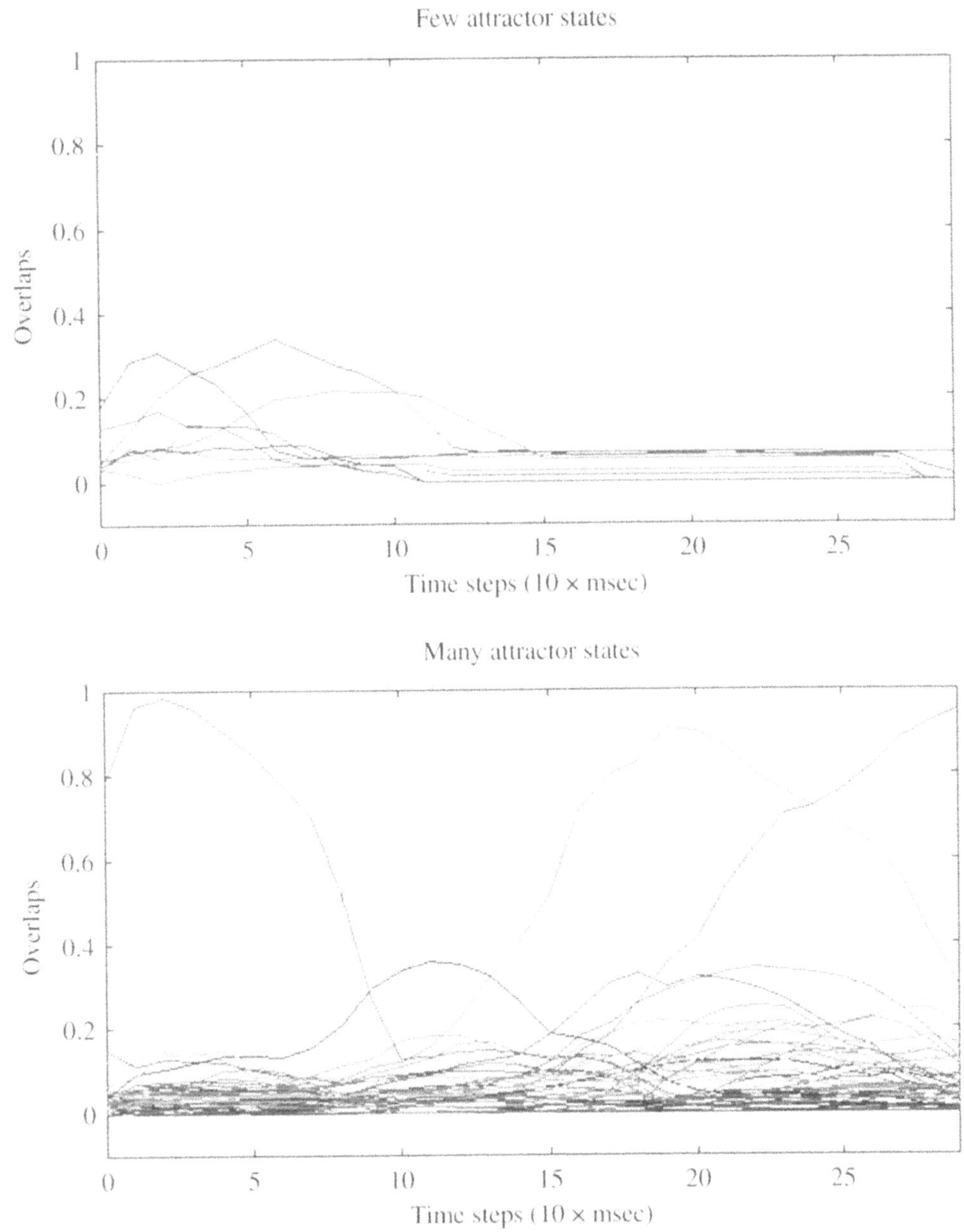

Figure 2. *Examples of global attractor retrieval with and without ensuing structured transitions among attractor states. Both examples were produced by simulating a Potts model with $M = 300$ units, $S = 10$, global patterns generated by a multifactor model with inverse eigenvalue decrease rate of 50 factors, and by applying a cue to 50% of the Potts units. (a) $c_M = 5$ and $P = 10$, and selective activity decays away after retrieval, as a second attractor is almost recruited, but it does not have a sufficient overlap with the first to emerge above an effective threshold. (b) $c_M = 25$ and $P = 50$, and a sequence of attractors dynamically replace each other, with the next one being recruited by its strong association with the previous one, thus generating structured transitions.*

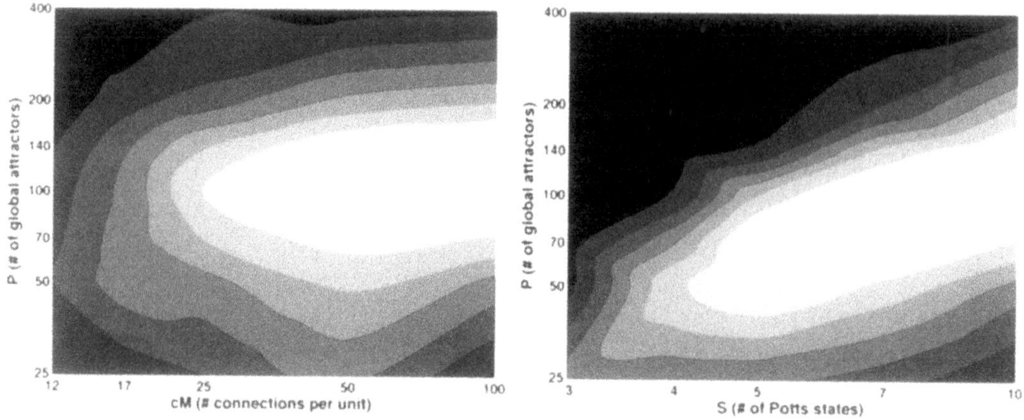

Figure 3. *Simulation results expressed as phase diagrams similar to Figure 1, again plotted on bi-logarithmic scales. In both the $P-c_M$ (left) and the $P-S$ plane (right), what is plotted in shades of gray is the product of a measure of retrieval ability (the degree to which activity is still best correlated with the cued pattern after 7 time steps) with a measure of latching ability (the degree with which, after 30 time steps, activity is still specifically correlated with one pattern, but not with the one cued). Both measures run from 0 to 1, and white corresponds to their product being higher than .3. Each diagram was obtained with 5×7 simulation datapoints, interpolated by Matlab. A datapoint reports the average of many ($10 \times P$) simulations with identical parameters.*

Figure 3 summarises how these three parameters determine the network ability to combine the retrieval of the first, cued pattern with successive latching to different patterns. The light areas correspond to regions where both retrieval and latching occur frequently (averaging across many independent runs). In the dark areas either retrieval tends to fail (towards the top of both plots) or latching tends to die out (towards the bottom of both plots). The simulations clearly demonstrate the existence of a limit P_c on the storage load, beyond which retrieval of the pattern that best matches a partial cue is not possible (the striped regions of Figure 1, and the top portions of Figure 3). Note that Figure 1 presupposes a sharp transition at a value P_c linear in c_M and quadratic in S, while the simulations, on a relatively small system, indicate a smeared transition at a value that, while ill-defined, is clearly sublinear in c_M (in part because of the reverberation of the noise around closed loops, cp. Treves & Rolls, 1991) and subquadratic in S (in part because of the logarithmic correction above) Below the P_c limit (e.g., at the marked points on the $P-c_M$ and $P-S$ planes in Figure 1) cued retrieval does occur, and latching can occur as well if P is high enough, but still below P_c, hence inside the right "wedges" appearing in both plots of Figure 1 and Figure 3. Note that Figure 3 represents the results of simulations limited in the size of the system but also in the time of each run (30 time steps), and this contributes to its smoother, more graded appearance than Figure 1. It is expected, though, that when comparing over longer runs behaviour corresponding to the marked points in Figure 1, long series of structured transitions will prevail only in the higher P regime (the upper marked point in each panel of Figure 1), possibly above a critical "percolation" point. This could be assessed quantitatively even looking at a limited time window only, by measuring the entropy of states that follow the activation of each attractor. For structured transitions, this entropy is smaller than for random transitions, thereby quantifying the metric content (Treves, 1997) of the underlying grammar. A fully analytic approach (Kropff, Roudi, & Treves, 2004) will allow clarification of these issues, beyond the limits of computer simulations and their dependence on specific choices of parameters.

CONCLUSIONS

I propose that a generic capacity for infinite recursion (intended in its basic meaning) may have evolved as a consequence of the refinement of the semantic system, a refinement allowed by the increase in connectivity among pyramidal cells in the cortex, particularly for some mammalian lineages including primates. Such a development was then accelerated in the frontal cortex, relative to the temporal lobe and its sensory semantics, because action semantics invoked more structure along the time dimensions. This may have led to a capacity for syntax in communication in humans, favoured by the further connectivity increase in their frontal cortex.

This proposal is still vague in several details, and not particularly original. Its two cornerstones have already been emphasised for several years. Chomsky and colleagues have pointed at infinite recursion as the key computational ability underlying human language, and Abeles has suggested that neurophysiologists look at structured transitions among network states, for the neural basis for this ability. Further, psychologists have speculated that language may have developed out of the declarative and procedural memory systems (Ullman, 2001), also on the spur of intriguing neurophysiological findings in primates (see Gallese & Lakoff, 2005 this issue). Recently it has been argued that the evolution of grammatical rules may have taken the sudden character of a phase transition, albeit with a very different variable, one quantifying the accuracy of language learning (Nowak, Komarova, & Niyogi, 2001). Computational linguists have laboured extensively at developing an adequate formalism for describing structured transitions in symbolic systems (see, e.g., Nowak, Komarova, & Niyogi, 2002), and chaos theorists have brought new impetus to this field by focusing on analogue systems, which are closer to neural networks (Afraimovich, Rabinovich, & Varona, 2004). Finally, in a series of remarkable papers, Elston has analysed the connectivity increase specific to frontal cortex (Elston, 2000) and highlighted its likely importance in human cognition (Elston, Benavides-Piccione, & DeFelipe, 2001). What I hope to contribute is a more explicit link among these ideas, based on the simple Potts model. Perhaps such a concrete model will serve to relate more intimately work in cognition and linguistics with neuroscience, and particularly with the analysis of the operation of cortical networks, the level at which, ultimately, mechanistic accounts have to be sought for any cognitive behaviour.

PrEview proof published online 10 January 2005

REFERENCES

Abeles, M. (1982). *Local cortical circuits.* New York: Springer.

Abeles, M. (1991). *Corticonics: Neural circuits of the cerebral cortex.* Cambridge: Cambridge University Press.

Abeles, M., Bergman, H., Gat, I., Meilijson, I., Seidemann, E., & Tishby, N. (1995). Cortical activity flips among quasi-stationary states. *Proceedings of the National Academy of Sciences, USA, 92,* 8616–8620.

Abeles, M., Bergman, H., Margalit, E., & Vaadia, E. (1993). Spatiotemporal firing patterns in the frontal cortex of behaving monkeys. *Journal of Neurophysiology, 70,* 1629–1638.

Afraimovich, V. S., Rabinovich, M. I., & Varona, P. (2004). Heteroclinic contours in neural ensembles and the winnerless competition principle. *International Journal of Bifurcation and Chaos, 14,* 1195–1208.

Allman, J. (1990). Evolution of neocortex. In E. G. Jones & A. Peters (Eds.), *Cerebral cortex, Vol. 8A: Comparative structure and evolution of cerebral cortex* (pp. 269–283). New York: Plenum Press.

Amit, D. J. (1995). The Hebbian paradigm reintegrated: Local reverberations as internal representations. *Behavioral Brain Science, 18,* 617–657.

Baker, M. C. (2002). *The atoms of language.* New York: Oxford University Press.

Bienenstock, E. (1995). A model of neocortex. *Network, 6,* 179–224.

Bollé, D., Cools, R., Dupont, P., & Huyghebaer, J. (1993). Mean-field theory for the Q-state Potts-glass neural network with biased patterns. *Journal of Physiology A, 26,* 549–562.

Bollé, D., Dupont, P., & Van Mourik, J. (1991). Stability properties of Potts neural networks with biased patterns and low loading. *Journal of Physiology A, 24,* 1065–1081.

Braitenberg, V. (1978). Cortical architectonics: General and areal. In M. A. B. Brazier & H. Petsche (Eds.), *Architectonics of the cerebral cortex* (pp. 443–465). New York: Raven.

Braitenberg, V., & Schüz, A. (1991). *Anatomy of the cortex*. Berlin: Springer-Verlag.

Brunel, N. (2003). Dynamics and plasticity of stimulus-selective persistent activity in cortical network models. *Cerebral Cortex, 13,* 1151–1161.

Buhmann, J., Divko, R., & Schulten, K. (1989). Associative memory with high information content. *Physical Review A, 39,* 2689–2692.

Cossart, R., Aronov, D., & Yuste, R. (2003). Attractor dynamics of network UP states in the neocortex. *Nature, 423,* 283–288.

DeFelipe, J., Alonso-Nanclares, L., & Arellano, J. I. (2002). Microstructure of the neocortex: Comparative aspects. *Journal of Neurocytology, 31,* 299–316.

Dehaene, S., Kerszberg, M., & Changeaux, J.-P. (1998). A neuronal model of a global workspace in effortful cognitive tasks. *Proceedings of the National Academy of Sciences, USA, 95,* 14529–14534.

Derrida, B., Gardner, E., & Zippelius, A. (1987). An exactly soluble asymmetric neural network model. *Europhysics Letters, 4,* 167–174.

Devlin, J., Gonnerman, L., Andersen, E., & Seidenberg, M. (1998). Category-specific semantic deficits in focal and widespread brain damage. A computational account. *Journal of Cognitive Neuroscience, 10,* 77–94.

Domany, E., Kinzel, W., & Meir, R. (1989). Layered neural networks. *Journal of Physics A, 22,* 2081–2102.

Douglas, R. J., & Martin, K. A. C. (1991). A functional microcircuit for cat visual cortex. *Journal of Physiology, 440,* 735–769.

Elston, G. N. (2000). Pyramidal cells of the frontal lobe: All the more spinous to think with. *Journal of Neuroscience, 20,* RC95(1–4).

Elston, G. N., Benavides-Piccione, R., & DeFelipe, J. (2001). The pyramidal cell in cognition: A comparative study in human and monkey. *Journal of Neuroscience, 21,* RC163(1–5).

Farah, M., & McClelland, J. (1991). A computational model of semantic memory impairment: Modality specificity and emergent category specificity. *Journal of Experimental Psychology: General, 120,* 339–357.

Fodor, J. A. (1983). *The modularity of mind*. Cambridge, MA: MIT Press.

Freedman, D. J., Riesenhuber, M., Poggio, T., & Miller, E. K. (2003). A comparison of primate prefrontal and inferior temporal cortices during visual categorization. *Journal of Neuroscience, 23,* 5235–5246.

Fulvi Mari, C., & Treves, A. (1998). Modeling neocortical areas with a modular neural network. *Biosystems, 48,* 47–55.

Fuster, J. M. (2002). Frontal lobe and cognitive development. *Journal of Neurocytology, 31,* 373–385.

Gallese, V., & Lakoff, G. (2005). The brain's concepts: The role of the sensory-motor system in conceptual structure. *Cognitive Neuropsychology, 22,* 455–479.

Hammersley, J. M. (1983). Origins of percolation theory. *Annals of the Israel Physical Society, 5,* 47–57.

Hauser, M. D., Chomsky, N., & Fitch, W. T. (2002). The faculty of language: What is it, who has it, and how did it evolve? *Science, 298,* 1569–1579.

Hauser, M. D., & McDermott, J. (2003). The evolution of the music faculty: A comparative perspective. *Nature Neuroscience, 6,* 663–668.

Hertz, J., & Prugel-Bennet, A. (1996). Learning synfire chains: Turning noise into signal. *International Journal of Neural Systems, 7,* 445–450.

Hopfield, J. J. (1982). Neural networks and physical systems with emergent collective computational abilities. *Proceedings of the National Academy of Sciences, USA, 79,* 2554–2558.

Kanter, I. (1988). Potts-glass models of neural networks. *Physical Review A, 37,* 2739–2742.

Kropff, E., Roudi, Y., & Treves, A. (2004). The storage capacity of Potts models for semantic memory retrieval. Manuscript in preparation.

Krubitzer, L. (1995). The organization of neocortex in mammals: Are species differences really so different? *Trends in Neuroscience, 18,* 408–417.

Laing, C. R., & Chow, C. C. (2002). A spiking neuron model for binocular rivalry. *Journal of Computational Neuroscience, 12,* 39–53.

Lorente de Nó, R. (1938). Architectonics and structure of the cerebral cortex. In J. F. Fulton (Ed.), *Physiology of the nervous system* (pp. 291–330). New York: Oxford University Press.

Marcus, G. F., Vouloumanos, A., & Sag, I. A. (2003). Does Broca's play by the rules? *Nature Neuroscience, 6,* 651–652.

Marr, D. (1970). A theory for cerebral neocortex. *Proceedings of the Royal Society of London B, 176,* 161–234.

Marr, D. (1971). Simple memory: A theory for archicortex. *Philosophical Transactions of the Royal Society of London B, 262,* 23–81.

Miyashita, Y., & Chang, H. S. (1988). Neuronal correlate of pictorial short-term memory in the primate temporal cortex. *Nature, 331,* 68–70.

Namikawa, J., & Hashimoto, T. (2004). Dynamics and computation in functional shifts. *Nonlinearity, 17,* 1317–1336.

Nowak, M. A., Komarova, N. L., & Niyogi, P. (2001). Evolution of universal grammar. *Science, 291,* 114–118.

Nowak, M. A., Komarova, N. L., & Niyogi, P. (2002). Computational and evolutionary aspects of language. *Nature, 417,* 611–617.

O'Kane, D., & Treves, A. (1992). Why the simplest notion of neocortex as an autoassociative memory would not work. *Network, 3,* 379–384.

Price, C. J., & Friston, K. J. (2002). Degeneracy and cognitive anatomy. *Trends in Cognitive Science, 6,* 416–421.

Pulvermuller, F. (2002). A brain perspective on language mechanisms: From discrete neuronal ensembles to serial order. *Progress in Neurobiology, 67,* 85–111.

Rempel-Clower, N. L., & Barbas, H. (2000). The laminar pattern of connections between prefrontal and anterior temporal cortices in the Rhesus monkey is related to cortical structure and function. *Cerebral Cortex, 10,* 851–865.

Renart, A., Parga, N., & Rolls, E. T. (1999). Associative memory properties of multiple cortical modules. *Network, 10,* 237–255.

Ringach, D. L., Hawken, M. J., & Shapley, R. (2003). Dynamics of orientation tuning in macaque V1: The role of global and tuned suppression. *Journal of Neurophysiology, 90,* 342–352.

Rockel, A. J., Hiorns, R. W., & Powell, T. B. S. (1980). The basic uniformity in structure of the neocortex. *Brain, 103,* 221–244.

Rolls, E. T., & Treves, A. (1998). *Neural networks and brain function.* Oxford: Oxford University Press.

Roudi, Y., & Treves, A. (2003). Disappearance of spurious states in analog associative memories. *Physical Review E, 67,* 041906.

Shu, Y., Hasenstaub, A., & McCormick, D. A. (2003). Turning on and off recurrent balanced cortical activity. *Nature, 423,* 288–293.

Sompolinsky, H., & Shapley, R. (1997). New perspectives on the mechanisms for orientation selectivity. *Current Opinion in Neurobiology, 7,* 514–522.

Treves, A. (1997). On the perceptual structure of face space. *Biosystems, 40,* 189–196.

Treves, A. (2003). Computational constraints that may have favoured the lamination of sensory cortex. *Journal of Computational Neuroscience, 14,* 271–282.

Treves, A., & Rolls, E. T. (1991). What determines the capacity of autoassociative memories in the brain? *Network, 2,* 371–397.

Tsodyks, M. V., & Feigel'man, M. V. (1988). The enhanced storage capacity in neural networks with low activity level. *Europhysics Letters, 6,* 101–105.

Tsodyks, M. V., & Markram, H. (1997). The neural code between neocortical pyramidal neurons depends on neurotransmitter release probability. *Proceedings of the National Academy of Sciences, USA, 94,* 719–723.

Ullman, M. T. (2001). A neurocognitive perspective on language: The declarative/procedural model. *Nature Reviews Neuroscience, 2,* 717–726.

Young, M. P., Scannell, J. W., Burns, G. A., & Blakemore, C. (1994). Analysis of connectivity: Neural systems in the cerebral cortex. *Reviews in the Neurosciences, 5,* 227–250.

Zanini, S., Rumiati, R. I., & Shallice, T. (2002). Action sequencing deficit following frontal lobe lesions. *Neurocase, 8,* 88–99.

APPENDIX A

To derive the storage capacity of the Potts model in the limit of large S one could start from eqs. (16–18) of Kanter (1988) but, as they contain typographical mistakes, it is more convenient to start from eqs. (28–30) of Bollé et al. (1993), considered without the "bias" terms. Such equations, as the authors note, can be reduced to a single equation in terms of their variable $m\surd(Q/\alpha r)$, which I denote as v, while, to be consistent with the notation I use in this paper, I write the parameter Q as S, and α as P/c_M. The single equation is the analogue of eqs. (23) and (27) of Treves and Rolls (1991), which apply to different degrees of connectivity in an autoassociative network. For simplicity I consider only the case of a highly "diluted-connectivity" network, for which the equation reads

$$E_1(v, S) = [SA_2(v; S) - 1]^2/(S-1)^2 - (P/c_M)v^2 A_3(v; S)[S(S-1)] = 0 \quad (9)$$

where I define the averages

$$A_2(v; S) = \int Dz \Phi(z+v)^{S-1}, \quad (10)$$

$$A_3(v; S) = \int Dz\, [\Phi(z+v)^{S-1} + (S-1) \times \Phi(z)^{S-2}\, \Phi(z-v)] \quad (11)$$

and

$$Dz \equiv dz \exp(-z^2/2)/\surd(2\pi) \quad \Phi(x) \equiv \int_{-\infty}^{x} Dy.$$

In general for $S > 2$, $E_1(0, S) > 0$ while $E_1(v \to \infty, S) < 0$. For low enough values of P, $E_1(v, S) = 0$ at three intersection points, the middle one of which represents a stable solution, corresponding to a Potts attractor. While the first intersection, for low v such that $A_2(v; S) < 1/S$, is always present (and it does not identify a stable solution), as P grows, at some point the two intersections for higher v disappear, and no stable attractor exists. The phase transition occurs at some value P_c at which both $E_1(v^*, S) = 0$ and $\partial E_1(v^*, S)/\partial v = 0$ (cp. Treves & Rolls, 1991). To leading order in S, these two equations determine $v^* \approx \surd \log S^4$ and $P_c \approx c_M S^2/\log S^4$. Note that the exact denominator, including the leading logarithmic correction, depends on the connectivity, which is full in the original Kanter model and highly diluted in the formulae above.

APPENDIX B

Global activity patterns were generated in the simulations by a two-step algorithm, which could be parametrically varied from producing independent to highly correlated patterns. In the first step, a number of underlying *factors* were generated, defined simply as distinct random subsets of the entire set of Potts units. In the simulations, each subset included 50 units out of the total 300 units, and a total of 200 such factors were generated. The overlaps in the spatial distribution of different factors therefore are purely random, and clustered around their mean value $50^2/300 = 8.33$.

In the second step, global patterns were generated from the factors, which had been indexed by r in order of decreasing mean importance. For each global pattern, the specific importance of each factor was given by a coefficient γ_r^μ obtained by multiplying the overall factor $\exp(\zeta r)$ by a random number, taken to be 0 with probability $1-a$, and otherwise drawn with a flat distribution between 0 and 1, specifically for pattern μ. A value taken by factor r, s_r, was randomly drawn among the S "genuine" attractors, and a contribution γ_r^μ was added to the field onto each Potts unit over which factor r was defined, in the direction s_r. After accumulating contributions from all factors, the direction in which each unit received the largest field was computed, and the *a*M units receiving the largest maximal fields were assigned the corresponding direction s_r in pattern μ, while the remaining

$(1-a)M$ units were assigned the null state in pattern μ.

With this procedure, pairs of Potts units have uncorrelated activity when averaged across patterns (because the different patterns that both engage the pair will span nearly evenly the different local states). Pairs of patterns, instead, can be highly correlated once averaged across units, particularly if they share one or a few most important factors; and positively correlated if these factors have been assigned the same direction in Potts space. Thus correlations among patterns will be higher if the importance of different factors decreases rapidly (e.g., in the simulations the value $\zeta = 0.02$ was used, equivalent to assuming of order 50 "important" factors); and they will tend to vanish if all factors are equally important ($\zeta = 0$). When correlations are very high each pattern tends to be significantly correlated with a specific subset of the others, those sharing the main factor that influences them, and positively correlated with a fraction $1/S$ of this subset. In this scheme, the number of memory items significantly overlapping with one recently retrieved, and which can be the target of a nonrandom transition, scales up as P/S, and does not depend on c_M. By contrast, the storage capacity for retrieval, although severely reduced by correlations, should still scale as in eq. (4).

COGNITIVE NEUROPSYCHOLOGY, 2005, 22 (3/4), 292–305

CONTEXT-DEPENDENT INTERACTIONS OF LEFT POSTERIOR INFERIOR FRONTAL GYRUS IN A LOCAL VISUAL SEARCH TASK UNRELATED TO LANGUAGE

Zina M. Manjaly
Forschungszentrum Jülich, Germany

John C. Marshall
Radcliffe Infirmary, Oxford, UK

Klaas E. Stephan
RWTH Aachen, Germany, and Wellcome Dept. of Imaging Neuroscience, London, UK

Jennifer M. Gurd
Radcliffe Infirmary, Oxford, and University of Hertfordshire, Hatfield, UK

Karl Zilles
Forschungszentrum Jülich and Heinrich-Heine-Universität Düsseldorf, Germany

Gereon R. Fink
Forschungszentrum Jülich and RWTH Aachen, Germany

The Embedded Figures Task (EFT) involves search for a target hidden in a complex geometric pattern. Even though the EFT is designed to probe local visual search functions, not language-related processes, neuropsychological studies have demonstrated a strong association between aphasia and impairment on this task. A potential explanation for this relationship was offered by a recent functional MRI study (Manjaly et al., 2003), which demonstrated that a part of the left posterior inferior frontal gyrus (pIFG), overlapping with Broca's region, is crucially involved in the execution of the EFT. This result suggested that pIFG, an area strongly associated with language-related functions, is also part of a network subserving cognitive functions unrelated to language. In this study, we tested this conjecture by analysing the data of Manjaly et al. for context-dependent functional interactions of the pIFG during execution of the EFT. The results showed that during EFT, compared to a similar visual matching task with minimal local search components, pIFG changed its interactions with areas commonly involved in visuospatial processing: Increased contributions to neural activity in left posterior parietal cortex, cerebellar vermis, and extrastriate areas bilaterally, as well as decreased contributions to bilateral temporo-parietal cortex, posterior cingulate cortex, and left dorsal premotor cortex were found. These findings demonstrate that left pIFG can be involved in nonlanguage processes. More generally, however, they provide a concrete example of the notion that there is no

Correspondence should be addressed to Prof. Gereon R. Fink, MD, Institut für Medizin, Forschungszentrum Jülich, 52425 Jülich, Germany (Email: g.fink@fz-juelich.de).

JCM and JMG are supported by the Medical Research Council (MRC), UK. KZ and GRF are supported by the Deutsche Forschungsgemeinschaft (DFG-KFO 112), Germany. KES is funded by the Wellcome Trust, UK. Additional support from the VolkswagenStiftung to JCM, KZ, and GRF is gratefully acknowledged.

general one-to-one mapping between cognitive functions and the activations of individual areas. Instead, it is the spatiotemporal pattern of functional interactions between areas that is linked to a particular cognitive context.

INTRODUCTION

In the Embedded Figures Task (EFT), initially developed by Gottschaldt (1926, 1929), participants are presented with two geometric figures on each trial: a complex and a simple one. The objective is to decide whether the simpler figure is "embedded" in the complex one (i.e., is a subpart thereof). The task thus requires one to search the complex figure for intrinsic patterns that could match the simpler figure, i.e., the subjects' visual search is guided and constrained by the simple figure and the local characteristics of the complex figure. In neuropsychological studies, the EFT has been used to investigate characteristics of local perception and visual search, both in normal subjects and various patient groups. One intriguing finding from these investigations is that both autistic subjects and unaffected relatives often show superior EFT performance as compared to normal controls (Baron-Cohen & Hammer, 1997; Happé, 1999; Shah & Frith, 1983). These results have been interpreted as evidence for the hypothesis of "weak central coherence" in autistic patients, i.e., the tendency to bias visual information processing towards the local rather than the global level (Frith, 1989; Happé, 1999).

While the application of the EFT in autism research has created long-lasting interest and has led to numerous applications, including functional imaging studies (Ring et al., 1999), it is less well known that some curious findings had been obtained when testing patients with acquired brain damage on the EFT. An interesting relationship between left-hemisphere lesions and EFT performance was first revealed in a clinical study by Teuber and Weinstein (1956): Patients suffering from aphasia unexpectedly showed greater impairment on the EFT than patients with other neuropsychological deficits. Subsequent studies replicated this finding, demonstrating additionally that (1) this association did not depend on the extent of brain damage as such, and (2) that the impairment was not due to failure to understand the task instructions (Orgass, Poeck, Kirchensteiner, & Hartje, 1972; Russo & Vignolo, 1967). These results were puzzling, since the EFT is not obviously related to language processing, but rather to local visuospatial processing. A convincing explanation for the association between aphasia and impaired EFT performance has been lacking for a long time, although the well-known left-hemisphere advantage for local processing (Fink et al., 1996, 1997; Marshall & Fink, 2001; Robertson, Lamb, & Knight, 1988) may at least in part contribute to this association.

Recently, a functional magnetic resonance imaging (fMRI) study that contrasted the EFT with a similar but simpler visual matching task that minimised the local search aspects identified the cortex around the left intraparietal sulcus (IPS) and, more interestingly, a region extending from the ventral part of the precentral gyrus across the precentral sulcus into the posterior part of the inferior frontal gyrus (pIFG) as areas crucially involved in the local search aspects of the EFT (Manjaly, Marshall, Stephan, Gurd, Zilles, & Fink, 2003). The spatial extent of the activation in the left pIFG overlapped with the dorsal part of Broca's region, i.e., areas 44 and 45, as defined by observer-independent cytoarchitectonic techniques (Amunts, Schleicher, Bürgel, Mohlberg, Uylings, & Zilles, 1999). Its local maximum ($x = -42$, $y = 10$, $z = 24$) possessed coordinates in good correspondence to those provided by previous fMRI studies on various aspects of language processing (e.g., Poldrack et al., 1999; Stephan et al., 2003). There is overwhelming evidence, both from lesion and functional imaging studies, that left pIFG is associated with various aspects of language function. Therefore, the strong activation of this region when subjects undertake the EFT provides an explanation for the association of aphasia and impaired EFT performance.

It remains to be explained, however, why a region like the left pIFG, which is normally found to be involved in language processing, should play any role at all during a local visual search task like the EFT, which does not seem to require any language-related processing. One possible explanation is that pIFG is involved in the EFT simply because the EFT contains a language-related component that we and previous researchers had not been aware of (the "hidden language component hypothesis"). But neither the simple nor the complex figures typically used in the EFT are easily nameable. An alternative hypothesis is that left pIFG participates in different cortical networks subserving different cognitive functions, depending on the context of the overall task. This idea of "neural context", i.e., the context-dependent binding of a given area into different networks, has previously been formulated by McIntosh (2000), who suggests that "a particular region in isolation may not act as a reliable index for a particular cognitive function. Instead, the neural context in which an area is active may define the cognitive function. Neural context emphasizes that the particular spatiotemporal pattern of neural interactions may hold the key to bridge between brain and mind." From this perspective, understanding the potential range of function of an area requires us to understand its *context-dependent interactions with other areas*. This view represents a change from the investigation of functional specialisation, as it has been conceived in the large majority of neuropsychological and functional imaging studies to date, towards the characterisation of *functional integration* in the brain (Friston, 1998).

In the present study, we have applied this concept to the fMRI study by Manjaly et al. (2003) and have re-analysed the data using a simple model of effective connectivity (Friston, 1994). Specifically, we have used "psychophysiological interactions" (PPI; Friston, Büchel, Fink, Morris, Rolls, & Dolan, 1997) to investigate the context-dependent functional contributions of left pIFG to brain responses elsewhere. If the "hidden language component hypothesis" is correct and pIFG function is indeed largely or entirely dedicated to language or language-like tasks, its pattern of functional interactions during the EFT, as compared to the control task, should include other language-related areas, e.g., in the left temporal lobe. On the other hand, if the hypothesis of "neural context" is correct, we would expect that comparing the functional interactions of left pIFG during the two different visuospatial search tasks of our experiment should reveal changes in pIFG connectivity only with areas associated with visuospatial rather than language processing, e.g., posterior parietal, extrastriate, and dorsal premotor regions.

MATERIAL AND METHODS

Details of the experimental design, data acquisition, and data analysis have been published previously (Manjaly et al., 2003). Here, we briefly summarise the methods and then focus on the analysis of effective connectivity, using psychophysiological interactions (PPIs; see Friston et al., 1997).

Subjects

Sixteen healthy, right-handed male volunteers (aged 20 to 36 years; mean age 24.3 years, $SD = 4.3$ years) with no history of neurological or psychiatric illness were studied. The study was approved by the ethics committee of the University Hospital Aachen. Informed written consent was obtained prior to participation.

Stimuli and experimental design

The initial aim of this experiment was to localise brain activations that were specific to the local search aspects of the EFT. Therefore, we compared the EFT to another closely related but easier visual search task (referred to as "control task") that operated on similar visual stimuli and also engaged visual search, shape analysis, visual matching, decisions about geometrical configurations, and motor responses, but which minimised local visual search processes as the stimuli were disambiguated, i.e., a figure within the complex figure was highlighted (see below). To investigate whether the spatial arrangement of the stimuli had an influence on how the tasks were performed, we used horizontally and vertically arranged pairs of stimuli equally often. We thus dealt with a 2×2 factorial design with task (EFT vs. control task) and stimulus orientation (horizontal vs. vertical) as experimental factors.

All stimuli were produced using a PC graphics program (Corel Draw 9.0, Corel Corp). Thirty-two geometrical figures consisting of 12 lines and of comparable complexity were created. Each of these complex figures was presented eight times throughout the course of the experiment, i.e., twice in each of the four conditions. In all conditions, each complex figure was accompanied by a simple target figure. These target figures were either embedded into the simultaneously presented complex figures (50% of trials) or were not part of any of the complex figures shown on any trial (50% of trials). Each correct target figure was only shown once throughout the entire experiment to minimise priming effects. Since the incorrect target figures were not embedded in any of the complex figures used in the experiment, they could safely be used twice, i.e., once in each task. Figure 1 shows examples of the figures used as stimuli during the EFT and the control task, and also summarises the factorial design of the experiment. For the EFT, subjects were instructed to indicate via right-hand button press whether or not the target was embedded in the complex figure. During the control task, subjects were presented with the same stimuli, which were, however, disambiguated: i.e., a simple figure within the complex figure was highlighted. For this task, subjects were instructed to indicate via right-hand button presses whether or not the target figure

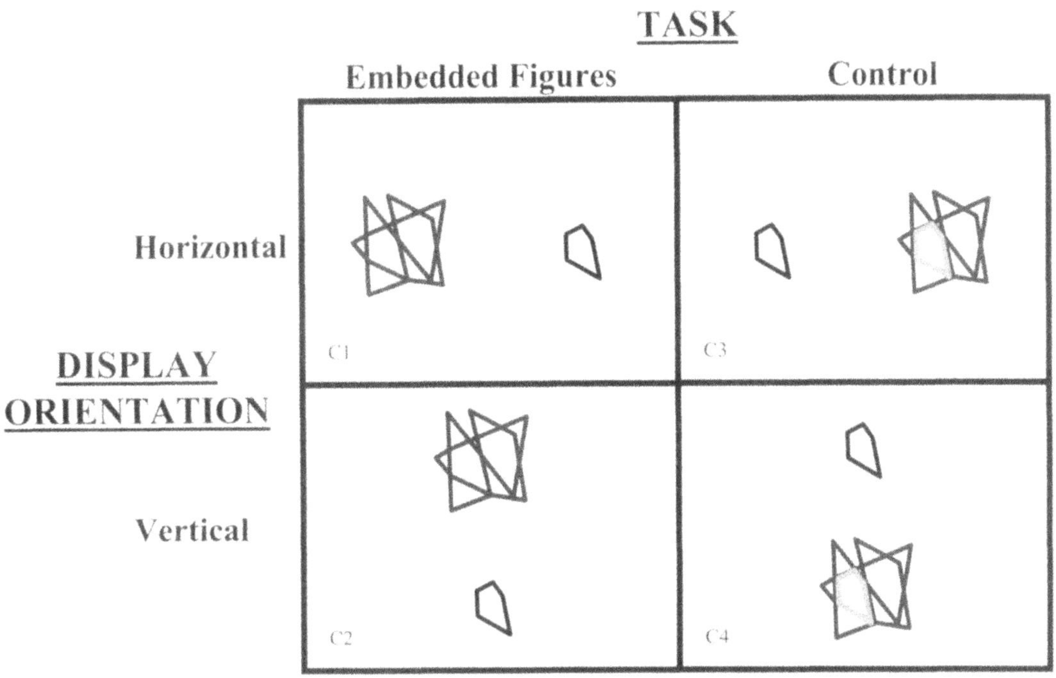

Figure 1. *Stimuli and study design. Examples of the stimuli used for the Embedded Figures Task and the control task. Stimuli were displayed either horizontally or vertically. In the EFT subjects judged whether the target figure was or was not embedded in the more complex figure. In the control task subjects judged whether the target figure did or did not match the highlighted figure (indicated in grey) within the complex figure. Adapted, with permission, from Figure 1 in Manjaly et al. (2003).*

matched the simple figure highlighted within the complex figure. The conditions were blocked, with each block containing eight trials (each with a stimulus on time of 3 s) and lasting 32 s in total. Between conditions, a "baseline" (lasting 24 s) was implemented, in which subjects viewed squares or triangles presented centrally and had to indicate via right-hand button presses whether or not the figure presented was a square. Before the beginning of each block, instructions of the subsequent task were given for 4 s, informing the subject which task to perform and whether the stimuli were arranged horizontally or vertically. The condition sequence was pseudorandomised and counterbalanced across subjects. In order to allow for short break periods, the experiment was split into four consecutive sessions. Each session consisted of eight task blocks alternating with eight baseline blocks. Thus, the experiment included 32 task blocks (16 EFT blocks, 16 control task blocks) and 32 baseline blocks altogether.

Behaviourally, reaction times and error rates were recorded as measures of task difficulty and task performance. Additionally, as the tasks were undertaken in free vision, we recorded eye movements in all subjects during the MR measurements to assess whether differential eye movements occurred in the Embedded Figures Task and control conditions. An fMRI-compatible infrared video-based eye-tracking device (ASL 504; Applied Science Laboratories, Bedford, MA, USA) was used for this purpose. Details of the analysis of the behavioural data can be found in our previous article (Manjaly et al., 2003).

MRI data acquisition

Magnetic resonance imaging was performed on a Magnetom Vision 1.5 Tesla scanner (Siemens Medical Systems GmbH, Erlangen, Germany) using a standard head coil. For each subject, a high-resolution, T1-weighted anatomical image was obtained using a MP-RAGE sequence. Functional images were obtained by means of an Echo Planar Imaging (EPI) sequence with the following parameters: gradient echo EPI; TE = 66 ms; TR = 4 s; FOV = 200 × 200 mm; flip angle = 90°; matrix size = 64 × 64; pixel size = 3.125 × 3.125 mm; slice thickness = 4.0 mm; inter-slice gap = 0.4 mm; 30 slices. At the beginning of each session, four dummy scans were obtained to allow the MR signal to reach a steady state.

fMRI data analysis

Spatial preprocessing and statistical analysis of fMRI data were performed using MATLAB 5.3 (The Mathworks Inc., Natick, MA, USA) and SPM99 software (Statistical Parametric Mapping; Wellcome Department of Imaging Neuroscience, London, UK; http://www.fil.ion.ucl.ac.uk/spm). The first four dummy images of each session were discarded. The remaining 128 volume images of each time-series were realigned to correct for head movements during scanning. Models of effective connectivity that are based on variants of regression analysis assume that data points from different time series have been acquired simultaneously. Since this is not the case in multi-slice acquisition fMRI, we corrected for differences in the acquisition times of the 30 slices by linear interpolation in time (slice timing), using the middle slice as a reference point. All functional images were then coregistered to the 3D anatomical image and transformed into the Montreal Neurological Institute (MNI) stereotactic space, which is based on the Talairach system (Talairach & Tournoux, 1988). Resampling after this nonlinear warping procedure (Ashburner & Friston, 1999; Friston et al., 1995a) led to a resulting pixel size of 2 × 2 × 2 mm. Transformed functional images were smoothed with a Gaussian kernel of 10 mm full width half maximum (FWHM) for the group analysis to meet the statistical requirements of the general linear model and to compensate for normal variation in individual brain size, shape, and sulcal/gyral anatomy.

Following spatial preprocessing, statistical analysis was performed using a general linear model in SPM99 (Friston et al., 1995b). Low-frequency signal drifts were removed by a high pass filter (cutoff: 0.0075 Hz). Global means were normalised by proportional scaling. Data were analysed by modelling the different conditions as reference waveforms (i.e., box car functions convolved with a canonical hemodynamic response function). For each subject, the design matrix included regressors for the 5 conditions (i.e., 4 task conditions, 1 baseline condition) and 12 regressors with realignment parameters (6 absolute and 6 differential parameters describing rotation and translation of the subject's head). Following parameter estimation, effects of interest were tested by applying appropriate linear contrasts, resulting in a *t*-statistic at each voxel. These *t*-statistics (transformed to *Z*-statistics) constitute a subject-specific statistical parametric map (SPM{Z}). The SPM{Z} maps were then interpreted by referring to the probabilistic behaviour of Gaussian random fields. In all analyses, areas of activation were identified as significant only if they passed a threshold of $p_c < .05$, corrected for multiple comparisons at the cluster level (Friston et al., 1995b; Poline, Worsley, Evans, & Friston, 1997).

For the fMRI data group analysis, the contrast images from the analyses of the individual subjects were analysed by one-sample *t*-tests. This constituted a random effects model, which allows inference to the population from which the 16 subjects were drawn (Friston, Holmes, & Worsley, 1999).

Details and results of the above analysis have been reported by Manjaly et al. (2003). Its methodological principles are briefly repeated here because the results form the starting point for the analysis of effective connectivity that is the central topic of this article. Specifically, in the present study we used a variant of psychophysiological interactions (Friston et al., 1997) to determine all brain areas that received a context-dependent contribution from the posterior part of the left inferior frontal gyrus (pIFG) cortex. First, the analysis described above was repeated for each subject, using the identical design matrix but smoothing the data spatially with a smaller kernel, i.e., 6 mm FWHM, to obtain a higher regional specificity for the left pIFG time series. For each subject, we then determined the local maximum of the left pIFG activation in the EFT vs. control task contrast that was closest to the group maximum in the random effects analysis for this contrast. In order to select voxels in which our model optimally explained the variance of the data, this local pIFG maximum was determined from an F-contrast spanning all effects of interest. Individual time series for the left pIFG were obtained by extracting the first principal component from all voxel time series within a sphere (6 mm radius) centred on the chosen pIFG coordinates. This procedure for extracting characteristic regional time series is widely used in analyses of effective connectivity (compare, for example, Büchel & Friston, 1997; Rowe et al., 2002; Stephan et al., 2003). The resulting time series were mean-corrected and high-pass filtered to remove low-frequency signal drifts, but were not manipulated otherwise. After these time series had been chosen, the actual PPI analysis could be prepared. The psychophysiological pIFG × task interaction term (referred to as "PPI regressor") was computed as the element-by-element product of the mean-corrected left pIFG time series and a mean-corrected task vector coding for the main effect of task (1 for each scan during the EFT, −1 for each scan during the control task, and 0 elsewhere). Prior to multiplication, this task vector was convolved with a canonical hemodynamic response function (to account for the hemodynamic lag) and mean-corrected. The PPI regressor was mean-corrected and orthogonalised with regard to the main effect of task and the pIFG time series. In addition to the PPI regressor and the pIFG time series per se, the model of effective connectivity included the main effects of task and stimulus orientation, the baseline condition, and effects of no interest (instruction periods, movement regressors). Altogether, our analysis of effective connectivity was thus specific for context-dependent pIFG influences that occurred over and above any task effects and context-independent pIFG influences (compare Macaluso, Frith, & Driver, 2000; Stephan et al., 2003). Brain sites receiving contextual pIFG influences that were stronger during EFT than during the control task were determined by testing for positive slopes of the PPI regressor, i.e., by applying a *t*-contrast that was 1 for the PPI regressor and 0 elsewhere. Conversely, areas receiving contextual pIFG influences that were weaker during the EFT than during the control task were found by testing for negative slopes of the PPI regressor, i.e., by applying a *t*-contrast that was −1 for the PPI regressor and 0 elsewhere. Subject-specific contrast images were smoothed spatially (using a Gaussian kernel of 8 mm FWHM; together with the initial 6 mm smoothing, this resulted in an overall smoothness of 10 mm FWHM) and then entered into random effects group analyses. As in the conventional SPM analysis described above, the significance of the results was assessed by correcting for multiple comparisons across the whole brain, using a corrected threshold of $p < .05$ at the cluster-level (with $p < .001$ at the voxel-level).

RESULTS

As reported in Manjaly et al. (2003) in detail, comparing Embedded Figures Task (EFT) vs. the control task (CT) showed significant clusters of activation in the posterior part of the left inferior frontal gyrus (pIFG; local maximum at $x = -42$, $y = 10$, $z = 24$; $t_{max} = 6.77$, $p < .05$, corrected) and along the left intraparietal sulcus (-24, -58, 54; $t_{max} = 5.15$, $p < .05$, corrected). Figure 2 summarises the results of this previous analysis.

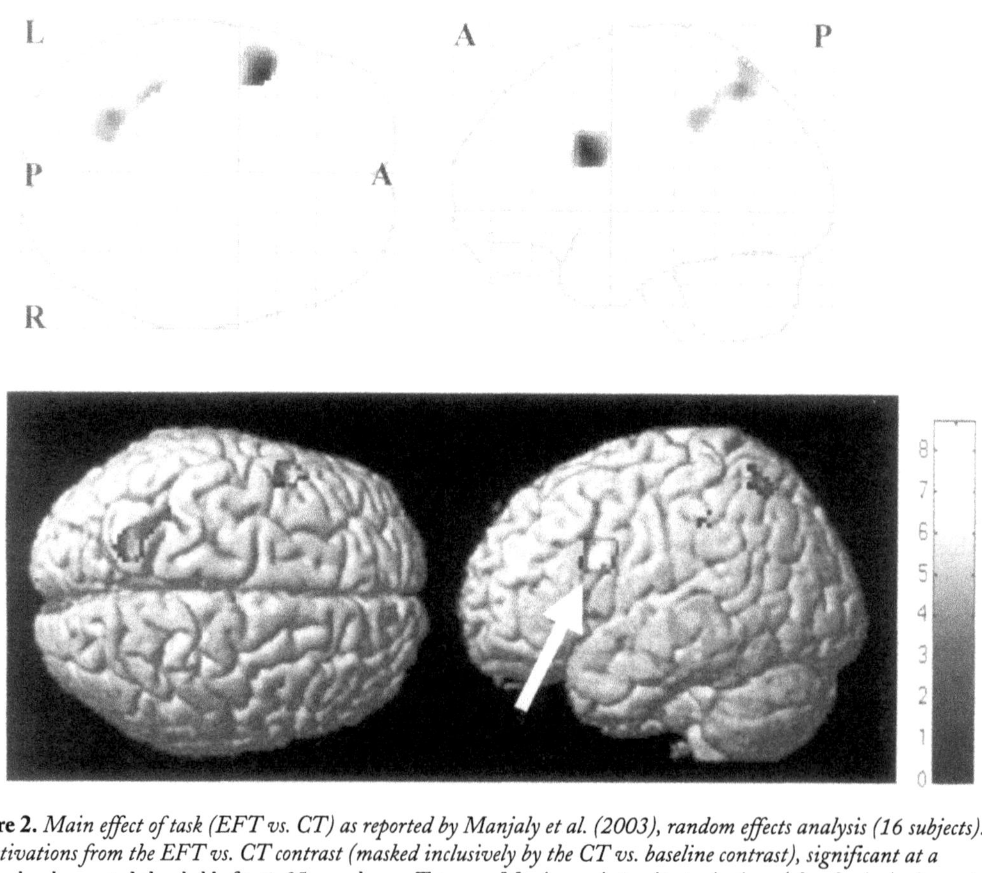

Figure 2. *Main effect of task (EFT vs. CT) as reported by Manjaly et al. (2003), random effects analysis (16 subjects). All activations from the EFT vs. CT contrast (masked inclusively by the CT vs. baseline contrast), significant at a cluster-level corrected threshold of p < .05, are shown. Top row: Maximum intensity projections (glass brains). A = anterior, P = posterior, L = left, R = right. Bottom row: Activations overlaid on a rendered template brain. The colour bar indicates t-values. The white arrow points to the activation in the posterior inferior frontal gyrus that represented the starting point for the analysis in this paper. Adapted, with permission, from Figure 3 in Manjaly et al. (2003). To view this figure in colour, please see the online issue of the Journal.*

The local maximum of this activation in the left pIFG served as the starting point for the PPI analysis in this paper. As described in the Methods section, for each subject we determined the local pIFG maximum in the "effects of interest" F-contrast that was closest to the group maximum of the EFT > CT contrast and extracted a characteristic regional time series as the basis for the subject-specific PPI analysis. The contrast images resulting from testing for positive and negative regression slopes of the PPI regressor (i.e., the pIFG × task interaction term), respectively, were then entered into standard random effects group analyses of all 16 subjects. All results reported below have been corrected for multiple comparisons across the whole brain, using a corrected cluster-level threshold of $p < .05$ (with $p < .001$ at the voxel-level).

In the random effects group analysis, areas that showed an *increased* contribution from left pIFG during EFT as compared to CT included the left posterior parietal cortex (local maximum at −18, −62, 58; $t_{max} = 6.77$, $p < .01$; Figure 3A,B), extrastriate areas bilaterally (left hemisphere: −18, −90, 26; $t_{max} = 5.47$, $p < .001$; right hemisphere: 26, −84, 22; $t_{max} = 4.63$, $p < .014$; Figure 3A,C), and the cerebellar vermis (2, −64, −50; $t_{max} = 4.60$, $p < .014$; Figure 3A). In contrast, areas that received a *decreased* contribution from the left pIFG during EFT relative to CT included the temporo-parietal cortex bilaterally (left hemisphere: −50, −56, 20; $t_{max} = 6.82$, $p < .001$; right hemisphere:

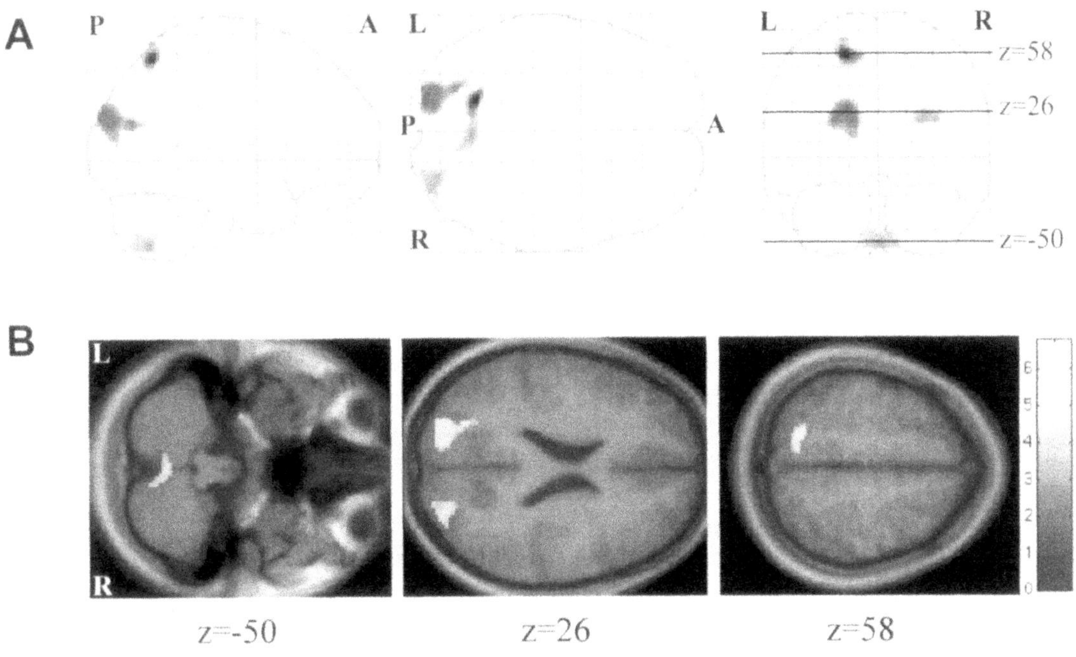

Figure 3. *Results of the PPI analysis, random effects analysis (16 subjects). All areas are shown that receive an increased influence from left pIFG during EFT relative to CT. Cluster-level threshold of p < .05, corrected for multiple comparisons across the whole brain (voxel-level threshold of p < .001). (A) Maximum intensity projections (glass brains) of the results: sagittal (left), horizontal (middle), and coronal (right) views. Red lines indicate the approximate locations of the sections in Figure 3B. Abbreviations as in Figure 2. (B) Horizontal sections showing significant increases of left pIFG contribution to the cerebellar vermis (left), extrastriate cortex (middle), and left posterior parietal cortex (right). Activations are overlaid on the averaged normalised structural image of all 16 subjects. z-coordinates denote the horizontal level from which sections were taken—see Figure 3A, right panel. To view this figure in colour, please see the online issue of the Journal.*

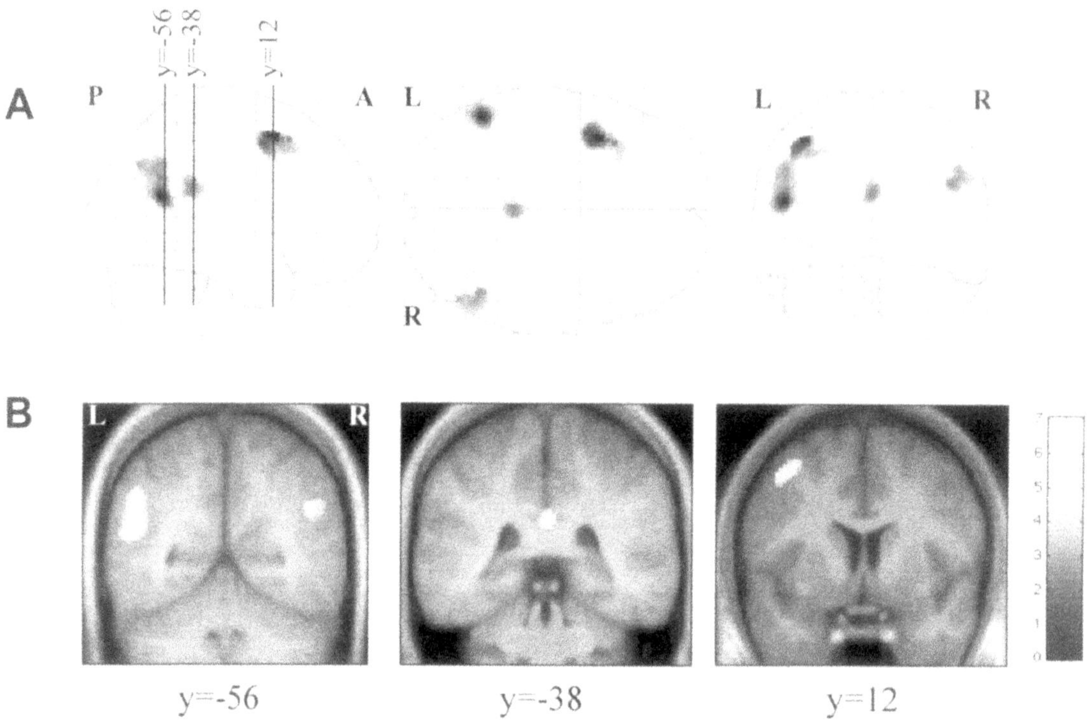

Figure 4. *Results of the PPI analysis for left pIFG, random effects analysis (16 subjects). All areas are shown that receive a decreased influence from left pIFG during EFT relative to CT. Conventions and abbreviations as in Figure 3. (A) Red lines indicate the approximate locations of the sections in Figure 4B. (B) Coronal sections showing significant decreases of left pIFG contribution to the bilateral temporo-parietal junction (left), posterior cingulate cortex (middle), and left dorsal premotor cortex (right). y-coordinates denote the coronal level from which sections were taken—see Figure 4A, left panel. To view this figure in colour, please see the online issue of the Journal.*

46, −56, 30; $t_{max} = 5.26$, $p < .001$; Figure 4A,B), the posterior cingulate cortex bilaterally (0, −38, 26; $t_{max} = 5.38$, $p < .007$; Figure 4A), and the left dorsal premotor cortex (−38, 12, 54; $t_{max} = 7.02$, $p < .001$; Figure 4A).

To complete the characterisation of context-dependent functional interactions in our paradigm, we performed analogous PPI analyses for the second area which, in the conventional SPM analysis, had demonstrated significantly higher activity during the EFT relative to the control task, i.e., the left IPS. In this second PPI analysis, the only area that showed an increased contribution from the left IPS during EFT as compared to CT was the right posterior parietal cortex (18, −62, 42; $t_{max} = 6.69$, $p < .001$; Figure 5A). Similar to the PPI results for the left pIFG, the left temporo-parietal cortex (−58, −50, 16; $t_{max} = 4.57$, $p < .001$; Figure 5B) was found to receive a decreased contribution from the left IPS during EFT compared to the control task.

DISCUSSION

The present study complements and extends the findings by Manjaly et al. (2003) in explaining a repeatedly observed association between aphasia (due to left-hemispheric lesions) and impaired performance on the EFT (Orgass et al., 1972; Russo & Vignolo, 1967; Teuber & Weinstein, 1956). Manjaly et al. demonstrated that a region in the left pIFG showed significantly higher activity during the EFT compared with a similar visual

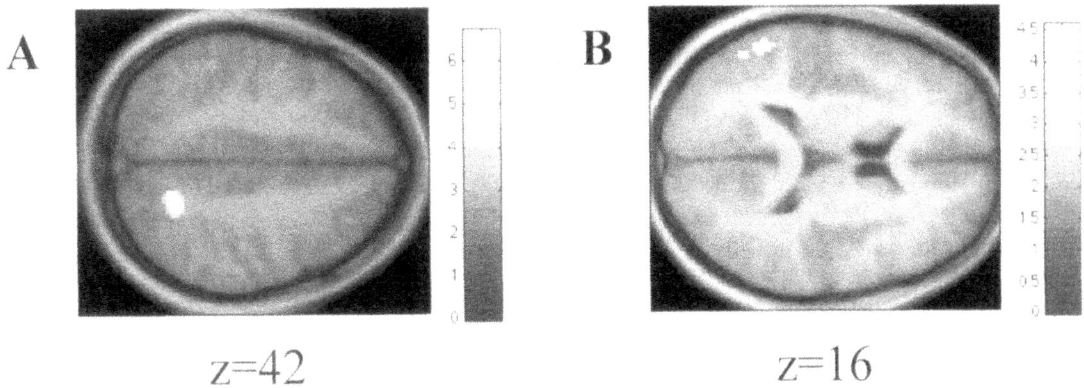

Figure 5. *Results of the PPI analysis for left IPS, random effects analysis (16 subjects). As in Figures 2–4, results are shown at a cluster-level threshold of* $p < .05$*, corrected for multiple comparisons across the whole brain (voxel-level threshold of* $p < .001$*). (A) The only area to receive an increased contribution from left IPS during EFT as compared to the control task was the right posterior parietal cortex (18, −62, 42;* $t_{max} = 6.69, p < .001$*). (B) Similar to the PPI results for the left pIFG (compare Figure 4), the left temporo-parietal cortex (−58 , −50, 16;* $t_{max} = 4.57, p < .001$*) was found to receive a decreased contribution from the left IPS during EFT relative to the control task. To view this figure in colour, please see the online issue of the Journal.*

matching control task that made only minimal use, however, of local visual search processes. In this study, we re-analysed the data by Manjaly et al. (2003) and investigated context-dependent functional interactions of the left pIFG to distinguish between two possible explanations why left pIFG, which is usually associated with language processing, might be involved in the execution of the EFT. One hypothesis was that pIFG is activated during the EFT because performing the EFT might involve a "hidden" language-related component that had simply gone unnoticed thus far. If this "hidden language component hypothesis" was correct and left pIFG function during the EFT was linked to language processes, we would expect to find significant changes in functional interactions with language-related areas, e.g., in the left temporal lobe, during the EFT as compared to the control task. The alternative hypothesis was based on the idea of "neural context" (McIntosh, 2000; McIntosh, Rajah, & Lobaugh, 2003), i.e., depending on task requirements: left pIFG may be able to participate in different cortical networks and could thus contribute to different cognitive processes. If this hypothesis was correct and left pIFG could also become involved in local visual search processes, we expected that comparing the functional interactions of left pIFG during the two different visuospatial tasks of our experiment should demonstrate significant changes in coupling, predominantly with areas typically involved in visuospatial processing.

In order to assess context-dependent functional interactions and decide between the two hypotheses above, we computed psychophysiological interactions of the left pIFG. Importantly, this method does not determine absolute degrees of coupling, but computes the *difference* in the functional contributions of a source area to voxels elsewhere between two different contexts (Friston et al., 1997). Since we had no strong hypotheses on the type of coupling changes induced by alternating between the two tasks, we determined the entire set of areas that showed a significant difference in coupling with left pIFG between the EFT and the control task, regardless of the direction of this difference.

The results of our PPI analyses provided evidence that pIFG function is not exclusively linked to language, but can cooperate with areas that commonly subserve visuospatial functions: During the EFT (relative to the control task), left pIFG increased its contribution to left posterior parietal cortex, bilateral extrastriate cortex, and the cerebellar vermis, and decreased its contribution to left and right temporo-parietal cortex, posterior cingulate cortex, and left dorsal premotor cortex (see Figures 3 and 4). The involvement of all these areas in various aspects of visuospatial processing has been demonstrated by a series of previous imaging studies (e.g., Corbetta, Kincade, Ollinger, McAvoy, & Shulman, 2000; Fink et al., 2000; Fink, Marshall, Weiss, & Zilles, 2001; Gitelman, Parrish, Friston, & Mesulam, 2002; Hopfinger, Buonocore, & Mangun, 2000; Kim et al., 1999; Yantis et al., 2002). In contrast, to our knowledge, only two of these areas have been implicated in language processing as well: left temporo-parietal cortex activation has previously been observed during the processing of spoken language (Binder et al., 1997), and the left dorsal premotor cortex has been linked to verbal working memory (Herwig et al., 2003). These cognitive processes, however, are highly unlikely to be part of any strategy that could be used to perform either the EFT or the control task: first, spoken words were not part of the stimulus material, and second, the use of verbal working memory was not an appropriate strategy to cope with our complex visuospatial displays (see Manjaly et al., 2003). Moreover, if language-related components had indeed played a role in our paradigm, one would not have expected the results from our analysis that showed higher left pIFG coupling with left temporo-parietal and left dorsal premotor cortex during the control task than during the EFT. In other words, why should the control task, which was a rather conventional matching task (with minimal visual search), use these putative language-related processes to a stronger degree than the more complex EFT?

We thus conclude that the changes in coupling with left pIFG that we have observed in the areas described above reflect the changes in a general visuospatial network that occur due to different demands of the two tasks on specific visuospatial subprocesses (e.g., direct matching of the target to a "pop-out" element in the control task compared to iterative matching during local search in the EFT). This interpretation is supported by the additional results from our analysis concerning the context-dependent interactions of the second region that was found by Manjaly et al. (2003) to be activated during the EFT relative to the control task, i.e., the left IPS. In contrast to left pIFG, there is much previous evidence that left IPS subserves visuospatial functions (e.g., Corbetta et al., 2000; Hopfinger et al., 2000). In our analysis, the left IPS showed an increased contribution to the right posterior parietal cortex, another "classical" visuospatial area, during EFT compared to the control task (see Figure 5A). Importantly, in analogy to the findings for left pIFG, the reverse comparison demonstrated higher left IPS coupling with the same left temporo-parietal region during the control task relative to EFT (Figure 5B).

At a more general level, our findings demonstrate that, depending on the context of the task, left pIFG can contribute to cognitive operations other than language processing. To some extent, this view had previously been suggested by functional imaging experiments of the human "mirror neuron system." These studies have demonstrated that the left pIFG is crucially involved in action understanding and action imitation (Binkofski et al., 2001; Buccino et al., 2001; Nishitani & Hari, 2001; Rizzolatti, Fogassi, & Gallese, 2001). However, although action understanding and imitation do not necessarily constitute language functions in a strict sense, some proposals have tried to bridge these two domains by suggesting that the acquisition of language skills may be linked to the imitation of mouth movements (e.g., Iacoboni et al., 1999; Rizzolatti & Arbib, 1998). Therefore, our current findings challenge the traditional view of pIFG as an area entirely dedicated to language much more radically than the results from the above studies of the "mirror neuron system."

Our results are in accordance with conceptual frameworks in cognitive neuroscience that stress the importance of context and interactivity for understanding the functional architecture of the brain (Friston, 1998, 2002; McIntosh, 2000). Although these approaches neither deny nor indeed question the existence of specialised computational modules in the brain, they posit that complex cognitive processes cannot be localised to a single region but result from context-dependent interactions within networks of areas. From the opposite perspective, the notion of a distributed architecture of brain function implies that a particular area may be part of different networks depending on a given task context. This view is corroborated by results from neuroanatomical and neurophysiological studies that, collectively, demonstrate that the computational role of any given cortical area cannot be derived from its behaviour in a single task or task comparison, but is characterised better through its multivariate response profile across a wide range of tasks (Passingham, Stephan, & Kötter, 2002). This "functional fingerprint" (Passingham et al., 2002) of a particular area critically depends on its unique pattern of anatomical connections with other areas. This is because the "connectional fingerprint" of an area necessarily constrains its functional interactions, i.e., where it receives information from and where the processed information can be sent to, and thus determines which networks the area can participate in (Kötter & Stephan, 2003; Passingham et al., 2002).

The notion that a particular area may contribute to more than one cognitive function by participating in more than one functional network represents a one-to-many structure-function relationship. It should be noted that the opposite principle, i.e., a many-to-one structure-function relationship, is also found in the human brain: There are some cognitive functions that can be mediated by means of different (partially overlapping or totally disjoint) networks (Friston & Price, 2003; Price & Friston, 2002; Tononi, Sporns, & Edelman, 1999). This concept of "degeneracy" is found at many different biological levels, ranging from the genetic code to the systems level of the brain, and represents a major problem for causal inferences based on behavioural deficits after brain lesions (Price & Friston, 2002; Young, Hilgetag, & Scannell, 2000). Both phenomena, particular areas participating in different cognitive functions and particular cognitive functions being mediated by different networks of areas, bear testimony to the highly distributed architecture of the human brain. Disentangling these complex structure-function relationships will require neurobiologically plausible and mathematically sophisticated models of brain function—a challenge that is only just beginning to be tackled (Friston, 2000; Friston, Harrison, & Penny, 2003; Tagamets & Horwitz, 1998).

PrEview proof published online 17 January 2005

REFERENCES

Amunts, K., Schleicher, A., Bürgel, U., Mohlberg, H., Uylings, H. B., & Zilles, K. (1999). Broca's region revisited: Cytoarchitecture and intersubject variability. *Journal of Comparative Neurology, 412,* 319–341.

Ashburner, J., & Friston, K. J. (1999). Nonlinear spatial normalization using basis functions. *Human Brain Mapping, 7,* 254–266.

Baron-Cohen, S., & Hammer, J. (1997). Parents of children with Asperger syndrome: What is the cognitive phenotype? *Journal of Cognitive Neuroscience, 9,* 548–554.

Binder, J. R., Frost, J. A., Hammeke, T. A., Cox, R. W., Rao, S. M., & Prieto, T. (1997). Human brain language areas identified by functional magnetic resonance imaging. *Journal of Neuroscience, 17,* 353–362.

Binkofski, F., Amunts, K., Stephan, K. M., Posse, S., Schormann, T., Freund, H. J., Zilles, K., & Seitz, R. J. (2001). Broca's region subserves imagery of motion: A combined cytoarchitectonic and fMRI study. *Human Brain Mapping, 11,* 273–285.

Buccino, G., Binkofski, F., Fink, G. R., Fadiga, L., Fogassi, L., Gallese, V., Seitz, R. J., Zilles, K., Rizzolatti, G., & Freund, H. J. (2001). Action observation activates premotor and parietal areas in a somatotopic manner: An fMRI study. *European Journal of Neuroscience, 13,* 400–404.

Büchel, C., & Friston, K. J. (1997). Modulation of connectivity in visual pathways by attention: Cortical interactions evaluated with structural equation modelling and fMRI. *Cerebral Cortex, 7,* 768–778.

Corbetta, M., Kincade, J. M., Ollinger, J. M., McAvoy, M. P., & Shulman, G. L. (2000). Voluntary orienting is dissociated from target detection in human posterior parietal cortex. *Nature Neuroscience, 3,* 292–297.

Fink, G. R., Halligan, P. W., Marshall, J. C., Frith, C. D., Frackowiak, R. S. J., & Dolan, R. J. (1996). Where in the brain does visual attention select the forest and the trees? *Nature, 382,* 626–628.

Fink, G. R., Halligan, P. W., Marshall, J. C., Frith, C. D., Frackowiak, R. S. J., & Dolan, R. J. (1997). Neural mechanisms involved in the processing of global and local aspects of hierarchically organized visual stimuli. *Brain, 120,* 1779–1791.

Fink, G. R., Marshall, J. C., Shah, N. J., Weiss, P. H., Halligan, P. W., Grosse-Ruyken, M., Ziemons, K., Zilles, K., & Freund, H. J. (2000). Line bisection judgments implicate right parietal cortex and cerebellum as assessed by fMRI. *Neurology, 54,* 1324–1331.

Fink, G. R., Marshall, J. C., Weiss, P. H., & Zilles, K. (2001). The neural basis of vertical and horizontal line bisection judgments: An fMRI study of normal volunteers. *NeuroImage, 14,* S59–S67.

Friston, K. J. (1994). Functional and effective connectivity: A synthesis. *Human Brain Mapping, 2,* 56–78.

Friston, K. J. (1998). Imaging neuroscience: Principles or maps? *Proceedings of the National Academy of Sciences USA, 95,* 796–802.

Friston, K. J. (2000). The labile brain. I. Neuronal transients and nonlinear coupling. *Philosophical Transactions of the Royal Society of London B: Biological Sciences, 355,* 215–236.

Friston, K. J. (2002). Functional integration and inference in the brain. *Progress in Neurobiology, 68,* 113–143.

Friston, K. J., Ashburner, J., Frith, C. D., Poline, J. B., Heather, J. D., & Frackowiak, R. S. J. (1995a). Spatial registration and normalization of images. *Human Brain Mapping, 3,* 165–189.

Friston, K. J., Büchel, C., Fink, G. R., Morris, J., Rolls, E., & Dolan, R. J. (1997). Psychophysiological and modulatory interactions in neuroimaging. *NeuroImage, 6,* 218–229.

Friston, K. J., Harrison, L., & Penny, W. (2003). Dynamic causal modeling. *NeuroImage, 19,* 1273–1302.

Friston, K. J., Holmes, A. P., & Worsley, K. J. (1999). How many subjects constitute a study? *NeuroImage, 10,* 1–5.

Friston, K. J., Holmes, A., Worsley, K. J., Poline, J. B., Frith, C. D., & Frackowiak, R. S. J. (1995b). Statistical parametric maps in functional imaging: A general linear approach. *Human Brain Mapping, 2,* 189–210.

Friston, K. J., & Price, C. J. (2003). Degeneracy and redundancy in cognitive anatomy. *Trends in Cognitive Sciences, 7,* 151–152.

Frith, U. (1989). *Autism: Explaining the enigma.* Oxford: Blackwell.

Gitelman, D. R., Parrish, T. B., Friston, K. J., & Mesulam, M. M. (2002). Functional anatomy of visual search: Regional segregations within the frontal eye fields and effective connectivity of the superior colliculus. *NeuroImage, 15,* 970–982.

Gottschaldt, K. (1926). Über den Einfluss der Erfahrung auf die Wahrnehmung von Figuren, I. *Psychologische Forschung, 8,* 261–317.

Gottschaldt, K. (1929). Über den Einfluss der Erfahrung auf die Wahrnehmung von Figuren, II. *Psychologische Forschung, 12,* 1–87.

Happé, F. (1999). Autism: Cognitive deficit or cognitive style? *Trends in Cognitive Science, 3,* 216–222.

Herwig, U., Abler, B., Schonfeldt-Lecuona, C., Wunderlich, A., Grothe, J., Spitzer, M., & Walter, H. (2003). Verbal storage in a premotor-parietal network: Evidence from fMRI-guided magnetic stimulation. *NeuroImage, 20,* 1032–1041.

Hopfinger, J. B., Buonocore, M. H., & Mangun, G. R. (2000). The neural mechanisms of top down attentional control. *Nature Neuroscience, 3,* 284–291.

Iacoboni, M., Woods, R. P., Brass, M., Bekkering, H., Mazziotta, J. C., & Rizzolatti, G. (1999). Cortical mechanisms of human imitation. *Science, 286,* 2526–2528.

Kim, Y. H., Gitelman, D. R., Nobre, A. C., Parrish, T. B., LaBar, K. S., & Mesulam, M. M. (1999). The large-scale neural network for spatial attention displays multifunctional overlap but differential asymmetry. *NeuroImage, 9,* 269–277.

Kötter, R., & Stephan, K. E. (2003). Network participation indices: Characterizing component roles for information processing in neural networks. *Neural Networks, 16,* 1261–1275.

Macaluso, E., Frith, C. D., & Driver, J. (2000). Modulation of human visual cortex by crossmodal spatial attention. *Science, 289,* 1206–1208.

Manjaly, Z. M., Marshall, J. C., Stephan, K. E., Gurd, J. M., Zilles, K., & Fink, G. R. (2003). In search of the hidden: An fMRI study with implications for the study of patients with autism and with acquired brain injury. *NeuroImage, 19,* 674–683.

Marshall, J. C., & Fink, G. R. (2001). Spatial cognition: Where we were and where we are. *NeuroImage, 14,* S2–S7.

McIntosh, A. R. (2000). Towards a network theory of cognition. *Neural Networks, 13,* 861–870.

McIntosh, A. R., Rajah, M. N., & Lobaugh, N. J. (2003). Functional connectivity of the medial temporal lobe relates to learning and awareness. *Journal of Neuroscience, 23,* 6520–6528.

Nishitani, N., & Hari, R. (2000). Temporal dynamics of cortical representation for action. *Proceedings of the National Academy of Sciences USA, 97,* 913–918.

Orgass, B., Poeck, K., Kirchensteiner, M., & Hartje, W. (1972). Visuo-cognitive performances in patients with unilateral hemispheric lesions. An investigation with three factorial reference tests. *Zeitschrift für Neurologie, 202,* 177–195.

assingham, R. E., Stephan, K. E., & Kötter, R. (2002). The anatomical basis of functional localization in the cortex. *Nature Reviews Neuroscience, 3,* 606–616.

Poldrack, R. A., Wagner, A. D., Prull, M. W., Desmond, J. E., Glover, G. H., & Gabrieli, J. D. (1999). Functional specialization for semantic and phonological processing in the left inferior prefrontal cortex. *NeuroImage, 10,* 15–35.

Poline, J. B., Worsley, K. J., Evans, A. C., & Friston, K. J. (1997). Combining spatial extent and peak intensity to test for activations in functional imaging. *NeuroImage, 5,* 83–96.

Price, C. J., & Friston, K. J. (2002). Degeneracy and cognitive anatomy. *Trends in Cognitive Sciences, 6,* 416–421.

Ring, H. A., Baron-Cohen, S., Wheelwright, S., Williams, S. C. R., Brammer, M., Andrew, C., & Bullmore, E. T. (1999). Cerebral correlates of perserved cognitive skills in autism. A functional MRI study of Embedded Figures Task performance. *Brain, 122,* 1305–1315.

Rizzolatti, G., & Arbib, M. A. (1998). Language within our grasp. *Trends in Neuroscience, 21,* 188–194.

Rizzolatti, G., Fogassi, L., & Gallese, V. (2001). Neurophysiological mechanisms underlying the understanding and imitation of action. *Nature Reviews Neuroscience, 2,* 661–670.

Robertson, L. C., Lamb, M. R., & Knight, R. T. (1988). Effects of lesions of temporal-parietal junction on perceptual and attentional processing in humans. *Journal of Neuroscience, 8,* 3757–3769.

Rowe, J. B., Stephan, K. E., Friston, K. J., Frackowiak, R. J. S., Lees, A., & Passingham, R. E. (2002). Attention to action in Parkinson's disease: Impaired effective connectivity among frontal cortical regions. *Brain, 125,* 276–289.

Russo, M., & Vignolo, L. A. (1967). Visual figure-ground discrimination in patients with unilateral cerebral disease. *Cortex, 3,* 113–127.

Shah, A., & Frith, U. (1983). An islet of ability in autistic children: A research note. *Journal of Child Psychology and Psychiatry, 24,* 613–620.

Stephan, K. E., Marshall, J. C., Friston, K. J., Rowe, J. B., Ritzl, A., Zilles, K., & Fink, G. R. (2003). Lateralized cognitive processes and lateralized task control in the human brain. *Science, 301,* 384–386.

Tagamets, M. A., & Horwitz, B. (1998). Integrating electrophysiological and anatomical experimental data to create a large-scale model that simulates a delayed match-to-sample human brain imaging study. *Cerebral Cortex, 8,* 310–220.

Talairach, J., & Tournoux, P. (1988). *Co-planar stereotactic atlas of the human brain.* Stuttgart, Germany: Thieme.

Teuber, H.-L., & Weinstein, S. (1956). Ability to discover hidden figures after cerebral lesions. *Archives of Neurology and Psychiatry, 76,* 369–379.

Tononi, G., Sporns, O., & Edelman, G. M. (1999). Measures of degeneracy and redundancy in biological networks. *Proceedings of the National Academy of Sciences USA, 96,* 3257–3262.

Yantis, S., Schwarzbach, J., Serences, J. T., Carlson, R. L., Steinmetz, M. A., Pekar, J. J., & Courtney, S. M. (2002). Transient neural activity in human parietal cortex during spatial attention shifts. *Nature Neuroscience, 5,* 995–1002.

Young, M. P., Hilgetag, C. C., & Scannell, J. W. (2000). On imputing function to structure from the behavioural effects of brain lesions. *Philosophical Transactions of the Royal Society of London B: Biological Sciences, 355,* 147–161.

COGNITIVE NEUROPSYCHOLOGY, 2005, 22 (3/4), 306–315

THE RIGHT PARIETAL CORTEX AND TIME PERCEPTION: BACK TO CRITCHLEY AND THE ZEITRAFFER PHENOMENON

Iona Alexander and Alan Cowey
University of Oxford, UK

Vincent Walsh
University College London, UK

We investigated the involvement of the posterior parietal cortex in time perception by temporarily disrupting normal functioning in this region, in subjects making prospective judgements of time or pitch. Disruption of the right posterior parietal cortex significantly slowed reaction times when making time, but not pitch, judgements. Similar interference with the left parietal cortex and control stimulation over the vertex did not significantly change performance on either pitch or time tasks. The results show that the information processing necessary for temporal judgements involves the parietal cortex, probably to optimise spatiotemporal accuracy in voluntary action. The results are in agreement with a recent neuroimaging study and are discussed with regard to a psychological model of temporal processing and a recent proposal that time is part of a parietal cortex system for encoding magnitude information relevant for action.

INTRODUCTION

The ability to register the temporal order and the temporal structure of events in the external world is important for coherent synchronous visual perception (Battelli, Cavanagh, Martini, & Barton, 2003; Nishida & Johnston, 2002; Walsh, 2002), in the timing of motor behaviour (Miall, 1996; Wing & Kristofferson, 1973), and in estimating the duration of intervals of time (Wearden, 1998, 1999). The brain areas identified as important for time perception have been associated with widely different ranges of time intervals: circadian rhythms depend on the suprachiasmatic nucleus; ultradian cycles are abolished by lesions to the paraventricular and retrochiasmatic nuclei; and much shorter intervals of seconds or milliseconds variously require cortical structures such as motor and supplementary motor areas, right parietal cortex, prefrontal cortex, and also the cerebellum (Harrington & Haaland, 1999; Hazeltine, Helmuth, & Ivry, 1997; Ivry, 1996; Lacruz, Artieda, Pastor, & Obeso, 1991; Rao, Mayer, & Harrington, 2001; Theoret, Haque, & Pascual-Leone, 2001). Several lines of evidence indicate that one of these regions, the right inferior parietal cortex (rIPC), is indispensable for time perception. For example, Rao et al. (2001) have observed rIPC activity specific to

Correspondence should be addressed to Vincent Walsh, Institute of Cognitive Neuroscience and Dept of Psychology, University College London, Alexandra House, 17 Queen Square, London WC1N 3AR, UK (Email: v.walsh@ucl.ac.uk).

This work was supported by The Medical Research Council, by The Oxford Centre for Cognitive Neuroscience, and an equipment grant from The Wellcome Trust to the Institute of Cognitive Neuroscience. Vincent Walsh is supported by the Royal Society.

prospective time judgements in fMRI experiments; patients with rIPC damage, but not left, have substantial time-related perception deficits (Battelli et al., 2003; Harrington, Haaland, & Knight, 1998); and electroencephalographic (EEG) recordings also implicate right posterior cortical areas in time perception (Mohl & Pfurtscheller, 1992). The occurrence of pure temporal deficits may be less salient or less common than spatial and visuomotor deficits following parietal lesions but, as Critchley (1953) noted, spatial and temporal deficits often coincide and parietal patients can display a wide range of errors in temporal experience. Such patients may be unable to judge the passage of time during a medical interview, time may appear to pass too quickly, objects may appear to move too quickly, too slowly, or too jerkily—phenomena that "may be merely a part of a more generalized distortion of the temporal sense, i.e. the 'time-grabbing' (*Zeitraffer*) phenomenon" (Critchley, 1953, p. 300; see also pp. 301–303). The parietal cortex is also emerging as an important locus of multimodal integration and some temporal phenomena hitherto regarded as purely visual have recently been shown to have auditory analogues (e.g., Hodinott-Hill, Thilo, Cowey, & Walsh, 2002), suggesting that time, like space, requires or involves multimodal algorithms. The association of time and spatial attributes in the parietal corex has also recently been discussed in a wider context, also encompassing number (see Walsh, 2003a, 2003b).

In this experiment, to test competing predictions that the right and left parietal cortex are important for time perception, we disrupted the normal activity of right or left IPC by applying low-frequency (1 Hz), repetitive transcranial magnetic stimulation (rTMS) over these regions. Stimulation at 1 Hz has been shown to decrease blood flow and cortical excitability in the region targeted by TMS for several minutes following stimulation (Chen et al., 1997; Paus, Jech, Thompson, Comeau, Peters, & Evans, 1997) and to impair performance on behavioural tasks that depend on the region stimulated (e.g., Kosslyn et al., 1999; Theoret et al., 2001). To make our interference study as closely comparable as possible with a recent neuroimaging study (Rao et al., 2001) we adapted the behavioural procedures described in that paper.

METHODS

Subjects

Six subjects, four male and two female, mean age 30.5 years, all right-handed, participated. All were screened for TMS exclusion criteria according to Wasserman (1998) and gave written informed consent to take part. All had previous experience as TMS subjects. They were paid for their participation. All procedures were approved by the Departmental Ethics Committee and by Oxford Research Ethics Committee (OXREC).

Experimental procedure

Subjects sat in a dark, quiet room 60 cm from a loudspeaker, which delivered the auditory discriminanda, and carried out a pitch discrimination task and a time discrimination task before receiving repetitive pulse TMS (rTMS). Magnetic stimulation was delivered for 10 minutes over the right or left parietal cortex or the vertex, as described below, and the subjects were then immediately retested on the two discrimination tasks. The order of tasks and TMS conditions was counterbalanced across subjects. Stimuli were generated from a Pentium II PC and delivered at 12dB[A] above background. All programs were written in E-Prime software and key-press responses for reaction times and accuracy were measured using a response box on which subjects made one of two presses with their right hand to indicate their decision of longer/shorter (time task) or higher/lower (pitch task). The motor demands of the two tasks were identical. There were 64 trials in each block and subjects carried out a control block per TMS block.

Time discrimination task

Two tones (700 Hz for 50 ms) separated by a standard interval of 1200 ms were followed by a delay of 1000 ms and by two further identical tones

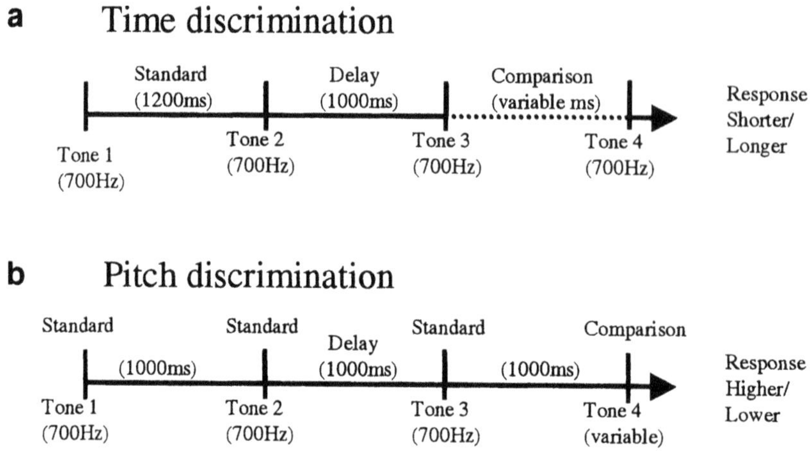

Figure 1. *The tone sequences and responses of (a) the time and (b) the pitch tasks. In each task the subject heard four tones. In the time task the subjects judged whether the interval between tones 3 and 4 was longer or shorter than between tones 1 and 2 (the interval difference was ±60, 120, 180, or 240 ms and the interval between tones 1 and 2 was always 1200 ms). In the pitch task, both intervals were 1000 ms and the subjects judged whether the fourth tone was higher or lower in frequency than the first three tones. Tones 1–3 were always 700 Hz and tone four was 700 ± 4, 8, 12, or 16 Hz.*

(700 Hz, 50 ms) separated by a comparison interval (1200 ± 60, 120, 180 or 240 ms). The subject's task was to indicate, by a key press, whether the comparison interval between the third and fourth tones was shorter or longer than the standard interval between the first two tones (Figure 1a).

Pitch discrimination task

Subjects were presented with three standard tones (each 700 Hz for 50 ms) separated by 1000 ms followed by a fourth comparison tone (700 ± 4, 8, 12 or 16 Hz), which subjects had to judge as either being higher or lower than the three standards (Figure 1b).

Magnetic stimulation

TMS was delivered at 1 Hz for 10 minutes using a Magstim Super-Rapid stimulator and a 70 mm figure-of-eight coil. The intensity was fixed at 65% of maximum stimulator output. In the TMS condition the behavioural task immediately followed the TMS. Before subsequent testing on a non-TMS or another TMS block the subjects had a 30-minute break to preclude the possibility of any TMS after-effects from having any effect on a subsequent block.

The parietal areas stimulated lie between the motor cortex and the visual cortex and it is difficult to select a level of TMS based on intrinsic excitability because there is no equivalent of a motor threshold or a phosphene threshold to use as a guide and the excitability of one region of cortex does not predict the level of stimulator output for another region of cortex (e.g., Stewart, Walsh, & Rothwell, 2000). Accordingly, the intensity and recovery periods were selected on the basis of other TMS studies that have used 1 Hz TMS in cognitive tasks (e.g., Kosslyn et al., 1999), disrupted parietal cortex function (Ashbridge, Walsh, & Cowey, 1997), or disrupted timing behaviour (Theoret et al., 2001).

The coil was fixed tangential to the skull with the handle pointing backwards at approximately 45° to the spinal cord. Subjects wore a tight-fitting lycra cap on which the relevant coordinates of the international 10/20 EEG system were marked. To select the region of stimulated parietal cortex, subjects first carried out a visual conjunction search task on a VDU at 60 cm distance, while receiving 10 Hz TMS for 500 ms over the P3 or P4 electrode site (left and right parietal cortex respectively). The coil stimulated sites on and around these locations for blocks of 20 trials until one region was found that consistently and markedly increased mean reaction times on the search task. This region was usually within 1 cm of the marked electrode site. We have described this "hunting procedure" in detail in several papers (e.g., Ashbridge et al., 1997). To compare our functional identification of the posterior parietal cortex with a measure of anatomical accuracy, before proceeding to the time experiment, we used the Brainsight Frameless Stereotaxic system (Rogue Research, Montreal, Canada) to identify the regions stimulated and to allow comparison with the parietal areas localised by Rao et al. (2001). Each subject was scanned to provide MRI T1 structural images. We then localised the intended site of stimulation on each subject. Figure 2 shows the Brainsight localisations of the parietal areas stimulated. As an additional control for nonspecific effects of TMS, the vertex was used as a stimulation site in four of the subjects to ensure that there were no effects due to the tactile or auditory sensations of TMS. Vertex was included purely as a check for nonspecific effects; the critical control condition was the lIPC stimulation. We thus carried out one analysis with lIPC vs. rIPC TMS and a separate analysis to ensure that behaviour following vertex TMS did not differ from no-TMS.

RESULTS

Reaction time data from correct trials were subjected to a two-factor Task (time/pitch) × Stimulation (lIPC, rIPC and no-TMS) repeated measures ANOVA to compare the effects of TMS

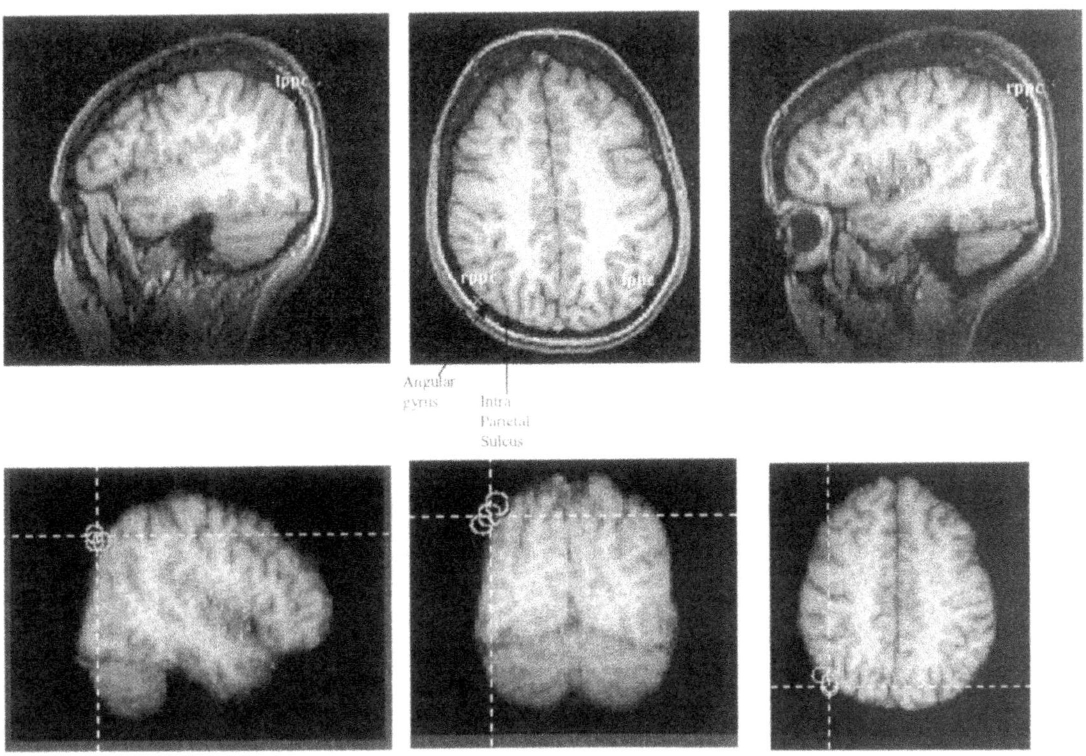

Figure 2. *Localisation of the rIPC stimulation site with Brainsight. The stimulated areas were the left and right inferior parietal cortices, ventral to the intraparietal sulcus and on the angular gyrus.*

on the two tasks, followed by post hoc tests to test directly the prediction that rIPC TMS would impair temporal discrimination. There was a significant main effect of stimulation, $F(2, 10) = 6.13$; $p < .02$, and a significant interaction effect between task and stimulation, $F(2, 10) = 5.128$; $p < .05$. There was a significant effect of TMS on time, $F(2, 15) = 5.56$; $p = .018$, but not pitch, $F(2\ 15) = 0.323$; $p = .729$. Figure 3a shows that the mean reaction times on the time discrimination task increased significantly, by 166 ms, when TMS was applied over rIPC, relative to no-TMS (Dunnett's test, $p < .05$). Left IPC simulation had no effect on reaction time relative to the no-TMS control (RT increase = 9 ms, $p > .05$).

Figure 3b shows the mean reaction time performance on the pitch discrimination task. In contrast to the time task, there was no significant effect of applying TMS over lIPC or rIPC compared to no-TMS controls ($p > .05$ in all cases), although left IPC stimulation slightly but insignificantly decreased reaction time (−20 ms), $p > .05$.

To examine the nonspecific effects of TMS, a two-factor Task (time/pitch) × Stimulation (vertex and no-TMS) repeated measures ANOVA was carried out. There was no significant main effect of task, $F(1, 3) = 1.418$; $p > .05$, or stimulation, $F(1, 3) = 1.841$; $p > .05$, and there was no significant interaction effect between task and stimulation, $F(1, 3) = 0.604$; $p > .05$.

The tasks were always performed at a high level of accuracy. Mean % correct responses in the pitch task were lIPC = 84.9%, rIPC = 83.55%, vertex = 93.6%, no-TMS = 91.2%. Mean errors in the time task were lIPC = 83%, rIPC = 89.6%, vertex = 84.37%, no-TMS = 92.8%. Error data were subjected to a two-factor Task (time/pitch) × Stimulation (IIPC, rIPC and no-TMS)) repeated measures ANOVA. There was no significant main effect of task, $F(1, 5) = 0.066$; $p > .05$, or stimulation, $F(2, 10) = 0.387$; $p > .05$, and there was no significant interaction effect between task and stimulation, $F(2, 10) = 3.072$; $p > .05$. A two-factor Task (time/pitch) × Stimulation (vertex and no-TMS) repeated measures ANOVA on error data from vertex and no-TMS conditions revealed no significant main effect of task, $F(1, 3) = 0.273$; $p > .05$, or stimulation, $F(1, 3) = 6.618$; $p > .05$, and there was no significant interaction effect between task and stimulation, $F(1, 3) = 1.744$; $p > .05$.

In summary, 1 Hz rTMS over the right IPC impaired time perception and this effect was specific when controlled by task (pitch perception) and TMS stimulation site (lIPC). The results are

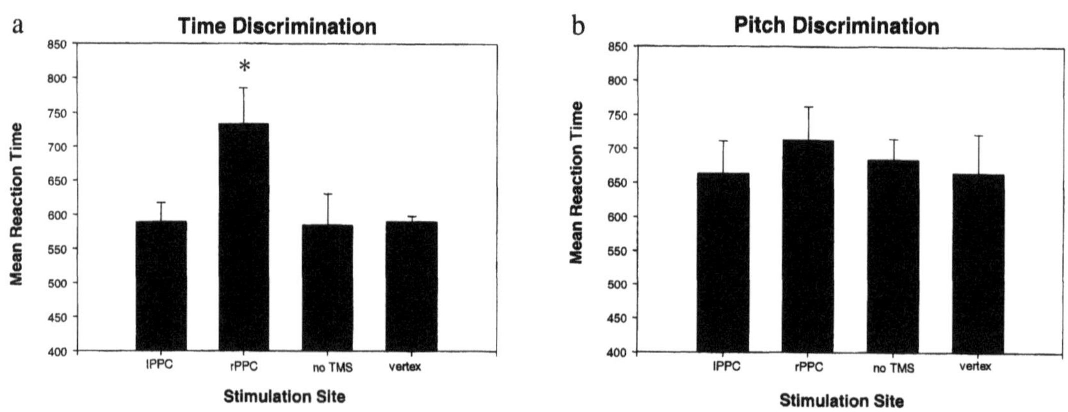

Figure 3. *The effects of rTMS on reaction time when judging (a) time and (b) pitch. Time: rTMS over the rIPC significantly delayed the response to categorise a temporal interval as longer or shorter than a standard. Stimulation over the vertex or the lIPC on the time discrimination task did not delay reaction times significantly. There were no effects of rTMS over left or right parietal cortex or vertex on the ability to make pitch judgements.*

not attributable to task difficulty. If time taken to reach a decision is taken as an index of difficulty, the pitch perception task was more difficult and therefore more likely to be disrupted by nonspecific aspects of magnetic stimulation. We can be sure that these effects of TMS are independent of motor effects because there was no effect of left parietal TMS even though all responses were made with the right hand. The effects were also specific to task, which is inconsistent with a motor artefact explanation of the data.

DISCUSSION

The effects of TMS show the right inferior parietal cortex to be necessary for rapid discrimination of temporal intervals. This is consistent with Critchley's observation of the judgement of time, the *Zeitraffer* phenomenon, following parietal cortex damage, with brain-imaging evidence (Rao et al., 2001), with temporal deficits observed in neuropsychological patients (Battelli et al., 2003; Harrington et al., 1998; Lacruz et al., 1991) and with EEG evidence (Mohl & Pfurtscheller, 1992).

Reaction time and error data were both analysed in this study. In several previous studies (e.g., Ashbridge et al., 1997) we have observed that tasks that are performed at a high level of correctness are likely to yield reaction time deficits rather than errors during TMS, whereas tasks close to the threshold of performance are also likely to produce increased errors in response to TMS. The reasons for this have been rehearsed at length in other publications (e.g., Walsh & Cowey, 1998; Walsh & Pascual-Leone, 2003), but before proceeding to our interpretation of the data it is perhaps worth stating what we understand a TMS disruption to mean in general terms. Briefly, if one considers the neural activity induced by TMS as highly unlikely to be organised in the pattern required for the brain area being stimulated to make its normal contribution to a task, the TMS can be considered to act as "neural noise." As a useful analogy, consider adding visual white noise to a display during, say, a visual identification task. With a little noise added, the subject might not immediately make misidentifications but might take longer to identify the target. If the noise level is increased, then the time required to identify the target will increase. If the noise level is increased again, subjects may begin to make errors. In other words, introducing noise to a signal is more likely to slow down correct performance than to force errors. One referee of this article asked whether a RT deficit without an error deficit could be considered as evidence that the stimulated area is *necessary* to perform the task. What we mean by necessary is *necessary for normal performance*. If the induced neural noise slows down performance then we would consider it as having induced an abnormal performance and thus have demonstrated the necessity of the area in normal performance.

The role(s) of the parietal cortex, or of cortex in general, in time perception have been investigated far less than those of subcortical structures. As a consequence, cortical processes have been loosely associated with all stages of temporal processing. In one model, for example, cortex is allocated a comparator role (decision unit in Figure 4) (Hazeltine et al., 1997; Meck, 1996). Although we agree that comparator processes may be cortical (see below), Meck's model applies to longer intervals (20 seconds or more) than those with which we are concerned here. Gibbon, Malapani, Dale, and Gallistel's model (1997) differentiates between prefrontal and premotor components but posterior parietal regions are not included. Rao et al. (2001, p. 317) also suggest that the parietal cortex may be required to encode or maintain temporal intervals (the memory component in Figure 4). Several studies emphasise the attentional role of parietal cortex in timing functions (Coull & Nobre, 1998; Rao et al., 2001). Other proposals suggest that attention may act at the level of the pacemaker (Timer in Figure 4), the switch between the pacemaker and accumulator (Zackay & Block, 1995), the level of the accumulator itself (Burle & Casini, 2001), or attention to expected or unexpected intervals in motor preparation (Coull & Nobre, 1998). Given the psychophysical success of certain models of time perception and timing behaviour (Gibbon et al., 1997; Wearden, 1999; Wing & Kristofferson, 1973), attention is clearly too vague a parameter to

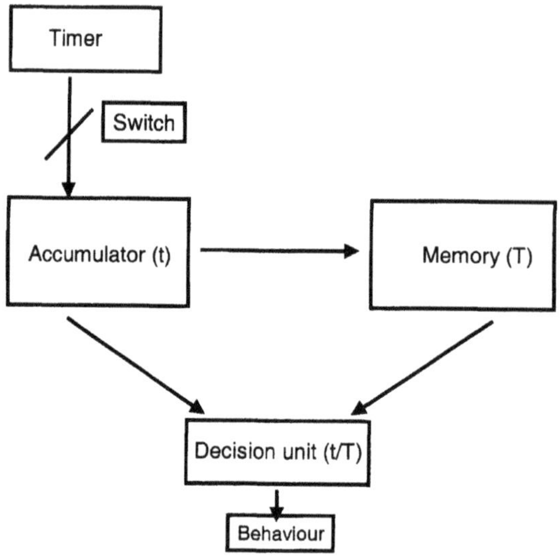

Figure 4. *A model of time perception containing the elements common to the major models of Gibbon, Meck, and Treisman. Terminology may change from paper to paper: the Timer is also termed "pacemaker" or "clock," the Accumulator "integrator" or "working memory," and the Memory Unit may sometimes be referred to as "reference memory."*

be of use in constraining explanations. The many degrees of freedom allowed by an attention-based explanation permit it to be applied alike to pacemaker, gating, integrating, encoding, maintaining, comparing, and decision stages of temporal models indiscriminately (see Walsh, 2003b).

There is some inconsistency in neuroimaging studies regarding which hemisphere is activated by temporal information processing. Rao et al. (2001) reported rIPC activity in a prospective task whereas Coull and Nobre (1998) reported left parietal activity. Our data, using a task similar to that of Rao et al., support their observations. The left hemisphere activity reported by Coull and Nobre was elicited by a task that confounded motor preparation and time processing and, as the authors suggest, is likely to be due to the motoric elements of the task rather than to anything concerned with temporal processing. Our data, then, support the suggestion by Rao et al. that the rIPC is important for encoding and maintaining temporal intervals. We propose that the right parietal cortex uses representational systems, perhaps spatially encoded (Walsh, 2003b), that are common to time, space, and quantity as relevant to action and that this representation is available to left hemisphere areas required for action selection and generation.

Figure 4 schematises a psychological model of time perception containing the core elements common to experimental studies (Gibbon et al., 1997; Meck, 1996; Treisman, 1963). The five elements of this model are Timer, Switch, Accumulator, Memory, and Decision Unit. In trying to account for the importance of rIPC in time perception, we have asked which of these functions seem to be closely related to already-known functions of the parietal cortex and also which known functions of parietal cortex might share computational or behavioural goals with some element of the time model.

In terms of temporal processing, being at the crossroads between perception and action places the role of the parietal cortex at the junction of central clock and peripheral effector processes. Hazeltine et al. (1997, p. 167) have observed that "in many cases, the distinction between time production and time perception is unclear" and where tasks fall within the range of motor decisions and actions (i.e., hundreds of milliseconds) this uncertainty may arise precisely because time information is used for action. Treisman (1963, 2002) also noted that "The coupling between perceiving durations and acting in time requires that similar pacemakers mediate both" (2002, p. 220). The parietal cortex, in its pivotal role in the "where" and "how" of spatial vision (Milner & Goodale, 1993), may also use temporal information to ensure that the metrics employed in space are employed at the right moment, which requires accurate spatiotemporal integration.

Our emphasis on the parietal cortex, at the interface of temporal transformations to be used with spatial information, raises the question of which components of models of timing (Gibbon et al., 1997; Meck, 1996; Treisman, 1963) best encapsulate its function. Our proposal that its importance lies in the need for convergence of space and time predicts an effect late in the processing hierarchy (Figure 4). This question is currently being pursued by assessment of inaccuracies made during time production tasks following 1 Hz rTMS. The pattern of inaccuracies may be more compatible with rIPC being the last stage of clock processing (in which case rTMS will bias judgements rather than increase variability) or the first stage of post-clock processes (in which case rTMS will increase variability more than bias). One might also predict that the behavioural pattern will fall between clock-like (increased bias) and effector-like (greater variability) patterns (Wing & Kristofferson, 1973) precisely because rIPC disruption could interfere with incoming clock signals or outgoing signals transformed to employ a metric compatible with spatial requirements. There is a clear consensus that where to look and reach (Ungerleider & Mishkin, 1982), and how to grasp (Milner & Goodale, 1993), require the integrity of the parietal cortex. However, not all objects to be fixated, pointed to, or grasped are stationary (e.g., tracking someone in a crowd; shaking someone's hand; catching something thrown; etc.), and behavioural accuracy often requires anticipation or temporal calculations: Behaviourally, space and time cannot easily be segregated (Campbell, 1994). In this context it is important to note that space and time processing are required in accurate motion perception and it is established that the right parietal cortex is involved in auditory spatial perception and higher-level motion perception (Battelli et al., 2001; Bisiach, Cornacchia, Sterzi, & Vallar, 1984; Griffiths et al., 1998). It would not be surprising if the sensory sources to be temporally decoded in these tasks involved the same region concerned with localisation, movement, and duration. Our data do not preclude a role for the left parietal cortex in temporal information processing in tasks other than the simple judgements made in our experiment. Indeed, when temporal information processing may have more motoric implications than in our task the left hemisphere is likely to be very important. A recent experiment showing such left hemisphere involvement in spatiotemporal integration (Assmus, Marshall, Ritzl, Noth, Zilles, & Fink, 2003) is one such example and how the left and right hemispheres contribute to other tasks is clearly an important question.

An important feature of cortical organisation relevant to this proposed convergence of space and time in behaviour is that wiring distances are kept to a minimum (Cowey, 1979), a consequence being that related computations are often performed in overlapping cortical areas or by near neighbours. We therefore suggest that the production of a time discrimination deficit with rIPC TMS reflects the fact that the need for a common metric of time and space to ensure accurate action requires that time information (in temporal ranges relevant for action) be closely associated with the visuospatial transformations carried out by the right posterior parietal cortex. Half a century after Critchley's comments concerning the *Zeitraffer* phenomenon, the parietal cortex has grabbed time back.

PrEview proof published online 17 January 2005

REFERENCES

Ashbridge, E., Walsh, V., & Cowey, A. (1997). Temporal aspects of visual search studied by transcranial magnetic stimulation. *Neuropsychologia, 35*, 1121–1131.

Assmus, A., Marshall, J. C., Ritzl, A., Noth, J., Zilles, K., & Fink, G. R. (2003). Left inferior parietal cortex integrates time and space during collision judgments. *Neuroimage, 20*, 82–88.

Battelli, L., Cavanagh, P., Intriligator, J., Tramo, M. J., Henaff, M. A., Michel, F., & Barton, J. J. (2001). Right parietal lesion leads to bilateral deficit for high level motion. *Neuron, 32*, 985–995.

Battelli, L., Cavanagh, P., Martini, P., & Barton, J. J. S. (2003). Bilateral deficits of transient visual attention in right parietal patients. *Brain, 126*, 2164–2174.

Bisiach, E., Cornacchia, L., Sterzi, R., & Vallar, G. (1984). Disorders of perceived auditory lateralisation after lesions of the right hemisphere. *Brain, 107*, 37–52.

Burle, B., & Casini, L. (2001). Dissocation between activation and attention effects in time estimation: Implications for internal clock models. *Journal of Experimental Psychology: Human Perception and Performance, 27*, 195–205.

Campbell, J. (1994). *Past, space and self.* Cambridge, MA: MIT Press.

Chen, R., Classen, J., Gerloff, C., Celnik, P., Wassermann, E. M., Hallett, M., & Cohen, L. G. (1997). Depression of motor cortex excitability by low frequency transcranial magnetic stimulation. *Neurology, 48*, 1398–1403.

Coull, J., & Nobre, A. C. (1998). Where and when to pay attention: The neural systems for directing attention to spatial locations and to time intervals as revealed by both PET and fMRI. *Journal of Neuroscience, 18*, 7462–7435.

Cowey, A. (1979). Cortical maps and visual perception: The Grindley Memorial Lecture. *Quarterly Journal of Experimental Psychology, 31*, 1–17.

Critchley, M. (1953). *The parietal lobes.* London: Hafner Press.

Gibbon, J., Malapani, C., Dale, C. L., & Gallistel, C. R. (1997). Toward a neurobiology of temporal cognition: Advances and challenges. *Current Opinion in Neurobiology, 7*, 170–184.

Griffiths, T. D., Rees, G., Rees, A., Green, G. R., Witton, C., Rowe, D., Buchel, C., Turner, R., & Frackowiak, R. S. J. (1998). Right parietal cortex is involved in the perception of sound movement in humans. *Nature Neuroscience, 1*, 74–79.

Harrington, D. L., & Haaland, K. Y. (1999). Neural underpinnings of temporal processing: A review of focal lesion, pharmacological and functional imaging research. *Reviews in Neuroscience, 10*, 91–116.

Harrington, D. L., Haaland, K. Y., & Knight, R. T. (1998). Cortical networks underlying mechanisms of time perception. *Journal of Neuroscience, 18*, 1085–1095.

Hazeltine, E., Helmuth, L. L., & Ivry, R. B. (1997). Neural mechanisms of timing. *Trends in Cognitive Science, 1*, 163–169.

Hodinott-Hill, I., Thilo, K., Cowey, A., & Walsh, V. (2002). Auditory chronostasis: Hanging on the telephone. *Current Biology, 12*, 1779–1781.

Ivry, R. B. (1996). The representation of temporal information in perception and motor control. *Current Opinion in Neurobiology, 6*, 851–857.

Kosslyn, S. M., Pascual-Leone, A., Felician, O., Camposano, S., Keenan, J. P., Thompson, W. L., Ganis, G., Sukel, K. E., & Alpert, N. M. (1999). The role of area 17 in visual imagery: Convergent evidence from PET and rTMS. *Science, 284*, 167–170.

Lacruz, F., Artieda, J., Pastor, M. A., & Obeso, J. A. (1991). The anatomical basis of somaesthetic temporal discrimination in humans. *Journal of Neurology, Neurosurgery and Neuropsychiatry, 54*, 1077–1081.

Meck, W. H. (1996). Neuropharmacology of timing and time perception. *Cognitive Brain Research, 3*, 227–242.

Miall, C. (1996). Models of neural timing. In M. Pastor & J. Artieda (Eds.), *Time, internal clocks and movement* (pp. 69–94). Amsterdam: Elsevier.

Milner, A. D., & Goodale, M. (1993). Visual pathways to perception and action. *Progress in Brain Research, 95*, 317–337.

Mohl, W., & Pfurtscheller, G. (1992). The role of the right parietal region in a movement time estimation task. *Neuroreport, 2*, 309–312.

Nishida, S., & Johnston, A. (2002). Marker correspondence, not processing latency determines spatial binding of visual attributes. *Current Biology, 12*, 359–368.

Paus, T., Jech, R., Thompson, C. J., Comeau, R., Peters, T., & Evans, A. C. (1997). Transcranial magnetic stimulation during positron emission tomography: A new method for studying connectivity of the human cerebral cortex. *Journal of Neuroscience, 17*, 3178–3184.

Rao, S. M., Mayer, A. R., & Harrington, D. L. (2001). The evolution of brain activation during temporal processing. *Nature Neuroscience, 4*, 317–323.

Stewart, L., Walsh, V., & Rothwell, V. (2000). Motor and phosphene thresholds: A transcranial magnetic stimulation correlation study. *Neuropsychologia, 39*, 415–419.

Theoret, H., Haque, J., & Pascual-Leone, A. (2001). Increased variability of paced finger tapping accuracy following repetitive magnetic stimulation of the cerebellum in humans. *Neuroscience Letters, 306*, 29–32.

Treisman, M. (1963). Temporal discrimination and the indifference interval: Implications for a model of the internal clock. *Psychological Monographs, 77*, 1–13.

Treisman, M. (2002). The perception of time. In J. Butterfield (Ed.), *Arguments of time* (pp. 217–246). London: The British Academy.

Ungerleider, L. G., & Mishkin, M. (1982). Two cortical visual systems. In D. J. Ingle, M. A. Goodale, & R. J. W. Mansfield (Eds.), *Analysis of visual behaviour*. Cambridge, MA: MIT Press.

Walsh, V. (2002). The when of perception. *Current Biology, 12,* R355–356.

Walsh, V. (2003a). Time: The back-door of perception. *Trends in Cognitive Sciences, 7,* 335–338.

Walsh, V. (2003b). A theory of magnitude: Common cortical metrics of time space and quantity. *Trends in Cognitive Sciences, 7,* 483–488

Walsh, V., & Cowey, A. (1998). Magnetic stimulation studies of visual cognition. *Trends in Cognitive Science, 2,* 103–110.

Walsh, V., & Pascual-Leone, A. (2003). *Transcranial magnetic stimulation: A neurochronometrics of mind.* Cambridge, MA: MIT Press.

Wassermann, E. M. (1998). Risk and safety of repetitive transcranial magnetic stimulation: Report and suggested guidelines from the International Workshop on the Safety of Repetitive Transcranial Magnetic Stimulation, June 5–7, 1996. *Electroencephalography and Clinical Neurophysiology, 108,* 1–16.

Wearden, J. (1998). Temporal generalization in humans. *Journal of Experimental Psychology, 18,* 134–144.

Wearden, J. H. (1999). "Beyond the fields we know . . .": Exploring and developing scalar timing theory. *Behavioural Processes, 45,* 3–21.

Wing, A., & Kristofferson, A. (1973). Response delays and the timing of discrete motor response. *Perception and Psychophysics, 14,* 5–12.

Zackay, D., & Block, R. A. (1995). An attentional gate model of prospective time estimation. In M. Richelle, V. De Keyser, G. d'Ydewalle, & A. Vandierendonck (Eds.), *Time and the dynamic control of behaviour* (pp. 167–178). Liege, Belgium: University of Liege Press.

COGNITIVE NEUROPSYCHOLOGY, 2005, 22 (3/4), 316–332

OUT OF SIGHT BUT NOT OUT OF MIND: THE NEUROPHYSIOLOGY OF ICONIC MEMORY IN THE SUPERIOR TEMPORAL SULCUS

C. Keysers*
University Groningen, The Netherlands
D.-K. Xiao*, P. Földiák, and D. I. Perrett
University of St Andrews, UK

Iconic memory, the short-lasting visual memory of a briefly flashed stimulus, is an important component of most models of visual perception. Here we investigate what physiological mechanisms underlie this capacity by showing rapid serial visual presentation (RSVP) sequences with and without interstimulus gaps to human observers and macaque monkeys. For gaps of up to 93 ms between consecutive images, human observers and neurones in the temporal cortex of macaque monkeys were found to continue processing a stimulus as if it was still present on the screen. The continued firing of neurones in temporal cortex may therefore underlie iconic memory. Based on these findings, a neurophysiological vision of iconic memory is presented.

GENERAL INTRODUCTION

Iconic memory and information persistence

In the world around us, many important events can be fleetingly brief. A gazelle might get a brief glimpse at a lion while the wind is moving the bush hiding the lion. How do we process such brief visual stimuli? Partial report paradigms (Loftus, Duncan, & Gehrig, 1992; Sperling, 1960) show that if a complex visual stimulus is flashed very briefly on a screen, subjects can continue processing this stimulus for 200–300 ms after it has gone. This phenomenon is called "information persistence" or "iconic memory" (Coltheart, 1980; Loftus et al., 1992). A suitable masking stimulus presented after the target is thought to overwrite this "icon" and therefore to terminate the information persistence of the previous stimulus. Despite the ubiquity of iconic memory in models of visual processing, little is yet known about the physiological basis of this phenomenon. In the present study, we examine the neural correlates of information persistence by comparing the performance of human subjects (Experiment 1) with that of single cells in the temporal cortex of macaque monkeys (Experiment 2) while rapid serial visual presentation (RSVP) was used to present naturalistic images to both groups.

Correspondence should be addressed to C. Keysers, BCN Neuro-Imaging Centre, University Groningen, A. Deusinglaan 2, 9713 AW Groningen, The Netherlands (Email: c.keysers@med.rug.nl).
*The first two authors contributed equally.
This work was supported by the BBSRC, the Wellcome Trust, the Boehringer Ingelheim Fond, and the Studienstiftung des deutschen Volkes. We thank E. Kohler and A. Perrett for critical comments, Mary Potter for suggesting that persistence might have an important role for higher brain functions, and the Sony Corporation for providing technical information about the GDM-20D11 computer screen.

RSVP with and without gaps

In RSVP, images are presented sequentially and continuously, with each image replacing the previous at the same location on the screen, one after another—much like a very rapid slide show. We have previously shown that human observers and pattern-sensitive neurones in the anterior superior temporal sulcus respond selectively to individual images in such RSVP sequences at presentation rates of up to one image every 14 ms (Keysers, Xiao, Földiák, & Perrett, 2001). Here we use the same technique to test how neurones and human subjects react to the introduction of gaps between successive frames in RSVP sequences. The experimental question is: If there is a gap between two images, will the iconic memory internally replace this gap with the "icon" of the preceding image? If so: How accurate is the icon, i.e., how does performance based on the icon compare to that based on the image itself?

To answer these two questions, two groups of RSVP sequences were tested (Figure 1a, left). Each group was composed of a set of three presentation conditions that could be compared. All stimuli were natural images (e.g., faces, real-world object), presented in the middle of a CRT computer screen with a refresh rate of 72 Hz. The images occupied only one quarter of the height of the video screen, and the phosphor decay time of the computer screen (Sony GDM-20D11) was short (≤ 1.2 ms to reach 10% of the original luminance, < 7.5 ms to reach 1% luminance). The presentation duration of a stimulus was varied by exposing it for an integer number of frames (1, 2, 4, or 8 consecutive frames) on the screen, and leaving 0, 3, or 6 frames of blank screen between consecutive stimuli (see Figure 1, left). When images are presented in the centre of a CRT screen, stimuli presented on consecutive frames are not actually continuously present on the screen (Bridgeman, 1998), but illuminated on the screen for ~4 ms on each frame, creating inevitable gaps of 9 ms between frames (see Figure 5). Since human subjects do not perceive these inevitable 9 ms gaps as gaps, in this paper conditions with 9 ms gaps will be called "nogap" conditions, while those with either 51 or 93 ms of blank screen will be called "gap" conditions.

The choice of conditions was dictated by a simple consideration. If human information processing based on the icon is as good as that based on the image itself, during the gaps human subjects should behave as if the stimuli had stayed on the screen. In addition to testing the performance in conditions with gaps, we therefore also tested performance in a condition referred to as "long-nogap," in which we left the stimulus on the screen during the time that had been a "gap" in the gap condition. If, on the other hand, human information processing based on the icon is very poor, information processing should be limited to the time during which the actual stimulus is present. A third condition was therefore added to each group in which the stimuli were shown for the same time as in the gap condition, but were immediately followed by the next stimulus ("short-nogap" condition). All three conditions were tested for two different durations, creating a slow and a fast group of comparison.

METHODS

Stimulus presentation

Stimuli (256×320 pixels) were presented centrally on a Sony GDM-20D11 monitor (72 Hz refresh rate, image size: $10^\circ \times 12.5^\circ$) attached to an Indigo2 Silicon Graphics workstation. Onset and duration of the stimuli were measured using light-sensitive diodes on the monitor screen, and found always to correspond to the intended duration. After a given pixel is presented on the screen, the P22 phosphor requires ≤ 1 ms to reach 10% and < 7.5 ms to reach 1% of the original luminance of the pixel (data provided by the Sony Corporation). Hence, given that the stimuli occupied $^1/_4$ of the height of the screen, the actual stimulus is shown for $^1/_4$ of the frame duration, i.e., $1\,\text{s} \times 72\,\text{Hz}^{-1} \times 4^{-1} = 3.4$ ms. Adding to that the duration for the last pixel to reach 10% of its original luminance, the stimulus duration is $\sim$4 ms. If one places the criterion at 1% of the original luminance, frame duration then reaches $\sim$11 ms (see Figure 5).

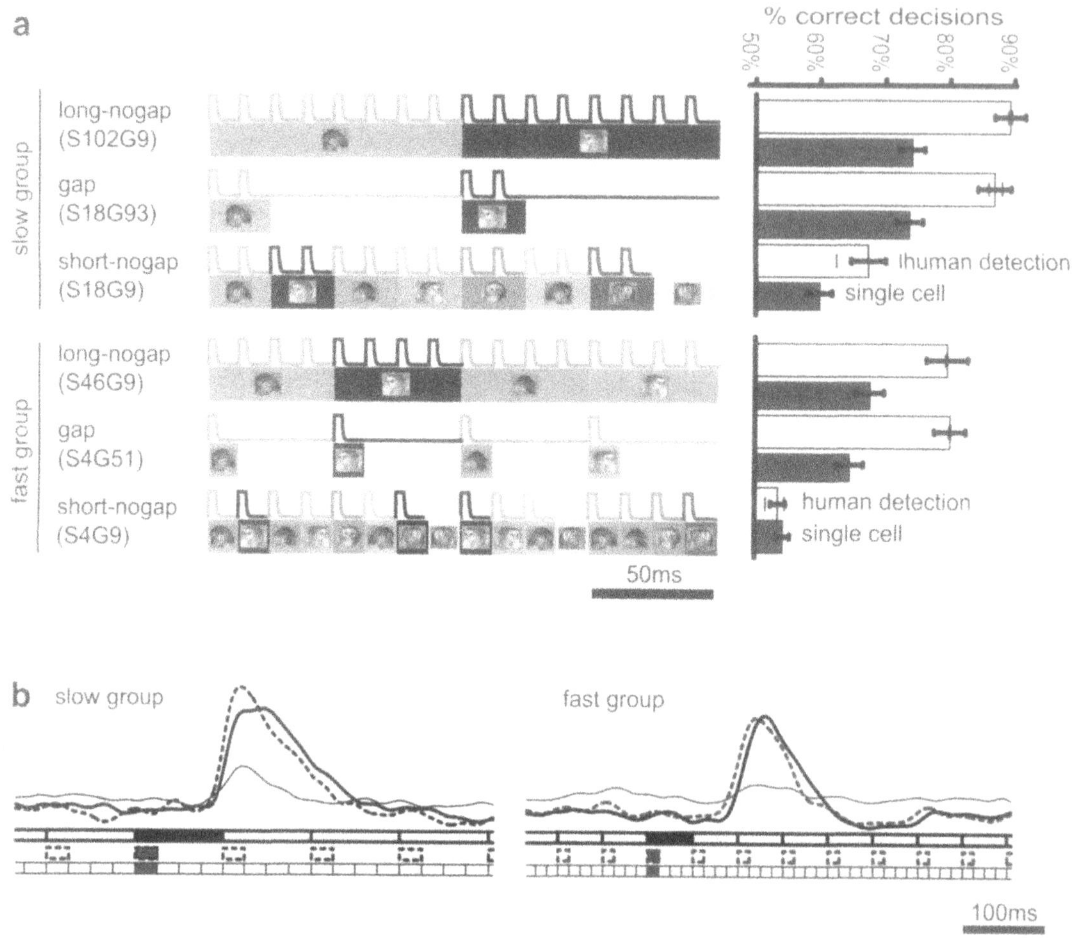

Figure 1. *(a) Stimulus timing (left) and the corresponding accuracy (right) with which a single stimulus can be detected in an RSVP sequence by human observers (open/green bars, the two black/red tick marks represent the individual mean accuracy for the two subjects) and by an ideal observer of STSa activity (grey/blue bars, as calculated using an ROC analysis). The x-axes of the left panel illustrate the stimulus timing in milliseconds, while the y-axes represent the energy on the screen of the stimulus shown below the curve. The timing of conditions is given as SxGy, where x is the duration in ms of the stimulus, and y that of the inter-stimulus gap. (b) Average normalised population response of the single neurones to the best stimulus in RSVP sequences of different timing. The x-axes represent time, the y-axes the mean averaged latency-aligned population response. The horizontal "ladders" under the response represent the stimulus timing, with the filled squares representing the timing of the best stimulus onto which responses were aligned, while the open squares represent adjacent stimuli in the sequence occupied at random by one of the eight stimuli. The space between two squares represents the gap in gap sequences. The dashed curves corresponds to the long gap condition, while the thin and thick continuous curves correspond to the short and long-nogap condition, respectively. See text for details. To view this figure in colour, please see the online issue of the Journal.*

For the monkeys, a fixation point appeared in the middle of the screen. Sequence presentation commenced when the subject's gaze remained within a fixation window of $\pm 5°$ of the monitor centre for >500 ms and terminated after 10 s or earlier if the monkey's gaze moved outside the fixation window. The fixation point was not visible during sequence presentation. The number of stimulus repetitions at a given presentation rate was adjusted to equate the total presentation time at each rate. On average, testing involved a total recording duration of approximately 1 hr per neurone. For humans, a fixation dot was shown together with a warning tone, the fixation dot then disappeared, and the target image was shown for 300 ms followed by a 500 ms gap. A sequence of seven images was then presented at rates shown in Figure 1. In 50% of the cases this sequence contained the target image in position 3, 4, or 5. Subjects pressed a button if the target image was in the sequence.

Physiological subjects and recording techniques

Awake subjects (two male *Macaca mulatta*, age 4–6 years) were seated in a primate chair and head restrained. Neural signals were recorded with standard methods (Oram & Perrett, 1992). Neurones were localised to the upper and lower banks of the STSa (12–18 mm anterior to the inter-aural plane) on the basis of x-ray visualisation of microelectrodes. Recording sites were confirmed through MRI and histology with markers placed at the site of neurone recording [MRI: Magnavist, Schering Health Care Ltd, Burgess Hill, UK; Histology: micro-lesions and DiI (as used in Snodderly & Gur, 1995), Molecular Probes, Europe]. The subjects' eye positions were monitored (accuracy ±1°; IView, SMI, Germany). A 486 PC and Cambridge Electronics CED 1401 interface recorded eye position and spike arrival times and measured stimulus onset times.

Human subjects

The subjects included one naïve subject (TJ) and one author, aged 35 and 26 respectively. Both were male and had normal vision. In a very similar task we tested five subjects and found no difference between naïve and author subjects (Keysers et al., 2001).

Neural response analysis

To measure the response to a particular stimulus in the sequence, we created peristimulus rastergrams by realigning the continuous recording on the time of each occurrence of the stimulus in the sequence. The average spike density functions obtained after the convolution with a SD = 10 ms Gaussian kernel then reflect the systematic response to the stimulus of alignment surrounded by activity evoked by all stimuli.

The responses of each neurone to each of the eight stimuli during the S102G9 condition were measured in a time window starting at 100 ms post-stimulus onset and lasting 111 ms. The stimulus eliciting the largest responses was defined as the neurone's "best" stimulus; the remaining seven stimuli were defined as "rest" stimuli. Response onset latency of a given neurone was computed off-line from trials for the "best" stimulus pooled across all presentation rates with 9 ms gaps. The latency of response onset was defined as the first 1 ms time bin of the spike density function (SDF) at which the firing rate exceeded the mean + 2.58 SD (i.e., $p < .005$) of activity measured in a control period 250 ms before stimulus onset, for at least 25 consecutive bins. Latency-aligned responses refer to responses time-shifted by the difference between an individual neurone's response onset latency and the population average (117 ms).

Population responses

Neurones differed in their response onset latency (56–171 ms). Hence, to investigate the duration of responses at population level, responses of all neurones were shifted onto the average latency of the population (117 ms). Neurones also differed with respect to their peak firing amplitude. In the S102G9 condition a post-stimulus time histogram (PSTH) of the response to the best stimulus was calculated with 1 ms bin-size. The bin with the largest spike count was then used to divide activity in all conditions.

Time window of interest

Based on the latency-aligned and normalised responses of the population of neurones, a window of analysis was defined separately for the fast and the slow comparison groups. The aim of this window is to identify the period of time during which responses are due to the stimulus of alignment, and not to the random stimuli occurring before or after the stimulus of alignment in the sequences. Hence, for each group, the period of time during which responses were different for different stimuli of alignment was identified. For each millisecond relative to response onset, the average normalised SDF values for each cell and stimulus were compared in an eight-stimulus within-cell ANOVA (see Figure 4). The window of analysis is then the period in which, from the three conditions of one group, at least one differentiates between stimuli, i.e., the period of time for which the ANOVA yields a p value for stimulus $< .01$. In the fast group, at least one condition showed stimulus discrimination in the -11 to 95 ms period, and in the slow group, in the -24 to 133 ms period, relative to response onset. These windows were then used to count spikes for the receiver operator curve (ROC) analysis and integrate the surface under the SDF for the response comparison. The windows started before $t = 0$, the no-gap response onset latency, because at the population level, the additional statistical power reveals significant differences between responses earlier than the less powerful single cell analysis used to determine the response onset latency.

Uncontaminated responses

Response to a stimulus X is considered "uncontaminated" if it was flanked by a sufficient number of consecutive "rest" stimuli (R, i.e., all but the best stimulus) to ensure that responses to nearby best stimuli did not contaminate the window of analysis for X. Contamination arises because response duration exceeds stimulus duration. The exact criterion therefore depended on presentation rate: RRXRR (S102G9, S18G93), RRRXRR (S46G9, S4G51), RRRXRRRR (S18G9, S4G9).

Neurometrics

For each of the 21 neurones tested, spike counts were obtained for uncontaminated stimulus sequences that were comparable to the target present and target absent sequences in the psychophysics. "Target present" and "target absent" spike counts were obtained by selecting uncontaminated responses to targets (i.e., the best stimuli) and distracters (i.e., any but the best stimulus), respectively. This selection was required because in the human psychophysics tasks there was at most one target stimulus per sequence. Spike count distributions for the target present and target absent sequences were calculated for each presentation rate separately. A receiver operator curve was then calculated using all possible thresholds, and the surface under this curve taken as the neurometric performance of an ideal observer (see Celebrini & Newsome, 1994, for details). The goal of the analysis is to determine the percentage of correct responses that would occur if an ideal observer used just the spike counts of that single neurone to determine whether the target was present or not. The mean trial number used for the ROC analysis in the slow group was 47 trials per stimulus and cell, and 95 trials per stimulus for the fast group. These large trial numbers lead to reliable ROC estimates.

EXPERIMENT 1: PSYCHOPHYSICS

Introduction

Information persistence and visual persistence

Coltheart (1980) introduced an important distinction between two seemingly identical phenomena: information persistence and visual persistence. Both phenomena refer to the fact that when a brief visual stimulus is flashed on a screen, the processing of this stimulus can outlast the stimulus itself. Information persistence refers to the fact that if a subject needs to process the brief stimulus, performance will be better if a masking stimulus is not presented immediately after the stimulus. This indicates that some processing is still going on after the end of the stimulus presentation, and that the mask interrupts this continued processing. Measurement of information persistence does not involve asking the subject to report if she still mentally "sees" the stimulus after it has ended. Visual persistence, on the other hand, refers to the fact that subjects subjectively have the impression that the stimulus doesn't suddenly vanish from the screen, but rather slowly fades. If one then measures the time from beginning of the subjective sensation of seeing the image to the end of this perception, the total subjective duration is substantially longer than the stimulus duration. It is intuitively appealing to believe that *information* persistence arises from the fact that the subjects process the *visual* persistence of the stimulus. Hence visual and information persistence should have similar time courses. Unfortunately, quantitative analyses of the two phenomena show that this is not the case (see Coltheart, 1980, and Loftus & Irwin, 1998, for reviews). In the present paper, information persistence will be examined, not visual persistence.

Human perception and gaps

The effect of gaps between stimuli in RSVP was measured in two male human observers using a simple target detection task. Only two subjects were used, because a previous psychophysical study (Keysers et al., 2001) using the same task had revealed that the performances of five subjects were so similar to one another, that two subjects were sufficient to yield very representative data. Figure 2a illustrates the time course of a single trial. In each trial, the subject viewed a "target" image for 306 ms (22 frames), followed after 500 ms by an RSVP sequence of seven stimuli containing either seven distracter images (i.e., images different from the target) or six distracter images and the original target image itself in the 3rd, 4th, or 5th position of the sequence. Images were photographs of humans and monkeys (e.g., Figures 1a and 2a), laboratory objects, and images drawn from image libraries on

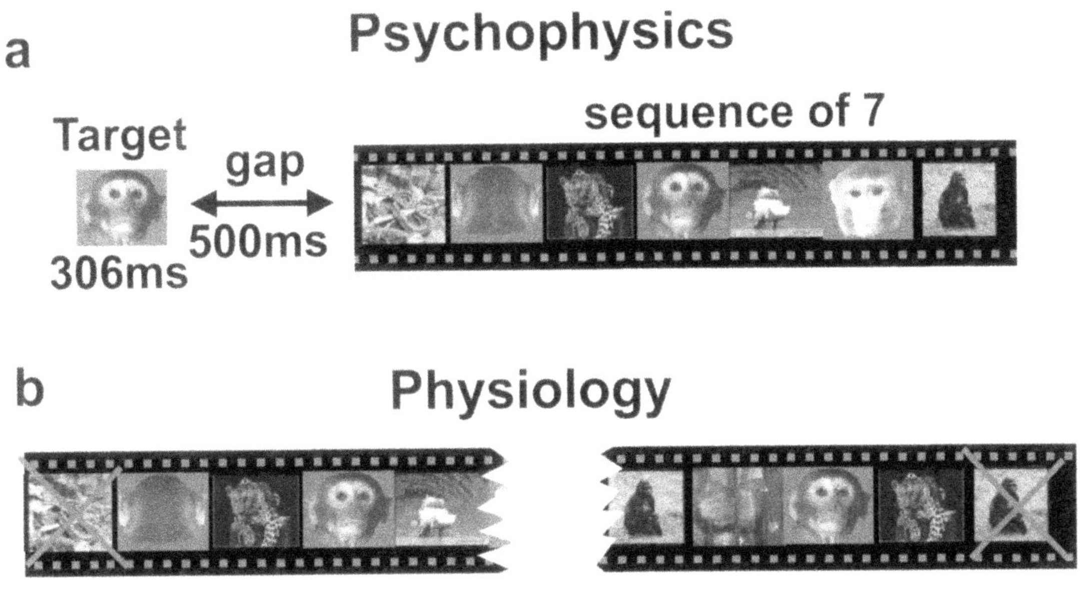

Figure 2. *Experimental design. (a) In the psychophysical detection task (Exp. 1), a single stimulus (the target) is shown for 306 ms, followed after a 500 ms gap by a sequence of seven stimuli presented using the different timing conditions. If this sequence contained the target stimulus, the subject had to press a button. (b) In the physiological recordings (Exp. 2), a continuous sequence of naturalistic images was presented to the monkey. For each neurone, eight stimuli were selected to range in effectiveness from that causing the strongest ("best") to that causing the weakest ("worst") responses for the cell. The "movie strip" represents schematically the RSVP sequence; the break in the strip represents the fact that in the physiology, the RSVP sequences were very long, containing up to 720 consecutive images. No report of perception was required. The first and last stimuli of each sequence were ignored in the analysis. To view this figure in colour, please see the online issue of the Journal.*

the Internet. All target images used in this study were the most effective stimuli for one neurone of the physiological study (Exp. 2) presented below. For 16 of the neurones, the best stimulus was a face. For 10/16 the face was that of a monkey, and in 6/16 it was the face of a human. Two of these cells selective for faces were tested with the target face mixed with 7 other faces, while the remaining 14 were tested against other stimuli including inanimate objects (e.g., apples, coca-cola cans, a newspaper). Five cells responded best to particular views of an entire body including the face. The remaining cells responded best to stimuli not associated with the face such as a syringe, an orange, an apple, a trash-bag, a bear, a spider, and a duck. If the observer recognised the target image in the sequence, he was required to press a button.

Figure 1 illustrates the stimulus timings used in the study. Six timing conditions were selected to fall into two comparison groups: a fast and a slow comparison group. The slow comparison group was composed of a "gap" condition, having a stimulus duration of 18 ms followed by 93 ms of blank screen; a "short-nogap" sequence, with the same stimulus duration (18 ms) but no gap (except the inevitable 9 ms); and a "long-nogap" sequence, having the same stimulus onset asynchrony (SOA = 111 ms) as the gap sequence but with the stimulus filling the entire SOA. The fast group was identical except that half as many frames were used for stimuli and gaps.

For precision, these groups and conditions are also referred to by the duration of stimulus (S) and blank screen (G) (i.e., slow group: gap S18G93, long-nogap S102G9, short-nogap S18G9; fast group: gap S4G51, long-nogap S46G9, short-nogap S4G9).

Twenty-one different target images were used with 16 trials each (8 target present and 8 target absent trials). These were tested for all six timing conditions. The distracter stimuli accompanying target stimuli were the same as those used in the testing of particular neurones described below.

Results

The results in terms of proportion correct decisions were calculated for each target image separately, but pooling trials from the two subjects (the performance of the two subjects did not differ, Binomial test $p > .05$). The results were then averaged over images and shown as the open bars ($\pm$ sem) in Figure 1a (right panel). To compare the performance in the three conditions of each group, due to the binary nature of the response (yes/no), a χ^2 statistic was adopted, comparing the total correct responses (i.e., pooled over stimuli and subjects) in one condition with those in another condition. For both groups, performance in the gap sequence was not different from that in the long-nogap sequence but was better than that in the short-nogap sequence. Slow group: null hypothesis H_0: S18G93 = S102G9, $\chi^2(1) = 1.82$, $p > .17$; H_0: S18G93 = S18G9, $\chi^2(1) = 72, p < .001$; Fast group, H_0: S4G51 = S46G9, $\chi^2(1) = 0.04$, $p > .83$; H_0: S4G51 = S4G9, $\chi^2(1) = 106, p < .001$.

Unsurprisingly, performance in gap and long-nogap conditions with long SOAs (111 ms) in the slow group was superior to comparable conditions in the fast group with shorter SOAs (55 ms), all $\chi^2(1) > 11, p < .001$. The lack of difference between the gap and long-nogap condition of the fast group cannot therefore be due to a ceiling effect.

Discussion

The performance in gap sequences was equal to that in long-nogap conditions and performance in gap sequences was much better than that in short-nogap conditions. Hence, when it comes to detecting the presence of a particular photograph in a sequence, humans perform as well based on the icon of the image as based on the photograph itself. The icon of the image is thus "as good" as having the image itself in the context of this task. This was true for gaps of up to 93 ms.

The retina and V1 cannot account for this persistence

Despite the central role played by the concept of information persistence and iconic memory in models of visual perception, little is yet known about the physiology of this phenomenon. In the

17th century, Newton suspected that the continuing activity in the eye was responsible for perceptual persistency. From such a perspective, the continuing activation in the retina would simply be sent on to all cortical areas processing this input.

Levick and Sacks (1970) measured the duration of responses in ganglion cells of the retina, and found those responses to be small and to last 50–70 ms for an 8 ms stimulus and to be strong and last about 180 ms for a 128 ms stimulus of the same intensity. Hence, for the stimuli used in the present experiment, responses should be much longer and stronger for the long-nogap compared to the gap condition. Stronger and longer responses would lead to better performance in the long-nogap condition if performance was based on the iconic properties of the retina alone. This was clearly not the case here. While it may be that the retina is responsible for part of the information persistence, retinal processing cannot by itself explain the strong persistence observed in Exp. 1.

Duysens, Orban, Cremieux, and Maes (1985) recorded the responses of single V1 neurones to optimally oriented bars. They found that the on-responses of the cells were either relatively transient, lasting for only ~25 ms independent of how long the optimally oriented stimulus was presented for. If responses were less transient, the on-responses to 100 ms stimuli were longer and stronger than those to 12.5 ms stimuli. These findings, too, would predict that an ideal observer of V1 activity would perform differently to 100 ms stimuli compared to 12.5 ms stimuli in psychophysical tasks. Duysens et al. and Levick and Sacks (1970) recorded from the cat, leading to results that may differ from those in the monkey. But Gur and Snodderly (1997) recorded from the macaque monkey, presented optimally oriented bars continuously on a 60 Hz monitor, and showed that the duration of the response of V1 cells actually reflects the duration of the stimulus on the screen, responding for only a few milliseconds on each refresh cycle of the screen. Taken together, these findings suggest that the time characteristics of responses in early visual cortex cannot account for the strong information persistence observed in Exp. 1. It should be noted, however, that this latter result was obtained from monkeys that were trained to fixate a light-emitting diode. The stimulus itself thus had no task relevance for the monkey. It might be that in the context of a different task where the stimuli were relevant, the timing of the V1 neuronal responses would have differed.

To be able to explain the psychophysical data of Exp. 1, a neural correlate of iconic memory would need to fulfil three requirements. First, it would need to provide a representation of a stimulus, which continues beyond the stimulus's physical duration. Second, presenting a new stimulus should terminate this persistence. Third, responses in gap conditions should be as informative as the responses to long-nogap conditions but substantially more informative than those to short-nogap conditions.

EXPERIMENT 2: PHYSIOLOGY

Introduction

STSa neurones and perception

Here we propose that iconic memory is implemented in the brain by the persistent firing of visual neurones in the higher stages of visual shape processing (e.g., in the temporal cortex). When a stimulus is flashed on a screen, it causes selective responses in visual cortex. The firing of neurones in macaque inferior temporal cortex (IT) and the cortex lining the anterior superior temporal sulcus (STSa) correlates with perceptual reports (Keysers et al., 2001; Logothetis, 1998). These same neurones are known to continue responding for some hundreds of milliseconds after the end of a briefly presented stimulus (Kovács, Vogels, & Orban, 1995; Rolls & Tovee, 1994). Finally, presenting a new stimulus is known to terminate the persisting responses to a previous stimulus for these neurones (Keysers et al., 2001; Kovács et al., 1995; Rolls & Tovee, 1994). Taken together, the response patterns of the temporal cortex neurones may thus provide adequate neural correlates of information persistence. It is surprising, therefore, that temporal cortex responses have not been explicitly tested in relation to iconic memory.

Iconic memory vs. working memory

Temporal cortex neurones have been implicated in working memory (Fuster & Jervey, 1981; Naya, Sakai, & Miyashita, 1996). A typical paradigm for the study of working memory is the delayed matching to sample task. A stimulus is shown first, and then, after a retention interval of several seconds, this "old" stimulus is shown together with another "new" stimulus. The monkey has to remember the old stimulus during the retention interval to be able to indicate which of the two stimuli shown afterwards is the old stimulus. In such paradigms, visual neurones in temporal cortex responding to the presentation of the old stimulus continue to fire, albeit to a lesser extent, for some seconds during the retention period. If the monkey has a different task, this delay activity disappears (Naya et al., 1996). Hence the delay activity observed in these tasks appears to reflect a deliberate retention of the stimulus, akin to working memory in humans. Iconic memory differs from working memory in that the former lasts for hundreds of milliseconds and is automatic, while the latter lasts for several seconds and is deliberate. If STSa neurones provide a neural correlate of iconic memory then they should show persistent activity even in the absence of a memory task.

Experimental paradigm

The responses of single neurones in the STSa of two macaque monkeys were tested using images and methods that have been described previously (Keysers et al., 2001). The data reported here were acquired at the same time as those presented in that paper. Briefly, 137 neurones were initially tested by presenting 60 different stimuli in RSVP sequences using a relatively slow presentation rate (8 frames per stimulus, S102G9). RSVP sequences were created by presenting all 60 stimuli once, then permuting their order and presenting them again and again, without pauses and in random order, while the monkey fixated the centre of the computer screen (±5 degrees). The monkeys were trained to fixate but were not trained in any memory-related tasks. Single cell responses to a particular stimulus were assessed by aligning responses to the onset of each occurrence of this stimulus and creating an average spike density function (SDF) of the response around the onset of this stimulus. If at least one of the 60 stimuli caused a visible response in the so-created SDF, the stimulus producing the largest response was selected as the "best" stimulus for that cell, and tested using the six timing conditions outlined in Figure 1. The best stimulus for the cell was presented with seven "rest" stimuli selected to span the range of responses from second best to worst stimulus out of the original 60 (see Figure 2b).

Results

For 72/137 of these neurones, none of the 60 stimuli were effective. Another 31/137 cells were lost before completing testing. Finally, 34/137 cells were tested in all conditions of the slow group, and 21 of these cells were also tested for the conditions of the fast group. The first 13 cells were not tested in the fast group because the ability to present sequences at one frame per image (S4G9) was not available before the 14th tested cell.

Results indicate that, in STSa, the response of neurones during the presentation of gap sequences is equal to that during the presentation of long-nogap sequences but better than that during short-nogap sequences (Fig. 1a grey/blue bars and Fig. 1b). The response of a single neurone to its best stimulus (the image of an apple) is shown in Figure 3. Note how the apparent end of the response (black arrow) depends not on the duration of the stimulus, but on the time of onset of the next stimulus. The response to a longer stimulus presentation (S213G9) also demonstrates that the similarity in the responses in the S102G9 and S18G93 conditions is not due to a ceiling effect: Longer stimuli are able to produce longer responses. The same pattern is evident in the population, and was assessed quantitatively using two analyses.

ROC analysis

First, a receiver operator analysis (ROC; see, for instance, Celebrini & Newsome, 1994) was

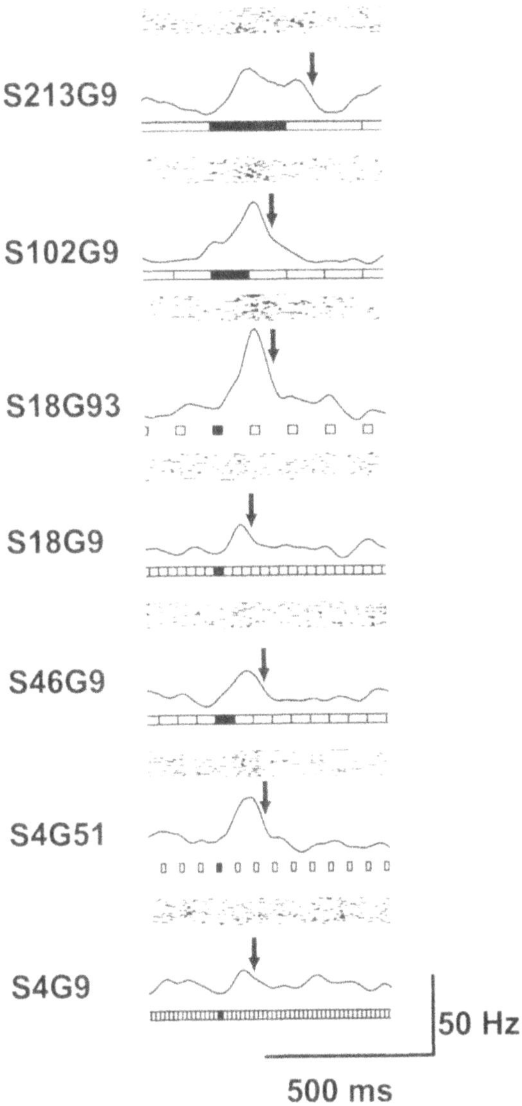

Figure 3. *Rastergram and sdfs of a single neurone response in STSa to the best stimulus for that cell (the image of an apple). Conventions as in Figure 1. For comparability only the first 21 trials are shown in each rastergram. The total trial numbers for this cell from top to bottom are 21, 42, 42, 168, 84, 84, 336. All trials are considered in the sdf. The duration of the responses decreases with decreasing SOA. The apparent ends of the responses are marked by black arrows. Comparing S102G9 with S18G93, two conditions with equal SOA (111 ms) but very different stimulus duration, the offset of the response (arrow) occurred at approximately the same time, despite the large difference in stimulus duration (102 vs. 118 ms). The same is true for S46G9 vs. S4G51. Surprisingly, in both cases the condition with the shorter stimulus had the larger peak firing rate but, as can be seen from Figure 1, this difference was not robust enough to be apparent at the population level. The response in the S132G9 condition is also shown in this figure to illustrate that the similarity between the S18G93 and S102G9 condition is not due to some ceiling effect: responses can last longer.*

performed for each neurone in each condition based on the spike count occurring in the "time window of interest." The time window of interest (see Methods for details) is the time during which the neurones discriminated between the best stimulus and the rest of the stimuli. Figure 4 shows the population response to the best and the rest of the stimuli, together with the probability that the cell discriminated between the best and the rest of the stimuli at that moment in time. Given that this window was slightly different for the different conditions, we considered the time window of interest to be the entire interval within each comparison group during which at least one of the conditions displayed significant stimulus discrimination. This time window reflects the interval during which the neurones respond to a particular stimulus, and was −24 to 133 ms (slow group) and −11 to 95 ms (fast group) relative to the response onset latency of each neurone. It might appear paradoxical that this time window contains negative values relative to the single cell latencies, but it should be noted that the latency is calculated cell by cell, while the time window of interest is calculated at the population level, with more statistical power. The ROC analysis yields a measure between 0 and 1, approximating how well an ideal observer of the activity of a single neurone could determine if the best or another stimulus had been presented in the sequence. Chance decision corresponds to .5 and a perfect decision corresponds to 1. To compare these results with those obtained in the psychophysical testing, this measure was calculated separately for each of the 21 cells tested in all conditions and whose best stimuli had been used as targets in the psychophysical experiment described above. Results are shown in Figure 1 as grey/blue bars (± sem). The results show that humans are better in their

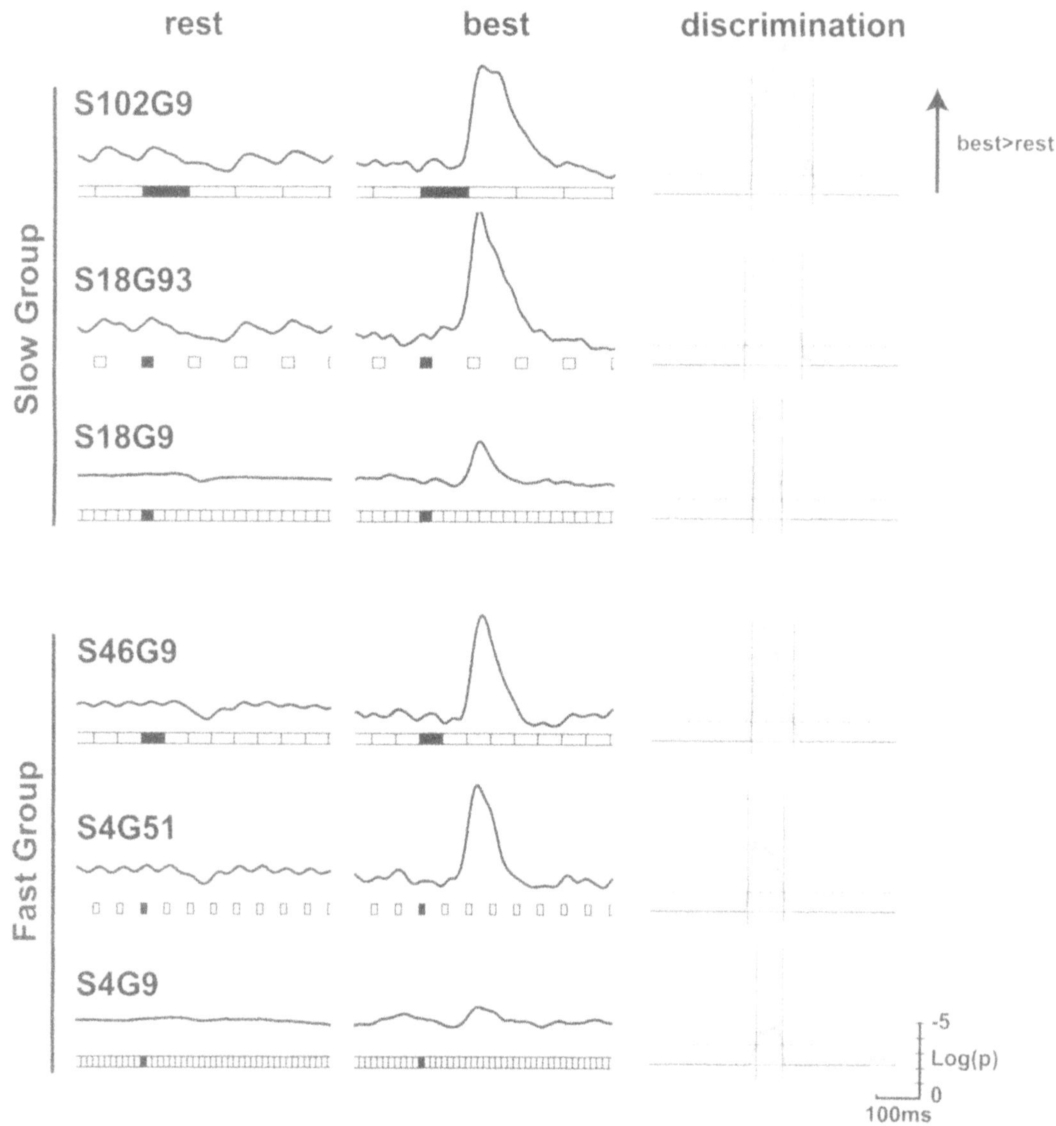

Figure 4. *Time window of interest. The black curves represent normalised, latency-aligned population sdf to the rest (left) and best stimuli (middle column) in the three conditions of the slow and the fast group. The rightmost column illustrates how well, over time, the population of neurones discriminates between the best and the rest of the stimuli. It shows the −Log(p) of the probability that the population of neurones does not discriminate between the stimuli, as assessed by a floating ANOVA (see Methods). High −Log(p) values thus suggest high discriminative capacity between the stimuli. The dotted horizontal lines represent the p = .05 threshold, the black solid line the p = 1 level, and the vertical lines, the beginning and end of the period during which discrimination is above p = .05. Only deflections in the direction best > rest are shown. The scale on the bottom right applies to the x-axes of all plots, and to the y-axes of all floating ANOVA plots (grey). ANOVA p-values are two-tailed and not Bonferroni corrected.*

proportion correct decisions than an ideal observer of the STSa single cell activity. Nevertheless, the ideal observer of STSa activity shows the *same pattern* of performance across conditions as that of the human observers: Performance in the gap conditions *does* differ from that in the short-nogap conditions but performance in the gap conditions does *not* differ from that in the long-nogap conditions. This effect was tested statistically using an ANOVA due to the parametric nature of the ROC values. The ANOVA (2 groups × 3 conditions × 21 neurones) indicated a main effect for group, $F(1, 20) = 58, p < .001$, and condition, $F(1, 20) = 61, p < .001$. The same results were found when all 34 neurones tested in the slow group were analysed only for the slow group condition. For both the fast and the slow groups, a Newman-Keuls post hoc analysis (criterion $p < .05$) indicated no difference between the gap and long-nogap conditions with equal SOA (S102G9 vs. S18G93 and S4G51 vs. S46G9, respectively). By contrast, for both the fast and the slow groups there was a significant difference between the gap condition and short-nogap conditions with equal stimulus duration but different SOAs (S18G9 vs. S18G93 and S4G9 vs. S4G51, respectively).

Population response

Single cell responses to a particular stimulus are assessed by aligning responses to the onset of each occurrence of the stimulus and creating an average spike density function (SDF) of the response around the onset of the stimulus.

A second form of analysis was based more directly on these SDFs (Figure 1b). Since the response onset latency of the 34 neurones varied considerably, responses were latency-aligned. The peak activity also varied between neurones. All SDFs of a given neurone were therefore normalised by dividing SDF values by the peak amplitude of the SDF of each neurone in the S102G9 condition. The average over all available neurones ($n = 34$ in the slow and $n = 21$ in the fast group) of these normalised and latency-aligned SDFs are shown in Figure 1b, bottom traces. As can be seen, the population response to gap sequences (S18G93 and S4G51; Figure 1b dashed/red lines) is very similar to the response to long-nogap sequences (S102G9 and S46G9, respectively, thick lines), while being much stronger than that to short-nogap sequences (S18G9 and S4G9, respectively, thin/green lines). To test this effect statistically, using the same time window of interest as in the ROC analysis, the surface under the normalised SDF to the best stimulus was integrated for each neurone, yielding one surface area value for each neurone in each of the six conditions. Within-subject F-tests comparing this surface over all available neurones confirmed that there was no difference between the responses during the gap and long-nogap sequence, but that the responses during the gap sequence differed from those during the short-nogap sequence. Slow group H_0: S102G9 = S18G93, $F(1, 33) = 0.16, p > .69$; H_0: S18G93 = S18G9, $F(1, 33) = 51, p < 10^{-7}$; fast group, H_0: S46G9 = S4G51, $F(1, 20) = 0.09, p > .76$; H_0: S46G9 = S4G51, $F(1, 20) = 15, p < .001$. These effects were also present in a majority of single neurones if tested separately.

It is also apparent that, in the slow group, the initial peak of the response appears larger in the S18G93 compared with the S102G9 condition. Again, we tested this effect statistically by comparing the surface under the curves, but this time looking at the first 60 ms of the response. This analysis showed that in the slow group the initial peak of the response was significantly higher in the gap condition, while in the fast group, only a trend in the same direction was visible: slow group, $F(1, 33) = 16.8, p < .0003$ and $F(1, 21) = 2.9, p > .09$. This effect then inverts in the second part of the responses, with the gap condition leading to slightly smaller responses. Overall the gap and long-nogap conditions then do not differ significantly.

We have repeated these analyses with both shorter (e.g., $SD = 5$ ms), and longer (e.g., $SD = 20$ ms) convolution windows for the SDF, and found virtually identical results. Indeed, even the 10 ms convolution used in the presented data is relatively short compared to the duration of the responses (~116 ms and 157 ms for the fast and slow group respectively).

Discussion

Overall, STSa activity was indistinguishable during gap conditions and long-nogap conditions with matched SOAs. This shows that neurones in STSa, unlike neurones in V1 (Gur & Snodderly, 1997), do not represent the duration of brief stimuli. Instead, neurones in STSa appear to process stimuli for as long as they can—unless a new stimulus is presented. This is compatible with the idea that the ventral processing stream extracts information about the shape of an object: Information about shape accumulates progressively over a period of at least 150 ms (Gershon et al., 1998), with less than 50% of the information present in the first 50 ms. If neurones responded only for the duration of brief stimuli (e.g., 18 ms), much less information about the stimulus would be extracted. While the persistence of responses in STSa therefore successfully maximises shape processing in STSa, other aspects of the stimulus, such as its duration, are lost for STSa neurones. Other cortical areas will need to provide this lost information if it is required.

The long persistence of the responses in STSa may also have another function (e.g., Földiák, 1991). When we observe an object or person rotating we have no problem understanding that the different views belong to the same object or to the same person. At a neural level, we know that most neurones in the temporal cortex respond only to certain views of faces (Perrett et al., 1991) or objects (Logothetis, Pauls, & Poggio, 1995). But how are these single views combined to enable us to understand that they all belong to a single object? The prolonged responses we observe in the STSa might be a key to this question. Our measurements showed STSa neuronal responses lasted ~60 ms longer than the SOA. This creates a temporal overlap between the neural responses of consecutive frames in the RSVP sequences. The rotation of an object on a screen can be seen as the consecutive presentation of the different views of that object. Neighbouring views will systematically occur one after another, and there will thus be overlap between the activity of neurones representing adjacent object views. This overlap could encourage Hebbian associations between the neurones responding to the different views of the same object. This scenario would predict that some neurones should then start to respond to all the views of an object. This implication has been confirmed for both faces (Perrett et al., 1991) and objects (Logothetis et al., 1995). In addition to linking the different views of an object, persistence could be a general way for the brain to connect visual events that systematically occur one after another. Connecting the different events in an action sequence or snapshots of biological actions might be interesting examples (Giese & Poggio, 2003; Jellema & Perrett, 2003). Future investigations will be needed to determine the duration of neural responses in RSVP sequences that resemble natural sequences such as walking or rotating, and compare these with sequences containing the same frames but in random order.

In addition, the responses of the STSa neurones recorded in the present study enable an ideal observer to perform as well in gap conditions as in long-nogap conditions. Hence, the "icon" of the stimulus used during the gap period to continue processing the stimulus is as informative as a continued retinal input. The retinal input would have stopped towards the second half of the response observed in STSa during the slow gap conditions: Retinal ganglion cells respond for only about 70 ms to stimuli lasting 18 ms without any masking stimulus (Levick & Sacks, 1970). In contrast, the STSa neurones reported here responded for at least 170 ms to these stimuli. The response of V1 neurones, too, would be different for 18 ms and 102 ms stimuli (Duysens et al., 1985; Gur & Snodderly, 1997). Hence, while early areas may contribute in part to the observed information persistence, some of the persistence has to derive from the response of neurones higher than V1 in the ventral visual processing stream. Whether such long persistence is only observed in STSa, or whether earlier areas occurring between V1 and STSa already show similarly long persistence remains for future investigations to explore. It should be kept in mind that, unlike our human observers, the monkey had no task to look for a particular target in the stream of images. The duration of neural

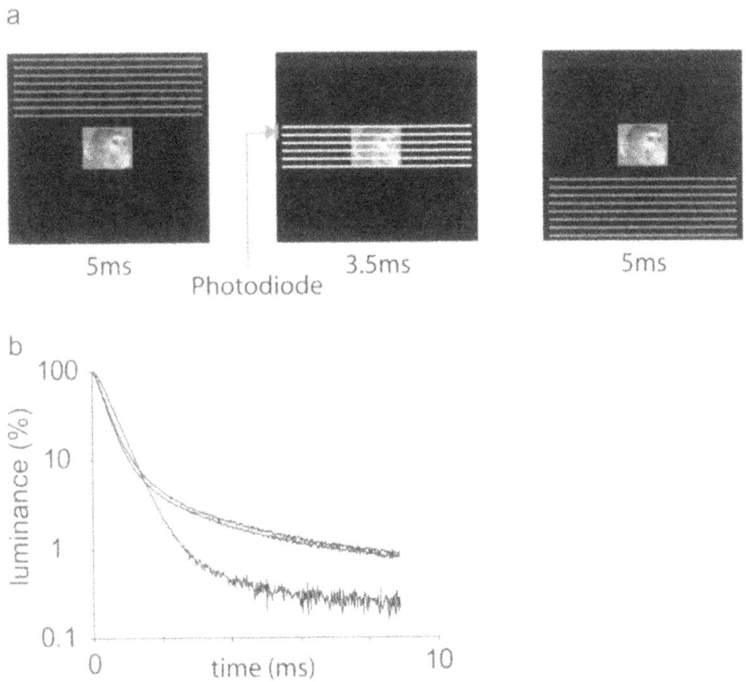

Figure 5. *Actual duration of a stimulus. (a) The stimuli occupied only the centre 1/4 of the screen. Of the 14 ms of total frame duration, 5.25 ms are spent sweeping the empty top and 5.25 ms the empty bottom of the screen. The actual image is swept for only 3.5 ms. Going back to the beginning of the next frame is virtually instantaneous. A photodiode on the side of the screen measured the actual beginning of the stimulus presentation. (b) After a given pixel has been illuminated on the screen (time 0 ms), the three coloured P22 phosphors of the screen progressively fade. The 10% luminance mark is reached after ~1 ms, the 1% luminance mark after ~8 ms (Graph: courtesy of the Sony Corporation). Physiological experiments in V1 suggest that at 10% contrast most, and at 1% all, neurones stop responding (Müller et al., 2001) to their preferred gratings. It is therefore reasonable to assume that the image is virtually "gone" ~4 ms after the beginning of its presentation (i.e., 3.5 ms of sweep time + 1 ms of decay time). This represents the timing from the beginning of the top left to the end of the bottom right corner of the stimulus. Indeed, the top left pixels are at less then 5% of their initial luminance by the time the bottom right pixel of the screen is illuminated. To view this figure in colour, please see the online issue of the Journal.*

responses may look slightly different if the monkey is looking for a particular target in the sequence. If responses do indeed last longer for a target stimulus in a sequence, this prolonged response could alter the processing of subsequent stimuli in the sequence and could be at the basis of the attentional blink observed in psychophysical investigations (Keysers & Perrett, 2002; Raymond, Shapiro, & Arnell, 1992). Physiological measurements are needed to answer this issue.

It should be noted, however, that in RSVP any stimulus is subjected both to forward and backward masking: Every stimulus is both followed and preceded by other stimuli in the sequence. Forward masking has been shown to depend both on the onset and the offset of the mask preceding the target stimulus (Crawford, 1947; Macknik & Livingstone, 1998). In the gap condition, the offset of the previous stimulus happened earlier than in the no-gap condition, and one might therefore expect less forward masking in gap conditions. The initially stronger response in the S18G93 condition seems to support this hypothesis. Pure backward masking experiments are needed to tell us if gap and long-nogap conditions produce equal responses even in the absence of a forward-masking advantage for the gap condition. Unfortunately, no such experiments have been done; neither Rolls and Tovee (1994) nor

Kovács et al. (1995) ever compared the responses of gap and no-gap conditions directly.

OVERALL CONCLUSIONS

STSa and iconic memory

Overall, our data demonstrates that when the task is to decide if a particular image is in a sequence of images, human subjects perform as well to a brief stimulus followed by a gap as to a much longer stimulus followed immediately by a mask. The icon underlying the continued processing of the stimulus is thus as informative as a continued retinal input.

Recordings from single cells show that, unlike the retina (Levick & Sacks, 1970) and V1 (Duysens et al., 1985; Gur & Snodderly, 1997), the STSa provides responses that would be adequate for supporting human psychophysical decisions in our detection task. That is to say, STSa neurones respond as well during the gap condition as during the long-nogap conditions. An ideal observer of STSa activity would perform as well in these two conditions. The monkeys from which STSa activity was recorded had never been trained for a memory task, and were not required to remember stimuli during the physiological recordings. The persistence of the responses of the neurones therefore reflects an automatic persistence that is characteristic of iconic memory. Further investigations will be needed to discover if the decay rate of the response of neurones in the STSa corresponds to the decay of information observed in humans (Loftus et al., 1992).

A multiplayer account of iconic memory

There has been a long-lasting debate on the exact information contained in iconic memory (see Coltheart, 1983, for a review). Is the icon like a slowly fading photograph of the stimulus, containing only pre-categorical information, or is it a description of the image containin post-categorical information (e.g., "a monkey face in the middle of the screen looking to the right," albeit in a nonverbal form)? Historically, answers to this question were limited to psychophysical considerations. In particular, two findings challenged the idea that there is a simple answer to this question. First, if subjects are shown a matrix containing digits and letters, and later asked to report all digits, they perform better than if asked to report all items (Duncan, 1983). Hence, the category of the stimulus (letter vs. digit) can be a cue for retrieval from iconic memory, and iconic memory must therefore contain some post-categorical (letter vs. digit) information. Second, when a spatial cue is used (i.e., "Tell me which item was present here in the matrix") subjects make two types of error: misidentification error, i.e., reporting an item that does not exist in the matrix; and mislocation errors, i.e., reporting a number that is in the matrix at a location that was close to but not exactly at the cued location (Townsend, 1973). Misindentification errors are compatible with the idea of a fading photograph that renders identification increasingly difficult; mislocation errors on the other hand are not: They require that the subject has identified the stimulus but has no clear information about the location of the item. Mislocation errors appear to occur predominantly if the cue is given relatively late after the original stimulus, suggesting that space and category information may fade at different rates in iconic memory.

Taking a physiological perspective on the issue may help the understanding of these two phenomena. The visual system can be described as being organised as a hierarchy of areas, with "early" areas such as V1 having small receptive fields and responding to simple features such as lines, and "later" visual areas having much larger receptive fields and much more complex visual properties, with single neurones representing objects as complex as faces. Hence early areas have precise spatial information due to their small receptive fields, but no information about the high-level category of an image (e.g., is it a face?). Late areas, on the other hand, lack the spatial information because of their large receptive fields, but have information about the high-level category of a stimulus. Indeed, given that between V1 and STSa the complexity of a stimulus required to drive cells appears to increase progressively (from simple edges to face patterns), the concept of pre- and post-categorical information used by psychophysicists should be replaced with the idea of a continuum of degrees of shape categorisation. The fact that responses in the later visual areas of the ventral stream have longer latencies and longer persistence compared to the earlier areas has implications for the processing of a brief stimulus. Directly after stimulus onset, only very elementary feature (pre-categorical) information about the stimulus is present, due to the longer latencies of neurones higher up in the hierarchy. Shortly thereafter, progressively more high-level information is added by higher visual cortex while the pre-categorical image is still available from the persisting responses of earlier neurones. At this time, objects can be identified based on their category. Some time later, the pre-categorical information represented in early visual cortex fades away leaving only the high-level, categorical, but poorly localised information embodied in the responses of higher visual cortex neurones with longer persistence and latencies. At this time, mislocation errors will be likely. Finally, after several hundred milliseconds, even this post-categorical information stored in higher visual cortex will fade away. Then only that information selected for working memory (Fuster & Jervey, 1981; Naya et al., 1996) will be kept alive, with weaker delay activity responses and limited memory capacity. Iconic memory in this neurophysiological perspective is thus a multilayered process, composed of a spectrum of levels of categorisation with different time courses. In addition to the layers of the ventral visual processing stream, the dorsal processing stream adds additional layers to the picture. Given that different areas have different persistence durations, the information available from different "layers" comes and goes with different time courses.

Comparative measurements of the rate of decay in the response to brief stimuli in the different areas along the ventral visual processing stream would be needed to make precise hypotheses about the time course of the different information layers that could underlie iconic memory.

PrEview proof published online 17 January 2005

REFERENCES

Bridgeman, B. (1998). Durations of stimuli displayed on video display terminals: $(n-1)/f$ plus persistence. *Psychological Science, 9,* 232–233.

Celebrini, S., & Newsome, W. T. (1994). Neuronal and psychophysical sensitivity to motion signals in extrastriate area MST of the macaque monkey. *Journal of Neuroscience, 14,* 4109–4124.

Coltheart, M. (1980). The persistences of vision. *Philosophical Transactions of the Royal Society of London B: Biological Sciences, 290,* 57–69.

Coltheart, M. (1983). Iconic memory. *Philosophical Transactions of the Royal Society of London B: Biological Sciences, 302,* 283–294.

Crawford, B. H. (1947). Visual adaptation in relation to brief conditioning stimuli. *Proceedings of the Royal Society of London, 134b,* 283–302.

Duncan, J. (1983). Perceptual selection based on alphanumeric class: Evidence from partial reports. *Perception and Psychophysics, 33,* 533–547.

Duysens, J., Orban, G. A., Cremieux, J., & Maes, H. (1985). Visual cortical correlates of visible persistence. *Vision Research, 25,* 171–178.

Földiák, P. (1991). Learning invariance from transformation sequences. *Neural Computation, 3,* 194–200.

Fuster, J. M., & Jervey, J. P. (1981). Inferotemporal neurons distinguish and retain behaviorally relevant features of visual stimuli. *Science, 212,* 952–955.

Gershon, E. D., Wiener, M. C., Latham, P. E., & Richmond, B. J. (1998). Coding strategies in monkey V1 and inferior temporal cortices. *Journal of Neurophysiology, 79,* 1135–1144.

Giese, M. A., & Poggio, T. (2003). Neural mechanisms for the recognition of biological movements. *National Review of Neuroscience, 4,* 179–192.

Gur, M., & Snodderly, D. M. (1997). A dissociation between brain activity and perception: Chromatically opponent cortical neurons signal chromatic flicker that is not perceived. *Vision Research, 37,* 377–382.

Jellema, T., & Perrett, D. I. (2003). Perceptual history influences neural responses to face and body postures. *Journal of Cognitive Neuroscience, 15,* 1–11.

Keysers, C., & Perrett, D. I. (2002). Visual masking and RSVP reveal neural competition. *Trends in Cognitive Science, 6,* 120–125.

Keysers, C., Xiao, D. K., Földiák, P., & Perrett, D. I. (2001). The speed of sight. *Journal of Cognitive Neuroscience, 13,* 90–101.

Kovács, G., Vogels, R., & Orban, G. A. (1995). Cortical correlate of pattern backward masking. *Proceedings of the National Academy of Sciences USA, 92,* 5587–5591.

Levick, W. R., & Sacks, J. L. (1970). Responses of the cat retinal ganglion cells to brief flashes of light. *Journal of Physiology, 206,* 677–700.

Loftus, G. R., Duncan, J., & Gehrig, P. (1992). On the time course of perceptual information that results from a brief visual presentation. *Journal of Experimental Psychology: Human Perception and Performance, 18,* 530–549 [discussion, 550–561].

Loftus, G. R., & Irwin, D. E. (1998). On the relations among different measures of visible and informational persistence. *Cognitive Psychology, 35,* 135–199.

Logothetis, N. K. (1998). Single units and conscious vision. *Philosophical Transactions of the Royal Society of London B: Biological Sciences, 353,* 1801–1818.

Logothetis, N. K., Pauls, J., & Poggio, T. (1995). Shape representation in the inferior temporal cortex of monkeys. *Current Biology, 5,* 552–563.

Macknik, S. L., & Livingston, M. S. (1998). Neural correlates of visibility and invisibility in the primate visual system. *Nature Neuroscience, 1,* 144–149.

Muller, J. R., Metha, A. B., Krauskopf, J., & Lennie, P. (2001). Information conveyed by onset transients in responses of striate cortical neurons. *Journal of Neuroscience, 21,* 6978–6990.

Naya, Y., Sakai, K., & Miyashita, Y. (1996). Activity of primate inferotemporal neurons related to a sought target in pair-association task. *Proceedings of the National Academy of Sciences USA, 93,* 2664–2669.

Oram, M. W., & Perrett, D. I. (1992). Time course of neural responses discriminating different views of the face and head. *Journal of Neurophysiology, 68,* 70–84.

Perrett, D. I., Oram, M. W., Harries, M. H., Bevan, R., Hietanen, J. K., Benson, P. J., & Thomas, S. (1991). Viewer-centred and object-centred coding of heads in the macaque temporal cortex. *Experimental Brain Research, 86,* 159–173.

Raymond, J. E., Shapiro, K. L., & Arnell, K. M. (1992). Temporary suppression of visual processing in an RSVP task: An attentional blink? *Journal of Experimental Psychology: Human Perception and Performance, 18,* 849–860.

Rolls, E. T., & Tovee, M. J. (1994). Processing speed in the cerebral cortex and the neurophysiology of visual masking. *Proceedings of the Royal Society of London B: Biological Sciences, 257,* 9–15.

Snodderly, D. M., & Gur, M. (1995). Organization of striate cortex of alert, trained monkeys (*Macaca fascicularis*): Ongoing activity, stimulus selectivity, and widths of receptive field activating regions. *Journal of Neurophysiology, 74,* 2100–2125.

Sperling, G. (1960). The information available in brief visual presentation. *Psychological Monographs, 74,* 1–29.

Townsend, V. M. (1973). Loss of spatial and identity information following a tachistoscopic exposure. *Journal of Experimental Psychology, 98,* 113–118.

COGNITIVE NEUROPSYCHOLOGY, 2005, 22 (3/4), 333–347

MENTAL IMAGES AND THE BRAIN

Stephen M. Kosslyn
Harvard University, Cambridge, MA, USA

One theory of visual mental imagery posits that early visual cortex is also used to support representations during imagery. This claim is important because it bears on the "imagery debate": Early visual cortex supports depictive representations during perception, not descriptive ones. Thus, if such cortex also plays a functional role in imagery, this is strong evidence that imagery does not rely exclusively on the same sorts of representations that underlie language. The present article first outlines the nature of a processing system in which such a dual use of early visual cortex (in perception and in imagery) makes sense. Following this, literature bearing on the claim that early visual cortex is used in visual mental imagery is reviewed, and key issues are discussed.

During the late 1970s and early 1980s there was vigorous debate about the nature of visual mental imagery. One position (championed primarily by Pylyshyn, 1973, 1981) held that representations that underlie the experience of mental imagery are the same type as those used in language; the other position (which my colleagues and I supported, e.g., Kosslyn, 1980, 1994) held that these representations serve to depict, not describe, objects. The debate evolved over time (for a summary, see Chapter 1 of Kosslyn, 1994), but always centred on the nature of the internal representations that underlie the experience of visualisation (e.g., Tye, 1991). The initial debate focused on conceptual issues and behavioural results, such as the finding that people require more time to scan farther distances in their visual mental images (Kosslyn, 1973; Kosslyn et al., 1978) and require more time to rotate objects in mental images by greater amounts (e.g., Shepard & Cooper, 1982). Interest in imagery waned by the mid-1980s, probably for several reasons (including the facts that definitive data had not been produced and other topics became fashionable). Nevertheless, research has continued on the topic, much of it in Europe (e.g., see Behrmann, Kosslyn, & Jeannerod, 1996), and progress has been made.

The debate moved into a new phase when neuroimaging began to be used to study the activation of early visual cortex during visual mental imagery (e.g., for review, see Kosslyn, Ganis, & Thompson, 2001a). Some studies found such activation, but others did not—and thus it was not clear how to interpret the full set of findings (for review, see Kosslyn & Thompson, 2003). At the same time, Pylyshyn (2002, 2003) rejected the very idea that neural evidence could bear on the imagery debate, and repeatedly claimed that

Correspondence should be addressed to S. M. Kosslyn, 830 William James Hall, Harvard University, 33 Kirkland Street, Cambridge, MA 02138, USA (Email: smk@wjh.harvard.edu).

This chapter summarises work supported by NIH grant 5 R01 MH60734, NSF grant REC-0106760, and NIMA grant NMA201-01-C-0032. I thank Marie Burrage for making many helpful and constructive comments on an earlier draft (but of course I must take responsibility for any muddled writing that persisted even after her careful edits).

there is no viable theory of mental imagery. Pylyshyn's general concept of a theory (never spelled out in any detail) appears to require something analogous to a theory of linguistic competence, and does not fully address the empirical results that have driven the field.

In this brief article I provide an overview of one attempt to develop a theory that captures the regularities underlying the empirical results, and show how it can help us to formulate testable predictions about brain function. The theory is not complete and may not even be accurate as far as it goes, but it is definitely a "theory of mental imagery." I focus here in particular on one aspect of the theory, namely the dual role of early visual cortex in perception and imagery. This is crucial for the debate because these brain areas are topographically organised, and hence patterns of activation in these areas serve specifically to depict objects.

We must begin by distinguishing between *visual mental imagery* and *visual perception*: Visual perception occurs while a stimulus is being viewed, and includes functions such as visual recognition (i.e., registering that a stimulus is familiar) and identification (i.e., recalling the name, context, or other information associated with the object). Two types of mechanisms are used in visual perception: "bottom-up" mechanisms are driven by the input from the eyes; in contrast, "top-down" mechanisms make use of stored information (such as knowledge, belief, expectations, and goals). Visual mental imagery is a set of representations that gives rise to the experience of viewing a stimulus in the absence of appropriate sensory input. In this case, information in memory underlies the internal events that produce the experience. Unlike afterimages, mental images are relatively prolonged.

The approach offered here is unabashedly reductionistic: In my view, "the mind is what the brain does." We will consider imagery in light of neural mechanisms that give rise to the internal phenomena that underlie both the experience of visualisation and the behaviour that accompanies such experiences (for reviews of such behaviour, see Finke, 1989; Kosslyn, 1980, 1994; Shepard & Cooper, 1982).

A BRAIN SYSTEM

In order to discuss the role of early visual cortex (i.e., Areas 17 and 18) in visual mental imagery, we first must put it in context. Imagery is not simply a pattern of activation in these areas, but arises when such activation is embedded in a larger system.

Visual imagery and visual perception

All of the mental functions that we label with a single word, such as perception, memory, reasoning, and imagery, are accomplished by systems of processes in the brain. Numerous distinct processes are used to accomplish such functions (see Kosslyn & Koenig, 1992/1995, for a characterisation of the concept of "process" in this context). We gain enormous leverage in understanding the system of processes used in visual mental imagery because numerous researchers have shown that many of the same processes are also used in visual perception, and much is known about perception (e.g., see Farah, 1988; Finke, 1989; Kosslyn, 1994). Two types of evidence support this inference.

First, patients with brain damage often show deficits in imagery that parallel their deficits in perception (see Farah, 1988; Kosslyn, 1994; Kosslyn & Koenig, 1992/1995). For example, patients with damage to the parietal lobes sometimes exhibit "unilateral visual neglect"—they ignore objects to one side of space. These patients often ignore objects at the same side of space in both perception and mental imagery (e.g., Bisiach & Luzzatti, 1978; Bisiach, Luzzatti, & Perani, 1979). However, Behrmann, Winocur, and Moscovitch (1992) and Jankowiak, Kinsbourne, Shalev, and Bachman (1992) have described patients who have disrupted perception but retain relatively intact imagery, which underscores the fact that the two systems are not identical: In particular, imagery is based on previously stored information, and thus it can operate effectively even if the processes that organise visual input are awry.

Second, researchers have used neuroimaging techniques, primarily positron emission tomography (PET) and functional magnetic imaging (fMRI), to assess brain activity while participants perform visual mental imagery tasks (for reviews, see Kosslyn et al., 2001a; Kosslyn & Thompson, 2003; Mellet, Petit, Mazoyer, Denis, & Tzourio, 1998). These studies have often reported activation in brain areas used in visual perception (e.g., Farah, Peronnet, Gonon, & Girard, 1988; Goldenberg, Podreka, Steiner, Willmes, Suess, & Deecke, 1989). Kosslyn, Thompson, and Alpert (1997) found that two thirds of all brain areas activated during either visual imagery or visual perception were activated in common; a more recent fMRI study from my lab, Ganis et al. (in press), demonstrated an even greater overlap in activation when the imagery and perception tasks were designed to be maximally similar. In this study, when the same task was performed in perception (with the stimuli visible) and during imagery (with eyes closed), approximately 90% of the same voxels were activated.

Perceptual processes used in visual imagery

Given the extant literature, I take it as a working assumption that imagery shares mechanisms with like-modality perception. In this section I provide a very brief overview of the major features of my current theory of visual mental imagery. The theory posits six major "components," as schematised in Figure 1. Each of these "components" is a coarsely described system of processes in its own right; each accepts input and transforms it in specific ways to produce output. Each component is also assumed to store information (in fact, the stored information plays crucial roles in producing the transformations). In my 1994 book I referred to the theory diagramed in Figure 1 as a "protomodel" because it is simply the bare bones of a theory. In that book I attempted to refine each of these major components, typically by dividing it into more specialised subcomponents, but I will not summarise that level of detail here. The motivation for positing each component rests largely on findings about the neurophysiology and neuroanatomy of visual perception. (The following summary has been adapted from that of Kosslyn, Alpert, Thompson, Chabris, Rauch, & Anderson, 1994.)

Visual buffer

Introspectively, visual mental images appear to embody the spatial layout of shapes. For example, consider what seems to occur when you try to

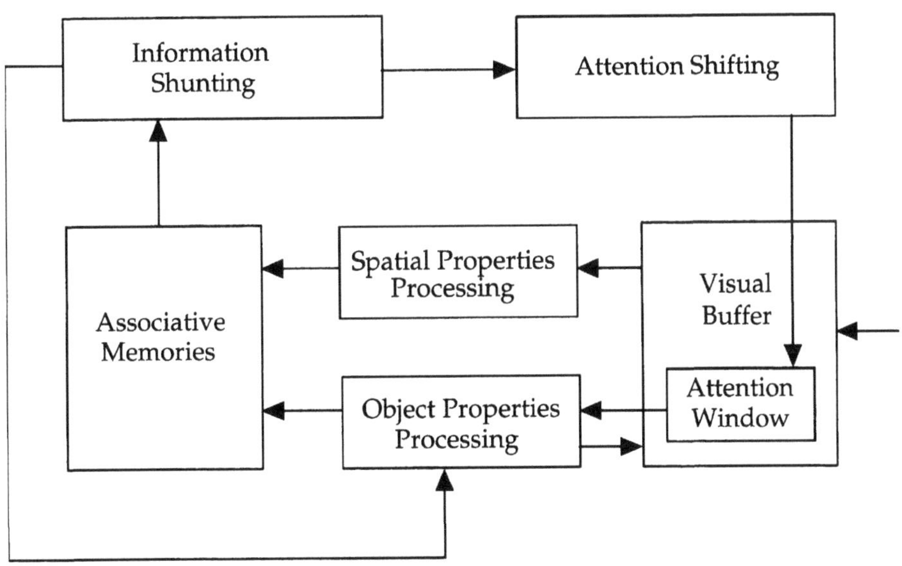

Figure 1. *The major processing systems posited to be used in visual imagery and the later phases of visual perception.*

answer questions such as, "Which is longer, a donkey's ears or an ear of corn?" "How many windows are in your living room?" "Which is wider, a light bulb or a tennis ball?" Most people report that they visualise the objects, and "see" the necessary properties. This sort of introspection suggests that visual mental images reconstruct the spatial geometry of objects. In fact, numerous areas of cerebral cortex are topographically organised; patterns of activity within these areas make explicit and accessible the spatial organisation of the planar projection of a stimulus. In these areas, the cortex is folded so that the fovea typically projects to the posterior part, with increasingly parafoveal regions projecting to increasingly anterior parts. The areas typically represent only the contralateral field, or even only a quandrant of the field. Neuroanatomical studies of nonhuman primates have revealed that about half of the cortical areas involved in vision are topographically organised, including Areas 17 and 18 (see Felleman & Van Essen, 1991; Heeger, 1999; Sengpiel & Huebener, 1999; Sereno et al., 1995; Tootell, Silverman, Switkes, & DeValois, 1982; Van Essen, 1985). Fox, Mintun, Raichle, Miezen, Allman, and Van Essen (1986) used PET to demonstrate that the largest such area, Area 17 (also known as primary visual cortex, striate cortex, area OC, and area V1), is topographically organised in humans (see also Heeger, 1999).

I group the topographically organised visual areas of cortex into a single functional structure, which I call the "visual buffer." A strong claim of the theory is that the brain areas that implement the visual buffer are also crucial during visual mental imagery (as will be discussed below). This is important because the visual buffer depicts shape. By "depict" I mean that each part of the representation corresponds to a part of the object such that the distances among the parts on the object are reflected (albeit not perfectly) by the distances among the representations of the parts (see Kosslyn, 1980).

Rather than thinking of the visual buffer as a simple "blackboard," a better analogy might be to a pegboard. As suggested by Tye (1991), at each location in the topographically organised buffer are a set of "symbolic" codes that indicate information such as the colour and luminance at that specific point. Thus, in addition to this "picture-like" depictive aspect of the representation, the visual buffer specifies information that is interpreted as nonspatial properties associated with each location. Finally, the visual buffer is not a passive screen, but rather serves to organise input in various ways, such as delineating figure from ground.

Attention window

There is far more information in the visual buffer than can be processed in detail. Thus, an "attention window" operates within this structure, which selects a region of the buffer and sends the pattern of activation in it to other areas for further processing (cf. Brefczynski & DeYoe, 1999; Moran & Desimone, 1985; Treisman & Gelade, 1980). The attention window can be covertly shifted, and allows one to scan over entire images in the visual buffer without moving one's eyes.

Processing object properties versus spatial properties

The information in the visual buffer would be useless if it could not be processed. In fact, such information is processed along two pathways. One runs from the occipital lobe ventrally to the inferior temporal lobe, while the other runs dorsally to the posterior parietal lobe. Many findings have shown that the ventral pathway acts as an object-properties processing subsystem whereas the dorsal pathway acts as a spatial-properties processing subsystem (e.g., Anderson, Essick, & Seigel, 1985; Hyvarinen, 1982; Maunsell & Newsome, 1987; Mountcastle et al., 1975; Ungerleider & Mishkin, 1982). By "object properties" I mean shape, colour, and texture; by "spatial properties" I mean relative positions in space of two or more objects or parts. The distinction between the two kinds of properties is not quite as straightforward as it may appear. For example, if you look closely at a TV screen, you will notice that the shapes are made up of individual pixels in specific locations—and thus location information gives rise to shape information. However, we can distinguish between the two types of properties in the following way: Spatial relations always include one point that has a privileged role; it is the "origin" from which the locations of other points are compared. Shapes, in contrast, emerge from the relations among all possible points—no one point has a privileged role. Instead, the local spatial relations give rise to higher-order patterns, such as contours, and it is these patterns (not the individual locations of constituent points) that define a shape.

Neuroimaging studies suggest that the middle temporal gyrus, inferior temporal gyrus, and fusiform gyrus may be the locus of visual memories in the human brain (see Haxby et al., 1991; Kosslyn et al., 1994; Sergent, Ohta, & MacDonald, 1992). These areas are selectively activated when one must recognise a stimulus. In addition, findings of Tanaka and colleagues (e.g., Fujita, Tanaka, Ito, & Cheng, 1992; Tanaka, Saito, Fukada, & Moriya, 1991) suggest that information is stored in the object-properties- processing system using a "population code" that, essentially, compresses the information. Shapes are stored by coding the presence or absence of each of a large set of attributes (which are not themselves interpretable in simple ways), and are not depicted in these areas.

According to our theory, images (i.e., topographically organised representations) are not stored in long-term memory. Rather, images in the visual buffer must be created by activating the stored memories in such a way that the implicit shape information is "unpacked" (for a detailed theory of how this may occur, see Kosslyn, 1994). Indeed, at least in the monkey brain, neural connections exist between the areas that store visual memory (nontopographically) and early visual cortex (which is topographically organised): Virtually every area involved in vision that has an afferent (forward) connection to another area also receives an efferent (backwards) connection from that area, and the forward and backward projections are of comparable size (e.g., Van Essen, 1985). These features of the anatomy imply that a great deal of information flows backwards in the visual system, from "higher-level" areas to the "lower-level," topographically organised areas. In fact, Douglas and Rockland (1992) have found direct connections from area TE (in the anterior inferior temporal lobe) to Area 17 in the macaque (see also Rockland, Saleem, & Tanaka, 1992). Such direct cortico–cortico connections from the higher-level areas to the lower-level areas are consistent with the hypothesis that visual mental images are formed by using stored information to reconstruct spatial patterns in topographically organised cortical areas. Similar ideas have long been popular (e.g., cf. Damasio, Damasio, Tranel, & Brandt, 1990; Hebb, 1968; James, 1890).

On the other hand, according to our theory, spatial representations in the dorsal system are often (but not always) used in the service of guiding movements (cf. Milner & Goodale, 1995). To this end, the spatial representation includes a "map," where the locations of parts and objects are represented by distinct points.

Associative memory

One of the advances of research on memory is the finding that different types of memories are often stored in different regions of the brain (e.g., Schacter, 1996; Squire, 1987). We can infer that there must be a long-term memory (LTM) representation that associates object properties with spatial properties; the mere fact that people can recall where furniture is located in their homes indicates that the two sorts of information must have been cross-indexed in memory. This memory representation is multimodal, associating not only visual object properties and spatial properties, but also auditory, tactile, and other sorts of information. Moreover, because many complex objects are encoded over the course of numerous eye movements, parts may be encoded separately as distinct shape representations in the object-properties-processing system, and a representation of the structure of the object is built up in associative memory as one's eyes move. Long-term associative memory appears to rely on cortex in the region of the angular gyrus and part of Area 19 (Kosslyn, Thompson, & Alpert, 1995a).

Information shunting

During perception, one sometimes cannot identify an object at first glance; the information encoded in a single eye fixation is not sufficient to match a stored representation (cf. Neisser, 1967). However, the input provides some indication of what is being viewed, and the partial match to stored representations may serve as a hypothesis. In this case, additional information is needed to identify the input. Frontal lobe processes apparently access information in long-term associative memory, and shunt this information to processes that guide further encodings, allowing one to seek a particularly diagnostic part or characteristic of an object. Many researchers have found that damage to the frontal lobe disrupts systematic search (e.g., Luria, 1980), and others have found that the frontal lobes are in fact active when one must access information in memory (see Berthoz, 1996; Nyberg, Cabeza, & Tulving, 1996).

Attention shifting and top-down priming

Finally, an attention-shifting system actually shifts attention to the location of a possibly distinctive part during perception, which allows one to encode it. And here is a crucial idea for the theory of imagery: At the same time that attention is shifted to the location of an expected part or characteristic, the representation of that part or characteristic in the object-properties processing system is primed. Such priming allows one to encode the sought part or property more easily (for evidence of such priming, see Kosslyn, 1994, pp. 287–289; McAuliffe & Knowlton, 2000; McDermott & Roediger, 1994).

According to the theory, in order to create an image representation in the visual buffer on the basis of stored information, frontal lobe processes access the stored representation of the structure of an object in associative memory, and send a signal to the object-processing system in the inferior temporal lobes to activate a representation of visual properties of the object. This activation process is identical to the priming that occurs during top-down hypothesis testing in perception, only now the priming is so strong that the activation propagates backwards and a depictive representation is formed in the visual buffer.

When visualising detailed objects or scenes, representations in associative memory of spatial relations among parts or characteristics (or objects, in scenes) lead one to shift attention to the appropriate location on the imaged object, and to visualise each part or characteristic at the correct relative locations, so that a composite image is built up sequentially over time (for further details, see Kosslyn, 1994). Kosslyn, Cave, Provost, and Von Gierke (1988) provide evidence that images are generated by building them up part-by-part over time. Indeed, the segments of letters are placed in the image in the same order that they typically are drawn when block letters are printed.

This theory has generated many predictions, some of which have been tested (e.g., Kosslyn et al., 1994, 1995a, 1997). In the context of the present article, all that is important is that after such tests the theory remains viable. It is indeed plausible that early visual cortex—the neural underpinnings of the visual buffer—is used in both imagery and perception, as hypothesised in the theory. Let us now focus on these topographically organised representations.

THE ROLE OF TOPOGRAPHICALLY ORGANISED VISUAL AREAS IN IMAGERY

All of the functions incorporated in the theory rely on areas that operate during both perception and imagery. However, the representation in the visual buffer plays a special role in this theory. These representations give rise to the depictive aspects of the experience of "seeing with the mind's eye." (Note: it is unlikely that consciousness arises directly out of activity in the earliest visual area, but rather from projections from that area to other parts of the brain; see Crick & Koch, 1994; Kosslyn, 1999.) Thus, a strong prediction of the theory is that the topographically organised areas in early visual cortex should be used in both imagery and perception. If so, they should be activated during imagery, and disrupting activity in these areas should disrupt imagery.

Activation of topographically organised visual areas

The first PET and fMRI neuroimaging studies of visual mental imagery were reported by Kosslyn et al. (1993) and LeBihan, Turner, Zeffiro, Cunod, Jezzard, and Bonnerot (1993), respectively. Although the two studies used very different tasks, both reported finding activation of Area 17 during imagery. The Kosslyn et al. task involved visualising letters in a grid and deciding whether the letter would cover an X in the grid, and the LeBihan et al. task involved simply visualising sets of stripes. Shortly thereafter, Damasio et al. (1993), using PET, and Menon et al. (1993) and Sabbah et al. (1995), using fMRI, also reported that Area 17 is activated during visual mental imagery.

My colleagues and I conducted numerous additional experiments to investigate whether Area 17 per se is activated during visual mental imagery. In the first follow-up study, Kosslyn et al. (1993, Experiment 3) adapted the logic of Fox et al. (1986) to an imagery experiment. Fox et al. showed that different-sized stimuli activated different portions of Area 17, as predicted from previous studies of which parts of the visual field were disrupted following damage to specific parts of this structure. Rather than varying the visual angle subtended by a perceived object, we varied the "visual angle" subtended by imagined patterns. If imagery activates topographically organised visual cortex, then we would expect different portions of it to be more strongly activated when objects are visualised at different sizes. In this experiment the participants closed their eyes and listened to names of letters of the alphabet along with cue words. Each cue specified one of four judgments (e.g., "all straight" was a cue to decide whether the upper-case letter has only straight lines or any curved lines). The participants visualised the letters at the smallest possible "visible" size in one condition and at the largest possible "nonoverflowing" size in another condition. In both cases, the letters were to be centred in front of them and maintained at the appropriate size until a probe was presented.

We were determined to find an appropriate baseline condition for this task. We decided that, given the question we wanted to answer, an ideal control task was another version of the task itself: If the participants form images of tiny letters directly in front of them, much spatial variation would occur in a small, foveal region of a topographically organised area. In contrast, if the participants formed images of large letters, this foveal region would contain little spatial variation (only part of one segment of a larger letter, at most). Hence we expected greater metabolic activity (and corresponding blood flow) within the foveal region for small images than for large ones. In contrast, large images should extend into more peripheral regions. Hence we expected greater metabolic activity farther from the foveal representation when large images were formed. This reasoning led us to subtract the blood flow in the large image condition from blood flow in the small image condition, which revealed regions that were more activated by small images. Similarly, we subtracted the blood flow in the small image condition from blood flow in the large image condition, which revealed regions that were more activated by large images.

The results were encouraging. First, when we examined selective activation when large images were formed (i.e., the pattern of blood flow for small images was subtracted from the pattern of blood flow for large images), we found greater blood flow in a region of Area 17 (as identified by the Talairach & Tournoux, 1988, atlas) that was about 69 mm posterior to the anterior commissure (AC, the origin of the coordinate space defined by the Talairach & Tournoux atlas). In contrast, when we examined selective blood flow when small images were formed (i.e., the pattern of blood flow from large images was subtracted from the pattern of blood flow from small images), we found greater activity in a region of Area 17 that was 89 mm posterior to the AC. Both areas of activation were to the right of the midline, which is consistent with Sergent's (1989) finding that participants perform this sort of task faster when the cues are presented to the left visual field. The activation we found in the large/small experiment is about where one would expect if Area 17 were in fact activated (based on the previous findings reported by Fox et al., 1986).

At this juncture, a new phase of the imagery debate began. Some researchers were not convinced by the results of the experiments just described. For example, some argued (informally, so far), that the large images and the small images actually activated different areas. Moreover, the fact that the two conditions were compared to each other only indicated relative amounts of activation during imagery; it did not allow one to localise activation due to imagery per se. And there appeared to be a more serious problem: Roland and Gulyas (1994) reported that when they performed similar experiments, they found no evidence of activation of topographically organised areas, and Mazoyer and his colleagues (e.g., Charlot, Tzourio, Zilbovicius, Mazoyer, & Denis, 1992; Mellet, Tzourio, Denis, & Mazoyer, 1995) also failed to find such activation.

We were greatly puzzled over the fact that our results were not replicated, and thus looked very carefully at what had actually been done. Kosslyn and Ochsner (1994) suggested a number of reasons why some researchers had failed to obtain the results we did, and Kosslyn, Thompson, Kim, and Alpert (1995b) tested one account that we found particularly plausible. We had noticed that Roland and his colleagues and Mazoyer and his colleagues always compared blood flow in imagery conditions to blood flow in a resting baseline condition. Indeed, Roland and colleagues asked participants to close their eyes in darkness and to "visualize blackness," and then subtracted cerebral blood flow in this condition from that in the imagery condition. We reasoned that Area 17 might be activated in this baseline condition, and thus subtracting activation in it from that in the imagery condition would remove evidence of activation during imagery.

To test this idea, we asked participants to take part in five conditions. There were two baseline conditions. One was the same resting baseline used by Roland and colleagues. The other required them to listen to stimuli of the following form, "anchor… right-higher" and to press a response pedal as soon as they heard the comparison terms; the participants received this baseline before having any idea about the nature of the experimental conditions. After participating in the listening baseline, the participants memorised a set of line drawings of common objects, and then received three imagery conditions. The imagery conditions had trials of the following form: The participants first heard the name of one of the drawings and visualised it (with their eyes closed), and then heard a comparison term, at which point they decided whether it characterised the drawing (e.g., whether the right side of the drawing was higher than the left?). Before each of the three imagery conditions the participants studied a different-sized square, which subtended either 0.25, 4, or 16 degrees of visual angle. They were told to form images, and hold them, at the size of that square during all the trials in that condition. Counterbalancing ensured that the same auditory stimuli occurred equally often in the listening baseline and in each of the imagery conditions, and also ensured that images at each size were formed equally often in each of the serial orders.

The most important results were as follows: First, when Kosslyn et al. (1995b) compared the imagery trials to the listening baseline, we found additional blood flow during imagery in Area 17. But more than that, the small images activated the portion of this area that registers central stimuli that subtend small visual angles during visual perception, the medium images activated cortex that registers medium-sized objects, and the large images activated cortex that registers objects that subtend large visual angles. Second, when we compared the imagery trials to the resting baseline, we found just what Roland and colleagues found: No additional blood flow during imagery in Area 17 (but instead evidence for parieto-occipital activation, in an area very close to the one reported by Roland & Friberg, 1985). Third, as expected, when we simply compared the two baseline conditions, we found that Area 17 was more activated during the resting baseline than during the listening baseline. Thus, our original conjecture was correct.

More than one kind of imagery

However, after we reported the research just described, it became clear that our story was far from complete. We initially thought that the difference in baselines was sufficient to explain why some researchers did not find activation of Area 17 during imagery. But this was not the case. For example, Mellet et al. (1996) report that they failed to find activation in Area 17 during imagery even when a listening baseline was used. Their task required participants to visualise rectangular blocks pointed in specific directions, building up a multi-armed 3-D figure (and later, after scanning, to recognise the figure). This task differs from the ones we have used in two important ways.

First, it is spatial; it requires keeping track of a set of directions. Such tasks may not activate the areas that underlie the object-properties-processing system or the visual buffer. Instead, such images require only spatial information and thus may be formed in parietal structures. Indeed, Levine, Warach, and Farah (1985) reported that a patient with damage to the parietal lobes could visualise objects (including faces) but not directions, and vice versa for a patient with damage to the temporal lobes. Thus, it is possible that the spatial nature of the task explains why Mellet et al. (1996) failed to obtain activation of medial occipital cortex (as they themselves hypothesise).

Second, this task required only very coarse resolution; the directions were very distinct, and the participants were not told that they would be tested after the scan. It is possible that Area 17 is activated during imagery only when patterns must be visualised with high resolution to perform the task. When less resolution is necessary to perform the task, areas with larger receptive fields, and hence presumably poorer resolution, may be adequate. D'Esposito et al. (1997) present the limiting case of this situation, where no task at all was required and participants were not allowed enough time to form images; in this case, images may be so vague that only temporal lobe activation is present (as was found, without medial occipital activation).

Kosslyn and Thompson (2003) reviewed the neuroimaging literature on visual mental imagery (over 50 studies have now been reported), and used a novel type of meta-analysis to analyse the conditions in which Areas 17 or 18 (both of which are topographically organised) are activated during visual imagery. We found that whether or not a study documented activation in Areas 17 or 18 can be accounted for by three variables: If the task requires high resolution images of the details of shape, Areas 17 or 18 will tend to be activated; if the task requires using spatial images, these areas will tend *not* to be activated; and if more sensitive techniques (such as 4-T fMRI) are used, activation will tend to be documented. Thus, the finding that topographically organised cortex is activated during visual mental imagery is not likely to be an artifact or an accident. More likely is the possibility that there is more than one way to form images, and that different mechanisms may be called into play in different circumstances (for similar views, see Mazard, Tzourio-Mazoyer, Crivello, Mazoyer, & Mellet, 2004; Mellet et al., 1998).

Indeed, a parallel issue has arisen in a related area of mental imagery, namely mental rotation. This issue concerns the role of primary motor cortex (Area M1). Some researchers have found activation in this area (especially when participants are to mentally rotate body parts) whereas others have not (e.g., for reviews, see Kosslyn, Thompson, Wraga, & Albert, 2001b; Wraga, Thompson, Albert, & Kosslyn, 2003). The resolution of this issue is now emerging: There is more than one way to mentally rotate objects. For example, participants can be told in advance to imagine that they mentally rotate by physically twisting the stimulus with their hands or can be told to imagine that they mentally rotate by observing an electric motor turn the stimulus (Kosslyn et al., 2001b). Although the behavioural data in both cases indicate that the participants mentally rotated the objects, only when the former strategy was used (when participants imagined that they were physically moving the stimuli) was primary motor cortex activated.

Epiphenomenal activation?

But what evidence do we have that imagery in fact relies on (as opposed to merely causes incidentally) activation in topographically organised brain areas that we identify with the visual buffer? We have three sorts. First, Farah, Soso, and Dasheiff (1992) used the Kosslyn (1978) technique to study the visual angle subtended by images in a patient before and after she had one occipital lobe removed (for medical reasons). The visual angle subtended by mental images shrank by about a half following the operation. In contrast, the vertical extent was preserved after surgery. This was as expected because the vertical extent is represented redundantly in topographically organised areas in the two hemispheres, whereas horizontal extent in each half field is represented preferentially in the areas in the contralateral hemisphere. We (unpublished data) have extended these results with a series of patients, and provided converging evidence that damage to Area 17 per se disrupts the ability to form sharp images in the affected visual field.

Second, Kosslyn et al. (1999) used repetitive transcranial magnetic stimulation (rTMS) to disrupt Area 17 in normal volunteers prior to an imagery task; this technique involves pulsing a strong magnetic field on a specific place on the scalp, directed inwards to disrupt a relatively small set of neurons. These tasks involved visualising or seeing sets of stripes and making judgments among them (such as which set had more stripes, longer stripes, etc.). A prior PET study had demonstrated that the task activated Area 17. We found that immediately after rTMS was used to disrupt activity in this area, the participants had deficits in both a visual imagery and a corresponding visual perception task. Moreover, these deficits were of comparable magnitude in imagery and perception—which is consistent with the claim that early visual cortex is used in both tasks.

Third, Kosslyn, Thompson, Kim, Rauch, and Alpert (1996) reasoned that if activation of Area 17 gives rise to imagery representations used in information processing, then characteristics of the neural activity ought to be reflected in performance. Thus, we re-examined the data from the 16 participants tested by Kosslyn et al. (1993, Experiment 3) in the original size-variation experiment. We now pooled the data over size, and normalised each person's brain to the same mean blood flow value. We then examined the relative amount of blood flow in Area 17 for each person (compared to the global mean), and correlated this measure with the mean time the participants required to evaluate the images (which was recorded while the participants were being scanned). We found that the slowest participants were in fact those who had the least amount of blood flow in Area 17 ($r = -.65$). Moreover, this effect persisted when we factored out the contributions of two other regions of interest that were correlated with response times. Klein, Paradis, Poline, Kosslyn, and Le Bihan (2000) performed a similar analysis, and also found a negative correlation between response times and activation in Area 17.

CONCLUSIONS

The rapid expansion of behavioural studies of mental imagery (from roughly 1965–1993) and then neuroimaging studies (1993–present) has vastly increased our understanding of the phenomena. Not only have the data become far richer, but also more constrained. The hypotheses being considered are more subtle than those previously offered, and the methods of testing those hypotheses are becoming increasingly refined. However, there are still many unresolved issues, surrounding questions about when depictive images are used, exactly how they are created, and their roles in cognition more generally. The existence of such open issues should not be discouraging; rather, the fact that the issues often are couched within a common conceptual framework seems to me to be evidence of genuine progress.

At this juncture, it is clear that the bulk of the evidence supports the claim that visual mental imagery not only draws on many of the same mechanisms used in visual perception, but also that topographically organised early visual areas play a functional role in some types of imagery. Many additional questions are sure to arise—but as long as these questions are empirically tractable I have confidence that we will continue to learn more about the nature of visual imagery and how it arises in the brain.

PrEview proof published online 20 December 2004

REFERENCES

Andersen, R. A. (1987). Inferior parietal lobule function in spatial perception and visuomotor integration. In F. Plum (Vol. Ed.) & V. B. Mountcastle (Sec. Ed.), *Handbook of physiology, Section 1: The nervous system, Vol. 5: Higher functions of the brain*. Bethesda, MD: American Physiological Society.

Andersen, R. A. (1989). Visual and eye movement functions of the posterior parietal lobe. *Annual Review of Neuroscience, 12*, 377–403.

Andersen, R. A., Essick, G. K., & Siegel, R. M. (1985). Encoding of spatial location by posterior parietal neurons. *Science, 230*, 456–458.

Baddeley, A. D. (1986). *Working memory*. Oxford: Oxford University Press.

Behrmann, M., Kosslyn, S. M., & Jeannerod, M. (Eds.). (1996). *The neuropsychology of mental imagery*. New York: Pergamon.

Behrmann, M., Winocur, G., & Moscovitch, M. (1992). Dissociation between mental imagery and object recognition in a brain-damaged patient. *Nature, 359*, 636–637.

Berthoz, A. (1997). *Le sens du mouvement*. Paris: Odile Jacob.

Bisiach, E., & Luzzatti, C. (1978). Unilateral neglect of representational space. *Cortex, 14*, 129–133.

Bisiach, E., Luzzatti, C., & Perani, D. (1979). Unilateral neglect, representational schema, and consciousness. *Brain, 102*, 609–618.

Brefczynski, J. A., & DeYoe, E. A. (1999). A physiological correlate of the "spotlight" of visual attention. *Nature Neuroscience, 2*, 370–374.

Charlot, V., Tzourio, N., Zilbovicius, M., Mazoyer, B., & Denis, M. (1992). Different mental imagery abilities result in different regional cerebral blood flow activation patterns during cognitive tests. *Neuropsychologia, 30*, 565–580.

Chatterjee, A., & Southwood, M. H. (1995). Cortical blindness and visual imagery. *Neurology, 45*, 2189–2195.

Cooper, L. A., & Shepard, R. N. (1975). Mental transformations in the identification of left and right hands. *Journal of Experimental Psychology: Human Perception and Performance, 1*, 48–56.

Corbetta, M., Miezin, F. M., Dobmeyer, S., Shulman, G. L., & Petersen, S. E. (1991). Selective and divided attention during visual discriminations of shape, color, and speed: Functional anatomy by positron emission tomography. *Journal of Neuroscience, 11*, 2383–2402.

Crick, F., & Koch, C. (1994). Are we aware of neural activity in primary visual cortex? *Nature, 375*, 121–123.

Damasio, A. R., Damasio, H., Tranel, D., & Brandt, J. P. (1990). Neural regionalization of knowledge access: Preliminary evidence. *Cold Spring Harbor Symposia on Quantitative Biology, LV: The Brain* (pp. 1039–1047). Plainview, NY: Cold Spring Harbor Laboratory Press.

Damasio, H., Grabowski, T. J., Damasio, A., Tranel, D., Boles-Ponto, L., Watkins, G. L., & Hichwa, R. D. (1993). Visual recall with eyes closed and covered activates early visual cortices. *Society for Neuroscience Abstracts, 19*, 1603.

Desimone, R., Albright, T. D., Gross, C. G., & Bruce, C. J. (1984a). Stimulus selective properties of inferior temporal neurons in the macaque. *Journal of Neuroscience, 4*, 2051–2062.

Desimone, R., Schein, S. J., & Albright, T. D. (1984b). Form, color, and motion analysis in prestriate cortex of the macaque monkey. In C. Chagas (Ed.), *Study group on pattern recognition mechanisms* (pp. 165–178). Vatican City: Pontifical Academy of Science.

D'Esposito, M., Detre, J. A., Aguirre, G. K., Stallcup, M., Alsop, D. C., Tippet, L. J., & Farah, M. J. (1997). A functional MRI study of mental image generation. *Neuropsychologia, 35*, 725–730.

Douglas, K. L., & Rockland, K. S. (1992). Extensive visual feedback connections from ventral inferotemporal cortex. *Society of Neuroscience Abstracts, 18*, 390.

Farah, M. J. (1984). The neurological basis of mental imagery: A componential analysis. *Cognition, 18*, 245–272.

Farah, M. J. (1988). Is visual imagery really visual? Overlooked evidence from neuropsychology. *Psychological Review, 95*, 307–317.

Farah, M. J., Peronnet, F., Gonon, M. A., & Girard, M. H. (1988). Electrophysiological evidence for a shared representational medium for visual images and visual percepts. *Journal of Experimental Psychology: General, 117*, 248–257.

Farah, M. J., Soso, M. J., & Dasheiff, R. M. (1992). Visual angle of the mind's eye before and after unilateral occipital lobectomy. *Journal of Experimental Psychology: Human Perception and Performance, 18*, 241–246.

Felleman, D. J., & Van Essen, D. C. (1991). Distributed hierarchical processing in primate cerebral cortex. *Cerebral Cortex, 1*, 1–47.

Finke, R. A. (1989). *Principles of mental imagery*. Cambridge, MA: MIT Press.

Fletcher, P. C., Frith, C. D., Baker, S. C., Shallice, T., Frackowiak, R. S. J., & Dolan, R. J. (1995). The mind's eye—precuneus activation in memory-related imagery. *NeuroImage, 2,* 195–200.

Fox, P. T., Mintun, M. A., Raichle, M. E., Miezen, F. M., Allman, J. M., & Van Essen, D. C. (1986). Mapping human visual cortex with positron emission tomography. *Nature, 323,* 806–809.

Fujita, I., Tanaka, K., Ito, M., & Cheng, K. (1992). Columns for visual features of objects in monkey inferotemporal cortex. *Nature, 360,* 343–346.

Ganis, G., Thompson, W. L., & Kosslyn, S. M. (in press). Brain areas underlying visual imagery and visual perception: An fMRI study. *Cognitive Brain Research.*

Goldenberg, G., Podreka, I., Steiner, M., & Willmes, K. (1987). Patterns of regional cerebral blood flow related to memorizing of high and low imagery words: An emission computer tomography study. *Neuropsychologia, 25,* 473–485.

Goldenberg, G., Podreka, I., Steiner, M., Willmes, K., Suess, E., & Deecke, L. (1989). Regional cerebral blood flow patterns in visual imagery. *Neuropsychologia, 27,* 641–664.

Goldman-Rakic, P. S. (1987). Circuitry of primate prefrontal cortex and regulation of behavior by representational knowledge. In F. Plum (Vol. Ed.) & V. B. Mountcastle (Sec. Ed.), *Handbook of physiology, Section 1: The nervous system, Vol. 5: Higher functions of the brain.* Bethesda, MD: American Physiological Society.

Goldman-Rakic, P. S. (1988). Topography of cognition: Parallel distributed networks in primate association cortex. *Annual Review of Neuroscience, 11,* 137–156.

Gross, C. G., Desimone, R., Albright, T. D., & Schwartz, E. L. (1984). Inferior temporal cortex as a visual integration area. In F. Reinoso-Suarez & C. Ajmone-Marsan (Ed.), *Cortical integration.* New York: Raven Press.

Haxby, J. V., Grady, C. L., Horwitz, B., Ungerleider, L. G., Mishkin, M., Carson, R. E., Herscovitch, P., Schapiro, M. B., & Rapoport, S. I. (1991). Dissociation of object and spatial visual processing pathways in human extrastriate cortex. *Proceedings of the National Academy of Sciences of the United States of America, 88,* 1621–1625.

Hebb, D. O. (1968). Concerning imagery. *Psychological Review, 75,* 466–477.

Heeger, D. J. (1999). Linking visual perception with human brain activity. *Current Opinion in Neurobiology, 9,* 474–479.

Hyvarinen, J. (1982). Posterior parietal lobe of the primate brain. *Physiological Review, 62,* 1060–1129.

James, W. (1890). *Principles of psychology.* New York: Holt.

Jankowiak, J., Kinsbourne, M., Shalev, R. S., & Bachman, D. L. (1992). Preserved visual imagery and categorization in a case of associative visual agnosia. *Journal of Cognitive Neuroscience, 4,* 119–131.

Jonides, J., Smith, E. E., Koeppe, R. A., Awh, E., Minoshima, S., & Mintun, M. A. (1993). Spatial working memory in humans as revealed by PET. *Nature, 363,* 623–625.

Klein, I., Paradis, A.-L., Poline, J.-B., Kosslyn, S. M., & Le Bihan, D. (2000). Transient activity in human calcarine cortex during visual imagery. *Journal of Cognitive Neuroscience, 12,* 15S–23S.

Kosslyn, S. M. (1973). Scanning visual images: Some structural implications. *Perception and Psychophysics, 14,* 90–94.

Kosslyn, S. M. (1975). Information representation in visual images. *Cognitive Psychology, 7,* 341–370.

Kosslyn, S. M. (1978). Measuring the visual angle of the mind's eye. *Cognitive Psychology, 10,* 356–389.

Kosslyn, S. M. (1980). *Image and mind.* Cambridge, MA: Harvard University Press.

Kosslyn, S. M. (1983). *Ghosts in the mind's machine.* New York: W. W. Norton.

Kosslyn, S. M. (1994). *Image and brain: The resolution of the imagery debate.* Cambridge, MA: MIT Press.

Kosslyn, S. M. (1999). Visual consciousness. In P. Grossenbacher (Ed.), *Finding consciousness in the brain: A neurocognitive approach.* New York: John Benjamins.

Kosslyn, S. M., Alpert, N. M., Thompson, W. L., Chabris, C. F., Rauch, S. L., & Anderson, A. K. (1994). Identifying objects seen from different viewpoints: A PET investigation. *Brain, 117,* 1055–1071.

Kosslyn, S. M., Alpert, N. M., Thompson, W. L., Maljkovic, V., Weise, S. B., Chabris, C. F., Hamilton, S. E., & Buonano, F. S. (1993). Visual mental imagery activates topographically organized visual cortex: PET investigations. *Journal of Cognitive Neuroscience, 5,* 263–287.

Kosslyn, S. M., Ball, T. M., & Reiser, B. J. (1978). Visual images preserve metric spatial information: Evidence from studies of image scanning. *Journal of Experimental Psychology: Human Perception and Performance, 4,* 47–60.

Kosslyn, S. M., Cave, C. B., Provost, D., & Von Gierke, S. (1988). Sequential processes in image generation. *Cognitive Psychology, 20,* 319–343.

Kosslyn, S. M., DiGirolamo, G., Thompson, W. L., & Alpert, N. M. (1998). Mental rotation of objects versus hands: Neural mechanisms revealed by positron emission tomography. *Psychophysiology, 35,* 1–11.

Kosslyn, S. M., Ganis, G., & Thompson, W. L. (2001a). Neural foundations of imagery. *Nature Reviews Neuroscience, 2,* 635–642.

Kosslyn, S. M., & Jolicoeur, P. (1981). A theory-based approach to the study of individual differences in mental imagery. In R. E. Snow, P. A. Federico, & W. E. Montague (Eds.), *Aptitude learning and instruction: Cognitive process analysis of aptitude.* Hillsdale, NJ: Lawrence Erlbaum Associates Inc.

Kosslyn, S. M., & Koenig, O. (1995). *Wet mind: The new cognitive neuroscience* (First published 1992). New York: Free Press.

Kosslyn, S. M., & Ochsner, K. (1994). In search of occipital activation during visual mental imagery. *Trends in Neurosciences, 17,* 290–292.

Kosslyn, S. M., Pascual-Leone, A., Felician, O., Camposano, S., Keenan, J. P., Thompson, W. L., Ganis, G., Sukel, K. E., & Alpert, N. M. (1999). The role of Area 17 in visual imagery: Convergent evidence from PET and rTMS. *Science, 284,* 167–170.

Kosslyn, S. M., & Thompson, W. L. (2003). When is early visual cortex activated during visual mental imagery? *Psychological Bulletin, 129,* 723–746.

Kosslyn, S. M., Thompson, W. T., & Alpert, N. M. (1995a). Identifying objects at different levels of hierarchy: A positron emission tomography study. *Human Brain Mapping, 3,* 107–132.

Kosslyn, S. M., Thompson, W. L., & Alpert, N. M. (1997). Neural systems shared by visual imagery and visual perception: A positron emission tomography study. *NeuroImage, 6,* 320–334.

Kosslyn, S. M., Thompson, W. L., & Ganis, G. (in press). *The case for mental imagery.* New York: Oxford University Press.

Kosslyn, S. M., Thompson, W. L., Kim, I. J., & Alpert, N. M. (1995b). Topographical representations of mental images in primary visual cortex. *Nature, 378,* 496–498.

Kosslyn, S. M., Thompson, W. L., Kim, I. J., Rauch, S. L., & Alpert, N. M. (1996). Individual differences in cerebral blood flow in Area 17 predict the time to evaluate visualized letters. *Journal of Cognitive Neuroscience, 8,* 78–82.

Kosslyn, S. M., Thompson, W. L., Wraga, M. J., & Alpert, N. M. (2001b). Imagining rotation by endogenous and exogenous forces: Distinct neural mechanisms for different strategies. *NeuroReport, 12,* 2519–2525.

LaBerge, D., & Buchsbaum, M. S. (1990). Positron emission tomography measurements of pulvinar activity during an attention task. *Journal of Neuroscience, 10,* 613–619.

LeBihan, D., Turner, R., Zeffiro, T. A., Cunod, C. A., Jezzard, P., & Bonnerot, V. (1993). Activation of human primary visual cortex during visual recall: A magnetic resonance imaging study. *Proceedings of the National Academy of Science, 90,* 11802–11805.

Levine, D. N., Warach, J., & Farah, M. J. (1985). Two visual systems in mental imagery: Dissociation of "what" and "where" in imagery disorders due to bilateral posterior cerebral lesions. *Neurology, 35,* 1010–1018.

Luria, A. R. (1980). *Higher cortical functions in man.* New York: Basic Books.

Marr, D. (1982). *Vision.* New York: W. H. Freeman.

Maunsell, J. H. R., & Newsome, W. T. (1987). Visual processing in monkey extrastriate cortex. *Annual Review of Neuroscience, 10,* 363–401.

Mazard, A., Tzourio-Mazoyer, N., Crivello, F., Mazoyer, B., & Mellet, E. (2004). A PET meta-analysis of object and spatial mental imagery. *European Journal of Cognitive Psychology, 16,* 673–695.

McAuliffe, S. P., & Knowlton, B. J. (2000). Long-term retinotopic priming in object identification. *Perception and Psychophysics, 62,* 953–959.

McDermott, K. B., & Roediger, H. L. (1994). Effects of imagery on perceptual implicit memory tests. *Journal of Experimental Psychology: Learning, Memory, and Cognition, 20,* 1379–1390.

Mellet, E., Petit, L., Mazoyer, B., Denis, M., & Tzourio, N. (1998). Reopening the mental imagery debate: Lessons from functional neuroanatomy. *NeuroImage, 8,* 129–139.

Mellet, E., Tzourio, N., Crivello, F., Joliot, M., Denis, M., & Mazoyer, B. (1996). Functional anatomy of spatial imagery generated from verbal instructions. *Journal of Neuroscience, 16,* 6504–6512.

Mellet, E., Tzourio, N., Denis, M., & Mazoyer, B. (1995). A positron emission tomography study of visual and mental spatial exploration. *Journal of Cognitive Neuroscience, 7,* 433–445.

Menon, R., Ogawa, S., Tank, D. W., Ellerman, J. M., Merkele, H., & Ugurbil, K. (1993). Visual mental imagery by functional brain MRI. In D. LeBihan, R. Turner, M. Mosley, & J. Hyde (Eds.), *Functional MRI of the brain: A workshop.* Arlington, VA: Society for Magnetic Resonance in Medicine.

Mesulam, M.-M. (1981). A cortical network for directed attention and unilateral neglect. *Annals of Neurology, 10,* 309–325.

Mesulam, M.-M. (1990). Large-scale neurocognitive networks and distributed processing for attention, language, and memory. *Annals of Neurology, 28,* 597–613.

Milner, A. D., & Goodale, M. A. (1995). *The visual brain in action.* London: Oxford University Press.

Moran, J., & Desimone, R. (1985). Selective attention gates visual processing in the extrastriate cortex. *Science, 229,* 782–784.

Mountcastle, V. B., Lynch, J. C., Georgopoulos, A., Sakata, H., & Acuna, C. (1975). Posterior parietal association cortex of the monkey: Command functions for operations within extrapersonal space. *Journal of Neurophysiology, 38,* 871–908.

Neisser, U. (1967). *Cognitive psychology.* New York: Appleton-Century-Crofts.

Nyberg, L., Cabeza, R., & Tulving, E. (1996). PET studies of encoding and retrieval: The HERA model. *Psychonomic Bulletin & Review, 3,* 134–148.

Paivio, A. (1971). *Imagery and verbal processes.* New York: Holt, Rinehart & Winston.

Petersen, S. E., Fox, P. T., Posner, M. I., Mintun, M., & Raichle, M. E. (1988). Positron emission tomographic studies of the cortical anatomy of single-word processing. *Nature, 331,* 585–589.

Petrides, M., Alivisatos, B., Evans, A. C., & Meyer, E. (1993). Dissociation of human mid-dorsolateral from posterior dorsolateral frontal cortex in memory processing. *Proceedings of the National Academy of Sciences USA, 90,* 873–877.

Plaut, D. C., & Shallice, T. (1993). Deep dyslexia: A case study of connectionist neuropsychology. *Cognitive Neuropsychology, 10,* 377–500.

Podgorny, P., & Shepard, R. N. (1978). Functional representations common to visual perception and imagination. *Journal of Experimental Psychology: Human Perception and Performance, 4,* 21–35.

Pohl, W. (1973). Dissociation of spatial discrimination deficits following frontal and parietal lesions in monkeys. *Journal of Comparative and Physiological Psychology, 82,* 227–239.

Posner, M. I., & Petersen, S. E. (1990). The attention system of the human brain. In W. M. Cowan, E. M. Shooter, C. F. Stevens, & R. F. Thompson (Ed.), *Annual review of neuroscience* (pp. 25–42). Palo Alto, CA: Annual Reviews.

Pylyshyn, Z. W. (1973). What the mind's eye tells the mind's brain: A critique of mental imagery. *Psychological Bulletin, 80,* 1–24.

Pylyshyn, Z. W. (1981). The imagery debate: Analogue media versus tacit knowledge. *Psychological Review, 87,* 16–45.

Pylyshyn, Z. W. (2002). Mental imagery: In search of a theory. *Behavioral and Brain Sciences, 25,* 157–238.

Pylyshyn, Z. (2003). Return of the mental image: Are there pictures in the brain? *Trends in Cognitive Sciences, 7,* 113–118.

Rockland, K. S., Saleem, K. S., & Tanaka, K. (1992). Widespread feedback connections from areas V4 and TEO. *Society for Neuroscience Abstracts, 18,* 390.

Roland, P. E., & Friberg, L. (1985). Localization of cortical areas activated by thinking. *Journal of Neurophysiology, 53,* 1219–1243.

Roland, P. E., & Gulyas, B. (1994). Visual imagery and visual representation. *Trends in Neurosciences, 17,* 281–296 (with commentaries).

Sabbah, P., Simond, G., Levrier, O., Habib, M., Trabaud, V., Murayama, N., Mazoyer, B. M., Briant, J. F., Raybaud, C., & Salamon, G. (1995). Functional magnetic resonance imaging at 1.5T during sensorimotor and cognitive task. *European Neurology, 35,* 131–136.

Schacter, D. L. (1996). *Searching for memory: The brain, the mind, the past.* New York: Basic Books.

Schwartz, E. L. (1980). A quantitative model of the functional architecture of human striate cortex with application to visual illusion and cortical texture analysis. *Biological Cybernetics, 37,* 63–76.

Sengpiel, F., & Huebener, M. (1999). Spotlight on the primary visual cortex. *Current Biology, 9,* R318–R321.

Sereno, M. I., Dale, A. M., Reppas, J. B., & Kwong, K. K. (1995). Borders of multiple visual areas in humans revealed by functional magnetic resonance imaging. *Science, 268,* 889–893.

Sergent, J. (1989). Image generation and processing of generated images in the cerebral hemispheres. *Journal of Experimental Psychology: Human Perception and Performance, 15,* 170–178.

Sergent, J., Ohta, S., & MacDonald, B. (1992). Functional neuroanatomy of face and object processing: A positron emission tomography study. *Brain, 115,* 15–36.

Shepard, R. N., & Cooper, L. R. (1982). *Mental images and their transformations.* Cambridge, MA: MIT Press.

Squire, L. R. (1987). *Memory and brain.* New York: Oxford University Press.

Talairach, J., & Tournoux, P. (1988). *Co-planar stereotaxic atlas of the human brain* (M. Rayport, Trans.). New York: Thieme.

Tanaka, K., Saito, H., Fukada, Y., & Moriya, M. (1991). Coding visual images of objects in the inferotemporal cortex of the macaque monkey. *Journal of Neurophysiology, 66,* 170–189.

Thompson, W. L., & Kosslyn, S. M. (2000). Neural systems activated during visual mental imagery: A review and meta-analyses. In J. Mazziotta & A. Toga (Eds.), *Brain mapping II: The systems* (pp. 535–560). New York: Academic Press.

Tootell, R. B. H., Silverman, M. S., Switkes, E., & De Valois, R. L. (1982). Deoxyglucose analysis of retinotopic organization in primate striate cortex. *Science, 218,* 902–904.

Treisman, A. M., & Gelade, G. (1980). A feature integration theory of attention. *Cognitive Psychology, 12,* 97–136.

Tye, M. (1991). *The imagery debate.* Cambridge, MA: MIT Press.

Ungerleider, L. G., & Mishkin, M. (1982). Two cortical visual systems. In D. J. Ingle, M. A. Goodale, & R. J. W. Mansfield (Ed.), *Analysis of visual behavior.* Cambridge, MA: MIT Press.

Van Essen, D. C. (1985). Functional organization of primate visual cortex. In A. Peters & E. G. Jones (Eds.), *Cerebral Cortex* (Vol. 3, pp. 259–329). New York: Plenum Press.

Van Essen, D. C., & Maunsell, J. H. (1983). Hierarchical organization and functional streams in the visual cortex. *Trends in Neurosciences, 6,* 370–375.

Van Essen, D. C., Newsome, W. T., & Maunsell, H. R. (1984). The visual field representation in striate cortex of the macaque monkey: Asymmetries, anisotropies, and individual variability. *Vision Research, 24,* 429–448.

Wexler, M., Kosslyn, S. M., & Berthoz, A. (1998). Motor processes in mental rotation. *Cognition, 68,* 77–94.

Wilson, F. A. W., O'Scalaidhe, S. P., & Goldman-Rakic, P. S. (1993). Dissociation of object and spatial processing domains in primate prefrontal cortex. *Science, 260,* 1955–1958.

Wraga, M. J., Thompson, W. L., Alpert, N. M., & Kosslyn, S. M. (2003). Implicit transfer of motor strategies in mental rotation. *Brain and Cognition, 52,* 135–143.

COGNITIVE NEUROPSYCHOLOGY, 2005, 22 (3/4), 348–363

THE ROLE OF THE PRIMARY MOTOR CORTEX IN MENTAL ROTATION: A TMS STUDY

Barbara Tomasino
Scuola Internazionale Superiore di Studi Avanzati (SISSA), Trieste, Italy
Paola Borroni
Istituto di Fisiologia Umana II, Milano, Italy
Alessio Isaja
Scuola Internazionale Superiore di Studi Avanzati (SISSA), Trieste, Italy
Raffaella Ida Rumiati
Scuola Internazionale Superiore di Studi Avanzanti (SISSA), Trieste, Italy, and Institute of Medicine, Research Center, Juelich, Germany

Mental rotation (MR) is sustained by a network of brain regions, including parietal, pre-motor and primary motor (M1) cortices. However it is still not clear whether M1 is recruited only when individuals mentally rotate hands or whether it is also enhanced by MR of non-body parts. Here we report two experiments in which the involvement of M1 in MR of hands and letters was tested using TMS. In Experiments 1a and 1b participants were asked to judge whether two line drawings, depicting either hands or letters, were the same or mirror images of each other ($N = 112$). Subjects were presented with pairs of stimuli with the same orientation (*baseline condition*) in half of the trials, while in the other half the stimulus in the right visual field was rotated (*rotation condition*). They performed the same–different task in three experimental situations: TMS of the primary motor hand area delivered at 400 ms after stimulus onset, sham TMS, and no-TMS. We stimulated the left M1 in Experiment 1a, and the right in Experiment 1b. Results showed that in Experiment 1a participants were slower after TMS when they performed MR of hands but not of letters. In Experiment 1b we failed to find an effect of TMS on MR of hands and letters. While in Experiment 1 the stimulus to be rotated was always presented in the right visual field, in Experiment 2 it was presented either in the left or in the right visual field. Results showed that only when TMS was delivered to the left M1, participants' ability to mentally rotate right and left hands slowed down. Taken together, these findings suggest that the left but not the right M1 plays a critical role in MR of hands.

INTRODUCTION

Mental rotation (MR) is the ability to manipulate mental representations, and it can take place either in an egocentric or an object-centred reference frame. MR is performed in the absence of real movements by imagining visual stimuli rotating into an orientation other than that in which they appear. The importance of this cognitive ability is in allowing individuals to predict the consequences of their own actions by continuously following and updating them. Several neuroimaging

Correspondence should be addressed to Raffaella Rumiati, Cognitive Neuroscience Sector, Scuola Internazionale Superiore di Studi Avanzati, SISSA, via Beirut 2–4, 34014 Trieste, Italy (Email: Rumiati@sissa.it).

studies, in which subjects had to decide whether two rotated pictures depict the same image or the mirror-image of each other has been adopted, show that MR is supported by a brain network involving *visual processing* areas, the *parietal lobe* (Cohen et al., 1996; Harris, Egan, Sonkkila, Tochon-Danguy, Paxinos, & Watson, 2000; Kosslyn, DiGirolamo, Thompson, & Alpert, 1998; Podzebenko, Egan, & Watson, 2002; Zacks, Ollinger, Sheridan, & Tversky, 2002; Zacks, Rypma, Gabrieli, Tversky, & Glover, 1999), and the *premotor cortex* (Cohen et al., 1996; Kosslyn et al., 1998; Kosslyn, Thompson, Wraga, & Alpert, 2001; Parsons & Fox, 1998). Whereas there is a general agreement that the premotor and parietal cortices are likely to be involved in MR, the role of M1 is still under debate.

IS M1 INVOLVED IN MR?

Traditionally, M1 has been thought to control voluntary movements. However, the idea that M1 can also be involved in higher motor functions has recently received support from studies using single-cell recording in the monkey (Alexander, & Crutcher, 1990; Ashe et al., 1993; Carpenter, Georgopoulos, & Pellizzer, 1999; Georgopoulos, Lurito, Petrides, Schwartz, & Massey, 1989; Pellizzer, Sargent, & Georgopoulos, 1995; Smyrnis, Taira, Ashe, & Georgopoulos, 1992; Wise, Moody, Blomstrom, & Mitz, 1998), brain imaging (Grafton, Hazeltine, & Ivry, 1995; Honda, Wise, Weeks, Deiber, & Hallett, 1998; Karni et al., 1998; Lotze et al., 1999; Tagaris, Richter, Kim, Pellizzer, & Anderson, 1998) and transcranial magnetic stimulation technique (TMS) in humans (Ganis, Keenan, Kosslyn, & Pascual-Leone, 2000). These studies suggest that M1 is engaged in motor imagery and spatial transformations, in addition to stimulus–response compatibility, plasticity, motor sequence learning and memory, and learning sensorimotor associations.

That MR, too, may in some instances require the involvement of action-related brain areas, including the M1 (e.g., Carpenter, Just, Keller, Eddy, & Thulborn, 1999; Ganis et al., 2000; Kosslyn et al., 1998), should surprise no-one. The idea that the manipulation of mental images is associated with a motor process was already intrinsic to the definition of MR given by Shepard and Cooper (1982). They pointed out that stimuli under MR appear to move in imagery, as they would if they were *physically rotated* by the subject. This simulated manipulation can be triggered implicitly by some classes of stimuli (e.g., hands) or explicitly by a strategy. Kosslyn et al. (2001), for instance, showed that the left M1 was selectively activated *only* when subjects were explicitly asked to imagine grasping and turning the 3-D object with their own hand (i.e., the motor strategy), but not when they just imagined the object rotating in the visual space (i.e., the visual strategy). Interestingly, in a different study in which subjects were not instructed to use any given strategy (Kosslyn et al., 1998), the left M1 was found to be activated during MR of hands and not of stimuli different from body parts, such as 3-D cubes.

So far the only neuropsychological evidence suggesting the involvement of the left M1 in MR of hands has been provided by Tomasino and Rumiati (2004). These authors found that patients with a tumour in the left M1 were impaired in MR of hands and succeeded in MR of letters; in contrast, patients with a tumour invading the right M1 succeeded in both MR tasks. Further evidence supporting a critical role of the left M1 in MR is provided by Ganis et al. (2000) who, using TMS, showed that stimulating the human hand area in the left M1 at 650 ms after stimulus onset significantly slowed down the subjects' latencies when they mentally rotated hands but not feet. Based on this evidence, these authors argued that the M1 must contain motor representations.

Yet, not everybody accepts that M1 has something to do with MR. In some imaging studies the activation found in M1 during MR was explained as just being due to the subjects responding by pressing the response button (Cohen et al., 1996; Richter et al., 2000). Other studies have failed to report any M1 activation when subjects performed tasks tapping MR (Barnes et al., 2000; Harris et al., 2000; Jordan, Heinze, Lutz, Kanowski, & Jancke, 2001; Parsons et al., 1995, 1998).

The reason why there are inconsistent findings concerning the involvement of M1 may be found in the variety of stimuli being used in the studies reported above. Indeed, the nature of the stimulus seems to affect the implicit selection of a particular type of mental transformation (i.e., motor or visual). In fact, an activation of M1 was observed, when subjects were explicitly requested to use a motor strategy in a mental rotation task (Kosslyn et al., 1998; Wraga, Thompson, Alpert, & Kosslyn, 2003). By contrast, the failure to find any enhancement of M1 in the studies of Barnes et al. (2000), Harris et al. (2000), and Jordan et al. (2001) could be due to the use of abstract pictures like alphanumeric character or an abstract 3-D shape as stimuli. Such stimuli can be transformed in a visual object-centred space without requiring motor processes (Zacks et al., 2002). However, there are other studies in which the M1 cortex was found to be enhanced during MR of external abstract objects, though subjects were not explicitly instructed to use a particular strategy (Carpenter et al., 1999; Cohen et al., 1996; Lamm, Windischberger, Leodolter, Moser, & Bauer, 2001; Richter et al., 2000; Tagaris, Kim, Strupp, Andersen, Ugurbil, & Georgopoulos, 1996; Vingerhoets, Santens, Van Laere, Lahorte, Dierckx, & De Reuck, 2001). Here the idea that subjects might have spontaneously adopted a motor strategy can account for these results. One of the above studies investigated MR of body parts by comparing pictures of hands and feet (Ganis et al., 2000). Since MR of stimuli other than body parts has not been tested, nobody can yet tell whether M1 is involved in MR of hands only or of external objects as well.

In the present study we carried out two experiments in which we applied the TMS to the left and the right hand area of healthy individuals who mentally rotated hands and external objects as stimuli, free to use any strategy. Based on the findings of Kosslyn et al. (1998) and Ganis et al. (2000), who both found that the left M1 is involved in MR of hands, we predicted that TMS on this region should significantly slow down the RTs of subjects when they mentally rotate hands but not letters. We also predicted an asymmetry between the left and the right M1 in sustaining MR of hands, with a direct involvement of the left M1 in MR of both the right and left hand stimuli. In Experiment 1a we stimulated the left M1 in one group of subjects, and in Experiment 1b the right M1 in a different group. In Experiment 2 both the left and the right M1 of the same individuals were stimulated in different blocks.

EXPERIMENT 1A: SINGLE PULSE TMS ON THE LEFT M1

If the left M1 were involved in MR of hands as stimuli, then single pulse TMS applied to the left M1 should slow down RTs during MR of hands but not of letters (Experiment 1a). Moreover we predicted that TMS over the left M1 should slow down RTs during MR of both the left and the right hand (as stimuli). This prediction is in alignment with the neuropsychological observations of patients suffering from ideomotor or ideational apraxia. The reduction in higher-level motor ability experienced by these patients affects both limbs and is typically caused by lesions of the left hemisphere (De Renzi, Faglioni, & Sorgato, 1982; De Renzi, Motti, & Nichelli, 1980). This suggests that the left hempishere is specialised in controlling higher motor activities. Similarly, the hand area of the left M1 seems to play an essential role in the imagination of movements of both hands, as suggested by the work of Fadiga, Buccino, Craighero, Fogassi, Gallese, and Pavesi (1999).

Method

Subjects

Ten right-handed (mean age = 26 years ± 6.4, 100/D, according to the Edinburgh Inventory, Oldfield, 1971) volunteers took part in the experiment. None of the subjects had any contraindications to TMS (e.g., metallic implants in their head or an implanted pacemaker; see Wassermann, 1998), or a history of neurological (e.g., seizures and a family history of epilepsy, chronic illnesses), psychiatric, or other medical disorders. Female participants were not pregnant. All participants gave informed consent prior to the experiment after being informed about the TMS procedure and risks but not about the specific hypotheses of the study. The study has been approved by the SISSA Ethical Commettee.

Stimuli

Subjects were presented with pairs of pictures on a computer screen and were required to judge whether stimuli of each pair were the same or different (i.e., mirror version of each other). Two experimental blocks, one of line drawings of hands ($N = 28$) and the other of letters ($N = 28$) were presented in a counterbalanced order across subjects. In the case of hands, the stimulus on the left side was always a left hand to avoid visuomotor interference (Ganis et al., 2000), whereas the stimulus on the right could be either a left (50%) or a right hand (50%). Hands varied for view (i.e., palms and backs of an open hand shape), handedness (i.e., left and right hands), and orientation. All ($N = 56$) stimuli could have either the same (*baseline condition*) or different orientations (*rotation condition*). In the rotation condition, the stimulus on the left was always upright, whereas the stimulus on the right could appear at four different orientations (60°, 150°, 210°, and 330°). In both conditions the pair stimuli were either the same (50%) or the mirror version of each other (50%), following Ganis et al.'s study (2000). Each participant performed two sessions of each task (i.e., MR of hand shapes $N = 28 \times 2$, and MR of letters $N = 28 \times 2$) in each of the three experimental situations (TMS, no-TMS and sham stimulation) for a total of 336 trials.

Design and procedure

Stimuli were presented on a 14" LCD monitor with a refresh rate of 60 Hz. Stimuli, responses, and TMS triggering were generated and collected by E-prime software. Subjects sat throughout the experiment in a comfortable, reclining armchair in front of a computer screen at a distance of 90 cm. They were instructed to keep their hands still and to be as relaxed as possible. After subjects were presented with some practice trials, they performed the experiment proper. Unlike other studies (Cohen et al., 1996; Richter et al., 2000), in which subjects responded by pressing a key, in the present study participants were required to respond verbally. Thus RTs of the subjects' voice onset (*Yes*! = same/ *No*! = mirror), and their accuracy were recorded. Of the three experimental situations, subjects performed the TMS and no-TMS in a counterbalanced order, and the sham stimulation in a different session on a different day (see Figure 1).

In each trial, the sequence of events was the following: A fixation point appeared on the screen for 200 ms, followed by the stimulus that remained visible until the response was given (see Figure 2). Single pulses of TMS were delivered at 400 ms after stimulus onset by means of a MagStim 200 Super Rapid Magnetic Stimulator (The Magstim Company, Wales, UK) on the hand area of the left motor cortex. For each trial the computer generated a TTL output pulse that triggered a stimulator (Grass Telefactor, S 88K, W. Warwick, RI, USA), and was then transferred to the MagStim with a 400 ms delay. The 400 ms delay was empirically driven. First, Iwaki, Ueno, Imada, and Tonoike (1999) showed that activity in M1 or SMA was detected (around 330–470 ms) after the activation in the occipital (at about 120–180 ms), inferior temporal (at 170–230 ms) and parietal cortices (at 200–270 ms). In addition, Ganis et al. (2000) found that TMS interfered with MR of hands at 650 ms after stimulus onset. Second, when in a pilot study we stimulated eight subjects at 250 ms after stimulus onset during a MR task, we failed to find any significant difference between the TMS and the no-TMS conditions, $F(1, 7) = 0.65, p > .05$, *ns*). Neither the two- nor three-way interactions were found significant (all $p > .05$, *ns*). RTs of MR of hands during the TMS (1036 ms) and during the no-TMS (1053 ms) conditions were similar to those of MR of letters in the same conditions (980 ms and 1005 ms, respectively).

The subject's head was restrained by a fitted support and a stereotactic apparatus held a figure-of-eight coil over the cortical focus for TMS

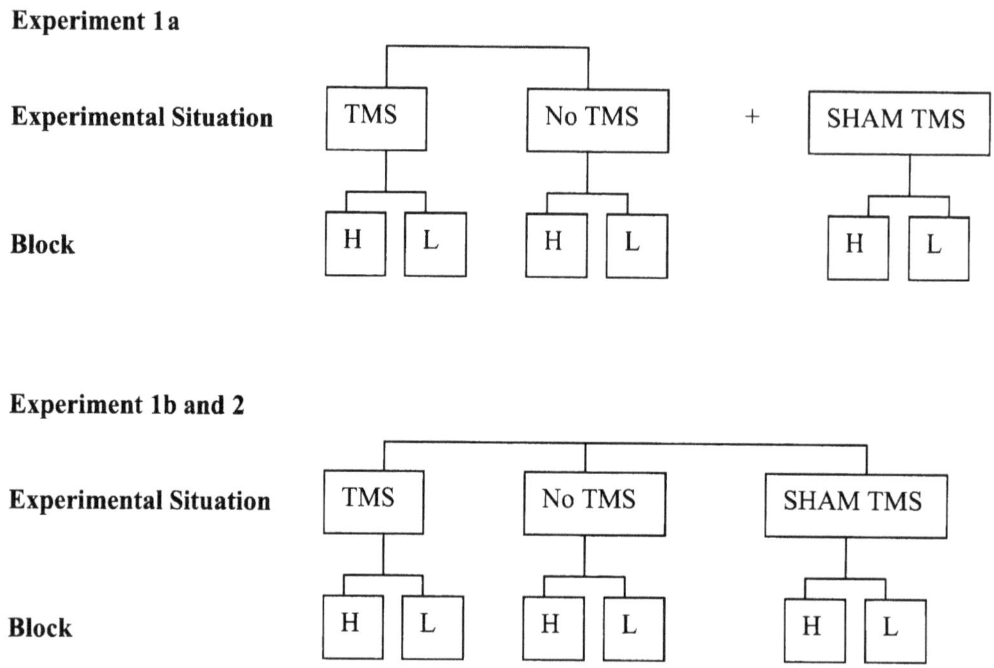

Figure 1. *Experimental design in Experiment 1a (upper panel) and in Experiment 1b (lower panel) using one possible counterbalancing order (H = MR of hands; L = MR of letters).*

activation of forearm muscles. The effectiveness of the TMS stimulation was verified by recording the compound muscle action potentials (CMAPs) from the right *extensor carpi radialis* muscle. The motor threshold for the target muscle was determined for each subject independently. The stimulation intensity was set at about 110% of the motor threshold and a CMAP was recorded for every single response accompanied by a TMS pulse. In the sham condition, the coil was placed more directly in front of the ear, and moved away from the surface of the head by 2 cm so that it was unlikely that the induced magnetic field would stimulate cortical neurons in M1, though the sound produced by the coil was comparable to that in the real TMS condition. The lack of effective stimulation in this condition was verified in each subject by the absence of an evoked CMAP. CMAPs were amplified, filtered (bandpass 10 to 3000 Hz), digitally converted (sampling rate 4 kHz).

Results

An ANOVA with experimental situation (TMS, sham TMS, and no-TMS), stimulus type (hands, letters), condition (baseline, rotation), and orientation (60°, 150°, 210°, and 330°) as factors was conducted on correct responses. Those trials in which subjects made an error (1.5%), RTs were 2 *SD*s above the mean for each cell (~3%), or in which the voice box was not triggered by the first response and subjects repeated the answer (2%), were not included in the analysis.

Accuracy

When stimulation was actually delivered, subjects made few errors (hands: 3.7%, letters: 3.6%), and were as accurate in carrying out the task with TMS as with no-TMS, $F(1, 9) = 0.16$, $p > .05$. No significant difference between MR of hands and letters was found, $F(1, 9) = 0.76$, $p > .05$.

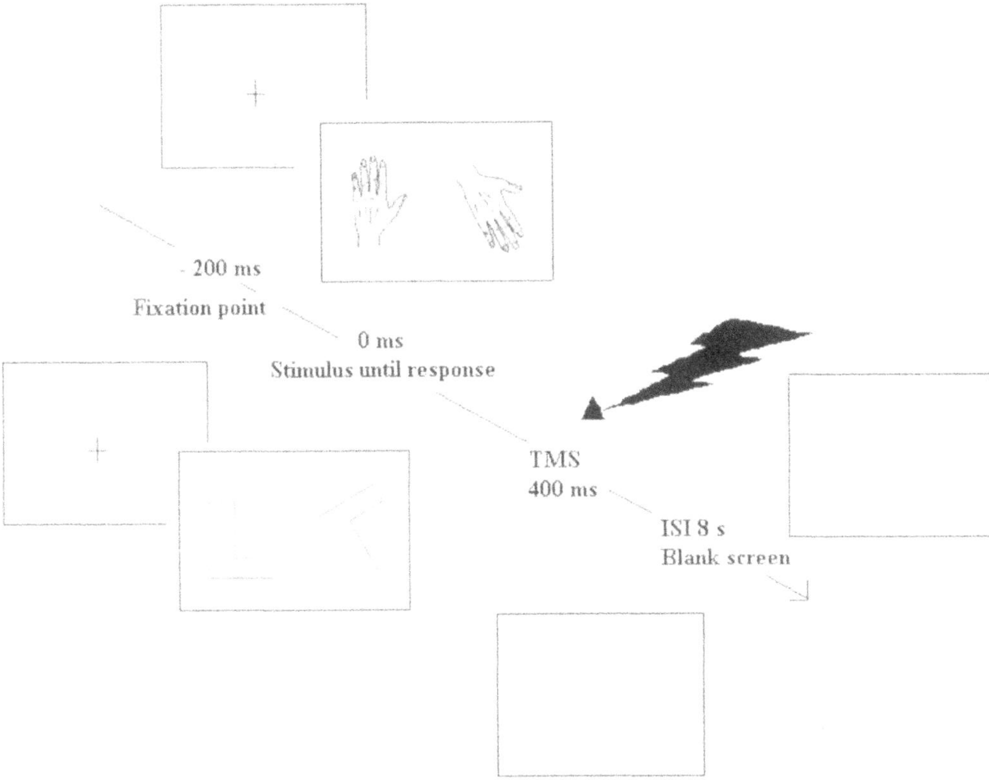

Figure 2. *Sequence of events in the experiment: A fixation point appeared on the screen for 200 ms, followed by the stimulus that remained visible until the response was given. Single pulses were delivered at 400 ms after stimulus onset on the hand area of the primary motor cortex.*

Reaction times

The main result was a significant three-way interaction: Experimental Situation × Stimulus Type × Condition, $F(2, 18) = 5.425, p = .014$. TMS slowed the RTs of MR of hands (i.e., in the rotation condition only, see Figure 3a), as suggested by the significant interaction Experimental Situation × Stimulus Type × Orientation, $F(6, 54) = 2.66$, $p = .025$. Within-subject contrasts revealed that RTs for MR of hands in the real TMS (1104 ms) were significantly slower, $F = 6.48, p < .05$, than those with no-TMS (999 ms), or when the sham stimulation was applied (1024 ms). RTs for MR of letters were similar in the real TMS (908 ms), in the no-TMS (956 ms), and in the sham stimulation (1019 ms).

In addition, significant main effects of condition, $F(1, 9) = 71.709, p < .001$, with RTs slower in the rotation condition than in the baseline, stimulus type, $F(1, 9) = 4.925, p < .05$, with MR slower for hands than for letters, and orientation, $F(3, 27) = 68.43, p < .001$, were found (see Figure 3b). The interaction Experimental Situation × Stimulus Type was also significant, $F(2, 18) = 10.43, p < .005$, with RTs for MR of hands slower in the real TMS (1013 ms) than in the sham stimulation (947 ms), and so was the interaction Condition × Orientation, $F(3, 27) = 28.72$, $p < .001$, with increasing RTs in the rotation condition only. The main effect experimental situation, $F(2, 18) = 1.11$, $p > .05$, and all the other interactions were not significant (all $p > .05$, *ns*).

Post hoc comparisons revealed a significant difference between RTs in the sham condition and RTs in the real TMS, $t(9) = 3.3$, $p < .009$, and between RTs in the no-TMS condition and in the TMS condition, $t(9) = 4.37$, $p < .005$, when subjects performed MR of hands. All the other planned comparisons did not reach significance.

A further ANOVA on RTs of MR of hands showed that the TMS effect was the same for left and right hands as stimuli. The interaction Experimental Situation × Handedness was not significant, $F(1, 9) = 1.00$, $p > .05$, *ns*, suggesting that the stimulation to the left hand area affected MR of both ipsi- and contralateral hand images (see Figure 3c).

EXPERIMENT 1B: SINGLE PULSE TMS ON THE RIGHT M1

In Experiment 1a we showed that TMS over the left M1 slowed down MR of hands but not of letters, suggesting that the hands are stimuli that implicitly engage motor processes. Moreover we observed that MR was affected by TMS irrespective of whether the stimuli were left or right hands. The next question to ask was whether this is a prerogative of the left M1 or whether it extends to the right M1 as well. To address this

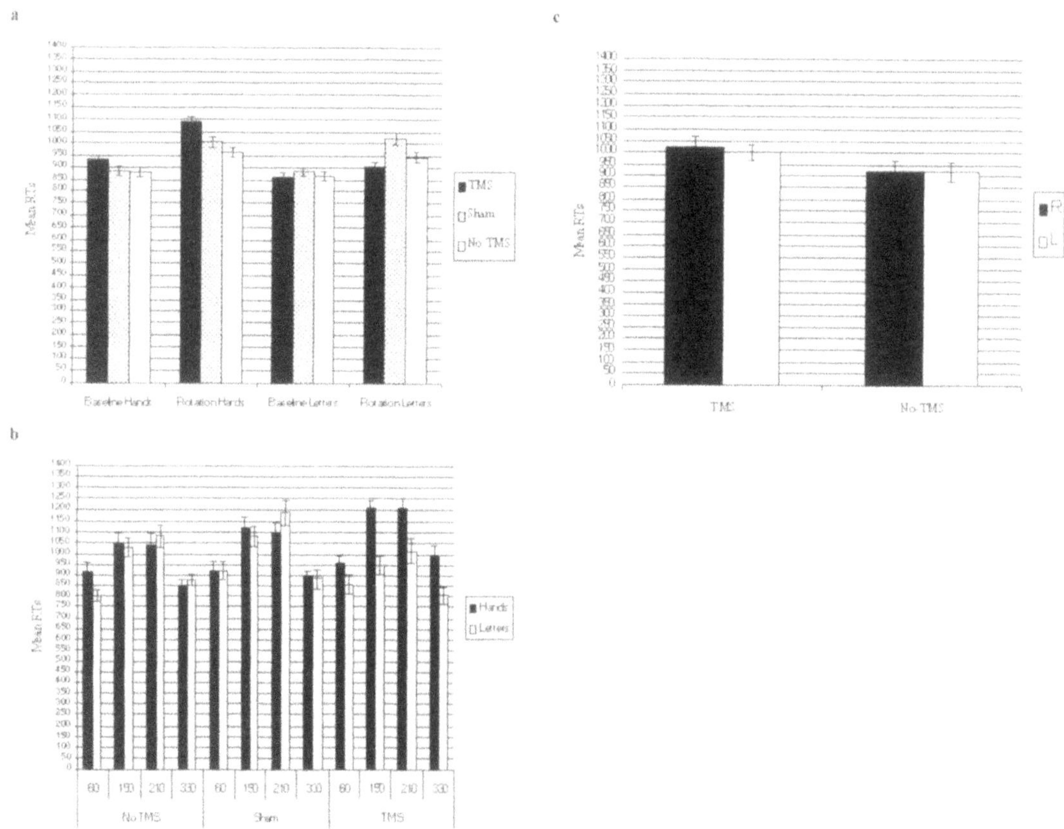

Figure 3. *a) Experiment 1a. Mean RTs (ms) and error bars (SD) are shown. TMS over the left-hand motor area slowed the RTs in the judgment task relative to hands in the rotation condition only. b) Interference effect of TMS in the rotation condition only, for each of the stimulus orientations. c) The TMS effect was the same for MR of left and right hands as stimuli. The stimulation of the left M1 hand area slowed RTs down MR of both the ipsi- and contralateral hand stimuli.*

issue in Experiment 1b we directly stimulated the right M1. Based on previous studies (Kosslyn et al., 1998; Wraga et al., 2003), single-pulse TMS to the right M1 was not expected to interfere with MR of left hands (or letters) as stimuli.

Stimuli, design, and procedure

In order to avoid possible learning effects, a different group of 10 right-handed subjects (mean age = 27.7 years ± 5.3, 100/D, according to the Edinburgh Inventory, Oldfield, 1971) was selected for Experiment 1b. Stimuli, design, and procedure were the same as in Experiment 1a except for the fact that the hand area in the right M1 was stimulated and that the three experimental conditions were performed in the same session and were counterbalanced across subjects (see Figure 1).

Results

An ANOVA with experimental situation (TMS, sham TMS, and no-TMS), stimulus type (hands, letters), condition (baseline, rotation), and orientation (60°, 150°, 210°, and 300°) as factors was performed. As for Experiment 1a, we discarded from the analysis those trials in which RTs were 2 *SDs* above the mean for each cell (~2%) as well as those in which the subject's voice did not trigger the voice box (2%).

Accuracy

Subjects were equally accurate in the baseline and the rotation conditions, $F(1, 9) = 0.84$, *ns*, irrespective of the experimental situations (TMS, sham, and no-TMS), $F(2, 18) = 2.02$, *ns*. Neither did their accuracy vary with the type of stimulus, $F(1, 9) = 0.212$, *ns*. Only the main effect of orientation was significant, $F(3, 27) = 6.77$, $p < .005$, with fewer errors at 150° and 210° stimulus orientations. None of the interactions was found significant (all $p > .05$, *ns*).

Reaction times

A significant main effect of condition, $F(1, 9) = 9.38$, $p < .05$, with slower RTs in the rotation condition, and of orientation, $F(3, 27) = 25.33$, $p < .001$, with RTs increasing as an effect of stimulus orientation (see Figure 4b), were found to be significant, as was the interaction Condition × Orientation, $F(3, 27) = 5.54$, $p < .001$, with an increase in RTs in the rotation condition. All the other main effects—experimental situation, $F(2, 18) = 1.7$; stimulus type, $F(1, 9) = 3.27$—and the remaining interactions did not reach significance (all $p > .05$). Post hoc comparisons between RTs concerning hands at 210° and 300° showed that subjects were slower in the TMS condition than in the sham TMS, $t(9) = 2.69$, $p < .05$, $t(9) = 2.81$, $p < .05$, respectively. None of the other comparisons reached significance.

Although we failed to observe any significant effect of TMS, we performed an ANOVA on RTs for MR of hands only in order to test whether RTs for MR of left and right hands as stimuli were different. Neither the Experimental Situation × Handedness, $F(2, 18) = 0.807$, $p > .05$, *ns*, nor the Experimental Situation × Condition × Handedness, $F(2, 18) = 0.013$, $p > .05$, *ns*, interactions were found significant, suggesting that the TMS did not affect RTs for either the ipsi- or the contralateral hand stimuli.

Discussion of Experiments 1a and b

Results from Experiment 1a clearly showed that TMS on the left M1 slowed RTs during MR of hand images but not of letters. This effect was the same for left and right hands as stimuli. Furthermore, results in Experiment 1b suggested that the right motor hand area does not seem to be recruited in MR of hands, not even when individuals imagine movements of the contralateral left hand. The specialisation of the left M1 for both the left- and right-hand movements has been observed also in the context of planning and execution of movements (Chen, Cohen, & Hallet, 1997; Kim et al., 1993; Kosslyn et al., 1998), as well as in the motor imagery domain (Fadiga et al., 1999).

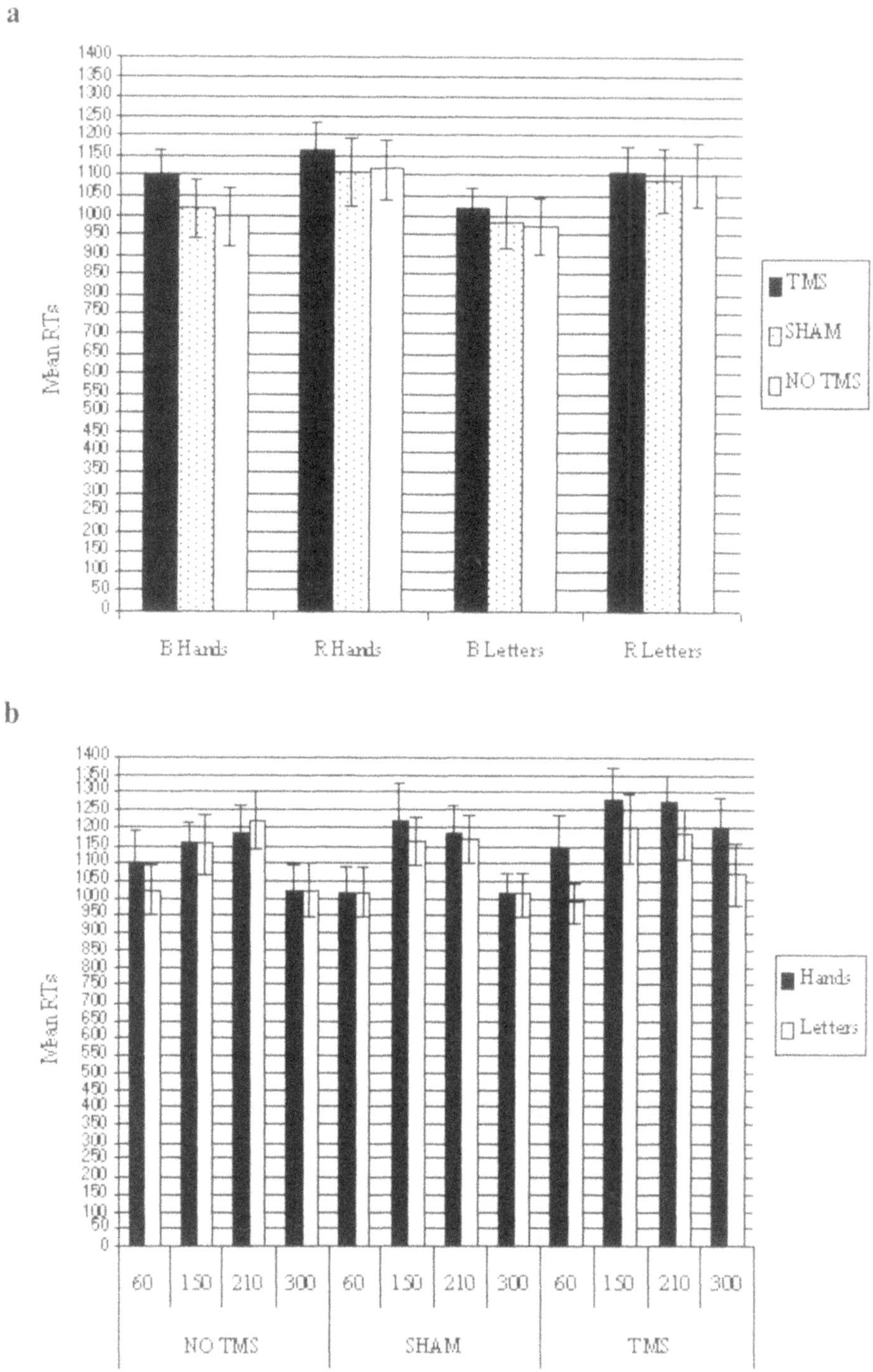

Figure 4. *a) Experiment 1b. Mean RTs (ms) and error bars (SD) are shown. TMS over the right motor hand area did not affect RTs for MR of either hands or of letters. b) RTs of the MR of hands and letters in the rotation condition only for each of the stimulus orientations.*

EXPERIMENT 2: TO-BE-ROTATED STIMULUS PRESENTED IN EITHER THE LEFT OR THE RIGHT VISUAL FIELDS

Results from Experiments 1a and 1b showed that the ability to perform MR of hands was altered when TMS was delivered to the left motor hand area but not to the same area in the right hemisphere. These results, however, may be constrained by the experimental design employed. In Experiment 1 the "comparison hand" was always presented in the left visual field, while the "rotating hand" was always shown in the right visual field, thus shading a potential role of the right motor cortex in MR. Even though this experimental design has been consistently used in many others MR studies (Cohen et al., 1996; Ganis et al., 2000; Kosslyn et al., 1998; Tagaris et al., 1996; Vingerhoets et al., 2001; Wraga et al., 2003), it could well be that the fixed location of the rotated stimulus may have influenced the participants to process all aspects of the task with the left hemisphere. To rule out the account that results in Experiment 1 were biased by the fixed location of the comparison hand we carried out an experiment in which the rotating hands (and letters) were presented in either the left or the right visual fields.

Subjects

A different group of six right-handed participants (mean age = 26.3 ± 3.3, 100/D, according to the Edinburgh Inventory, Oldfield, 1971) took part in the experiment. None of the subjects had any contraindications to TMS (see Method section in Experiment 1). Participants gave informed consent to the experiment after being informed about the TMS procedure and risks but not about the specific hypotheses of the study.

Method and procedure

In Experiment 2, stimuli, design, and procedure were the same as in Experiment 1 except for the fact that the three experimental conditions (TMS on the left motor hand area, TMS on the right motor hand area, and sham stimulation) were performed in the same session and were counterbalanced across subjects.

Results

An ANOVA with experimental situation (left M1 TMS, right M1 TMS, sham TMS), stimulus type (hands, letters), condition (baseline, rotation), rotating stimulus position (in the left or the right visual field), same–different (same or mirror images), and orientation (60°, 150°, 210°, and 330°) as factors was conducted on correct responses.

Accuracy

When stimulation was actually delivered, subjects made few errors (hands: 3.2%, letters: 3.4%) and they were as accurate in carrying out the task during TMS to the left and right M1 as during the sham TMS ($p > .05$). No significant difference between MR of hands and letters ($p > .05$) was found.

Reaction times

The effect of TMS was independent of whether the rotating stimulus was presented in the left or right visual field. None of the interactions were found to be significant (all $p > .05$) except for the Experimental Situation × Stimulus Type × Condition interaction, $F(2, 10) = 6.009$, $p = .019$, suggesting that TMS over the left M1 slowed down RTs for MR of hands only, just like in Experiment 1a (see Figure 5). The main effects of condition, $F(1, 5) = 25.37$, $p < .005$, orientation, $F(3, 15) = 23.45$, $p < .001$, and stimulus type, $F(1, 5) = 9.832$, $p < .05$, were significant. All the other main effects were not significant (all $p > .05$, n.s.). The Stimulus Type × Rotating Stimulus Position, $F(1, 5) = 12.8$, $p < .05$, Condition × Orientation, $F(3, 15) = 11.606$, $p < .001$, Condition × Same–Different, $F(1, 5) = 15.568$, $p < .05$, and the Stimulus Type × Condition × Orientation, $F(3, 15) = 4.36$, $p < .05$, interactions were all found significant.

Within-subject contrasts revealed that RTs were slower in the rotation than in the baseline condition, $F(1, 5) = 25.37, p < .005$, increased with the increase of the stimulus angle, $F(1, 5) = 62.38$, $p < .005$ for 60° vs. 150°, $F(1, 5) = 1.68, p > .05$, *ns* for 150° vs. 210°, and $F(1, 5) = 16.14, p < .05$ for 210° vs. 60°, and slowed down during MR of hands with respect to letters, $F(1, 5) = 9.8, p < .05$. In addition, subjects were slower when hands were presented in the right visual field, but were slower when letters were presented in the left visual field, $F(1, 5) = 12.821, p < .05$.

Discussion of Experiment 2

Results in Experiment 2 proved that the left primary motor cortex does play a critical role in MR of hands. Moreover, we demonstrated that the hemispheric lateralisation within the M1 cortex during MR tasks is not simply a consequence of the position in the visual field (i.e., left or right) of the rotating stimulus. A lateralisation effect has been found also in Kawamichi, Kikurchi, Endo, Takeda, and Yoshizawa's (1998) and in Parsons et al.'s (1995) studies in which a single hand was tachistoscopically presented to right-handed subjects in either the left or the right visual field. In these studies a stronger activation in the left premotor cortex, but not in M1, was observed, irrespective of the visual field or body side of the hand stimulus. The role of the left and the right M1 will be addressed in the General Discussion.

GENERAL DISCUSSION

Left M1 is involved in MR

The main finding of the present study is that the ability of healthy subjects to perform MR of hands but not of letters was affected by the temporary disruption of the neural activity in the left motor hand area by means of single-pulse TMS. The finding that the left M1 is recruited in MR of

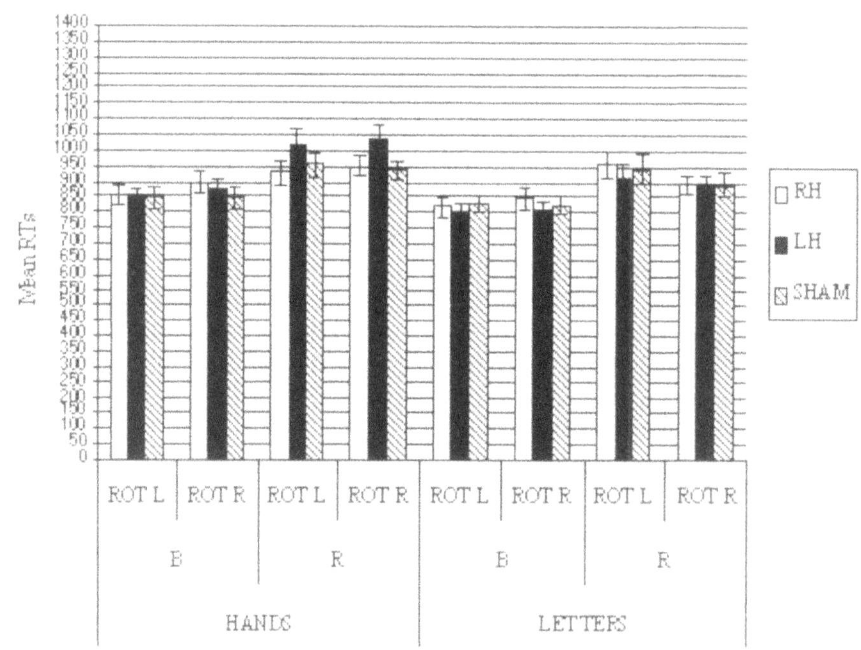

Figure 5. *Experiment 2: Mean RTs (ms) and error bars (SD) are shown. TMS over the hand motor area of the right-hand, the left-hand, and the sham stimulation when stimuli were presented in the left (Rot L) or the right visual field (Rot R).*

hands is consistent with some neuroimaging results (Kosslyn et al., 1998) and with a previous TMS study (Ganis et al., 2000) in which MR of hands and feet but not of external objects was studied.

This specificity should not be taken as evidence that discrete brain areas are selectively recruited according to the *type of stimulus* to be rotated. Neuropsychological (Tomasino & Rumiati, 2004) and neuroimaging (Kosslyn et al., 2001) studies have shown that the left M1 is recruited not just for body parts such as hand shapes, but also for non-body-part stimuli such as 3D cubes, providing that subjects use a *motor strategy* in MR. In particular, Tomasino and Rumiati found that patients with left M1 lesions exhibited a selective deficit when solving MR of either hands or external objects only when instructed to use a motor strategy (i.e., as a consequence of their manual activity).

In the present study, subjects were free to apply one or the other strategy, with the instructions requiring them to mentally rotate the stimulus on the right, and decide whether it was the same or a mirror image of the other one. Since an interference effect due to stimulation was obtained only during MR of hands, we argue that hands *implicitly* require a mental motor transformation. This account is consistent with the activation of M1 found in some brain imaging studies in which subjects mentally simulated a motor act (Abruzzese, Trompetto, & Schieppati, 1996; Decety et al., 1994; Gerardin et al., 2000; Lang et al., 1994; Lotze et al., 1999; Porro et al., 1996; Roth et al., 1996; Stephan et al., 1995).

By contrast, since TMS did not interfere with MR of letters, we argue that alphanumeric characters do not implicitly require a mental motor strategy (i.e., viewer-based), but rather a visuospatial strategy (i.e., object-based). This view is compatible with Harris and Miniussi's (2003) finding that MR of external objects is lateralisated to the right parietal lobe. In their study, subjects performed MR of alphanumeric characters while undergoing repetitive TMS. While the right parietal lobe stimulation slowed down the MR performance, the left parietal stimulation did produce no significant interference. We therefore suggest that the type of stimulus (i.e., hands or external objects) may implicitly triggers one or the other strategy (i.e., motor or visual respectively; see also Tomasino & Rumiati, 2004), and that the left M1 supports the former.

Left M1 is involved in simulating the movements of both left and right hands

We showed that the left M1 plays an essential role in MR of both the left and the right hands. In sharp contrast with Parsons et al.'s (1995) study in which M1 was not found activated, we demonstrated the involvement of the left M1 cortex in MR when the rotating hand is fixed in the right visual field (Experiment 1a) as well as when it is shown randomly in the left and right visual fields (Experiment 2). However, in Parsons et al.'s study, where the visual and the somatic processing were dissociated by presenting left-hand stimuli to the right hemisphere and right-hand stimuli to the left hemisphere, the authors found that the activation in SMA and in the premotor cortex was stronger in the left hemisphere, regardless of whether the hand was left or right. We proposed here that the left hemisphere specialisation for MR of both the ipsi- and contralateral hand movements is consistent with the specialisation of left hemisphere for higher motor control of both left and right limbs. Consistently, ideomotor and ideational apraxia affect both limbs and it is typically caused by lesions of the left hemisphere (DeRenzi et al., 1980, 1982).

Right M1 hand area does not seem to be involved in MR

The stimulation of the right M1 did not interfere with MR of hands not even when the subjects simulated the rotation of the contralateral hand. This functional left–right asymmetry within M1 is consistent with neuroimaging results (e.g., Kosslyn et al., 1998; Wraga et al., 2003) in which the right M1 hand area was not found activated during MR of hands and with an fMRI study by Porro et al. (1996), in which an activation of the left and right M1 was found while subjects performed kinaesthetic motor imagery involving the contralateral hand, with a greater activation in the left MI during left-hand movement and imagery.

Our results are at variance with the view that the right M1 would play a role in MR at least of the left-hand movements (Chen et al., 1997). In fact, when we stimulated the right M1 hand area we failed to find a significant effect on MR of either hands, though RTs tended to be slower in the TMS than in the sham or in the no-TMS conditions. One interpretation holds that the right M1 hand area participates in MR of hands, but its involvement is weaker than that of the left M1. If we interfere with the neuronal activity of the right M1, the effect may not reach significance because the left M1 can, alone, complete MR. Likewise Beisteiner, Hollinger, Lindinger, Lang, and Berthoz (1995) recorded direct current (DC) brain potentials during a motor imagery task and found that they were larger in the left than in the right hemisphere both when subjects performed or imagined performing hand movements.

Which computations are sustained by the M1?

Overall our findings strenghten the idea that the left M1 hand area, whose primary function is known to be the execution of hand movements, is involved in at least one type of MR. Thus within the brain network supporting MR, the left M1 can be recruited at a final stage of the object rotation. The interference produced by the TMS was found at about 400 ms after stimulus onset and there are other studies reporting M1 involvement at 650 ms (Ganis et al., 2000) or even later at 900 ms (Thayer, Johnson, Corballis, & Hamm, 2001, using ERPs). These differences in between-studies timing can be explained by different stimuli used (i.e., open hand shapes and finger configurations). MR of open hand shapes is known to require a rotation on the picture plane. By contrast, MR of finger configurations might involve the simulation of a movement through a longer trajectory, and for this reason, more time is needed.

We do not wish to claim that M1 represents a module in the brain dedicated to MR. We share the view that MR is performed by a host of subprocesses sustained by different parts of the brain (visual areas, parietal lobe, and premotor cortex). However, depending on the nature of the task, various components of this network may become more or less important. What does M1 do then? The parietal lobe plays a role in processing the 3D visual information in ego-, allo- and object-centred reference frames; it can select the movement, guide attention to motor performance, and anticipate the consequences of the action by simulating the movement. This information is then transferred to premotor areas, involved in the planning of motor acts, and probably to M1. M1 may contribute to MR during somatotopic, dynamic remapping, a process in which individuals mentally track and continuously update the transformation of the hand motor image by comparing the actual position of their own hands to the final position of the hand stimulus. It is known from neurophysiological studies that M1 neurons code the intended direction of the movements (e.g., Georgopuolos et al., 1989). Thus the fact that subjects usually report kinaesthetic feelings specific to the imagined limb suggests that this representation is of a kinaesthetic-motor type.

PrEview proof published online 10 January 2005

REFERENCES

Abruzzese, G., Trompetto, C., & Schieppati, M. (1996). The excitability of the human motor cortex increases during execution and mental imagination of sequential but not repetitive finger movements. *Experimental Brain Research, 111,* 465–72.

Alexander, G. E., & Crutcher, M. D. (1990). Neural representations of the target (goal) of visually guided arm movements in three motor areas of the monkey. *Journal of Neurophysiology, 64,* 164–178.

Ashe, J., Taira, M., Smyrnis, N., Pellizzer, G., Georgakopoulos, T., Lurito, J. T., & Georgopoulos, A. P. (1993). Motor cortical activity preceding a memorized movement trajectory with an orthogonal bend. *Experimental Brain Research, 95,* 118–130.

Barnes, J., Howard, R. J., Senior, C., Brammer, M., Bullmore, E. T., Simmons, A., Woodruff, P., & David, A. S. (2000). Cortical activity during rotational and linear transformations. *Neuropsychologia, 38,* 1148–1156.

Beisteiner, R., Hollinger, P., Lindinger, G., Lang, W., & Berthoz, A. (1995). Mental representations of movements. Brain potentials associated with imagination of hand movements. *Electroencephalography Clinical Neurophysiology, 96,* 183–193.

Carpenter, A. F., Georgopoulos, A. P., & Pellizzer, G. (1999). Motor cortical encoding of serial order in a context-recall task. *Science, 283,* 1752–1757.

Carpenter, P. A., Just, M. A., Keller, T. A., Eddy, W., & Thulborn, K. (1999). Graded functional activation in the visuospatial system with the amount of task demand. *Journal of Cognitive Neuroscience, 11,* 9–24.

Chen, R., Cohen, L. G., & Hallett, M. (1997). Role of the ipsilateral motor cortex in voluntary movement. *Canadian Journal of Neurological Science, 24,* 284–291.

Cohen, M. S., Kosslyn, S. M., Breiter, H. C., DiGirolamo, G. J., Thompson, W. L., Anderson, A. K., Bookheimer, S. Y., Rosen, B. R., & Belliveau, J. W. (1996). Changes in cortical activity during mental rotation: A mapping study using functional MRI. *Brain, 119,* 89–100.

Decety, J., Perani, D., Jeannerod, M., Bettinardi, V., Tadary, B., Woods, R., Mazziotta, J. C., & Fazio, F. (1994). Mapping motor representations with positron emission tomography. *Nature, 371,* 45–52.

De Renzi, E., Faglioni, P., & Sorgato, P. (1982). Modality specific and supramodal mechanisms of apraxia. *Brain, 105,* 301–312.

De Renzi, E., Motti, F., & Nichelli, P. (1980). Imitating gestures. *Archives of Neurology, 37,* 6–10.

Fadiga, L., Buccino, G., Craighero, L., Fogassi, L., Gallese, V., & Pavesi, G. (1999). Corticospinal excitability is specifically modulated by motor imagery: A magnetic stimulation study. *Neuropsychologia, 37,* 147–158.

Ganis, G. Keenan, J. P., Kosslyn, S. M., & Pascual-Leone, A. (2000). Transcranial magnetic stimulation of primary motor cortex affects mental rotation. *Cerebral Cortex, 10,* 175–180.

Georgopoulos, A. P., Lurito, J. T., Petrides, M., Schwartz, A. B., & Massey, J. T. (1989). Mental rotation of the neuronal population vector. *Science, 243,* 234–236.

Gerardin, E., Sirigu, A., Lehericy, S., Poline, J. B., Gaymard, B., Marsault, C., Agid, Y., & Le Bihan, D. (2000). Partially overlapping neural networks for real and imagined hand movements. *Cerebral Cortex, 10,* 1093–1104.

Grafton, S. T., Hazeltine, E., & Ivry, R. (1995). Functional mapping of sequence learning in normal humans. *Journal of Cognitive Neuroscience, 7,* 497–510.

Harris, I. M., Egan, G. F., Sonkkila, C., Tochon-Danguy, H. J., Paxinos, G., & Watson, J. D. G. (2000). Selective right parietal lobe activation during mental rotation. *Brain, 123,* 65–73.

Harris, I. M., & Miniussi, C. (2003). Parietal lobe contribution to mental rotation demonstrated with rTMS. *Journal of Cognitive Neuroscience, 15,* 315–323.

Honda, M., Wise, S. P., Weeks, R. A., Deiber, M. P., & Hallett, M. (1998). Cortical areas with enhanced activation during object centred spatial information processing: A PET study. *Brain, 121,* 2145–2158.

Iwaki, S., Ueno, S., Imada, T., & Tonoike, M. (1999). Dynamic cortical activation in mental image processing revealed by biomagnetic measurement. *NeuroReport, 10,* 1793–1797.

Jordan, K., Heinze, H. J., Lutz, K., Kanowski, M., & Jancke, L. (2001). Cortical activations during the mental rotation of different visual objects. *NeuroImage, 13,* 143–152.

Karni, A., Meyer, G., Rey-Hipolito, C., Jezzard, P., Adams, M. M., Turner, R., & Ungerleider, L. G. (1998). The acquisition of skilled motor performance: Fast and slow experience-driven changes in primary motor cortex. *Proceedings of the National Accademy of Sciences of the United States of America, 95,* 861–868.

Kawamichi, H., Kikurchi, Y., Endo, H., Takeda, T., & Yoshizawa, S. (1998). Temporal structure of implicit motor imagery in visual hand-shape discrimination as revealed by MEG. *NeuroReport, 9,* 1127–1132.

Kim, S., Ashe, J., Hendrich, K., Ellermann, J. M., Merkle, H., Ugurbil, K., & Georgopoulos, A. P. (1993). Functional magnetic resonance imaging of motor cortex: Hemispheric asymmetry and handedness. *Science, 261,* 615–617.

Kosslyn, S. M., DiGirolamo, G. J., Thompson, W. L., & Alpert, N. M. (1998). Mental rotation of objects versus hands: Neural mechanisms revealed by positron emission tomography. *Psychophysiology, 35,* 151–161.

Kosslyn, S. M., Thompson, W. L., Wraga, M., & Alpert, N. M. (2001). Imagining rotation by endogenous versus exogenous forces: Distinct neural mechanisms. *NeuroReport, 12,* 2519–2525.

Lamm, C., Windischberger, C., Leodolter, U., Moser, E., & Bauer, H. (2001). Evidence for premotor cortex activity during dynamic visuospatial imagery from single-trial functional magnetic resonance imaging and event-related slow cortical potentials. *NeuroImage, 14,* 268–83.

Lang, W., Petit, L., Hollinger, P., Pietrzyk, U., Tzourio, N., Mazoyer, B., & Berthoz, A. (1994). A positron emission tomography study of oculomotor imagery. *NeuroReport, 5,* 921–924.

Lotze, M., Montoya, P., Erb, M., Hulsmann, E., Flor, H., Klose, U., Birbaumer, N., & Grodd, W. (1999). Activation of cortical and cerebellar motor areas during executed and imagined hand movements: An fMRI study. *Journal of Cognitive Neuroscience, 11,* 491–501.

Oldfield, R. C. (1971). The assessment and analysis of handedness: The Edinburgh inventory. *Neuropsychologia, 9,* 97–113.

Parsons, L. M., & Fox, P. T. (1998). The neural basis of implicit movements used in recognizing hand shape. *Cognitive Neuropsychology, 15,* 583–615.

Parsons, L. M., Fox, P. T., Downs, J. H., Glass, T., Hirsh, T. B., Martin, C. C., Jerabeck, P. A., & Lancaster, J. L. (1995). Use of implicit motor imagery for visual shape discrimination as revealed by PET. *Nature, 375,* 54–58.

Pellizzer, G., Sargent, P., & Georgopoulos, A. P. (1995). Motor cortical activity in a context-recall task. *Science, 269,* 702–705.

Podzebenko, K., Egan, G. F., & Watson, J. D. G. (2002). Widespread dorsal stream activation during a parametric mental rotation task, revealed with functional magnetic resonance imaging. *NeuroImage, 15,* 547–558.

Porro, C. A., Francescato, M. P., Cettolo, V., Diamond, M. E., Baraldi, P., Zuiani, C., Bazzocchi, M., & Prampero, P. E. (1996). Primary motor and sensory cortex activation during motor performance and motor imagery. *Journal of Neuroscience, 16,* 7688–7698.

Richter, W., Somorjai, R., Summers, R., Jarmasz, M., Menon, R. S., Gati, J. S., Georgopoulos, A. P., Tegeler, C., Ugurbil, K., & Kim, S. G. (2000). Motor area activity during mental rotation studied by time-resolved single-trial fMRI. *Journal of Cognitive Neuroscience, 12,* 310–320.

Roth, M., Decety, J., Raybaudi, M., Massarelli, R., Delon-Martin, C., Segebarth, C., Morand, S., Gemignani, A., Decorps, M., & Jeannerod, M. (1996). Possible involvement of primary motor cortex in mentally simulated movement: A functional magnetic resonance imaging study. *NeuroReport, 7,* 1280–1284.

Sekiyama, K., Miyauchi, S., Imaruoka, T., Egusa, H., & Tashiro, T. (2000). Body image as a visuomotor transformation device revealed in adaptation to reversed vision. *Nature, 407,* 374–377.

Shepard, R. N., & Cooper, L. A. (1982). *Mental images and their transformations.* Cambridge, MA: MIT Press.

Smyrnis, N., Taira, M., Ashe, J., & Georgopoulos, A. P. (1992). Motor cortical activity in a memorized delay task. *Experimental Brain Research, 92,* 139–151.

Stephan, K. M., Fink, G. R., Passingham, R. E., Silbersweig, D., Ceballos-Baumann, A. O., Frith, C. D., & Frackowiak, R. S. J. (1995). Functional anatomy of the mental representation of upper extremity movements in healthy subjects. *Journal of Neurophysiology, 73,* 373–386.

Tagaris, G. A., Kim, S. G., Strupp, J. P., Andersen, P., Ugurbil, K., & Georgopoulos, A. P. (1996). Quantitative relations between parietal activation and performance in mental rotation. *NeuroReport, 29,* 773–776.

Tagaris, G. A., Kim, S. G., Strupp, J. P., Andersen, P., Ugurbil, K., & Georgopoulos, A. P. (1998). Mental rotation by functional magnetic resonance imaging at high field (4 tesla): Performance and cortical activation. *Journal of Cognitive Neuroscience, 9,* 419–432.

Tagaris, G. A., Richter, W., Kim, S. G., Pellizzer, G., & Andersen, P. (1998). Functional magnetic resonance imaging of mental rotation and memory scanning: A multidimensional scaling analysis of brain activation patterns. *Brain Research Reviews, 26,* 106–112.

Thayer, Z. C., Johnson, B. W., Corballis, M. C., & Hamm, J. P. (2001). Perceptual and motor mechanisms for mental rotation of human hands. *NeuroReport, 12,* 3433–3437.

Tomasino, B., & Rumiati, R. I. (2004). Effects of strategies on mental rotation and hemispheric specialization: Neuropsychological evidence. *Journal of Cognitive Neuroscience, 16,* 878–888.

Tomasino, B., Rumiati, R. I., & Skrap, M. (2004). *The role of the human motor hand area in mental rotation: Neuropsychological evidence.* Manuscript submitted for publication.

Vingerhoets, G., Santens, P., Van Laere, K., Lahorte, P., Dierckx, R. A., & De Reuck, J. (2001). Regional brain activity during different paradigms of mental rotation in healthy volunteers: A position emission tomography study. *NeuroImage, 13,* 381–391.

Wassermann, E. M. (1998). Risk and safety of repetitive transcranial magnetic stimulation. *Electroencephalograpy Clinical Neurophysiology, 105,* 1–17.

Wise, S. P., Moody, S. L., Blomstrom, K. J., & Mitz, A. R. (1998). Changes in motor cortical activity during visuomotor adaptation. *Experimental Brain Research, 121,* 285–299.

Wraga, M., Thompson, W. L., Alpert, N. M., & Kosslyn, S. M. (2003). Implicit transfer of motor strategies in mental rotation. *Brain and Cognition, 52,* 135–143.

Zacks, J. M., Ollinger, J. M., Sheridan, M. A., & Tversky, B. (2002). A parametric study of mental spatial transformations of bodies. *NeuroImage, 6,* 857–872.

Zacks, J., Rypma, B., Gabrieli, J. D. E., Tversky, B., & Glover, G. H. (1999). Imagined transformations of bodies: An fMRI investigation. *Neuropsychologia, 37,* 1029–1040.

COGNITIVE NEUROPSYCHOLOGY, 2005, 22 (3/4), 364–386

PROCESSING OF VISUAL SEMANTIC INFORMATION TO CONCRETE WORDS: TEMPORAL DYNAMICS AND NEURAL MECHANISMS INDICATED BY EVENT-RELATED BRAIN POTENTIALS

Hein T. van Schie
University of Nijmegen and University of Groningen, The Netherlands

Albertus A. Wijers, Rogier B. Mars, Jeroen S. Benjamins, and Laurie A. Stowe
University of Groningen, The Netherlands

Event-related brain potentials were used to study the retrieval of visual semantic information to concrete words, and to investigate possible structural overlap between visual object working memory and concreteness effects in word processing. Subjects performed an object working memory task that involved 5 s retention of simple 4-angled polygons (load 1), complex 10-angled polygons (load 2), and a no-load baseline condition. During the polygon retention interval subjects were presented with a lexical decision task to auditory presented concrete (imageable) and abstract (nonimageable) words, and pseudowords. ERP results are consistent with the use of object working memory for the visualisation of concrete words. Our data indicate a two-step processing model of visual semantics in which visual descriptive information of concrete words is first encoded in semantic memory (indicated by an anterior N400 and posterior occipital positivity), and is subsequently visualised via the network for object working memory (reflected by a left frontal positive slow wave and a bilateral occipital slow wave negativity). Results are discussed in the light of contemporary models of semantic memory.

Generally, people find concrete words (e.g., lion) easier to understand and to remember than abstract words (e.g., idea). This phenomenon, which is known as the concreteness effect, is a well-known empirical finding that has been observed in a large variety of experimental studies and conditions

Correspondence should be addressed to H.T. van Schie, Nijmegen Institute for Cognition and Information, PO Box 9104, 6500 HE Nijmegen, The Netherlands (Email: h.vanschie@nici.kun.nl).

This study was performed at the Department of Experimental and Work Psychology, University of Groningen, The Netherlands. At the time of the study, Hein T. van Schie, Albertus A. Wijers, Rogier B. Mars, and Jeroen S. Benjamins were affiliated with the Department of Experimental and Work Psychology, University of Groningen, The Netherlands; Laurie A. Stowe and Hein T. van Schie were affiliated with the Department of Linguistics, University of Groningen, The Netherlands.

Hein T. van Schie is now at the Nijmegen Institute for Cognition and Information, Nijmegen University, The Netherlands. Rogier B. Mars is now at the FC Donders Centre for Cognitive Neuroimaging, Nijmegen, The Netherlands. Jeroen S. Benjamins is now at the Helmholtz Research Institute, University of Utrecht, The Netherlands.

This research was supported by a grant from the Netherlands Organization for Scientific Research (NWO) awarded to L.A. Stowe for the Pioneer Project "The Neurological basis of language."

(review in Paivio, 1991). However, the discussion on the origin of the concreteness effect is an old one, and is still far from settled. Several theoretical models have been proposed that may explain the concreteness effect, building on evidence from behavioural, neuropsychological, and, more recently, neuroimaging studies.

On the behavioural level there remain two contenders: dual coding theory (Paivio, 1971) and context availability theory (Schwanenflugel & Shoben, 1983). Dual coding theory is perhaps the most widely known theory of the concreteness effect. According to this theory the fundamental difference between concrete and abstract words is that concrete words may be translated into a mental (visual) image, while abstract words can only activate a verbal or linguistic code of representation. Dual coding theory posits two systems, one verbal and one imagistic, that are functionally distinct yet interconnected. Because concrete words are more imageable than abstract words, dual coding theory proposes that concrete words are processed by both the verbal (left hemisphere) and the imagery system (right hemisphere), as an account for the superiority of concrete words over abstract words.

Context availability theory, on the other hand, proposes the existence of a single amodal semantic system for word meanings. This theory argues that concrete words benefit from a more extensive propositional organisation that may include additional perceptual properties or stronger contextual support for concrete items than for abstract items (e.g., Kieras, 1978). According to the context availability theory, abstract words presented in isolation need more contextual support than concrete words because they are inherently more ambiguous or vague, and therefore harder to process. Concrete words, on the other hand, are said to exhibit stronger or more extensive associative links in semantic memory.

Others have sought to understand the organisation of semantic memory by investigating neuropsychologically impaired patients (e.g., Breedin, Saffran, & Coslett, 1994; Coltheart, Inglis, Cupples, Michie, Bates, & Budd, 1998; Damasio, Grabowski, Tranel, Hitchwa, & Damasio, 1996; Saffran & Schwartz, 1994; Tranel, Damasio, & Damasio, 1997). Warrington's sensory/functional theory of semantic representation (Warrington & Shallice, 1984) proposes that semantic knowledge is organised in separate modality-specific brain areas that represent the sensory (i.e., visual) and functional (i.e., motor) features of objects (also see Farah & McClelland, 1991; Warrington & McCarthy, 1983, 1987). This theory attempts to explain the occurrence of category-specific deficits for living and nonliving things. Living things (e.g., animals) are hypothesised to rely on visual features such as colour, shape, size, texture, etc., whereas for nonliving things (e.g., tools) functional or motor features are thought to be important. According to the sensory/functional theory of semantic memory, lesions in visual or motor areas may respectively impair semantics for living or nonliving items. This theory may be classified as a multicode theory of semantic memory that is more similar to dual coding theory than to (single code) context availability theory.

In direct opposition to the multicode theory of semantics is the OUCH (organised unitary content hypothesis) model (Caramazza, Hills, Rapp, & Romani, 1990; Hillis, Rapp, & Caramazza, 1995) that argues for a unitary semantic system that is organised in clusters that develop because of correlations and overlap between the properties of objects (e.g., properties of fruits and vegetables tend to be represented in adjacent neural tissue because they have many properties in common). Category-specific deficits may occur because of circumscribed lesions to cortical areas representing conceptual knowledge of objects. Although the OUCH model is mostly concerned with the properties of concrete objects, there is an obvious resemblance to the context availability theory. Both theories argue for a single-code semantic system, with an internal organisation based upon associations between object properties.[1]

[1] Note that the list of neuropsychological theories discussed here is not meant to be exclusive (for a more complete overview, see Caramazza, 1998).

With the availability of neuroimaging techniques such as PET and fMRI, more detailed information on the specific brain areas involved in the processing and representation of semantic knowledge has accumulated. Typically, results of neuroimaging have provided support for a distributed or multimodal account of semantic memory (Martin, 1998; Martin & Chao, 2001; Pulvermüller, 2001). The presentation of objects from different semantic categories such as animals and tools have been indicated to elicit distinct patterns of neural activation. Animals are typically associated with increased activation in occipital and fusiform (shape) areas, whereas tools generate more activation in areas that support motor function and perception of object motion (Chao & Martin, 1999, 2000; Gabrowski, Damasio, & Damasio, 1998; Martin, Wiggs, Ungerleider, & Haxby, 1996; Perani et al., 1995). Importantly, similar and overlapping patterns of neural activation have been found in conditions where no perceptual object was presented, but in which subjects retrieved semantic information about the visual or functional properties of objects on the basis of verbal cues (e.g., Chao & Martin, 1999; Martin et al., 1995; Perani, Schnur, Tettamanti, Gorno-Tempini, Cappa, & Fazio, 1999; Thompson-Schill, Aguirre, D'Esposito, & Farah, 1999). This has been interpreted to suggest that semantic knowledge about visual and functional properties of objects are stored in close proximity to sensory and motor areas that are activated when when perceiving or performing actions with these objects (e.g., see Martin et al., 1995).

In general, these results are taken to be consistent with the idea that the development of meaning for concrete objects, such as plants, animals, and tools, originates in everyday life experience with these objects. According to Pulvermüller (1999), when the meaning of a concrete content word is being acquired, the learner may be exposed to sensory information through various modalities, which becomes associated to the word. The same goes for action words, which may become associated with the actions that are performed by the learner at the time that the word is learned. This process of coactivation is believed to result in the development of a distributed functional unit or cell assembly that links the word's phonological features with visual and action properties in sensory and motor areas of the cortex (also see Allport, 1985). Consistent with this perspective, neuroimaging results showed that visual or motor activation to concrete items followed automatically from the presentation of their names (e.g., Hauk, Johnsrude, & Pulvermüller, 2004; Martin, 1998; Thompson-Schill et al., 1999).

Although we consider the distributed account of semantic memory to be promising, we feel that the approach is still very generally formulated. There is little known about the neurophysiological mechanisms that enable retrieval and activation of concrete semantic knowledge. One reason for this lack of detail is that PET and fMRI have a low temporal resolution that only allow visualisation of averaged neural activity over a certain period of time. The technique of event-related brain potentials (ERPs) may serve to fill in some of the gaps by providing a high-resolution view on the timing of separate brain processes associated with the retrieval of semantic information for concrete words. The purpose of the present study is to investigate the retrieval of visual semantic information of concrete words, and to learn more about the functional mechanisms that may assist in this process.

One main candidate as a mechanism for the activation of visual semantic information from concrete words is visual working memory (Baddeley, 1986; Logie & Baddeley, 1990). Previous neuroimaging experiments with human subjects distinguished between object working memory and spatial working memory (Belger, Puce, Krystal, Gore, Goldman-Rakic, & McCarthy, 1998; Courtney, Petit, Haxby, & Ungerleider, 1998; Owen, Milner, Petrides, & Evans, 1996; Smith & Jonides, 1997), showing a left hemisphere dominance for object working memory with emphasis on the ventro-lateral frontal cortex and inferior occipito-temporal lobe. Although neuroimaging research on working memory is still very much in progress, these results have typically been interpreted to reflect a cortical network for the retention of object shape, with specialisation for object recognition in inferior temporal regions (Ungerleider & Mishkin, 1982) extending into ventro-lateral frontal cortex, which serves to maintain an active representation of the object after the stimulus has been removed from view (Ungerleider, Courtney, & Haxby, 1998) (see also Courtney et al., 1998; D'Esposito, Postle, & Lease, 1999). Consistent with these findings, electrophysiological studies using event-related brain potential measurements showed that retention of visual objects in working memory is associated with a sustained negative slow wave over visual occipital areas (Ruchkin, Canoune, Johnson, & Ritters, 1995; Ruchkin, Grafman, Krauss, Johnson, Canoune, & Ritters, 1994; Ruchkin, Johnson, Grafman, Canoune, & Ritters, 1992; Ruchkin, Johnson, Grafman, Canoune, & Ritters, 1997; Uhl, Goldenberg, Lang, Lindinger, Steiner, & Deeck 1990) accompanied by a positive slow wave over frontal areas (Berti, Geissler, Lachmann, & Mecklinger, 2000; Klaver, 1999; Nielsen-Bohlman & Knight, 1999; see also Mecklinger & Muller, 1996; Löw, Rockstroh, Hauk, Berg, & Maier, 1999, for slow wave effects of object retention with a different placement of the reference electrode).[2] Similar results have been obtained in experiments where there is no external visual stimulus to be remembered, but which require internal visualization, as is the case with mental imagery. Here too, the evidence seems to point towards the importance of the left inferior occipito-temporal lobe (review in Farah, 1995). Consistent with these results is a large literature which suggests that the left inferior frontal and left ventral occipito-temporal areas are important for semantic memory concerning the visual properties concrete objects (Breedin et al., 1994; Damasio et al., 1996; Martin & Chao, 2001; Wiggs, Weisberg, & Martin, 1999).[3] The overall picture that emerges from these findings is that there is a cortical network specialised for object representation that is involved in object working memory, mental imagery, and visual semantics for concrete objects.

In the current study we will investigate the cognitive mechanisms that are involved in the activation of visual semantic information from concrete words. It is hypothesised that concrete words will activate their visual representation via the cortical network for object working memory. This hypothesis is investigated by presenting concrete (imageable) words and abstract (nonimageable) words in various conditions that differ in the amount of load that is put on the object working memory system. When words are presented in conditions where object working memory load is high, difficulty in the activation of concrete visual representations is expected, as compared to words presented in conditions where there is no load on object working memory.

Important groundbreaking work on the concreteness effect, using ERPs, was performed by Holcomb and colleagues (Holcomb, Kounios, Anderson, & West, 1999; Kounios & Holcomb, 1994; West & Holcomb, 2000), who conducted a number of studies to investigate processing differences between concrete and abstract words. Kounios and Holcomb (1994) observed that concrete words generated a larger N400 amplitude over frontal areas than abstract words. The N400 effect was larger over the right hemisphere than over the left hemisphere, which was taken to be consistent with the dual coding theory, which predicts imagistic processing to concrete words in the right hemisphere. However, the frontal distribution of the concreteness effect was difficult to reconcile with the proposed locus of mental imagery in the left occipito-temporal lobe (e.g., D'Esposito et al., 1997). In a later publication by West and Holcomb (2000), this led to an attempt to separate concreteness effects from imageability. While replicating the N400 effect of concreteness, imageability was found to be accommodated by a later posterior negativity that was larger over the left hemisphere.[4] This second effect is consistent

[2] Note that Berti, Geissler, Lachmann, and Mecklinger (2000) interpreted the effect over the frontal lobe as a negative slow wave to less complex patterns, instead of a positive slow wave to more complex patterns.

[3] Notice that these results are inconsistent with the dual coding theory (Paivio, 1991), which proposes that imagistic processes are lateralised to the right hemisphere.

[4] Note that this effect was marginal, and was only observed when abstract imageable words were compared with abstract nonimageable words.

with ERP correlates of object working memory and mental imagery, and is much closer to what one would expect for the visualisations to concrete words.

In the present study we aim to obtain a clearer perspective on the functional significance of the different ERP effects that have been reported in the previous studies. The main innovation made in the present design is that we compare directly the effects of concreteness to the effects of object working memory, and investigate the interference between these two cognitive processes. Based on previous results by West and Holcomb (2000), and ERP studies directed at object working memory (e.g., Klaver, 1999), we predict that, following the effect on the N400, concrete words will activate their visual representation via object working memory, resulting in slow wave effects over frontal and posterior visual areas. In order to reliably find these effects, we will record and analyse ERPs over a longer time interval (Holcomb et al., 1999, restricted analysis to 1200 ms after word onset), consistent with ERP studies of object working memory and mental imagery that found slow wave effects to extend over several seconds (Farah, Peronnet, Weisberg, & Monheit, 1989; Mecklinger & Pfeifer, 1996; Ruchkin et al., 1997). Furthermore, we predict that visualisation to concrete words will be inhibited by the concurrent load of the object working memory conditions, resulting in a reduction of slow wave effects to concrete words over frontal and occipital areas.

METHOD

Participants

A total of 21 participants (10 male, 11 female) took part in the experiment. Most were students of the University of Groningen. The average age of participants was 22 years (*SD* = 3.17). All were native speakers of the Dutch language, were right-handed, healthy, and had normal or corrected-to-normal vision.[5] Participants were paid a standard experimental fee (7 euros per hour) for participation.

Stimuli and materials

Polygons

Object working memory load was manipulated by creating polygons (Attneave & Arnoult, 1956) with two levels of complexity: simple 4-angled polygons, and more complex 10-angled polygons, which had to be retained in memory for a delayed matching to sample task. Four-angled polygons were created in a two-axis coordinate system (see Figure 1, left), with one axis running from the upper left to the lower right, and the other axis running from the lower left to the upper right, orthogonal to the first. The centre of the polygon was defined by the intersection of the two axes. For each direction of the coordinate system (upper left, upper right, lower left, and lower right), a random number was chosen that defined the distance of an angular point to the polygon's centre. The maximum distance between an angular point and the centre of the polygon was set at 100 pixels. The minimal distance was chosen at 4 pixels. Polygons were realised by a line-drawing algorithm that connected the four resulting angular points with one another.

In order to be included as a stimulus in the experiment, each polygon had to fulfil a number of requirements. To restrict inter-polygon variability, each polygon's surface was kept between 500 and 1500 pixels. In addition, each of the polygon's angles was selected to be between 45–135 degrees, to ensure that every angle was clearly visible to the participants. This resulted in 600 different 4-angled polygons.

Ten-angled polygons were created within a five-axis coordinate system to afford polygons with 10 angular points (see Figure 1, right). The procedure was similar to that of the 4-angled polygons. For each individual angular point of a polygon, a random distance between 4 and 100 pixels was chosen, which defined the outline of the polygon.

[5] Handedness was assessed informally through verbal enquiry.

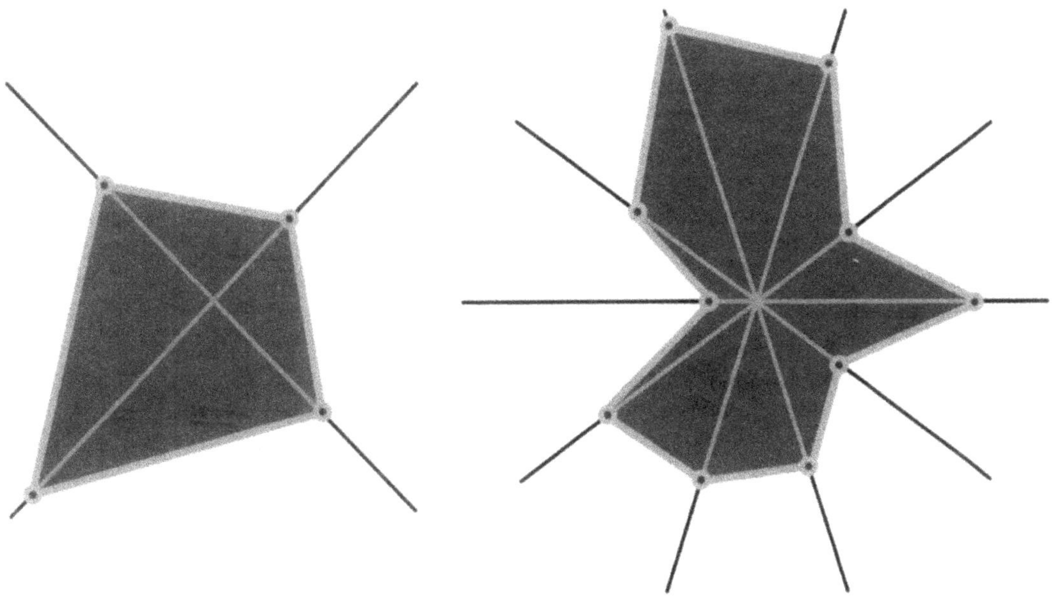

Figure 1. *Example of stimuli used for the object working memory task. Depicted on the left side is a simple polygon with 4 angles, and on the right side is a complex polygon with 10 angles. Both the axes and the circles that define the vertexes of the polygons were not displayed in the experiment.*

Ten-angled polygons had to meet the same requirements as the 4-angled polygons. In order to ensure accurate comparison between both types of polygons, 10-angled polygons were equated in size with 4-angled polygons. For each of the 600 simple polygons that had already been created, a 10-angled polygon was generated with the same size.

The maximum distance from the centre of a polygon to its outline was 100 pixels. This corresponds to a maximum of 6.06 visual degrees on a 17-inch screen with a resolution of 640 by 480 pixels at a viewing distance of 50 cm. For each polygon we calculated the exact centre of gravity and presented it on the fixation point. Polygons to be memorised (memory objects) were presented with a dark grey surface and a green outline, displayed on black background. Polygons that were used to test participants' memory for objects (test objects) were displayed with a dark grey surface and a light grey outline. The different colours of the memory and test objects were used to emphasise the difference between the two objects.

Words

Concrete and abstract words were selected from a list generated by Van Loon-Vervoorn (1985), which contains 4600 Dutch nouns, 1000 verbs, and 500 adjectives that were all tested on their imageability. Three hundred abstract nouns were selected from the list that had an imageability rating of 3.3 or lower on a 7-point scale. Similarly, 300 concrete nouns were selected with an imageability rating of 6.6 or higher. In order to constrain word length variability, only one- or two-syllable words were used. Abstract and concrete words were matched on number of syllables (concrete words: 1.61, abstract words: 1.74), number of phonemes (concrete words: 5.01, abstract words: 5.11), and on their written frequency (concrete words: 694.4, abstract words: 696.6) in a 42 million word database (Burnage, 1990). In addition, we created a set of 300 pseudowords that were matched with abstract and concrete words for mean number of syllables and word length.

Words and pseudowords were then recorded as wave files (16 bits) with a sample frequency of

44.1 kHz, spoken by a female voice. A profile was made of the amount of noise for recorded words and pseudowords and noise reduction was carried out to minimise differences in noise level across conditions. Recordings were filtered to approximate natural speech. Individual words were selected and saved as separate wave files that were enveloped to ensure smooth onset and offset. A normalisation of amplitude was performed to equate the volume of all wave files. The speed of articulation was then digitally altered to 115% of the original tempo. Resulting average file lengths were 643 ms ($SD = 115$ ms) for concrete words, 683 ms ($SD = 116$ ms) for abstract words, and 662 ms ($SD = 114$ ms) for pseudowords.

Half of all materials (words and polygons) were selected for presentation in the present experiment. The other half was presented in a second experiment in which subjects made concrete–abstract decisions to words instead of a lexical decision (not reported here). Across participants all materials were balanced over the two experiments.

Procedure

Participants were seated in a dimly lit, sound attenuated, and electrically shielded cabin facing a computer screen at a distance of 50 cm, with their head in a chin-rest. Chair and chin-rest were adjusted to fit individual demands. The index fingers of the participant's right and left hands rested on two touch-sensitive response boxes, which recorded a response when one of the fingers was lifted.

The experiment involved a dual task paradigm in which participants were required to remember a visually presented polygon for a short period of time (5 s delayed match to sample). During object retention, a second task was administered in which a spoken word that required lexical decision was presented to participants (see below).

The object working memory task involved two objects, a memory object (a dark grey polygon with a green outline) and test object (a second polygon with a light grey outline), that were presented on a computer screen (see Figure 2). The participant was instructed to retain the shape of the memory object in short-term memory, and compare it with the test object. Participants responded to both matching and nonmatching test objects, using either a left or a right hand response (response hands were balanced across participants). For the object working memory task three levels of difficulty, or load, were used. In the load 1 condition, participants were presented with relatively simple 4-angled polygons that had to be maintained in short-term memory. The load 2 condition involved the retention of the more complex 10-angled polygons. In addition to the load 1 and load 2 conditions, a third condition was administered (load 0), which involved visual presentation of 4-angled and 10-angled polygons, but participants were instructed not to carry out the object working memory task. The load 0 condition served as a control or baseline condition with which to compare effects of object working memory in the load 1 and load 2 conditions.

During the polygon retention interval, intermediate between the memory object and the test object, participants performed a second task that involved the presentation of a word via headphones.

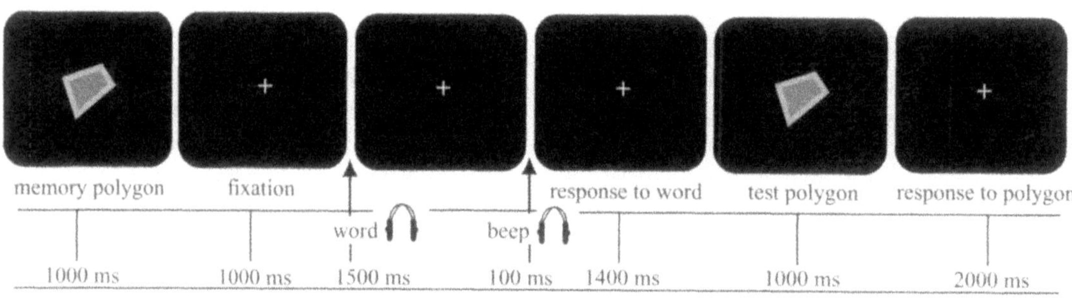

Figure 2. *Example of a possible trial, showing the presentation of consecutive visual and auditory frames.*

For each word that was presented, subjects indicated whether the word was a real existing word (lexically valid), or whether a pseudoword had been presented (lexically invalid), by responding either with their left or right hand (response hands were balanced across participants). Four different word conditions were presented with equal probability (25% each): (1) abstract words, (2) concrete words, (3) pseudowords, and (4) no word. The no-word condition was included to enable a clean view on the single task effect of object working memory, without interruption from auditory presented words.

Timing of stimuli was identical in all trials (see Figure 2). First a memory object was presented for 1000 ms, followed by a single fixation point that remained on screen for 4000 ms; 1000 ms after offset of the memory object (during the fixation interval), a word could be presented via the headphones (average word length = 663 ms). In some cases no word was presented. Then, 1500 ms after onset of the word, a 100 ms beep was presented, after which participants were allowed to respond to the word. The delayed response to words was included because differences in reaction times to concrete and abstract words may cause differences in the ERPs to both word-types that may be confounded with the early ERP effects to abstract and concrete words. The length of the response interval following the beep was 1400 ms. Subsequent to the word response interval, a test object was presented that was identical to the memory polygon in half of the trials. In other cases, one of the polygon's angular points had been moved along the trajectory of one of the axes, either 50 pixels away, or 50 pixels towards the origin of the object.

The load 0, load 1, and load 2 conditions were presented as blocks, and block order was balanced over participants. Each block was presented in four consecutive experimental runs of 50 trials each, taking about 6 minutes and 40 seconds per run. Participants rested between runs. Before participants began with the actual experiment they were allowed to practice until both the experimenter and the participant felt that the task was performed in a confident manner (with practice conditions similar to the first block of the experiment). With every change in block, e.g., changing from 4-angled polygons to 10-angled polygons, participants performed one practice run to familiarise themselves with the new stimulus properties or task instructions.

Data recording and analysis

Behavioural recordings and analysis

Each trial involved two response intervals; one to record behaviour to words, and one to measure participants' performance to polygon matching. Subjects' manual behaviour was continuously sampled at 1000 Hz, and analysed off-line. Responses to both types of stimuli were analysed separately, with tests for significance (MANOVA repeated measurements) for reaction times, and errors (wrong response). Main analysis of behaviour to abstract and concrete words included two within-subject factors: word-type (abstract versus concrete words), and load (load 0, load 1, and load 2). Main analysis of responses to polygons involved word-type (abstract, concrete, and no-word conditions), and load (load 1 versus load 2) as within-subject factors.

EEG recordings and analysis

The electroencephalogram (EEG) was recorded with 37 Sn-electrodes placed in an electrocap (Electro-Cap International) at positions Fp1, Fp2, Fz, F3, F4, F7, F8, FC3, FC4, FC7, FC8, Cz, C3, C4, T7, T8, TP7, TP8, Pz, P3, P4, P7, P8, P9, P10, POz, PO3, PO4, PO7, PO8, PO9, PO10, Oz, O1, O2, O9, and O10 according to the revised 10–20 system as presented by Pivik, Broughton, Coppola, Davidson, Fox, and Nuwer (1993). Electrodes were referred to the left and right (electronically averaged) mastoids. Horizontal EOG was recorded via two Sn-electrodes positioned lateral to the outer canti of the left and the right eye. Vertical EOG was recorded with two Sn-electrodes placed above and below the left eye, one on the cheekbone and one above the eyebrow. The ground electrode was on the sternum. Electrode resistance was kept below 2K-Ohm. EEG and EOG signals were amplified (EEG: 0.2 mV/V; EOG: 0.5 mV/V; time constant: 10 s), sampled at 1000 Hz, digitally lowpass filtered with a cutoff frequency of 30 Hz and reduced to a sample frequency of 100 Hz on-line.

Trials with artefacts (amplifier or subject induced artefacts), and trials with incorrect responses were rejected from further analysis.[6] The eye movement correction procedure of Gratton, Coles, and Donchin (1983) was used to correct EEG for blinks and small saccades. Separate ERPs were calculated, synchronised to the onset of memory polygons and to the onset of words. In both cases, individual trials were aligned using a 100 ms pre-stimulus baseline interval. Separate averages per stimulus category (see below) were calculated for each individual participant. ERPs to memory objects included most of the trial, running from 100 ms before onset of the memory object until 100 ms before offset of the test object, including a 6 s interval. ERPs to words covered 4 s, running from 100 ms before word onset until 100 ms before offset of the memory object.

For both the analysis of polygons and words, ERPs were pooled over conditions with matching and nonmatching test polygons. For the load 0 condition, ERPs were pooled for 10-angled polygons and 4-angled polygons. The analysis of ERPs to the object working memory task was restricted to conditions in which no word was presented, resulting in three stimulus categories for the three different levels of object load (load 0, load 1, and load 2). The analysis of ERPs to words excluded conditions with pseudowords, and conditions in which no word was presented, resulting in total of six stimulus categories, based on the combinations of object working memory load (load 0, load 1, and load 2), and word-type (abstract, concrete) that were included for statistical testing.

Averaged ERPs to memory polygons and words were divided into intervals of 50 ms that were exported and tested for significance using MANOVA repeated measurements analysis. Separate analyses were performed for midline electrodes (Fz, Cz, Pz, POz, and Oz), frontal electrodes (Fp1, Fp2, F3, F4, F7, and F8), central electrodes (FC3, FC4, FT7, FT8, C3, C4, T7, T8, TP7, and TP8), posterior electrodes (P3, P4, P7, P8, PO3, PO4, PO7, PO8, O1, and O2), and cerebellar electrodes (P9, P10, PO9, PO10, O9, and O10). To correct for chance capitalisation (that is, correcting for the number of tests of significance being performed) only three consecutive significant intervals ($\alpha < .05$) of 50 ms were accepted as truly significant. For both the analysis of ERPs to polygons and ERPs to words, within-subject factors were: load (load 0, load 1, and load 2), hemisphere (left versus right) and electrode. The analysis of word ERPs additionally included word-type (concrete versus abstract words) as a within-subject factor.

RESULTS

Behaviour

Behaviour to words

Table 1 shows the average response times and percentage of errors for lexical decisions to abstract words, concrete words, and pseudowords presented under different object load conditions.

Although participants had to withhold their responses to words until the presentation of a beep, this did not take away behavioural differences between abstract and concrete words. Participants'

Table 1. *Mean response times in ms (SD in brackets), and percentage of errors to abstract words, concrete words, and pseudowords presented under different object load conditions*

	Load 0	*Load 1*	*Load 2*
Response times			
Abstract words	447 (176)	403 (139)	397 (119)
Concrete words	416 (197)	377 (151)	383 (124)
Pseudowords	470 (200)	416 (137)	427 (133)
Errors			
Abstract words	4.29	6.48	7.13
Concrete words	1.33	1.05	1.05
Pseudowords	3.04	2.95	2.95

[6] Artefacts were detected in 9.2% of all trials.

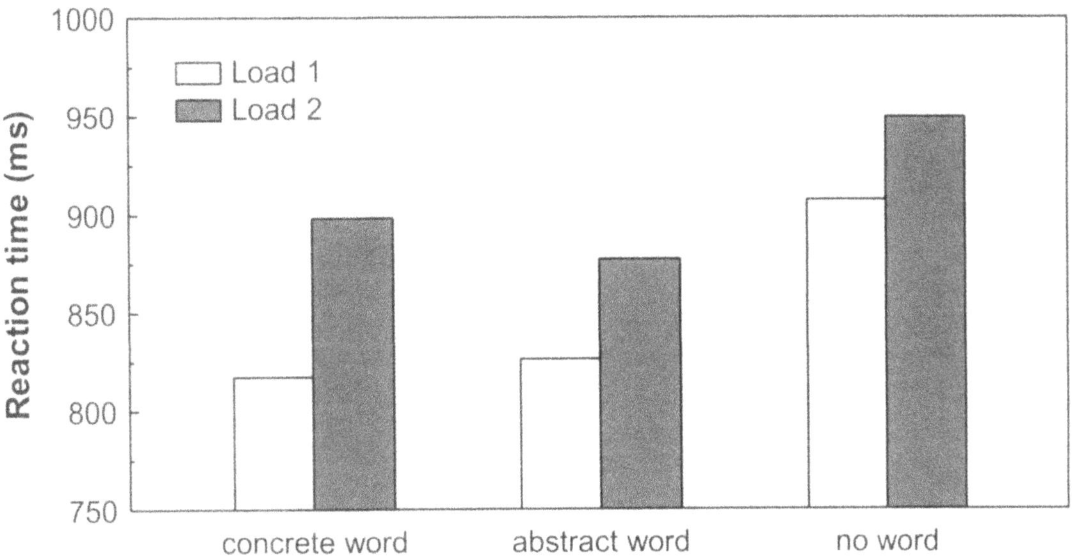

Figure 3. *Reaction times to polygon matching for simple polygons (load 1) and complex polygons (load 2), separate for conditions with concrete words, abstract words, and no words intervening the memory interval.*

responses were faster, $F(1, 20) = 12.42$, $p < .002$, and more accurate, $F(1, 20) = 36.82$, $p < .001$, to concrete words (RT = 392 ms; percentage of errors = 1.14%) than to abstract words (RT = 416 ms; percentage of errors = 5.97%). No significant effects of load or interaction between load and word-type was found in the analysis of subjects' responses to the lexical decision task.

Behaviour to polygons

Table 2 shows the average response times and the percentage of errors to different conditions of the polygon matching task.

The analysis of participants' responses to polygons showed a main effect of load reflecting prolonged reaction times, $F(1, 20) = 4.97$, $p < .037$, and more errors, $F(1, 20) = 47.23$, $p < .001$, for the load 2 condition (RT = 909 ms; percentage of errors = 17.71%) than for the load 1 condition (RT = 851 ms; percentage of errors = 9.32%).

Dual task conditions resulted in faster response times and more errors than single task conditions. Trials with intervening words were accompanied by faster responses to polygons (856 ms) than trials in which no word was presented (929 ms), main effect of word-type: $F(2, 19) = 9.87$, $p < .001$. However, trials that included words also generated more errors (error percentages = 14.26%), as compared to trials in which no word was presented (error percentage = 12.05%), suggesting a speed–accuracy tradeoff.

Table 2. *Mean response times in ms (SD in brackets), and percentage of errors for the polygon matching task, under conditions in which subjects made lexical decisions to abstract words, concrete words, and pseudowords, or conditions in which no words were presented*

	Load 1	*Load 2*
Response times		
Abstract words	827 (241)	878 (273)
Concrete words	818 (262)	899 (296)
Pseudowords	888 (249)	933 (266)
No words	908 (250)	950 (266)
Errors		
Abstract words	10.57	18.67
Concrete words	8.86	18.95
Pseudowords	13.71	22.10
No words	8.48	15.62

In addition to the more general effects of word-type on the performance of the object retention task described above, the analysis of reaction times to polygons showed a significant interaction between word-type and load, $F(2, 19) = 5.07$, $p < .017$. Intervening concrete words resulted in a large difference between load 1 and load 2 conditions: 818 ms (load 1) versus 899 ms (load 2); as compared to abstract words: 827 ms (load 1) versus 878 ms (load 2); and conditions in which no words intervened: 908 ms (load 1) versus 950 ms (load 2). See Figure 3 for the reaction times to load 1 and load 2 polygons, intervened by concrete words, abstract words, and conditions without words.

Event-related potentials

The results section on event-related potentials involves two parts. In the first part the ERP effects of object working memory load will be identified. In the second part we will focus on the concreteness effects by looking at the ERP differences between abstract and concrete words, and describe the influence of object working memory load on the processing of concrete words.

ERP effects of object working memory

Figure 4 displays the ERPs recorded to the three different object working memory load conditions in which no words were presented. The figure depicts the entire 6 s trial interval, showing ERP components evoked by presentation of memory objects (onset at 0 s), and test objects (onset at 5 s).

Manipulations of object working memory load were found to result in a clear pattern of slow wave effects over frontal, occipital, and parietal areas. Over frontal areas, object working memory load was found to be accompanied by a positive slow wave that showed increased amplitude with increasing load. Over occipital areas the opposite pattern was found: a negative slow wave that increased in amplitude with increasing object load. Parietal areas showed a sustained positivity in object working memory load conditions (load 1 and load 2) as compared to the load 0 condition where no memory of polygons was required. Figure 5 (left) shows the distribution of the effects over frontal, occipital, and parietal areas in the 1300–1500 ms interval following onset of the memory object.

Frontal effects of object working memory. Over frontal areas, larger object working memory load was found to be accompanied by a positive slow wave that showed increased amplitude with increasing load. In comparison with the no-load condition, both the load 1 and load 2 conditions generated a positive slow wave, strongest over ventro-lateral parts of the frontal cortex (electrodes F7 and F8 in Figure 4). Frontal effects of object working memory are reflected by a main effect of load that was significant from 150–2000 ms following onset of the memory object, $F(2, 19) = 29.78$, $p < .001$. Pairwise comparisons between the two load conditions (load 1 and load 2) and the no-load condition showed effects of object working memory to continue until 3200 ms (load by electrode interaction), $F(2, 19) = 8.26, p < .003$. The difference between load 1 and load 2 conditions was found to be distributed more broadly over the frontal lobe (main effect of load, 450–1400 ms), $F(1, 19) = 12.10$, $p < .002$, with a maximum centred over the Fz electrode (see Figure 5).

During the final part of the retention interval, slow wave effects to the load 1 and load 2 conditions were accompanied by a CNV component (contingent negative variation) over fronto-central electrodes, reflecting anticipation to the upcoming test stimulus. This effect is best seen at the Fz electrode in Figure 4. Following the onset of the test polygon, both the load 1 and load 2 conditions generated a large P3 component over parietal areas. Parallel to the selective P3 for the load 1 and load 2 conditions, a frontal slow wave difference between load 1 and load 2 emerged that was similar to the slow wave difference found in the retention interval (see the Fz electrode in Figure 4). Pairwise comparisons between load 1 and 2 showed the frontal effect of load to be significant from 5500–6000 ms (midline: load by electrode interaction), $F(4, 17) = 5.72, p < .004$.

Occipital effects of object working memory. Over occipital areas, object working memory was found to be reflected in a sustained negative slow wave

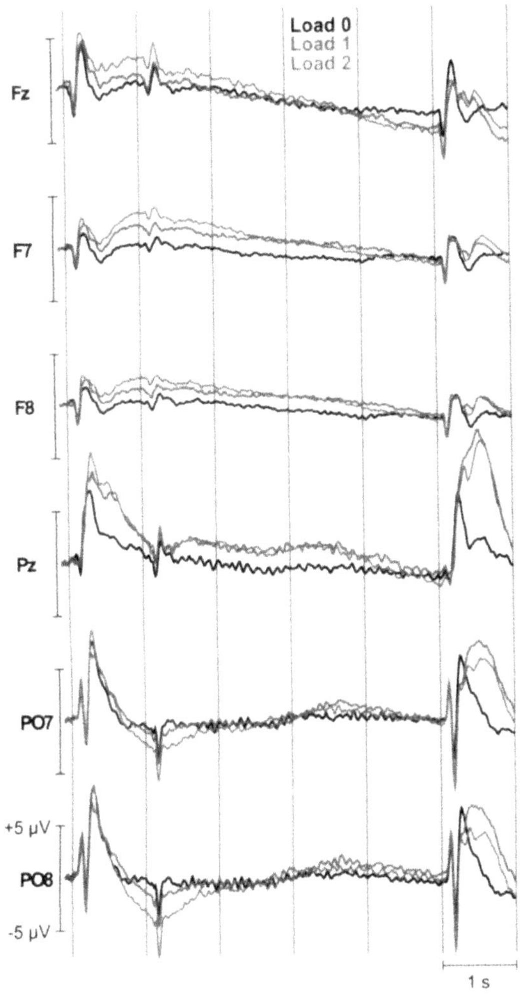

Figure 4. *ERPs aligned to memory objects, showing the 6 s trial interval from 100 ms before onset of the memory polygon until 100 ms before offset of the test polygon, for trials in which no words were presented. Red lines indicate ERPs for the condition in which subjects remembered simple 4-angled polygons (load 1), and green lines indicate ERPs for the condition in which subjects remembered complex 10-angled polygons (load 2). Black lines indicate ERPs for the condition in which objects did not have to be remembered (load 0).*

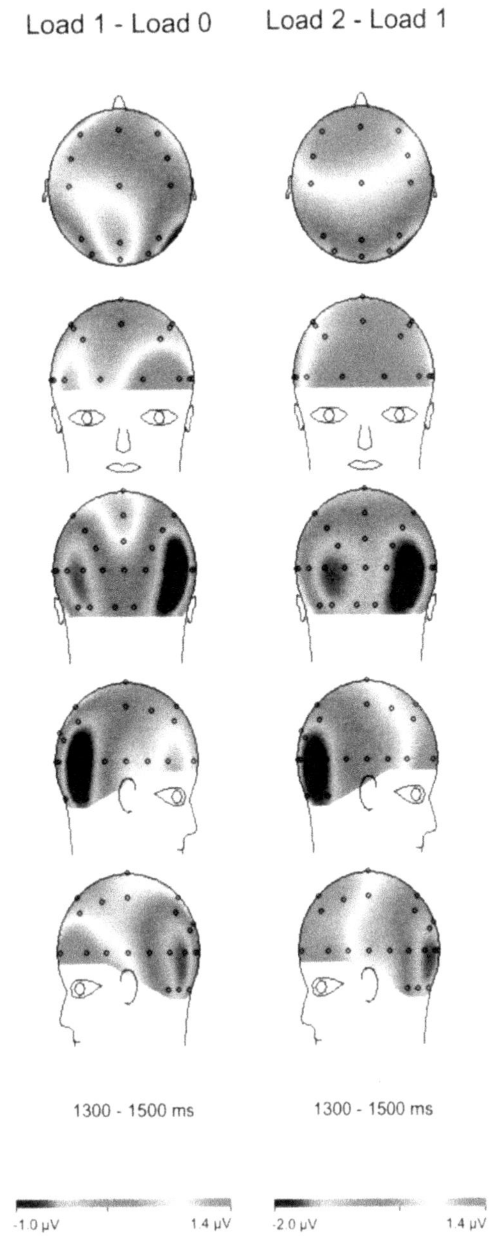

Figure 5. *Topographic maps showing the distribution of the effects of object working memory from 1300–1500 ms following onset of the memory polygon. The left panel shows the topographic distribution of the ERP difference between load 1 (retain 4-angled polygon) and load 0 (no retention) object working memory conditions. The right panel shows the difference between retaining the more complex 10-angled polygons (load 2), and the less complex 4-angled polygons (load 1).*

that increased in amplitude with increasing object load. The negative slow wave started to develop in the latency of the P3 evoked by the memory object, reaching a maximum negative difference at around 1200 ms, $F(8, 13) = 29.63, p < .001$ (load by electrode interaction); see electrodes PO7 and PO8 of Figure 4. In addition, the main analysis of posterior electrodes, which included both occipital and parieto-occipital electrodes,[7] showed an interaction between load and hemisphere (1100–1250 ms), $F(2, 19) = 4.36, p < .028$, reflecting the presence of a larger slow wave negative difference over the right occipital lobe than over the left (compare PO7 with PO8 in Figure 4). After reaching its maximum shortly after the offset of the memory polygon, the occipital slow wave negativity gradually decreased over the following 1 s period (see Figure 4). A small occipital difference between load 1 and load 2 conditions, however, persisted throughout the retention interval (load by electrode, significant from 300–1650 ms, 2800–2950 ms, and 3550–3700 ms), $F(4, 17) = 19.37, p < .001$.

Similar to effects observed over frontal electrodes, presentation of the test object resulted in the re-emergence of a slow wave negative difference over posterior occipital electrodes. The pairwise comparison of load 1 and load 2 conditions showed a significant interaction between load and electrode in the 5350–6000 ms interval, $F(4, 17) = 7.20, p < .001$.

Parietal effects of object working memory. Over central parietal areas (see Figure 4, electrode Pz) a sustained positive slow wave was observed for the load 1 and load 2 conditions, as opposed to the load 0 condition. Whether we can classify this effect as a genuine effect of object working memory is questionable since there is no parietal difference between load 1 and load 2 conditions during the retention interval. Rather than signalling the amount of short-term memory load within object working memory, the effect seems to correlate with the presence of a task, as opposed to the load 0 conditions where there is no working memory task associated with polygons.

ERP effects of concreteness

Figure 6 displays the ERPs to abstract and concrete words. The figure depicts a 4 s period from word onset until the end of the trial, showing ERP components evoked by presentation of auditory words (onset at 0 s), beep (onset at 1.5 s), and test objects (onset at 3 s).

ERPs to concrete words were found to be clearly different from ERPs to abstract words, resulting in a number of subsequent effects over different cortical areas. Early effects of concreteness resulted in an enhanced N400 amplitude over mid-frontal regions, together with a posterior positivity overlying left cerebellar electrodes. Subsequent to these early effects, ERPs to concrete words were found to generate a left frontal positive slow wave and a prolonged negative slow wave over visual areas, as compared to abstract words. These latter effect are comparable with the effects of object working memory described above. The left frontal effect of concreteness was found to be reduced under conditions of object load.

N400 and posterior positivity. The earliest difference between concrete and abstract words was found on the N400. Concrete words generated a stronger N400 effect over anterior electrodes. The N400 effect is distinctly visible at the Fz electrode in Figure 6, and lasted from about 950 ms until 1600 ms post word onset. Notice that with auditory word presentation, as compared to visually presented words, the relative timing of ERP components with respect to stimulus onset is delayed, as auditory words cannot be presented at a single moment. Whereas with visually presented words, the N400 effect reaches its maximum at around 400 ms after word onset, the N400 effect to auditory words in the present experiment was found to peak at 900 ms after word onset. Notice, however, that the latency of the N400 component with respect to the auditory N1 component is within the normal range (the N400 reaches its maximum some 400 ms after the peak of the auditory N1).

[7] In the subsequent text we will refer to these as posterior or occipital sites.

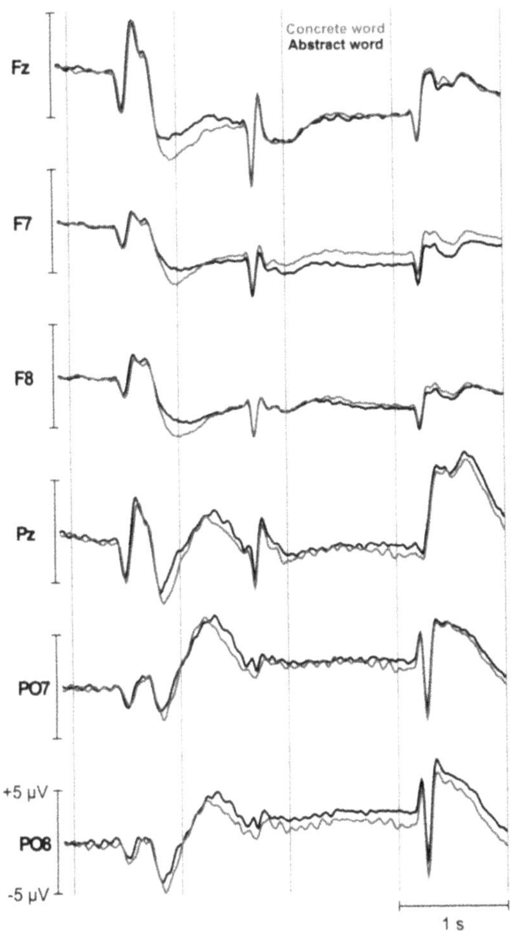

Figure 6. *ERPs to words over a 4 s interval, from 100 ms before word onset until 100 ms before offset of the test object. Red lines indicate ERPs to concrete words, and black lines indicate ERPs to abstract words.*

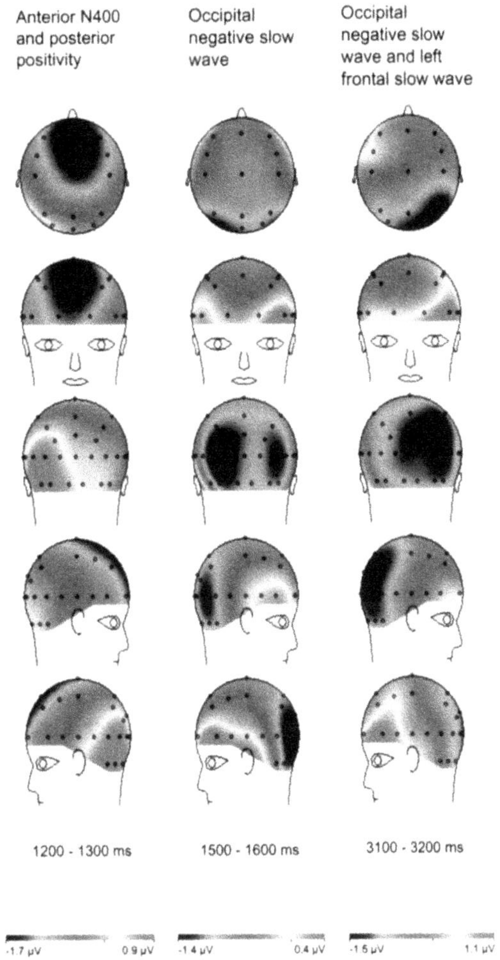

Figure 7. *Topographic maps showing the distribution of concreteness at different latencies following word presentation, from 1200–1300 ms (left), 1500–1600 ms (middle), and 3100–3200 ms (right). The left panel shows the topographic distribution of the anterior N400 that was found to be larger for concrete words, as opposed to abstract words. The same panel shows the distribution of a posterior positivity that was found in parallel to the anterior N400 effect. The middle panel shows the bilateral distribution of the occipital negative slow wave that was found as a difference between concrete words and abstract words. An additional (small) effect is seen bilaterally over the frontal lobes. The third panel shows the distribution of (right lateralised) occipital and (left lateralised) frontal slow wave effects of concreteness at a subsequent time.*

The larger N400 to concrete words over frontal areas was significant. The analysis of word ERPs over frontal areas showed a main effect of word-type in the 950–1350 ms interval, $F(1, 20) = 71.47, p < .001$, along with an interaction between word-type and electrode in the 1050–1700 ms interval, $F(2, 19) = 25.68, p < .001$. The topographic distribution of the N400 effect to concrete words is presented in Figure 7 (left panel).

Parallel to the N400 effect, a positivity was noted over the left posterior cortex. Concrete words generated a positive wave as compared to abstract words. The effect was significant in the analysis of cerebellar electrodes in the 1050–1300 ms post-word interval (word-type by hemisphere interaction), $F(1, 20) = 15.44, p < .001$. See Figure 7 for the distribution of the posterior positivity.

Clearly, it is not the case that the posterior positivity and the anterior N400 effect are a manifestation of the same cortical source. The duration of the N400 effect is much longer than the posterior effect. Furthermore, we find that the posterior slow wave effect is lateralised to the left hemisphere, while there is no lateralisation for the anterior effect on the N400.

Neither the N400 effect to concrete words, nor the posterior positivity effect to concrete words, were found to be influenced by the object working memory task. Main analysis of word ERPs over frontal electrodes showed no significant interactions between word-type and load in the interval of the N400, and no significant interactions between load and word-type were found in the analysis of cerebellar electrodes in the interval of the posterior positivity.

Frontal and occipital slow wave effects of concreteness. Subsequent to the early effects of concreteness (N400 and posterior positivity), concrete words were found to generate slow wave effects over frontal and occipital areas. The frontal effect of concreteness was found maximally over the left inferior frontal cortex, where concrete words generated a positive slow wave as compared to abstract words. The effect can be observed in Figure 6 (electrode F7). The left frontal slow wave set in shortly after the N400 effect, and lasted throughout most of the ERP interval. In the main analysis of frontal electrodes the left frontal effect is reflected by a word-type by hemisphere interaction from 1900–4000 ms, $F(1, 20) = 19.35, p < .001$, and a word-type by electrode by hemisphere interaction from 1700–1900 ms, $F(2, 19) = 4.43, p < .026$. Figure 7 (right panel) shows the distribution of the slow wave effect over the left frontal hemisphere.

Over occipital electrodes, concrete words were found to generate a robust slow wave negative difference, as compared to abstract words (see Figure 6, electrodes PO7 and PO8). The effect set in at around 1300 ms, some 400 ms after the peak of the N400. After an initial bilateral distribution over the left and right occipital hemispheres, the slow wave negativity dominated over the right occipital lobe. See Figure 7 for the distribution of the occipital slow wave negativity to concrete words in the early stages of the slow wave (middle panel), and the distribution of the effect at a later time (right panel). Statistically, the occipital slow wave negativity is reflected in the analysis of posterior electrodes, which showed a main effect of word-type significant from 1400–1600 ms and 3050–3300 ms, $F(1, 20) = 12.19, p < .002$. The lateralisation to the right hemisphere is reflected by the interaction between word-type and hemisphere, which was found significant in the 3350–3550 ms post-word interval, $F(1, 20) = 8.52, p < .008$.

The occipital slow wave effect to concrete words was not found to be influenced by the object working memory task. No significant interactions were found between word-type and load, in the interval of the occipital slow wave over posterior electrodes.

Importantly, the concreteness effect over the left frontal hemisphere was found to be modulated by object working memory load. As is reflected in Figure 8, the size of the slow wave effect to concrete words is significantly reduced in conditions that required object retention in working memory. The reduction was found maximally over the FT7 electrode, just posterior to the F7 electrode overlying the left inferior prefrontal cortex. Statistically, the suppression of the concreteness effect over the FT7 electrode is reflected in the main analysis of central electrodes, which showed an interaction between

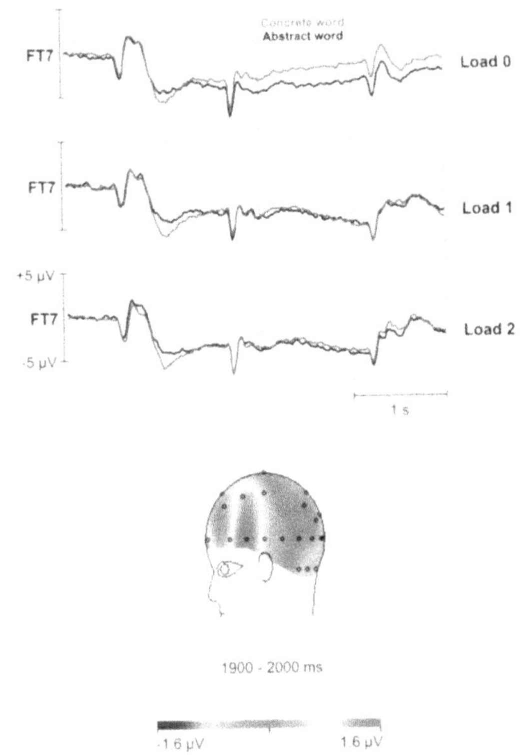

Figure 8. *(Top) ERPs to words, recorded at the FT7 electrode, under conditions of different object working memory load. Red lines indicate ERPs to concrete words, and black lines indicate ERPs to abstract words. Top, middle, and bottom graphs show ERPs recorded in load 0, load 1, and load 2 conditions respectively. (Bottom) Topographic map showing the difference between the left frontal slow wave effect of concreteness recorded in the load 0 condition, as compared to the reduced frontal effect of concreteness observed in the load 1 and load 2 conditions, from 1900–2000 ms following word onset.*

word-type, load, electrode, and hemisphere (from 1700–2050 ms), $F(8, 13) = 9.45, p < .001$. Figure 8 displays the topographic distribution of the left frontal slow wave effect in the load 0 condition, as compared to the effect in the load 2 condition.

DISCUSSION

This study investigated the neural mechanisms that are involved in the activation of visual semantic information to concrete words. It was hypothesised that concrete words activate their visual representation via the cortical network for object working memory.

Both behavioural and electrophysiological measures were found to be consistent with the above hypothesis. Concrete words were found to generate a series of ERP components which reflect the timing of specific neurophysiological mechanisms that are involved in the activation of visual semantic information to concrete words.

Behaviour

On the behavioural level, responses to words and polygons were found to display the expected effects of concreteness and object working memory. Participants' responses to polygons showed the expected effects of object working memory load, with prolonged reaction times and more errors to the visually complex polygons (load 2 condition), than to the more simple polygons (load 1 condition). Behavioural results to the language task were also consistent with our expectation. Lexical decision responses to concrete words were faster and more accurate than responses to abstract words.

Subjects' behaviour to words was found to be unaffected by the dual task requirement to retain polygons in working memory. On the contrary, materials presented for lexical decision did affect subjects' performance in the working memory task. A specific interaction was observed between the type of intervening word and the working memory requirements. Load effects were found to be more pronounced for trials with intervening concrete words, as compared to trials with intervening abstract words (Figure 3). This result is consistent with the hypothesis that processing of visual semantic information to concrete words is functionally overlapping with cognitive mechanisms for object working memory.

ERPs

ERP effects of object working memory

ERP effects accompanying object working memory were found to display slow wave potentials over frontal, occipital, and parietal areas. Both object load conditions involving the retention of simple and complex polygons generated a slow wave positivity over bilateral inferior frontal areas (electrodes F7 and F8), as compared to the load 0 condition where no memory for polygon shape was required. Retention of more complex polygons resulted in a pronounced slow wave with a broad medial frontal distribution (around Fz) as compared to the retention of simple polygons. Shortly after onset of the frontal slow wave, a bilateral occipital negative slow wave was observed that was found to grow in amplitude with increasing object load. Although distributed bilaterally, the effect was found to be stronger over the right occipital lobe than over the left. At parietal sites object retention was accompanied by a positive slow wave (centred around the Pz electrode), as compared to conditions where no object retention was required. The slow wave effect over the parietal cortex was of similar size in the load 1 and load 2 conditions.

The ERP effects of object working memory over frontal and occipital areas observed in the present study are consistent with previous ERP studies (e.g., Klaver, 1999) and neuroimaging results (e.g., Smith & Jonides, 1997), which suggest the existence of a cortical network for object memory in ventro-lateral parts of the prefrontal cortex and inferior occipito-temporal lobe. It is important to note that the frontal and occipital effects of object working memory cannot be explained by a single source of neural activation (there are clear differences in timing, amplitude, and lateralisation between both effects), but appear to reflect the separate activation of prefrontal and visual areas for object working memory. Interestingly, the activation over frontal areas appears to be preserved over a longer period of time, as compared to the occipital activation. This suggests that object information may be retained more efficiently in prefrontal areas of the brain after the object has been removed from view.

Whereas both the frontal and occipital slow wave effects of object working memory have been reported frequently, the parietal slow wave positivity that was found for the retention of both simple and complex polygons has not been reported before. Both the lack of earlier studies reporting this effect, and the fact that the amplitude of the parietal slow wave was unaffected by the amount of object load, suggest that the parietal slow wave is not a direct correlate of the amount of information that has to be retained in object working memory. Rather, the parietal slow wave may be associated with the control of visual information in working memory. This interpretation is consistent with suggestions that parietal areas assist in visual imagery (Kosslyn, 1994) and are important for the control of visual attention (Smith & Jonides, 1997).

ERP effects of concreteness

ERP correlates of concreteness were found to be reflected in a number of slow wave effects over different cortical areas. The earliest ERP effect of concreteness was found on the amplitude of the N400 over the frontal cortex (950–1600 ms after word onset). Parallel to the anterior N400 effect, a posterior positivity was found, maximal over left cerebellar electrodes (1050–1300 ms). Subsequent to the N400 and posterior positivity, concreteness effects were found in the form of slow wave effects over occipital areas (onset at 1400 ms) and left frontal areas (onset at 1700 ms). Over occipital areas, concrete words generated a prolonged negative slow wave as compared to abstract words, while over the left frontal cortex concrete words generated a positive slow wave.

N400 and posterior positivity. The present results successfully replicated the N400 effect of concreteness over frontal cortical areas as observed by Kounios and Holcomb (1994). However, a difference between the results of the present study and the study by Kounios and Holcomb is that they found the N400 effect to concrete words to be lateralised to the right frontal lobe, while in the present results we found the effect on the N400 to be distributed centrally over the frontal cortex (also see Kellenbach, Wijers, Hovius, Mulder, & Mulder, 2002). As an explanation we note the possibility that the distribution of the N400 effect in the Kounios and Holcomb (1994) study may have shifted to the right anterior cortex due to positive slow wave effects over the left frontal lobe. Although the effect over the left frontal lobe, as observed in the current study, was only significant after the N400 interval had finished, it is possible that the left frontal positivity may have had an earlier onset in the Kounios and Holcomb study, which may as a result have affected the distribution of the N400 negativity to concrete words.

Previous research has shown the existence of an N400-like ERP effect for pictures with a more anterior distribution as compared to the N400 effect to words that is generally found over the posterior parietal lobe (Barrett & Rugg, 1990; Ganis, Kutas, & Sereno, 1996). Although the exact function and cortical origin of the frontal negativity is still under debate (e.g., Schendan, 2002) it seems clear that the effect is involved in the processing of picture- or object-specific information. McPherson and Holcomb (1999) suggested that the anterior N400 may originate from the dorsolateral prefrontal cortex (cf. Kosslyn, Alpert, Thompson, Chabris, Rauch, & Anderson, 1994), which, among other things, may act to look up stored properties of objects that are difficult to identify. A similar suggestion has been made by Schendan (2002), who proposed that "the frontal N350 reflects [. . .] searching for a stored description that matches the perceived image" (p. 943), but they speculated on a neuroanatomical locus in the occipitotemporal and mid-fusiform regions, as these areas have been proposed to hold the structural descriptions of objects (see also Doninger et al., 2000). As discussed above, similar effects have been found for the processing of concrete versus abstract words (e.g., Kounios & Holcomb, 1994), in conditions where no actual picture is being presented. In line with these studies we concur that the anterior negativity may index processes that are specifically associated with high-level analysis and retrieval of visual descriptive information about objects.

One important advance that is made in the current study, as compared to previous studies, is that our results suggest that the anterior N400 to concrete words is not a direct measure of visual processing, but appears to be associated to pre-visual processing (possibly retrieval or encoding of descriptive object information within semantic memory).

Possibly, the left lateralised posterior positivity that was found to concrete words as compared to abstract words, parallel to the N400 effect over anterior areas, is associated with this process. A similar posterior effect, parallel to the anterior N400, was observed by McPherson (McPherson & Holcomb, 1992, 1999), and was hypothesised to be associated with activation within an early visual buffer (in areas 17 and 18), which is believed to be involved in the retention of mental images (Kosslyn et al., 1994). In our view this is unlikely since mental imagery and visual working memory have consistently been associated with negative slow waves over the posterior cortex, and almost never with positive waves. Instead we propose that the posterior positivity over the occipital cortex is functionally related to the N400 effect over the anterior lobe, as both effects are consistently observed together. Possibly the posterior positivity is associated with the retrieval of structural descriptions of objects in the left occipitotemporal lobe (cf. Damasio et al., 1996). The lateralisation of the effect overlying the ventral posterior area of left hemisphere is consistent with this possibility.

Frontal and occipital slow wave effects of concreteness. Although the present study successfully replicated the anterior N400 effect of concreteness and the associated posterior positivity, we do not considered these effects as a direct manifestation of visualisation. Rather, the results of the present study suggest that the activation of object information in the visual system is signalled by (frontal and occipital) slow wave effects that follow on the N400.

Following the anterior N400, and posterior slow wave positivity, ERPs to concrete words were found to generate a slow wave negativity over bilateral occipital cortices, shortly followed by the onset of a slow wave positivity over the left frontal cortex. These effects appear to be consistent with previous reports of object working memory and mental imagery, which have been observed to result in slow wave effects over several seconds (Farah et al., 1989; Mecklinger & Muller, 1996; Ruchkin et al.,

1997). The similarity between the effects of object working memory, as observed in the present study, and the slow wave effects to concreteness, as recorded in the lexical decision task, suggest that concrete words activate their visual representation via the existing network for object memory. Slow wave effects over the left frontal cortex may signal activation of object representations in left ventrolateral prefrontal cortex (Smith & Jonides, 1997). The finding of additional slow wave negativity over bilateral occipital cortices supports a frontal-posterior network for object representation, where the visual representations of concrete words are activated in the ventral occipito-temporal pathway (cf. Ungerleider et al., 1998).

Since concreteness effects were hypothesised to use the same neural system as object working memory, we expected to find interactions between object load and effects of concreteness. Results showed that the requirement to maintain an object in working memory affected the amplitude of the left frontal slow wave to concrete words. This result is important because it is consistent with the hypothesis that object working memory and concreteness effects to words use overlapping neural structures.

Our results, however, did not show a significant influence of object working memory on the visual slow wave negativity to concrete words. A possible explanation for the absence of an interaction is that the main occipital slow wave to the object retention task ended just before the presentation of words (see Figure 4). Frontal effects of the object retention task, on the other hand, largely continued throughout the ERP interval for words. As a consequence, the interactions between object working memory and concreteness may have been confined to the frontal area.

CONCLUSION

The results of the present study provide a processing view on the (timing of) neurophysiological mechanisms involved in the activation of visual semantic information to concrete words. Our data indicate a model of visual semantics in which visual descriptive information to concrete words is first encoded in semantic memory (indexed by the anterior N400, and the left posterior positivity), and is subsequently visualised via the cortical network for object working memory (reflected by a left frontal positive slow wave and bilateral occipital slow wave negativity).

Our ERP results provide an important addition to the data of neuroimaging studies that examine the brain's metabolic activity over several seconds. Although the latter techniques offer a high spatial localisation with respect to the different (sub)areas of the brain that are activated, it is difficult for these techniques to determine the order in which areas were activated. As a consequence, activation in modality-specific areas (e.g., visual) may be interpreted to derive automatically from the activation of a word's phonological code, whereas in reality the modality-specific activation may be delayed and only occurs after semantic processing in some other area. Although the present results are consistent with neuroimaging studies that indicate modality specific activations to concrete words, the exact mechanisms that are hypothesised to underly this activation are different.

Whereas neuroimaging results are typically interpreted to be consistent with the existence of cell-assemblies that associate verbal information to, for example, visual and functional features in modality-specific areas of the brain (e.g., Hauk et al., 2004; Martin, 1998), the current ERP data argue for a different mechanism. ERPs indicate that visual representations to concrete words are not activated directly from a verbal code, but rather through an intermediate process reflected by the anterior N400 and posterior positivity. Although the exact functional nature of the anterior N400, and its neural origin need further investigation, it appears likely that the component reflects processing of visual semantic information in the form of high-level descriptions of the visual properties of concrete objects, which allow for subsequent visualisation via object working memory.

Our data furthermore suggest that modality-specific activations to concrete words (object working memory in our case) do not reflect visual semantics proper, as is often suggested, but are merely visualisations or mental images derived from earlier activation of visual semantic knowledge (indicated by the anterior N400 and posterior positivity). Consistent with this suggestion, the visualisation to concrete words (as reflected by slow wave effects) was found to be suppressed by the concurrent (nonsemantic) object working memory task. The anterior N400 and posterior positivity effects of concreteness, on the other hand, were not affected by the object working memory task, which is consistent with the hypothesis that these effects do not reflect visual activation, but represent higher-level semantic processing.

The present data suggest that visual information to concrete words is activated at two different levels of representation. As such, our results are consistent with both amodal and multimodal accounts of semantic representation. Although we consider the (modality-specific) visualisation to concrete words not to be semantic in the true sense, visualisation to concrete words does appear to follow automatically when a word is heard or identified for lexical decision (also see, e.g., Hauk et al., 2004; Martin, 1998; Thompson-Schill et al., 1999). This suggests that the modality-specific effects to concrete words are closely associated to the semantic process concerned with word comprehension.

In conclusion, we believe that our data provide new and exciting insight into the neurocognitive mechanisms involved in word comprehension and visual semantics. Further research will have to determine whether the two-step model that was identified here to underly the visualisation of concrete words is selective for the visual domain, or whether similar principles are used for other semantics (e.g., activation of motor representations to action words).

PrEview proof published online 17 January 2005

REFERENCES

Allport, D. A. (1985). Distributed memory, modular subsystems and dysphasia. In S. K. Newman & R. Epstein (Eds.), *Current perspectives in dysphasia* (pp. 32–60). Edinburgh, UK: Churchill Livingstone.

Attneave, F., & Arnoult, M. D. (1956). The quantitative study of shape and pattern perception. *Psychological Bulletin, 53,* 452–471.

Baddeley, A. D. (1986). *Working memory.* Oxford: Oxford University Press.

Barrett, S. E., & Rugg, M. D. (1990). Event-related potentials and the semantic matching of pictures. *Brain and Cognition, 14,* 201–212.

Belger, A., Puce, A., Krystal, J. H., Gore, J. C., Goldman-Rakic, P., & McCarthy, G. (1998). Dissociation of mnemonic and perceptual processes during spatial and nonspatial working memory using fMRI. *Human Brain Mapping, 6,* 14–32.

Berti, S., Geissler, H., Lachmann, T., & Mecklinger, A. (2000). Event-related brain potentials dissociate visual working memory processes under categorical and identical comparison conditions. *Cognitive Brain Research, 9,* 147–155.

Breedin, S. D., Saffran, E. M., & Coslett, H. B. (1994). Reversal of the concreteness effect in a patient with semantic dementia. *Cognitive Neuropsychology, 11,* 617–660.

Burnage, G. (1990). *Celex: A guide for users.* Centre for Lexical Information, University of Nijmegen, The Netherlands.

Caramazza, A. (1998). The interpretation of semantic category-specific deficits: What do they reveal about the organization of conceptual knowledge in the brain? *Neurocase, 4,* 265–272.

Caramazza, A., Hillis, A. E., Rapp, B., & Romani, C. (1990). The multiple semantics hypothesis: Mulitiple confusions. *Cognitive Neuropsychology, 7,* 161–189.

Chao, L. L., & Martin, A. (1999). Attribute-based neural substrates in temporal cortex for perceiving and knowing about objects. *Nature Neuroscience, 2,* 913–919.

Chao, L. L., & Martin, A. (2000). Representation of man-made objects in the dorsal stream. *Neuroimage, 12,* 478–484.

Coltheart, M., Inglis, L., Cupples, L., Michie, P., Bates, A., & Budd, B. (1998). A semantic system specific to the storage of information about the visual attributes of animate and inanimate objects. *Neurocase, 4,* 353–370.

Courtney, S. M., Petit, L., Haxby, J. V., & Ungerleider, L. G. (1998). The role of prefrontal cortex in working memory: Examining the contents of consciousness. *Philosophical Transactions of the Royal Society of London, 353,* 1819–1828.

Damasio, H., Grabowski, T. J., Tranel, D., Hitchwa, R. D., & Damasio, A. R. (1996). A neural basis for lexical retrieval. *Nature, 380,* 499–505.

D'Esposito, M. D., Detre, J. A., Aguirre, G. K., Stallcup, M., Alsop, D. C., Tippet, L. J., & Farah,

M. J. (1997). A functional MRI study of mental image generation. *Neuropsychologia, 35,* 725–730.
D'Esposito, M. D., Postle, B. R., & Lease, J. (1999). Maintenance versus manipulation of information held in working memory: An event-related fMRI study. *Brain and Cognition, 41,* 66–86.
Doninger, G. M., Foxe, J. J., Murray, M. M., Higgins, B. A., Snodgrass, J. G., Schroeder, C. E., & Javitt, D. C. (2000). Activation time course of ventral visual stream object-recognition areas: High density electrical mapping of perceptual closure processes. *Journal of Cognitive Neuroscience, 12,* 615–621.
Farah, M. J. (1995). Current issues in the neuropsychology of image generation. *Neuropsychologia, 33,* 1455–1471.
Farah, M. J., & McClelland, J. L. (1991). A computational model of semantic memory impairment: Modality specificity and emergent category specificity. *Psychological Review, 120,* 339–357.
Farah, M. J., Peronnet, F., Weisberg, L. L., & Monheit, M. (1989). Brain activity underlying mental imagery: Event-related potentials during mental image generation. *Journal of Cognitive Neuroscience, 1,* 302–316.
Gabrowski, T. J., Damasio, H., & Damasio, A. R. (1998). Premotor and prefrontal correlates of category-related lexical retrieval. *Neuroimage, 7,* 232–243.
Ganis, G., Kutas, M., & Sereno, M. I. (1996). The search for "common sense": An electrophysiological study of the comprehension of words and pictures in reading. *Journal of Cognitive Neuroscience, 8,* 89–106.
Gratton, G., Coles, M. G., & Donchin, E. (1983). A new method for off-line removal of ocular artifact. *Electroencephalography and Clinical Neurophysiology, 55,* 468–484.
Hauk, O., Johnsrude, I., & Pulvermüller, F. (2004). Somatotopic representation of action words in human motor and premotor cortex. *Neuron, 41,* 301–307.
Hillis, A. E., Rapp, B. C., & Caramazza, A. (1995). Constraining claims about theories of semantic memory: More on unitary versus multiple semantics. *Cognitive Neuropsychology, 12,* 175–186.
Holcomb, P. J., Kounios, J., Anderson, J. E., & West, W. C. (1999). Dual-coding, context-availability, and concreteness effects in sentence comprehension: An electrophysiological investigation. *Journal of Experimental Psychology: Learning, Memory, and Cognition, 25,* 721–742.
Kellenbach, M. L., Wijers, A. A., Hovius, M., Mulder, J., & Mulder, G. (2002). Neural differentiation of lexico-syntactic categories or semantic feature? Event-related potential evidence for both. *Journal of Cognitive Neuroscience, 14,* 561–577.
Kieras, D. (1978). Beyond pictures and words: Alternative information-processing models for imagery effects in verbal memory. *Psychological Bulletin, 85,* 532–554.
Klaver, P. (1999). Representations in human visual short-term memory: An event-related potential study. *Neuroscience Letters, 268,* 65–68.
Kosslyn, S. M. (1994). *Image and brain: The resolution of the imagery debate.* Cambridge, MA: MIT Press.
Kosslyn, S. M., Alpert, N. M., Thompson, W. L., Chabris, C. F., Rauch, S. L., & Anderson, A. K. (1994). Identifying objects seen from different viewpoints. A PET investigation. *Brain, 117,* 1055–1071.
Kounios, J., & Holcomb, P. J. (1994). Concreteness effects in semantic processing: ERP evidence supporting dual-coding theory. *Journal of Experimental Psychology: Learning, Memory, and Cognition, 20,* 804–823.
Logie, R. H., & Baddeley, A. D. (1990). Imagery and working memory. In P. J. Hampson, D. F. Marks, & J. T. Richardson (Eds.), *Imagery: Current developments* (pp. 103–128). London: Routledge.
Löw, A., Rockstroh, B., Hauk, O., Berg, P., & Maier, W. (1999). Determining working memory from ERP topography. *Brain Topography, 12,* 39–47.
Martin, A. (1998). Organization of semantic knowledge and the origin of words in the brain. In N. G. Jablonski & L. C. Aiello (Eds.), *The origin and diversification of language* (pp. 69–88). *Memoirs of the California Academy of Sciences, Number 24.* San Francisco: California Academy of Sciences.
Martin, A., & Chao, L. L. (2001). Semantic memory and the brain: Structure and processes. *Current Opinion in Neurobiology, 11,* 194–201.
Martin, A., Wiggs, C. L., Ungerleider, L. G., & Haxby, J. V. (1995). Discrete cortical regions associated with knowledge of color and knowledge of action. *Science, 270,* 102–105.
Martin, A., Wiggs, C. L., Ungerleider, L. G., & Haxby, J. V. (1996). Neural correlates of category-specific knowledge. *Nature, 379,* 649–652.
McPherson, W. B., & Holcomb, P. J. (1992). Semantic priming with pictures and the N400 component. *Psychophysiology, 29,* S51.
McPherson, W. B., & Holcomb, P. J. (1999). An electrophysiological investigation of semantic priming with pictures of real objects. *Psychophysiology, 36,* 53–65.
Mecklinger, A., & Muller, N. (1996). Dissociations in the processing of "what" and "where" information in working memory: An event-related potential analysis. *Journal of Cognitive Neuroscience, 8,* 453–473.

Mecklinger, A., & Pfeifer, E. (1996). Event-related potentials reveal topographical and temporal distinct neuronal activation patterns for spatial and object working memory. *Cognitive Brain Research, 4,* 211–224.

Nielsen-Bohlman, L., & Knight, R. T. (1999). Prefrontal cortical involvement in visual working memory. *Cognitive Brain Research, 8,* 299–310.

Owen, A. M., Milner, B., Petrides, M., & Evans, A. C. (1996). Memory for object features versus memory for object locations: A positron-emission tomography study of encoding and retrieval processes. *Proceedings of the National Academy of Sciences USA, 93,* 9212–9217.

Paivio, A. (1971). *Imagery and verbal processes.* New York: Holt, Rinehart, & Winston.

Paivio, A. (1991). Dual coding theory: Retrospect and current status. *Canadian Journal of Psychology, 45,* 255–287.

Perani, D., Cappa, S. F., Bettinardi, V., Bressi, S., Gorno-Tempini, M., Matarrese, M., & Fazio, F. (1995). Different neural systems for the recognition of animals and man-made tools. *Neuroreport, 6,* 1637–1641.

Perani, D., Schnur, T., Tettamanti, M., Gorno-Tempini, M., Cappa, S. F., & Fazio, F. (1999). Word and picture matching: A pet study of semantic category effects. *Neuropsychologia, 37,* 293–306.

Pivik, R. T., Broughton, R. J., Coppola, R., Davidson, R. J., Fox, N., & Nuwer, M. R. (1993). Guidelines for the recording and quantitative analysis of electroencephalographic activity in research contexts. *Psychophysiology, 30,* 547–558.

Pulvermüller, F. (1999). Words in the brain's language. *Behavioral and Brain Sciences, 22,* 253–279.

Pulvermüller, F. (2001). Brain reflections of words and their meaning. *Trends in Cognitive Sciences, 5,* 517–524.

Ruchkin, D. S., Canoune, H. L., Johnson Jr, R., & Ritter, W. (1995). Working memory and preparation elicit different patterns of slow wave event-related brain potentials. *Psychophysiology, 32,* 399–410.

Ruchkin, D. S., Grafman, J., Krauss, G. L., Johnson Jr, R., Canoune, H., & Ritters, W. (1994). Event-related brain potential evidence for a verbal working memory deficit in multiple sclerosis. *Brain, 117,* 289–305.

Ruchkin, D. S., Johnson Jr, R., Grafman, J., Canoune, H., & Ritters, W. (1992). Distinctions and similarities among working memory processes: An event-related potential study. *Cognitive Brain Research, 1,* 53–66.

Ruchkin, D. S., Johnson Jr, R., Grafman, J., Canoune, H., & Ritters, W. (1997). Multiple visuospatial working memory buffers: Evidence from spatiotemporal patterns of brain actvity. *Neuropsychologia, 35,* 195–209.

Saffran, E. M., & Schwartz, M. F. (1994). Of cabbages and things: Semantic memory from a neuropsychological perspective—a tutorial review. In C. Umiltà & M. Moscovitch (Eds.), *Attention and performance, Vol. XV* (pp. 507–536). Cambridge, MA: MIT Press.

Schendan, H. E. (2002). Neurophysiological evidence for two processing times for visual object identification. *Neuropsychologia, 40,* 931–945.

Schwanenflugel, P., & Shoben, E. (1983). Differential context effects in comprehension of abstract and concrete verbal materials. *Journal of Experimental Psychology: Learning, Memory, and Cognition, 9,* 82–102.

Smith, E. E., & Jonides, J. (1997). Working memory: A view from neuroimaging. *Cognitive Psychology, 33,* 5–42.

Thompson-Schill, S. L., Aguirre, G. K., D'Esposito, M., & Farah, M. J. (1999). A neural basis for category and modality specificity of semantic knowledge. *Neuropsychologia, 37,* 671–676.

Tranel, D., Damasio, H., & Damasio, A. R. (1997). A neural basis for the retrieval of conceptual knowledge. *Neuropsychologia, 35,* 1319–1327.

Uhl, F., Goldenberg, G., Lang, W., Lindinger, G., Steiner, M., & Deecke, L. (1990). Cerebral correlates of imagining colours, faces and a map—II. Negative cortical DC potentials. *Neuropsychologia, 28,* 81–93.

Ungerleider, L. G., Courtney, S. M., & Haxby, J. V. (1998). A neural system for human visual working memory. *Proceedings of the National Academy of Sciences USA, 95,* 883–890.

Ungerleider, L. G., & Mishkin, M. (1982). Two cortical visual systems. In J. Ingle, M. A. Goodale, & R. J. W. Mansfield (Eds.), *Current perspectives in dysphasia* (pp. 594–586). Edinburgh: Churchill Livingstone.

Van Loon-Vervoorn, W. (1985). *Voorstelbaarheidswaarden van nederlandse woorden.* Lisse, The Netherlands: Swets & Zeitlinger.

Warrington, E. K., & McCarthy, R. A. (1983). Category-specific access dysphasia. *Brain, 106,* 859–878.

Warrington, E. K., & McCarthy, R. A. (1987). Categories of knowledge: Further fractionation and an attempted integration. *Brain, 110,* 1273–1296.

Warrington, E. K., & Shallice, T. (1984). Category-specific semantic impairment. *Brain, 107,* 829–854.

West, W., & Holcomb, P. (2000). Imaginal, semantic and surface-level processing of concrete and abstract words: An electrophysiological investigation. *Cognitive Neuroscience, 12,* 1024–1037.

Wiggs, C. L., Weisberg, J., & Martin, A. (1999). Neural correlates of semantic and episodic memory retrieval. *Neuropsychologia, 37,* 103–118.

COGNITIVE NEUROPSYCHOLOGY, 2005, 22 (3/4), 387–407

EXPERIMENTING WITH THE ACTING SELF

Manos Tsakiris and Patrick Haggard
Institute of Cognitive Neuroscience, University College London, UK

Recent neuroscientific research has developed the concept of the embodied agent as a scientifically viable approach to the psychological concept of the self. Both the awareness of one's own actions and awareness of one's own body are necessary conditions for the experience of selfhood. The relative contributions of efferent and afferent information in self-awareness are yet to be fully understood. We review experimental evidence that highlights the phenomenological and functional differences between the "acting self" and the "sensory self." These differences may underlie the ubiquitous modulation of perception in voluntary action. We focus on three main research fields: somatosensory perception, time-awareness, and self-recognition. A series of experiments, designed so as to dissociate afferent from efferent information, are reviewed. As a whole the results suggest that intentional action functions as a general context for awareness, modulating the perception of one's own body. The "acting self," owner of the efferent information, modulates the phenomenal experience of the "sensory self" because of the intrinsically agentic nature of voluntary movement. Finally, it is suggested that this sense of agency is efferent-driven, originating from pre-action processes.

INTRODUCTION

The quest to understand what is "the body in the brain" (Berlucchi & Aglioti, 1997) is intrinsically linked to the emergence of a new topic in neuroscientific research: the embodied agent. The aim of the present review is to investigate the way in which perception of one's own body is modulated by the intentional and agentic nature of voluntary action.

In this context, agency is defined according to the phenomenological distinction between "sense of agency" and "sense of ownership" proposed by Gallagher (2000a, 2000b). Sense of agency is the sense of intending and executing an action, whereas ownership refers to the sense that one's own body experiences a certain sensation, either externally or self-generated. A crucial phenomenological observation is that sense of ownership is present not only during voluntary actions, but also during externally or passively generated bodily experiences. In contrast, only voluntary actions can produce a sense of agency. Following these operational definitions, the sense of agency involves a strong *efferent* component, because actions are centrally generated. The sense of ownership involves a strong *afferent* component, because the content of body-awareness originates mostly by the plurality of multisensory peripheral signals. We do not normally experience the efferent and afferent components separately. Instead, we have a general awareness of our body that involves both components. This body-awareness can be defined as a nonconceptual and prelinguistic form of self-awareness, which is ontogenetically more primitive than the higher

---

Correspondence should be addressed to Manos Tsakiris, Institute of Cognitive Neuroscience, Alexandra House, 17 Queen Square, London, WC1N 3AR, UK (Email: e.tsakiris@ucl.ac.uk).

The authors would like to thank three anonymous reviewers, as well as Julie Grèzes, Dorothée Legrand, and Dan Zahavi, for their helpful comments and suggestions.

form of reflectional self-consciousness (Bermúdez, 1998; Rochat, 2003; Zahavi, 2002).

There is a clear link between body-awareness and self-consciousness. My experience of my body reflects the fact that this particular body responds to my intentional actions, and is the site of my bodily feelings (Merleau-Ponty, 1962). Therefore, the sense of agency arising from controlling one's own body movements is quite different from the feeling of controlling an independent object, such as a machine. We deal here with the first, "embodied" variety of agency. The main issue under investigation is the exact contribution of this sense of embodied agency to body-awareness in general.

This emphasis on the agentic self is justified and supported by a renewed interest of cognitive neurosciences in the functional and phenomenological properties of sensory and motor processes. The concept of agency underlies many recent research trends, including the primacy of goal-directed movement in cognitive development (for a review, see Rochat & Striano, 2000), the constitution of a "sense of agency" and its relation to bodily self-awareness (for a review, see Blakemore, Frith, & Wolpert, 2002), the status of "free will" (Libet, Gleason, Wright, & Pearl, 1983), and the neural processes underpinning the understanding of actions (Decety & Grèzes, 1999). The sensorimotor functions of the brain are no longer considered as low-level processes that cannot account for the existence of self-consciousness, agency, and symbolic thought. For example, the discovery of mirror neurons demonstrated that the firing of these special classes of pre-motor neurons is not related to a command for action, but to an internal representation of the motor behaviour they code (for a review, see Rizzolatti, Fogassi, & Gallese, 2001). The presence of a motor vocabulary within area F5, which operates by means of neuronal sensitivity to specific actions performed with different effectors (Buccino et al., 2001) and across different modalities (Kohler, Keysers, Umiltà, Fogassi, Gallese, & Rizzolatti, 2002), implies that these actions are represented at the level of goals rather than at the level of movements (Gallese, Fadiga, Fogassi, & Rizzolatti, 1996). Such evidence suggests that motor systems might be representational systems, as well as executive (for a review, see Gallese, 2000).

As a result of this re-conceptualisation of sensory and motor processes, "motor" theories of cognition are currently widespread and popular (Blakemore et al., 2002; Cruse, 2003; Frith, 1992; Paillard, 1999). A common presumption among diverse "motor theories" is that our perception of the world is guided by sensorimotor dependences, in other words "[...] perception consists of perceptually guided action" (Varela, 1999, p. 12; for a similar argument, see also O'Regan & Noë, 2001). It is postulated that these recurrent sensorimotor patterns that guide our actions give birth to higher cognitive structures. The same basic initial mechanisms, which are used by our sensorimotor system in the execution and understanding of simple goal-directed actions, can be generalised to higher cognitive tasks (Rizzolatti & Gallese, 1997). Within this theoretical framework, recent neuroscientific research has developed the concept of the embodied agent as a scientifically viable approach to the psychological concept of the self.

Almost every human activity involves voluntary movements. Central motor signals (i.e., efferent) and peripheral sensory signals (i.e., afferent) are ever present. As agents, we act upon the world with our bodies, and at the same time we experience ourselves, and the world, through the same bodies. The fact that the body is this "intentional arc" (Merleau-Ponty, 1962) between the agent and the world implies that the sense of self is crucially dependent on sensory-motor signals. In effect, a long-standing debate regarding the influence of efferent and afferent information on action-awareness started more than 100 years ago. In the "Williams debate" (see Petit, 1999), W. James argued that knowledge of our movements originates from peripheral information, whereas W. Wundt emphasised the role of a central corollary efference of the motor command. Traditionally, proprioception is conceptualised as the modality of the self *par excellence*, especially in relation to body awareness (Bermúdez, 1998; Gibson, 1979), because proprioceptive information unambiguously pertains to the sensing subject. On the other hand, efferent information (Helmholtz, 1995) and the function of the internal models of the motor system have been linked to the sense of agency (Blakemore, Frith, & Wolpert, 1999a; Wolpert, 1997). These two sources may produce the distinctive phenomenologies of the "sensory self" and the "acting self" respectively. Although the "Williams debate" originally concerned the representation of actions, it has wider implications: Is the "self" primarily a *proprioceptive* experience of our bodies, or primarily a *motor* experience of our actions?

In an attempt to answer this question, we will review experimental evidence that highlights the phenomenological and functional differences between the "acting self" and the "sensory self." The "acting" self is the author of an action and also the owner of the consequent bodily sensations. The "sensory" self is solely the owner of bodily sensations that were not intentionally generated, but on the contrary were passively experienced. This distinction is principally a methodological one, because the experience of one's self in the world does not entail these two separate entities. Nevertheless, this distinction can be of great use for a neuroscientific approach on agency, because it allows for the comparison between purely afferent events and similar afferent events that are voluntarily generated (i.e., efferent-driven).

We focus on recent experiments from three main research paradigms: sensory suppression, time-awareness, and self-recognition. By sensory suppression we refer to the well-known phenomenon of attenuating the sensory consequences of self-generated movements. Recent studies link sensory suppression to prediction of the consequences of action, perhaps within a forward model of the motor system (Blakemore et al., 2002). The question we address is whether such attenuation occurs even when the motor system *cannot* accurately predict the sensory consequences of self-generated movements. By time-awareness we refer to the perceived time of actions and their sensory effects (Haggard, 2003). The question we address is whether the time perception of voluntary actions and their effects is different from the time-perception of involuntary movements and comparable effects. By self-recognition, we refer to the process of integrating different sources of information (i.e., intentions, efference and afference) in order to ascribe a visual representation of a body-part to its proper agent (Jeannerod, 2003). The question we address refers to the specific role of efferent information in such experimental tasks.

In all three research areas, we use a single simple experimental design to compare the "acting" and the "sensory" self. This design involves manipulating efference, and maintaining afference constant (Tsakiris & Haggard, 2003; Tsakiris, Haggard, Franck, Mainy, & Sirigu, in press). Such studies suggest a distinctive contribution of efference to body- awareness, based on laboratory experiments in which both subjective experience and objective performance has been compared across conditions in which efference was either present or absent. We propose a theoretical model of agency based on a synthesis of these three research areas.

SENSING WHEN I AM ACTING: THE PERCEPTION OF SENSORY STIMULATION IS MODULATED BY AUTHORSHIP OF ACTION

In this section we focus on the processes underlying the perception of self-generated bodily effects. Touching and being touched at the same time characterise our tactile relations with the world. An active and a receptive element coexist, which generate a computational problem for the brain of separating these two elements. Especially during action, one should pay attention not to the self-generated bodily effects, but to the externally generated bodily effects and also to the effects in the external world. The process of separating and distinguishing self-generated from externally generated events has been linked to the sense of selfhood and agency (Blakemore et al., 1999a).

This process seems to begin early in life. Developmental studies showed that newborn infants (24 hours old) are able to discriminate between double touch stimulation combined with proprioception, and single touch of exogenous origin (Rochat & Hespos, 1997). It seems that even at birth, infants can discriminate between external and self-stimulation, suggesting, that an early sense of the body as a differentiated entity exists, and even more importantly, that self-generated sensory stimulation is processed and perceived differently from externally generated stimulation.

Sensory suppression is a key concept in recent accounts of the link between perception and action, because it highlights the way that perception of sensory events is modulated by the voluntary nature of the movement. Numerous studies have shown that the perceptual consequences of self-generated actions are attenuated (Blakemore et al., 1999a; Blakemore, Wolpert, & Frith, 1998, 1999b, 2000; Claxton, 1975; Collins, Cameron, Gillard, & Prochazka, 1998; Weiskrantz, Elliot, & Darlington, 1971). The reasons for sensory suppression are probably twofold. First, any body movement potentially increases the amount of afferent information to the brain. Sensory suppression would reduce the possibility of computational overload. Second, the sensory consequences of my own actions can be predicted internally, so there is no need to sense them. The phenomenon of sensory suppression suggests that the acting self is hierarchically positioned above the passive, sensory self, since the acting self can temporarily block afferent sensation.

Blakemore and colleagues (1998, 1999a, 1999b, 2000) investigated the way that somatosensory consequences of our own actions are perceived differently from identical somatosensory inputs that are externally generated in a series of psychophysical and neuroimaging experiments. The perceptual consequences of self-generated actions are attenuated because internal models of the motor system use the efference copy to predict the consequences of our own actions, and subsequently an internal "forward model" (Wolpert, 1997) compares the predicted sensory outcome of our own actions with the actual somatosensory feedback. It has been suggested that the intact function of this comparative mechanism is a prerequisite for correct attribution of actions and recognition of agents (Blakemore et al., 2002).

At the core of this model lies the concept of an "efference copy" or copy of the motor command (Sperry, 1950; Von Holst & Mittelstaedt, 1950, cited in Nelson, 1996). The concept of efference copy was initially proposed in answer to Helmholtz's (1995) question: "how is it that, when we move our eyes, the world remains stable, despite the fact that the retinal image has moved?" In other words, how do we know whether the movement can be attributed to the eye or to the object; whether the perceived movement originates from us or from the world (Pachoud, 1999)? By generating an efference copy of the motor command, the motor system can simulate the motor execution, and therefore it can predict and anticipate the sensory consequences of self-generated movements. Any sensory input that is not predicted from the motor command would reflect an external event.

In the study by Blakemore and colleagues (1999a), tactile stimulation by means of a piece of foam was applied to the participant's right hand. The stimulation was either produced by a voluntary movement of the participant's left hand, or it was externally generated. Crucially, for the self-generated condition, between the movement of the right hand and the stimulated left hand a robotic interface was mediated, so that the experimenters could manipulate and parametrically vary (a) the delay between movement and stimulation, and (b) the degrees of trajectory perturbations. Participants' task was to judge the "ticklishness" of the sensory stimulation. Participants perceived the tactile stimulation as significantly less ticklish when it was self-generated compared to the externally generated condition, suggesting that relevant perceptual attributes of stimulation were attenuated. When a time delay of 200 ms was artificially introduced between the motion and the resulting sensation, the attenuation effect was absorbed. The authors attributed this absence of attenuation to sensory discrepancy, or the error between the predicted sensory feedback during voluntary action and the *actual* sensory feedback from the right hand. The results showed that even in the case of self-generated stimulation, the tactile sensation and its causative movement should correspond in time and space for the attenuation to take place.

Follow-up imaging experiments suggested that the cerebellum is crucially involved in the comparison between predicted and actual sensory feedback (Blakemore, Frith, & Wolpert, 2001), and that it provides the signal used for sensory attenuation in the somatosensory cortex (Blakemore et al., 1998, 1999b). According to this model (Blakemore et al., 2002), awareness of our own actions is largely dependent on the outcome of the comparison between the predicted and the actual state of our bodies. In the case of little or no discrepancy between predicted and actual state, one can be reassured that she was the agent. Therefore, it may seem as if ascription of agency is a post-action verificational judgment.

Of course, under normal circumstances, the mere presence of efferent information should constitute an infallible, or at least a necessary, index of the ownership of action, and it is debatable whether agency attribution is a post hoc judgment. One way to investigate this hypothesis is to create a situation where the efferent copy cannot directly predict the sensory outcome. It is an empirical question whether similar sensory attenuation would occur in such conditions.

In a recent experiment (Tsakiris & Haggard, 2003) we showed that identical somatic effects, induced with transcranial magnetic stimulation (TMS) over the motor cortex, are perceived as less intense when caused by a voluntary action than when caused by an involuntary movement. Figure 1 shows the experimental set-up.

A key press triggered the TMS, which was applied over the motor cortex of the participant, producing a twitch of the right index finger 270 ms later. The key was pressed either voluntarily by the participant's left index finger (voluntary condition) or by a mechanical motor pressing the participant's finger on to the key (involuntary condition), or by the experimenter (control condition). Participants were asked to judge the *intensity* of the TMS

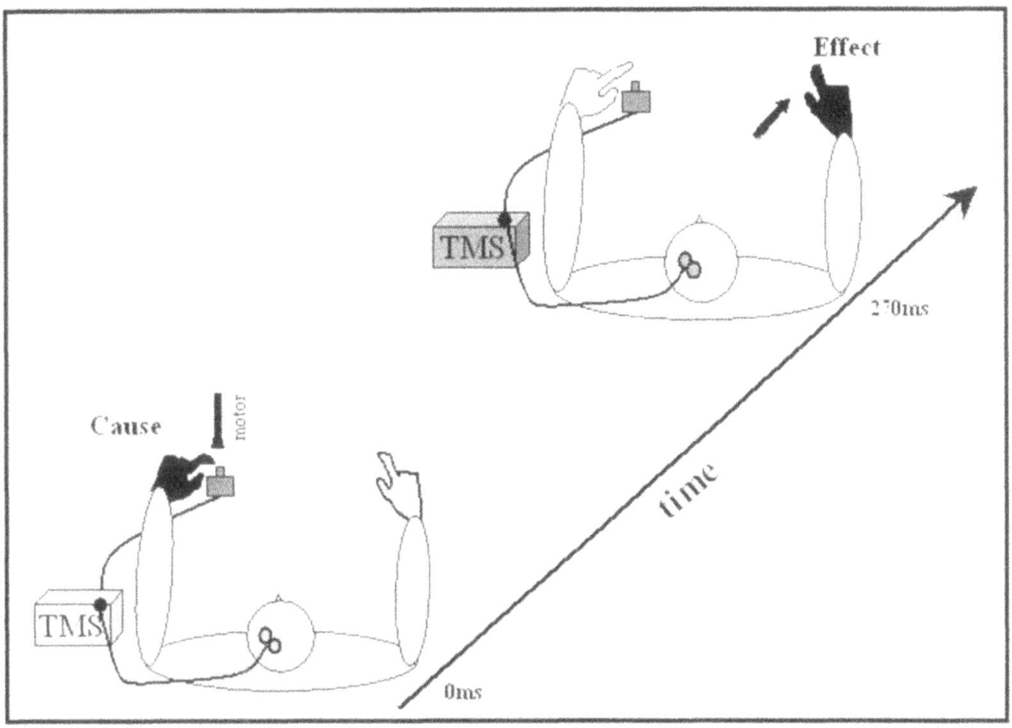

Figure 1. *Experimental set-up from Tsakiris and Haggard (2003). A key press triggered the TMS, which was applied over the motor cortex of the participant, producing a twitch of the right index finger 270 ms later. The key was pressed either voluntarily by the participant's left index finger or by an involuntary movement (e.g., the motor was pressing the participant's finger onto the key). Participants had to judge the intensity of the TMS-induced twitch.*

induced twitch of their right index finger by using a subjective scale from 1 to 10, 1 being not intense at all, and 10 extremely intense. To achieve a wide range of actual twitch intensities, the TMS output was varied randomly across trials between 110%, 130%, and 150% of relaxed motor threshold in the first dorsal interosseus. The participants were unaware of the TMS intensity that would be used in each trial. In both voluntary and involuntary conditions, a physically comparable movement of the left hand preceded the somatic effect. However, only in the voluntary condition did the subject intentionally cause the somatic effect. No prior movement of the left hand occurred in the control condition.

Mean subjective intensity ratings and mean objective MEP sizes across conditions are shown in Figure 2.

Participants perceived the TMS twitches in the control condition as more intense than a physically comparable twitch occurring as a somatic effect of a previous movement. More interestingly, somatic effects that were induced involuntarily were judged to be significantly more intense than when caused voluntarily. This finding confirms the sensory suppression observation of Blakemore and other authors. However, by separating the action and its sensory consequences in both space and time, our study provides a more controlled experiment. For example, previous measures of sensory suppression have confounded agency with predictability, by comparing the perceived intensity of highly predictable somatic effects of action with less predictable external events. Our result shows that sensory suppression is not an artefact of predictability because across conditions, the intensity of the somatic effect was unpredictable, whereas its time-occurrence was the same. Moreover, intentional action, and not mere body movement, is a necessary condition of sensory suppression.

We also investigated *how* sensory suppression occurs. Does it act as a proportional attenuator, or does it shift perceived intensity of all somatic effects by a fixed amount? Because we varied the actual size of the somatic effect in a measurable way, we could address this problem by regressing perceived intensity on objective MEP size, and investigating whether the slopes or intercepts of this regression changed across conditions, using dummy regression analysis (Kleinbaum, Kupper, & Muller, 1988).

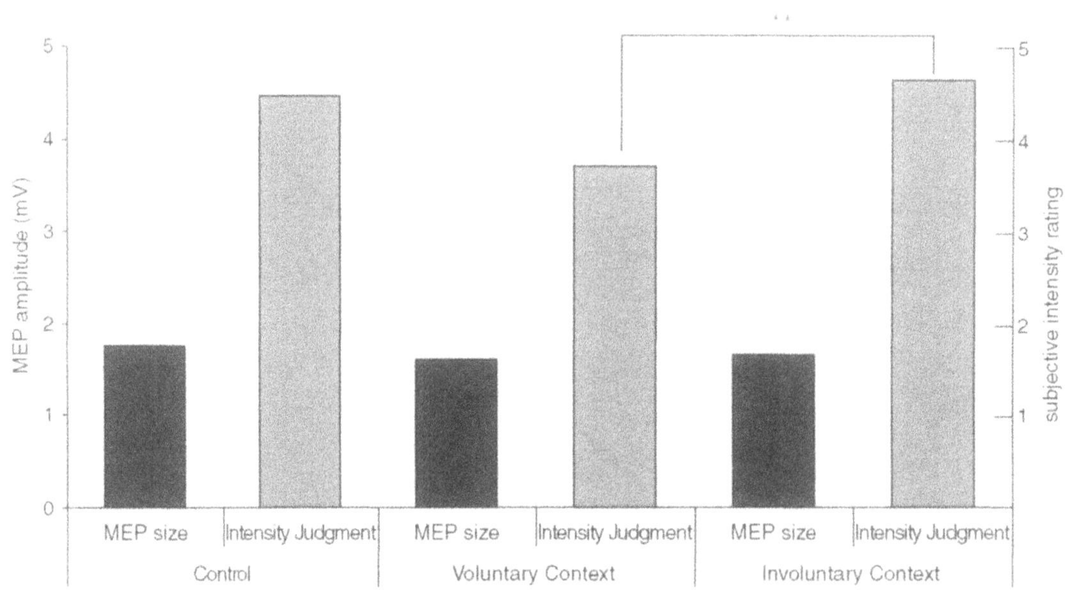

Figure 2. *Mean MEP size (mV) and subjective intensity rating across conditions. Asterisks indicate significant differences.*

This revealed that there was a significant effect on the intercept of the psychophysical relation between perceived intensity and objective MEP size, with significantly lower perceived intensity after voluntary action than after passive involuntary movement. However, the slope coefficients did not differ significantly between voluntary and involuntary conditions. Therefore, we concluded that agency shifts the perceived intensity of all subsequent somatic effects by a fixed amount, but does not attenuate percepts in a proportional manner. It is due to the operation of the forward model 392 that sensory events are attenuated in a proportional manner, because of the detailed comparison between motor parameters, predicted, and actual sensory feedback.

In the light of this evidence, intention and efference act as a general context for awareness, shifting the perceived intensity by fixed amounts. This context effect could be applied predictively in the form of a "sensory bias." We have shown that this bias occurs quite generally, even when the details of the action do not predict the details of its sensory consequences. The mere intention to act would therefore be sufficient to apply this bias. Sensory suppression may be an important index of agency (Blakemore et al., 2002). Our sensory suppression results suggest that the sense of agency could arise at an early stage in the planning of action, and before the precise details of the impending movement are determined.

TIMING WHEN I AM ACTING: THE TIME-AWARENESS OF SENSORY EFFECTS IS MODULATED BY AUTHORSHIP OF ACTION

Apart from perceiving the somatic effects of self-generated actions, we also perceive the time occurrence of these events. Voluntary actions have a distinctive temporal structure: generation of intention, "translation" of the intention to the motor command and the accompanying efference copy, execution, and perception of the effects. Early neuroscientific research on time-awareness focused on the perceived time of intending to act (Libet et al., 1983). However, both the methodology of the "psychophysics of intention" and the interpretation of Libet's experiments have been criticised on various neuroscientific and philosophical grounds (see Libet, 1985, commentaries).

Investigation of the time-awareness of action, rather than intention, might be a more viable research topic for two main reasons (Haggard, Aschersleben, Gehrke, & Prinz, 2002a). First, actions and effects can be self-generated or externally generated. Therefore, by comparing the perceived times of self-generated vs. externally generated events we can investigate the role of agency on time-awareness, using the basic experimental design proposed in the introduction. Moreover, studying the perceived time of *actions* offers an indirect way of studying *intentions*, by comparing awareness of intentional movements with awareness of physically identical movements, which are nonintentional.

A series of experiments on the time-awareness of actions has demonstrated the anticipatory nature of the acting self (Haggard & Eimer, 1999; Haggard & Magno, 1999; Haggard et al., 2002a; Libet et al., 1983). Overall, these studies show that the perceived time of action is influenced by intentional processes preceding the action itself. The perceived time of sensory effects of operant actions is also modulated by the intentional nature of the action that caused them (Haggard et al., 2002a; Haggard, Clark, & Kalogeras, 2002b; Tsakiris & Haggard, 2003).

By using a modified version of the Libet method (Libet et al., 1983), subjects were asked to make time judgments for actions (such as a key press) or for sensory stimuli caused by the action after a short delay. Haggard and colleagues (2002b) compared the perceived times of voluntary actions with the perceived times of involuntary movements induced by TMS over the motor cortex (single-event conditions), as well as the perceived times of these events (voluntary action vs. TMS-induced movement) when they triggered an auditory stimulus (operant conditions). An additional sham TMS condition was used as control. Judgment errors were defined as the difference between the actual time of occurrence of the judged event and the perceived time of its occurrence, and they were calculated for each trial and averaged. By subtracting the judgment error for an event in the single-event baseline condition (i.e., only one of the three possible events occurred in each trial) from the perceived time of the same event in a causal, operant context, Haggard and colleagues calculated the perceptual shifts for each context. These perceptual shifts represent the effect of operant context on the perceived time of each event. Moreover, they control for factors such as the sensory transmission and division of attention of each participant, and differences in the salience or perceptual center of judged events. Figure 3 shows the perceptual shifts across conditions.

The analysis of perceptual shifts showed that the perceived times of voluntary actions and their sensory consequences (auditory tones) were attracted together. Participants perceived voluntary movements as occurring *later* and their sensory consequences as occurring *earlier*, when these events occurred together compared to when they occurred in isolation. Approximately comparable *involuntary* movements caused by TMS over the motor cortex reversed this attraction effect between the movement and the auditory tones, producing a perceptual repulsion in the opposite direction. Haggard and colleagues (2002b) concluded that only truly operant intentional actions elicit perceptual attraction or binding effects between the action and its sensory auditory consequence.

Recently, Tsakiris and Haggard (2003) also compared the perceived times of voluntary actions or involuntary movements and of a subsequent somatic effect. The experimental design compared somatic effects of agentic movement to those of nonagentic movement: A voluntary action and its somatic effect were compared with a physically comparable involuntary passive movement and identical somatic effect. A response key positioned under the left index finger was connected to a transcranial magnetic stimulator (TMS) placed over the left motor cortex (see Figure 1). Participants were informed that the key could be pressed either voluntarily or passively by the index finger of their left hand, according to condition. In both cases, the

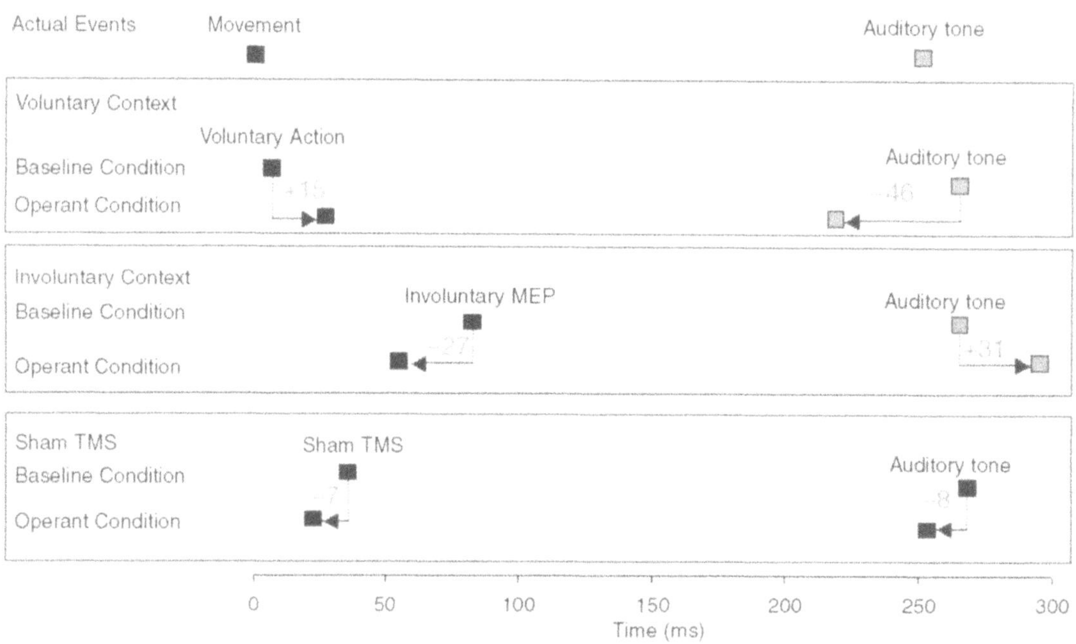

Figure 3. *The pattern of perceptual shifts (in ms) from Haggard et al. (2002b).*

key press would produce a TMS pulse 250 ms later, inducing a twitch of their right index finger approximately 270 ms after the key press. Thus, the key press was defined as the causative action, and TMS-induced twitch was the somatic effect of this action. In the experimental blocks, the same events were arranged in an operant context so that the somatic effect followed either the voluntary action or the passive movement of the left hand. For each operant condition, only one event was judged, either the action or the effect, in separate blocks. In additional single-event baseline conditions participants judged the onset of voluntary key press, involuntary key press, or TMS-induced twitches when only one of these events occurred in each trial. The parameters of movement were identical across conditions, and the spatiotemporal relation between the key press and the TMS pulse was also identical. Only the authorship of the action was different across conditions.

Figure 4 shows the mean perceptual shifts across conditions. As in the experiment of Haggard et al. (2002b), participants perceived voluntary actions as occurring later and their bodily effects as occurring earlier in the agency context, compared to single-event baseline conditions. When the voluntary action was replaced by a passive, involuntary movement this attraction effect reversed. This study adds several additional facts to our knowledge of this binding process. First, we showed that the binding process works with a different, and more ecological, modality of effect (i.e., somatomotor), in addition to auditory tones. Second, it does not work with involuntary movements and their identical somatic effects. The binding mechanism is engaged by intention, but not by mere body movement. In this experiment, the sense of agency was manipulated by design: The key-press could be effected either voluntarily or involuntarily. By contrast, the sense of ownership (e.g., the TMS-induced somatic effect) was maintained constant across conditions. The results suggest that the sense of our body is modulated by the intentional context of a prior action. In particular, intention, or "sense of agency," is necessary for binding, while "sense of ownership" is not.

Consistent results obtained from all these studies suggest that (1) awareness of action depends on central signals, which precede actual bodily movement, and (2) the volitional character of the movement modulates not only the perception of the action, but also the perception of the sensory stimulus following that action. Briefly, voluntary

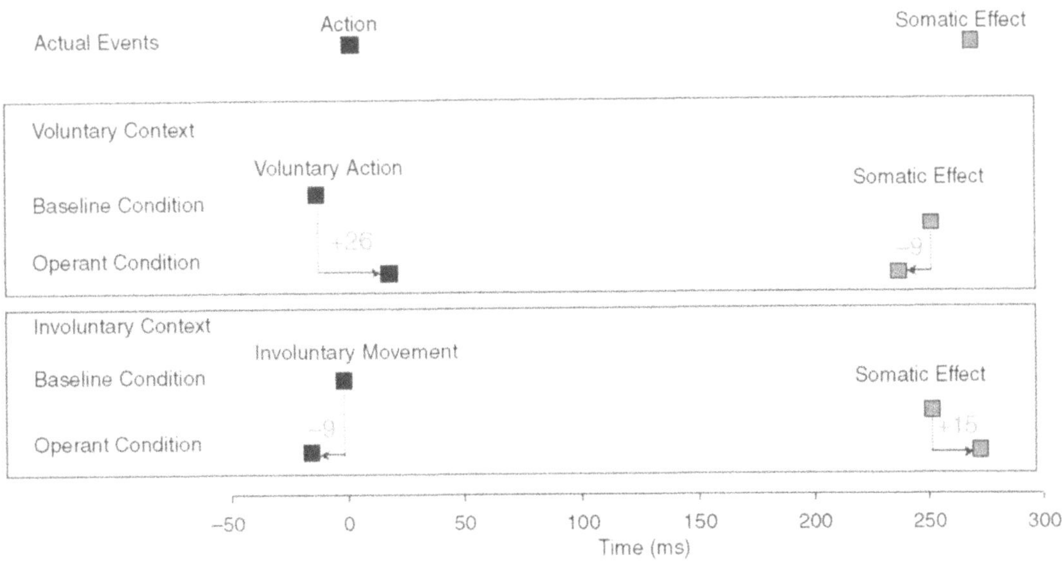

Figure 4. *The pattern of perceptual shifts (in ms) from Tsakiris and Haggard (2003), adapted with permission.*

actions that produced an external effect were perceived to occur *later* than voluntary actions that produced no effect. Conversely, external events produced by one's own voluntary action were perceived to occur *earlier* than comparable events that occurred without agency. Thus, awareness of actions and effects showed an attraction in time towards each other, termed "intentional binding" (Haggard et al., 2002a, 2002b; Tsakiris & Haggard, 2003).

In summary, by manipulating both causality (Haggard et al., 2002b) and agency (Tsakiris & Haggard, 2003), we showed that the perceived times of voluntary actions and their effects are bound together. The results reviewed provide support for the existence of a CNS process that operates only when a subject is the active agent of her actions. This "intentional binding" process integrates the conscious representations of actions and events. A series of experiments have consistently shown that this process is specific to actions, thereby underlying its intentional nature, and does not reflect general perceptual attraction. This "intentional binding" mechanism might underlie the way in which the mind constructs a strong association between intentions, actions, and consequences so as to generate the unique and private phenomenological experience of self-agency.

RECOGNISING WHEN I AM ACTING: THE ROLE OF AFFERENT AND EFFERENT INFORMATION IN SELF-RECOGNITION TASKS

Whereas in the previous sections we reviewed recent experiments that dealt separately with sensory and time perception, self-recognition tasks provide an opportunity of combining these two elements. In most studies of self-recognition, participants are presented with a visual stimulus that may or may not be related to their own body. The task is to judge whether they see themselves or not. The information available to support this judgment is systematically varied across conditions, for example by moving the hand. Self-recognition requires the *monitoring* and *integration* of various sources of information such as intention, motor command, and somatic perception in a short time-window.

Visual stimuli have predominated in this area, because ambiguities regarding visual representations of the body are both fairly convincing phenomenologically and also easy to produce via mirrors or virtual reality. This is the main reason behind the use of mirrors and video monitors in self-recognition experiments on dolphins (Reiss & Marino, 2001), chimpanzees (Kitchen, Denton, & Brent, 1996), infants (for a review, see Rochat & Striano, 2000), and adults (for a review, see Jeannerod, 2003).

Developmental studies suggest that explicit self-awareness in infants comes between the 14th and 18th month: At this period, infants will be embarrassed when they see in a mirror that there is a rouge spot on their face (Bertenthal & Fisher, 1987). However, from the 4th month, infants start playing in front of mirrors and therefore attending to the visuoproprioceptive contingencies that accompany self-generated movements. In numerous studies, visuoproprioceptive incongruence was introduced, and the results suggested that infants were able to discriminate temporal incongruence (Bahrick & Watson, 1985) and that they were also sensitive to spatial calibration of their own body movements (Rochat, 1998; Rochat & Morgan, 1995). More recently, it has been shown that infants as young as 4 months of age were able to discriminate between self- and other's mirror images (Rochat & Striano, 2002). This evidence demonstrates the presence of a preconceptual self-awareness that is bodily in its nature. It is possible that this play with movements, vision, and proprioception contributes to the prereflective awareness of the same self who will be embarrassed some months later, during more explicit self-reflecting situations, like the "rouge task."

In cases of abnormal self-awareness, the ability to correctly recognise intentions, actions and their effects, or even one's own body parts is often disturbed, as shown in cases of "anarchic hand syndrome" (Hari et al., 1998), somatoparaphrenia (Bottini, Bisiach, Sterzi, & Vallar, 2002), and schizophrenia (Daprati et al., 1997; Fourneret, Franck, Slachevsky, & Jeannerod, 2001; Franck et al., 2001). These pathological cases suggest that both action and bodily cues need to be integrated in order to generate the normal experience of will, agency and body-ownership that we entertain in our daily lives.

Schizophrenics and parietal patients were the focus of interest in previous self-recognition experiments, because of the deficits these groups show in action attribution and action recognition. Daprati et al. (1997) and Sirigu, Daprati, Pradat-Diehl, Franck, and Jeannerod (1999) investigated the perception of simple and complex gestures in schizophrenic and in parietal patients respectively. The experimental design was the same in both experiments. Participants were instructed to perform simple or complex self-generated movements (extension of one or two fingers) without direct visual image of their hand. An experimenter, sitting in a similar cabin, performed either the same or a different gesture at the same time. Two cameras were filming the experimenter's and the participant's hands, thus enabling the manipulation of the visual feedback. Participants could see (a) their *own* hand, (b) the experimenter's hand performing the *same* gesture as the participant, or (c) the experimenter's hand performing a *different* gesture. Participants were asked to judge whether the hand they saw was theirs or not.

The pattern of results was the same across the two experiments. Patients and controls performed almost perfectly when they saw their *own* hand, and when they saw the experimenter's hand performing a *different* movement. This suggests that the detection of a mismatch between visual and proprioceptive/efferent information is a relatively easy task, even for patients who display impaired awareness of action. However, both schizophrenics and parietal patients were significantly worse, compared to controls, when they saw the experimenter's hand performing the *same* movements as them. In this case, the patients tended to misattribute the experimenter's hand to themselves. Presumably, the patients were less able than normal subjects to detect or interpret small spatiotemporal and kinematic differences between the observed movement and their own actions as represented proprioceptively or via efferent information.

Daprati et al. (1997) suggested that this pattern of results revealed a wide deficit in reading other people's intentions. A defective internal model for action attribution (Fourneret et al., 2001; Franck et al., 2001) may also underlie the impaired performance of schizophrenics. Sirigu et al. (1999) suggested that parietal cortex contains an internal model that compares internal and external feedback about one's own movements, and therefore parietal damage would impair the on-line monitoring of actions. The common point in these two interpretations is that a process of coordinating egocentric and allocentric representations underlies self-recognition.

In these two studies, proprioceptive and efferent information were not dissociated, and therefore the relative contribution of each signal was not directly tested. Efferent and proprioceptive information were the same and present across all conditions, because the movements were self-generated. Only the visual feedback was manipulated. It is debatable whether visual manipulations alone can distinguish if the critical proprioceptive information about one's own action, which is required for the matching process, is afferent or efferent in origin. Subjects might recognise themselves in the visual display using purely afferent information. For example, if the proprioceptive and visual afference that they receive match each other perfectly, they might conclude they are watching themselves. If some mismatch occurs, they might conclude they are watching someone else's hand. Equally, efferent information could make a key contribution to this matching process.

In a recent study, Van den Bos and Jeannerod (2002) attempted to separate the contribution of afferent and efferent information to self-recognition. In this study, both the participant's and the experimenter's hands were presented on a monitor simultaneously. *Visual* afferent information was operationalised by rotating the hand image (0°, 90°, −90°, 180°) on the screen and the efferent information was manipulated by creating three action conditions: (1) participant and experimenter performed the *same* movement, (2) participant and experimenter performed a *different*

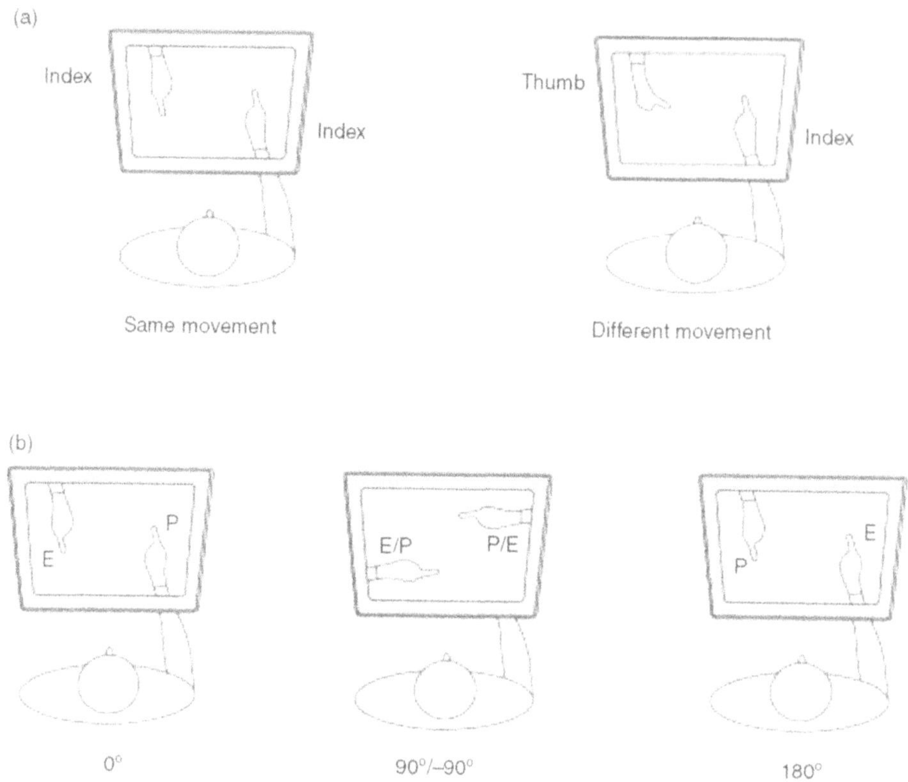

Figure 5. *The experimental set-up used in Van den Bos and Jeannerod (2002), adapted from Knoblich (2002) with permission.*

movement, and (3) participant and experimenter made *no movement* (see Figure 5).

As in previous studies (Daprati et al., 1997; Sirigu et al., 1999), participants performed perfectly when the experimenter made a different movement, across all rotation conditions. The authors suggested that "when distinctive movements are available, subjects tend to recognize actions, and not just hands" (Van den Bos & Jeannerod, 2002, p. 185). When, the movements of both hands were the same, performance was influenced by the rotation factor. The main conclusion of the authors is that action cues are used when distinctive movements are made, and that bodily cues are used when action cues are ambiguous.

But still, in this study, efferent information was not dissociated from proprioceptive afferent information because movements were self-generated, and therefore their relative contributions were not clarified. As shown in the studies of schizophrenic (Daprati et al., 1997) and parietal patients (Sirigu et al., 1999), it is relatively easy to detect the kind of mismatch produced when experimenter and participant perform *different* movements. Furthermore, it is questionable whether the manipulation of visual afference was an appropriate way to operationalise the "sense of body," because proprioceptive afference may be more important for self-consciousness (Bermúdez, 1998). Only in the "same movement" condition can the role of efference and proprioceptive afference be properly addressed. By implementing a situation where proprioceptive information is constant, whereas efference is manipulated, we can clarify the distinctive contribution of central signals. In the design used by Van den Bos and Jeannerod, differences in performance across conditions are not informative for the respective contribution of central and peripheral signals, since "in the same movement condition" efference was always present, proprioception was the same, and only the visual orientation of the hand image was manipulated.

An alternative way of investigating the distinctive role of efferent and afferent signals in action awareness and body awareness is to examine patients who are deprived of afferent signals. Deafferented patients, such as GL, have been extensively tested in a variety of experimental designs. GL was tested in the "action conflict task" developed by Fourneret and Jeannerod (1998). In this experimental paradigm, participants are asked to trace a continuous line, as straight as possible, with a stylus on a surface hidden from direct view. The visual feedback, manipulated by the experimenters who introduce angular biases, is presented on a monitor screen. There are two issues under investigation. The first one refers to the motor performance: Will the participants be able to compensate for the angular biases after a certain number of trials? The second issue refers to the content of motor awareness. Normal participants are able to compensate after some trials and therefore to produce the desired straight line (Fourneret & Jeannerod, 1998), and they do become aware of their actual behaviour only when the biases are large. When GL was tested in the same paradigm (Fourneret, Paillard, Lamarre, Cole, & Jeannerod, 2002), she was able to compensate for the angular biases in a similar way as the control participants, suggesting that her motor performance was intact. However, "GL never became aware of the bias and, consequently, of any strategy of correction she had to apply to correct" (Fourneret et al., 2002, p. 545), suggesting that the *content* of awareness of one's own movements is derived not from the efferent signals, but from the comparison of the predicted to the real sensory consequences of the executed movement. In a deafferented patient like GL, this process never takes place, since she is deprived of any afferent signals. GL was also tested in a self-recognition task developed by Farrer and colleagues (Farrer, Franck, Paillard, & Jeannerod, 2003). The results were consistent with GL's performance in the action conflict task. Her motor performance was not significantly different compared to controls, but her motor awareness was significantly impaired. GL was also tested in a "sense of effort" task (Lafargue, Paillard, Lamarre, & Sirigu, 2003). Controls and GL were asked to produce and judge isometric forces: The force was produced with one hand and, 3 s later, participants were asked to match the force with the other hand. Again, GL's motor performance was not significantly different compared to controls, suggesting that she did have a sense of muscular effort derived from efferent signals, even though she reported been unaware of any fatigue or of how hard she tried to match the produced forces. These consistent results seem to suggest that the *content* of body awareness is largely dependent on afferent signals. However, the fact that GL's performance was accurate, and that she did have a sense of effort, suggest that the sense of agency may be crucially dependent on efferent, rather than afferent, signals (for a similar argument, see Marcel, 2003).

An equally critical issue is what would happen if, instead of being deprived of afferent information, subjects were deprived of efferent information. To that extent, efferent information was systematically manipulated in a recent study, where the self-recognition task developed by Daprati and colleagues was used (Tsakiris et al., in press). We manipulated the efference by dissociating an action from its effect, using the same logic as in Tsakiris and Haggard (2003). Separating the action in space and/or time from its somatic effect allowed us to investigate whether the recognition of the somatic effect depends primarily on the afferent information generated during the body movement itself, or whether it also depends on efferent information from the spatially remote action that produced the somatic effect.

In a 2×2 factorial design, an action performed with the left hand produced a passive displacement of the right hand. There were two experimental factors. The first factor was the authorship of action that caused the passive displacement of the right hand (self-generated vs. externally generated), and the second factor was the visual feedback of the right hand (view participant's hand vs. view other's hand).

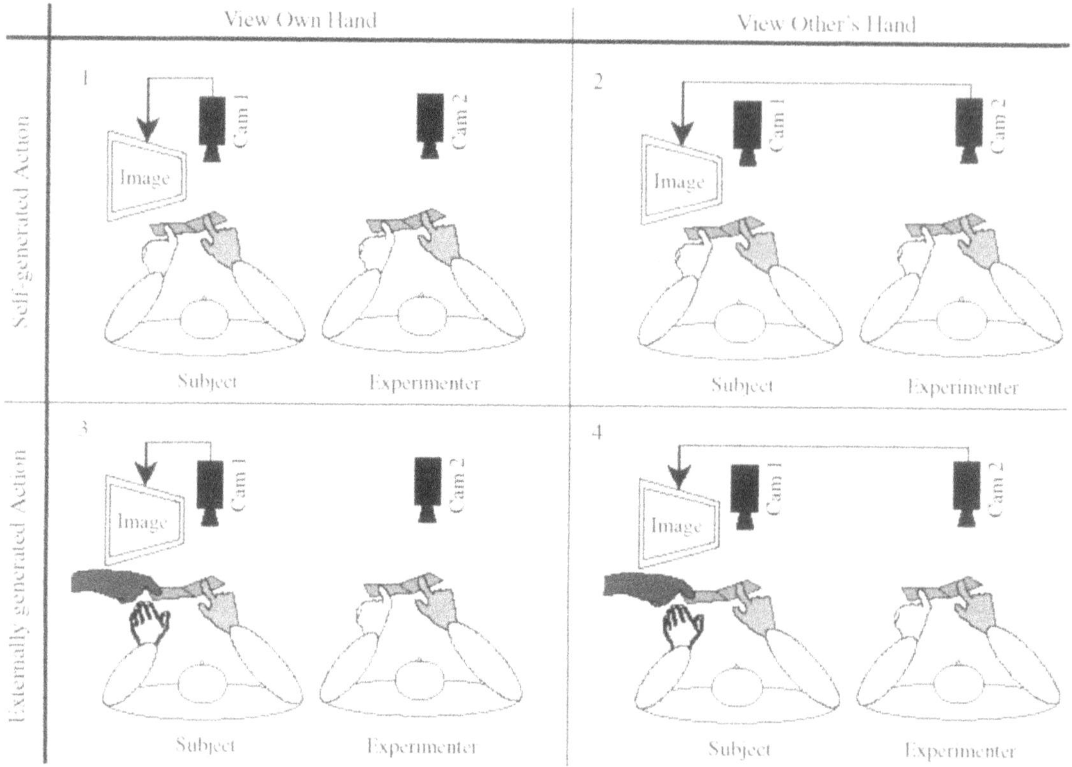

Figure 6. *The experimental set-up and design used in Tsakiris et al. (in press). The participant and the experimenter are sitting in similar cabins. The task was to produce a passive displacement of the right index finger by pressing on a lever (length 15 cm, angle 45°), and consequently to recognise the identity of the viewed hand. The movement of the right hand was always effected passively, and can therefore be seen as a somatic effect of the left hand action. The lever could be pressed either by the subject's left hand (self-generated condition) or by the experimenter (externally generated condition). Each box represents a different condition. The displacement of the right index finger was self-generated by the participant herself, and she saw her own right hand (condition 1). The displacement of the right index finger was self-generated, but the participant saw the experimenter's right hand (condition 2). The displacement of the right index finger was externally generated by another experimenter, and the participant saw her own right hand (condition 3). Finally, the displacement of the right index finger was externally generated by another experimenter, and the participant saw the experimenter's right hand (condition 4). Both hands were covered with identical gloves in order to eliminate morphological differences.*

Efferent information was manipulated because the right hand's displacement could be effected either by the participant or by the experimenter. In the former case, participants had two kinds of information about the passive displacement of the right hand: efferent information from the left hand that caused the displacement of the right hand, and also afferent information from the right hand itself. When the displacement of the right hand was externally generated, the afferent information was similar, but efferent information was absent. Participants viewed only the effect of the action in visual display of the right hand, and never saw the left hand or left side of the lever. As in previous experiments, they saw either their *own* right hand or *someone else's* right hand undergoing the *same* passive displacement (see Figure 6). Participants were asked to judge whether the right hand they saw was theirs or not, as a measurement of self-recognition.

Figure 7 shows the mean correct rates across conditions. Overall, performance was significantly better when the passive displacement of the right index finger was self-generated across both viewing conditions. Authorship of action had a significant effect on self-recognition judgments,enabling the subjects to better recognise their own hand.

In the critical condition where participants saw someone else's right hand and the displacement of their right hand was externally generated, they incorrectly attributed the viewed hand to themselves in 55% of the trials. When the passive displacement was self-generated and they saw someone else's hand, incorrect attribution to self occurred in 38% of the trials. The difference between these two conditions shows the specific role of efferent information in self-recognition.

Therefore, efferent information clearly contributed to the ability to match proprioceptive and visual representations of a remote bodily effect. This significant contribution of efferent information was present in both the "view own hand" and "view other's hand" conditions. This could occur for two reasons. First, efferent information might provide an advantage in monitoring the timing of sensory events. In the case of a self-generated action, forward models of the motor system use the efferent information so as to generate a prediction about the anticipated sensory feedback (Wolpert, 1997). Second, efference might modulate the on-line comparison between vision and proprioception by providing detailed temporal and kinematic information, and integrating these signals in posterior parietal areas (MacDonald & Paus, 2003; Sirigu et al., 1999).

Interestingly, efferent information has a significant contribution not only in the conscious and/or unconscious processing of various aspects of action per se, but also in the perception of the effects of the action. Thus, in this experiment, the movements of the right hand, which subjects used to recognise themselves, were not actions but rather the effects of an action performed by either the subject or the experimenter on the other end of the lever. This is consistent with recent experiments on action recognition and prediction, where an authorship effect

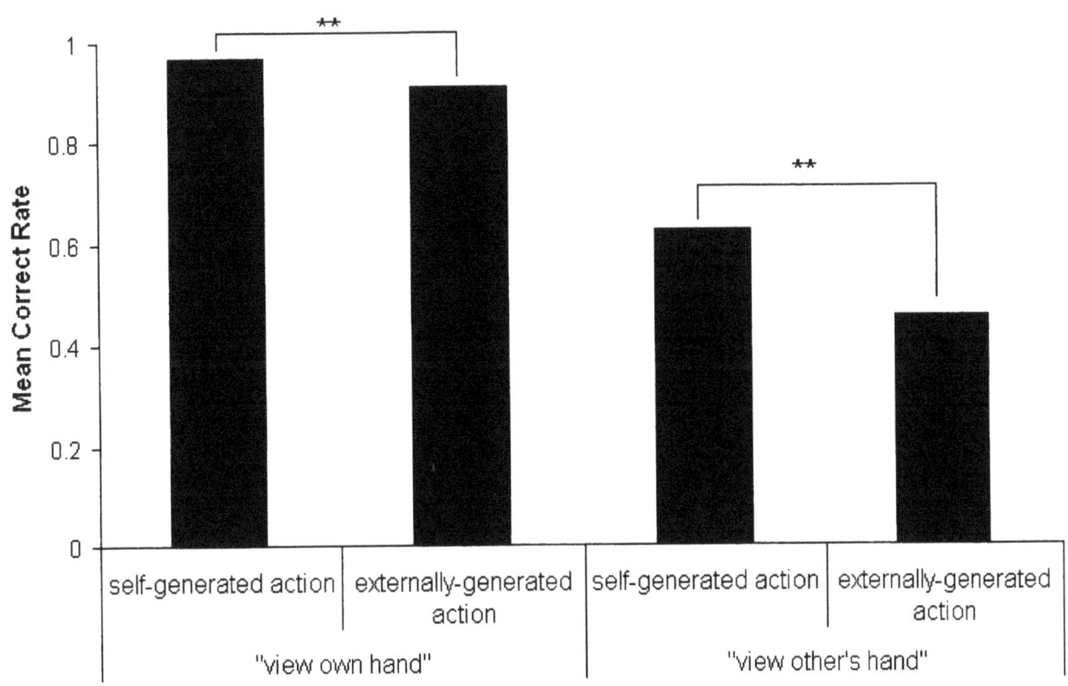

Figure 7. *Mean correct responses across conditions in Tsakiris et al. (in press). Asterisks indicate significant differences across conditions.*

was observed in recognising and predicting actions that were performed by the participants themselves, when compared to actions performed by other agents (for a review, see Knoblich & Flach, 2003). This finding suggests that efferent information might also be important for self-recognition and self-awareness, and not only for motor control (see also Blakemore et al., 2002; Tsakiris & Haggard, 2003). This distinctive role of efference in self-recognition experiments suggests that central signals are highly accurate in detecting the appropriate afferent signals that pertain to one's self, and that even though the content of our body awareness is mostly afferent in its origin, it is nevertheless modulated by efferent-driven processes.

A MODEL OF EMBODIED AGENCY

The task of a cognitive neuroscience of the embodied self is to explain the sense in which percepts of action and bodily effects are so clearly and inexorably "mine." There are two methodological issues that need to be carefully treated, if research on action is meant to be informative not only for the underlying brain processes, but also for the phenomenology of "acting." Not only is the very concept of intention problematic in the neuroscientific field (see Breitmeyer, 1985; Haggard & Libet, 2001; Libet, 1985), but so is the investigation of the interplay between motor and sensory neural processes, which accompany every voluntary action.

In this review, we highlighted the importance of experimental designs that separate efferent and afferent information. Of course both awareness of one's own actions and one's own body are indispensable for the experience of agency and selfhood. But it is also true that one can have afferent information without efferent information, as in the case of externally generated stimulation. The empirical question that we have addressed is whether the presence of efferent information modulates the perception of afference (especially proprioception) and, if so, in what way. Is the presence of efferent information indispensable only for the prediction of sensory stimulation, or is it linked to the sense of self in an intrinsic way, even before afference arrives? We have investigated this possible role of efference in three different aspects: somato-sensory perception, time awareness, and self-recognition.

In "sensing when I am acting," the aim was to examine whether an intentional modulation of sensory perception occurs whenever an effect is self-generated. To that extent, an artificial situation was created (Tsakiris & Haggard, 2003), where the motor system was not able to accurately predict the sensory consequences of a self-generated action. By using the TMS and randomly varying its output, participants could only have a vague idea about the intensity of the twitch (a typical MEP). The fact that the perceived intensity of the TMS twitches was attenuated when actively generated by the subject, compared to when similar TMS-twitches were generated passively by an identical movement of the subject's left hand, indicates that there is a "sensory bias" in the perception of the somatosensory system. This bias is present even when the motor system cannot accurately predict the sensory consequences. It is as if the system tags the forthcoming event as being "mine", before the motor system starts predicting and correcting the various sensory-motor parameters of the movement. This sensory bias is expected to be present whenever a sensory consequence can unambiguously be attributed to oneself. It was also suggested that the mere presence of intention and "raw" efferent information suffice for this sensory bias to be generated. This finding is not contradictory to the functional role of the forward model. It simply suggests that in the case of self-generated actions, the movement is tagged as "mine" by virtue of the presence of efference. If there is more information available for processing the sensory outcome, then the forward model will produce accurate predictions. The discrepancy between predicted and actual outcome will function in a proportional manner in the resulting perceptual attenuation, whereas the sensory bias derived from efference seems to function as general contextual modulation, because in Tsakiris and Haggard (2003) the perceived intensity of all subsequent somatic effects shifted by a fixed amount.

In "timing when I am acting," the review focused on the neuroscientific investigation of time-awareness. The results showed the operation of a temporal attraction process between the perceived time of voluntary actions and their sensory effects, called "intentional binding." Because intentional binding is specific to intentional operant actions (Haggard et al., 2002b) and it operates independently of whether the produced sensory effects of the action can be predicted by the motor system (Tsakiris & Haggard, 2003), it seems that the sense of agency is generated as part of the process of "translating" the intention to the efferent copy of the motor command. Intention to act also influences the awareness of non-operant voluntary actions (for a review, see Haggard, 2003). More recently, it has been shown that the mere presence of preceding but uncompleted intentions (i.e., intentions that did not lead to voluntary movements, but that were interrupted by TMS-induced movements) does not suffice for the operation of intentional binding (Haggard & Clark, 2003). If the intentional binding was a by-product of a reconstructive self-ascription of agency (Wegner, 2003), then some form of intentional binding should be evident in the case of a preceding, but interrupted, intention. The sense of agency, which generates our experience of actions, seems to be efferent driven, and it can be thought of as the first crucial step towards the realisation of intentions.

In "recognising when I am acting," the main focus was on the role of efference in self-recognition (Tsakiris et al., in press). While proprioception is considered to be intrinsically linked to the constitution of bodily self-awareness (Bermúdez, 1998), we suggest that the role of efference in self-awareness has not been properly addressed in previous studies of self-recognition. The main reason is the methodological difficulties encountered in the attempt to dissociate these two sources of information in experimental designs. However, when proprioceptive afference was separated from efference in a self-recognition task, self-recognition was significantly more accurate when participants were the authors of the action, even though the felt and seen movements had comparable forms in both conditions and despite the fact that it was the effect and not the action *per se* that the subjects were watching. Efferent information therefore played a key role in self-recognition, most probably by improving the visuoproprioceptive comparison.

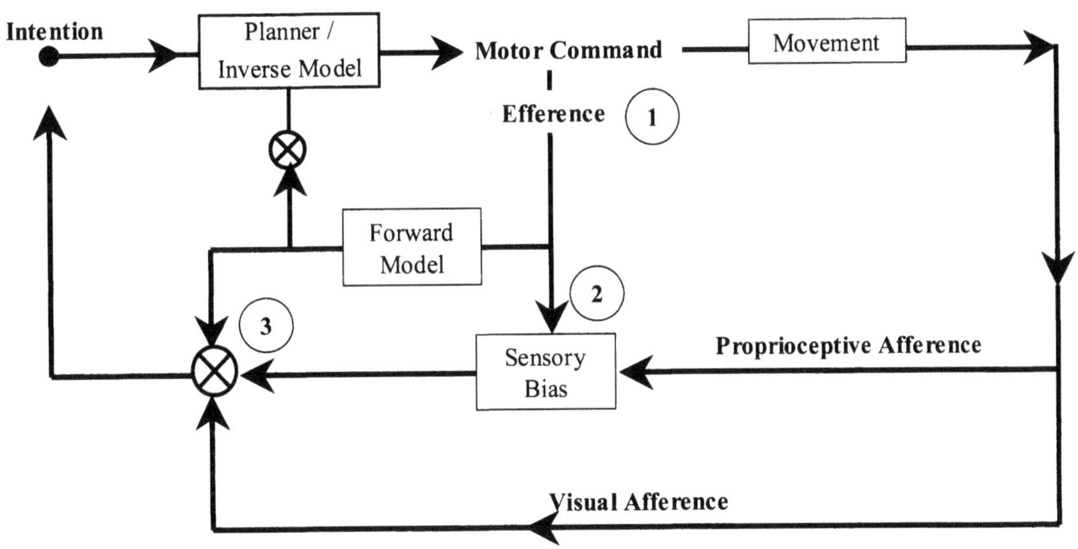

Figure 8. *A schematic model of the embodied agent.*

Taken overall, the results across these three sections are consistent and can be used to create a preliminary model of embodied agency. Figure 8 represents this model.

Intention refers to the desired state of the system's motor behaviour, which is translated into a motor command through the inverse model. When the motor command is generated, an efferent copy of this command is generated in parallel. This efferent copy seems to be sufficient condition for the raw sense of agency (point 1), as suggested by the experiment on time-perception of voluntary actions and their sensory consequences (Haggard et al., 2002a, 2002b; Tsakiris & Haggard, 2003). The experiment by Tsakiris and Haggard on sensory suppression showed that even when the motor system cannot actually predict the final state, the sensory consequences are still attenuated. This suggest that a sensory bias is introduced in the system, and that possibly the generation of efference is sufficient for this bias to occur (point 2). This bias might reflect the knowledge of the system that "it is me who is acting" as a direct consequence of an efferent-driven sense of agency, and does not need specifications of the actual motor parameters. The experiment on self-recognition (Tsakiris et al., in press) highlighted the critical role of efference in correctly attributing a visual representation to oneself. We suggest that efference modulates the comparison between proprioception and visual afference (point 3). An alternative possibility, that efference directly improves the quality of the proprioceptive signals, is rejected on the grounds of inconsistency with the established efferent down-regulation of proprioceptive afference (point 2). Whereas it seems that efference provides an intrinsic sense of agency, it is suggested that the contents of body awareness are derived from the multisensory on-line comparisons between efferent and afferent signals. The better the integration of these signals, the more accurate the self-recognition performance will be.

Overall, the "agentic self" seems to be constituted by voluntary movement, and it is experienced as a "perspectival source" (Gallagher & Marcel, 1999; Marcel, 2003) that modulates the phenomenal experience of peripheral and central signals. Our results suggest that this sense of agency is efferent-driven, whereas the contents of body awareness may be predominantly afferent in their origins. At the beginning of this paper we argued for a methodological separation between "acting" and "sensory" self. This distinction can be implemented by dissociating efferent and afferent information in order to investigate the interplay between these two sources in self-awareness. Efference intrinsically modulated the perception of afferent events. This is not surprising since normally we actively explore our environment, rather than passively perceiving it. The body is only rarely an object of perception; it is normally a subject. In that sense, body awareness is not simply another form of object consciousness (Zahavi, 2002). Models of self-awareness based on the privileged nature of proprioception as the "sense of the self" (Bermúdez, 1998) ignore the mere fact that my body is not so much an object of perception, but rather it is given to me as a subject; it is my being-in-the-world (Merleau-Ponty, 1962). And this might be so because, in both phylogenetic and ontogenetic terms, perception and cognition begin with movement.

PrEview proof published online 20 December 2004

REFERENCES

Bahrick, L. E., & Watson, J. S. (1985). Detection of intermodal proprioceptive-visual contingency as a potential basis of self-perception in infancy. *Developmental Psychology, 21,* 963–973.

Berlucchi, G., & Aglioti, S. (1997). The body in the brain: Neural bases of corporeal awareness. *Trends in Neurosciences, 20,* 560–564.

Bermúdez, J. L. (1998). *The paradox of self-consciousness.* Cambridge, MA: MIT Press.

Bertenthal, B., & Fisher, K. (1987). Development of self-recognition in the infant. *Developmental Psychology, 14,* 44–50.

Blakemore, S.-J., Frith, C. D., & Wolpert, D. (1999a). Spatio-temporal prediction modulates the perception of self-produced stimuli. *Journal of Cognitive Neuroscience, 11,* 551–559.

Blakemore, S.-J., Frith, C. D., & Wolpert, D. (2001). The cerebellum is involved in predicting the sensory consequences of action. *NeuroReport, 12,* 1879–1884.

Blakemore, S.-J., Frith, C. D., & Wolpert, D. (2002). Abnormalities in the awareness of action. *Trends in Cognitive Sciences, 6,* 237–242.

Blakemore, S.-J., Wolpert, D. M., & Frith, C. D. (1998). Central cancellation of self-produced tickle sensation. *Nature Neuroscience, 1,* 635–640.

Blakemore, S.-J., Wolpert, D. M., & Frith, C. D. (1999b). The cerebellum contributes to somatosensory cortical activity during self-produced tactile stimulation. *NeuroImage, 10,* 448–459.

Blakemore, S.-J., Wolpert, D. M., & Frith, C. D. (2000). Why can't you tickle yourself? *NeuroReport, 11,* R11–R16.

Bottini, G., Bisiach, E., Sterzi, R., & Vallar, G. (2002). Feeling touches in someone else's hand. *NeuroReport, 13,* 249–252.

Breitmeyer, B. (1985). Problems with the psychophysics of intention. *Behavioural and Brain Sciences, 8,* 539.

Buccino, G., Binkofski, F., Fink, G. R., Fadiga, L., Fogassi, L., Gallese, V., Seitz, R. J., Zilles, K., Rizzolatti, G., & Freund, H. J. (2001). Action observation activates premotor and parietal areas in a somatotopic manner: An fMRI study. *The European Journal Of Neuroscience, 13,* 400–404.

Claxton, G. (1975). Why can't we tickle ourselves? *Perceptual and Motor Skills, 41,* 335–338.

Collins, D. F., Cameron, T., Gillard, D. M., & Prochazka, A. (1998). Muscular sense is attenuated when humans move. *Journal of Physiology, 508,* 635–643.

Cruse, H. (2003). The evolution of cognition: A hypothesis. *Cognitive Science, 27,* 135–155.

Daprati, E., Franck, N., Georgieff, N., Proust, J., Pacherie, E., Dalery, J., & Jeannerod, M. (1997). Looking for the agent. An investigation into consciousness of action and self-conciousness in schizophrenic patients. *Cognition, 65,* 71–86.

Decety, J., & Grèzes, J. (1999). Neural mechanisms subserving the perception of human actions. *Trends in Cognitive Sciences, 3,* 172–178.

Fadiga, L., Fogassi, L., Pavesi, G., & Rizzolatti, G. (1995). Motor facilitation during action observation: A magnetic stimulation study. *Journal of Neurophysiology, 73,* 2608–2611.

Farrer, C., Franck, N., Paillard, J., & Jeannerod, M. (2003). Action recognition in a deafferented patient. *Consciousness and Cognition, 12,* 609–619.

Fourneret, P., Franck, N., Slachevsky, A., & Jeannerod, M. (2001). Self-monitoring in schizophrenia revisited. *NeuroReport, 12,* 1203–1208.

Fourneret, P., & Jeannerod, M. (1998). Limited conscious monitoring of motor performance in normal subjects. *Neuropsychologia, 36,* 1133–1140.

Fourneret, P., Paillard, J., Lamarre, Y., Cole, J., & Jeannerod, M. (2002). Lack of conscious recognition of one's own actions in a haptically deafferented patient. *NeuroReport, 13,* 541–547.

Franck, N., Farrer, C., Georgieff, N., Marie-Cardine, M., Daléry, J., d'Amato, T., & Jeannerod, M. (2001). Defective recognition of one's own actions in patients with schizophrenia. *American Journal of Psychiatry, 158,* 454–459.

Frith, C. D. (1992). *The cognitive neuropsychology of schizophrenia.* Hove, UK: Lawrence Erlbaum Associates Ltd.

Gallagher, S. (2000a). Self-reference and schizophrenia: A cognitive model of immunity to error through misidentification. In D. Zahavi (Ed.), *Exploring the self: Philosophical and psychopathological perspectives on self-experience.* Amsterdam & Philadelphia: John Benjamins.

Gallagher, S. (2000b). Philosophical concepts of the self: Implications for cognitive sciences. *Trends in Cognitive Sciences, 4,* 14–21.

Gallagher, S., & Marcel, A. (1999). The self in contextualized action. *Journal of Consciousness Studies, 6,* 4–30.

Gallese, V. (2000). The inner sense of action. *Journal of Consciousness Studies, 7,* 23–40.

Gallese, V., Fadiga, L., Fogassi, L., & Rizzolatti, G. (1996). Action recognition in the premotor cortex. *Brain, 119,* 593–609.

Gibson, J. J. (1979). *The ecological approach to visual perception.* Boston: Houghton Mifflin.

Haggard, P. (2003). Conscious awareness of intention and of action. In J. Roessler & N. Eilan (Eds.), *Agency and self-awareness* (pp. 111–127). Oxford: Oxford University Press.

Haggard, P., Aschersleben, G., Gehrke, J., & Prinz, W. (2002a). Action, binding, and awareness. In W. Prinz & B. Hommel (Eds.), *Common mechanisms in perception and action: attention and performance XIX.* Oxford & New York: Oxford University Press.

Haggard, P., & Clark, S. (2003). Intentional action: Conscious experience and neural prediction. *Consciousness and Cognition, 12,* 695–707.

Haggard, P., Clark, S., & Kalogeras, J. (2002b). Voluntary action and conscious awareness. *Nature Neuroscience, 5,* 382–385.

Haggard, P., & Eimer, M. (1999). On the relation between brain potentials and the awareness of voluntary movements. *Experimental Brain Research, 126,* 128–133.

Haggard, P., & Libet, B. (2001). Conscious intention and brain activity. *Journal of Consciousness Studies, 8,* 47–63.

Haggard, P., & Magno, E. (1999). Localizing awareness of action with transcranial magnetic stimulation. *Experimental Brain Research, 127,* 102–107.

Hari, R. et al. (1998). Three hands: Fragmentation of human bodily awareness. *Neuroscience Letters, 240,* 131–134.

Helmholtz, H. (1995). *Science and culture: Popular and philosophical essays.* Chigaco: University of Chicago Press.

Jeannerod, M. (2003). The mechanism of self-recognition in humans. *Behavioural Brain Research, 142,* 1–15.

Kitchen, A., Denton, D., & Brent, L. (1996). Self-recognition and abstraction abilities in the common chimpanzee studied with distorting mirrors. *Proceedings of the National Academy of Sciences of the United States of America, 93,* 7405–7408.

Kleinbaum, D. G., Kupper, L. L., & Muller, K. E. (1988). *Applied regression analysis and other multivariate methods.* Boston: PWS-KENT.

Knoblich, G. (2002). Self-recognition: Body and action. *Trends in Cognitive Sciences, 6,* 447–449.

Knoblich, G., & Flach, R. (2003). Action identity: Evidence from self-recognition, prediction, and coordination. *Consciousness and Cognition, 12,* 620–632.

Kohler, E., Keysers, C., Umiltà, M. A., Fogassi, L., Gallese, V., & Rizzolatti, G. (2002). Hearing sounds, understanding actions: Action representation in mirror neurons. *Science, 297,* 846–848.

Lafargue, G., Paillard, J., Lamarre, Y., & Sirigu, A. (2003). Production and perception of grip force without proprioception: Is there a sense of effort in deafferented subjects? *European Journal of Neuroscience, 17,* 2741–2749.

Libet, B. (1985). Unconscious cerebral initiative and the role of conscious will in voluntary action. *Behavioural and Brain Sciences, 8,* 529–566.

Libet, B., Gleason, C. A., Wright, E. W., & Pearl, D. K. (1983). Time of conscious intention to act in relation to onset of cerebral activity (readiness-potential): The unconscious initiation of a freely voluntary act. *Brain, 106,* 623–642.

MacDonald, P. A., & Paus, T. (2003). The role of parietal cortex in awareness of self-generated movements: A transcranial magnetic stimulation study. *Cerebral Cortex, 13,* 962–967.

Marcel, A. J. (2003). The sense of agency: Awareness and ownership of action. In J. Roessler & N. Eilan (Eds.), *Agency and self-awareness* (pp. 48–93). Oxford: Oxford University Press.

Merleau-Ponty, M. (1962). *The phenomenology of perception* (C. Smith, trans.). London: Routledge.

Nelson, R. J. (1996). Interactions between motor commands and somatic perception in sensorimotor cortex. *Current Opinion in Neurobiology, 6,* 801–810.

O'Regan, J. K., & Noë, A. (2001). A sensorimotor account of vision and visual consciousness. *Behavioural and Brain Sciences, 24,* 883–975.

Pachoud, B. (1999). The teleological dimension of perceptual and motor intentionality. In J. Petitot, F. J. Varela, B. Pachoud, & J.-M. Roy (Eds.), *Naturalizing phenomenology: Issues in contemporary phenomenology and cognitive science* (pp. 196–219). Stanford, CA: Stanford University Press.

Paillard, J. (1999). Motor determinants of a unified world perception. In G. Aschersleben, T. Bachmann, & J. Müsseler (Eds.), *Cognitive contributions to the perception of spatial and temporal events* (*Advances in Psychology, 129,* pp. 95–111). Amsterdam: Elsevier.

Petit, J.-L. (1999). Constitution by movement: Husserl in light of recent neurobiological findings. In J. Petitot, F. J. Varela, B. Pachoud, & J.-M. Roy (Eds.), *Naturalizing phenomenology: Issues in contemporary phenomenology and cognitive science* (pp. 220–245). Stanford, CA: Stanford University Press.

Prinz, W., & Hommel, B. (Eds.). (2002). *Common mechanisms in perception and action: Attention and performance XIX.* Oxford & New York: Oxford University Press.

Reiss, D., & Marino, L. (2001). Mirror self-recognition in the bottlenose dolphin: A case of cognitive convergence. *Proceedings of the National Academy of Sciences of the United States of America, 98,* 5937–5942.

Rizzolatti, G., Fogassi, L., & Gallese, V. (2001). Neurophysiological mechanisms underlying the understanding and imitation of action. *Nature Review Neuroscience, 2,* 661–670.

Rizzolatti, G., & Gallese, V. (1997). From action to meaning. In J.-L. Petit (Ed.), *Les neurosciences et la philosophie de l'action.* Paris: Vrin.

Rochat, P. (1998). Self-perception and action in infancy. *Experimental Brain Research, 123,* 102–109.

Rochat, P. (2003). Five levels of self-awareness as they unfold early in life. *Consciousness and Cognition, 12,* 717–731.

Rochat, P., & Hespos, S. J. (1997). Differential rooting response by neonates: Evidence for an early sense of self. *Early Development and Parenting, 6,* 105–112.

Rochat, P., & Morgan, R. (1995). Spatial determinants in the perception of self-produced leg movements by 3- to 5-month-old infants. *Developmental Psychology, 31,* 626–636.

Rochat, P., & Striano, T. (2000). Perceived self in infancy. *Infant Behavior and Development, 23,* 513–530.

Rochat, P., & Striano, T. (2002). Who's in the mirror? Self-other discrimination in specular images by four- and nine-month-old infants. *Child Development, 73,* 35–46.

Sirigu, A., Daprati, E., Pradat-Diehl, P., Franck, N., & Jeannerod, M. (1999). Perception of self-generated movement following left parietal lesion. *Brain, 122,* 1867–1874.

Sperry, R. W. (1950). Neural basis of the spontaneous optokinetic response produced by visual inversion. *Journal of Comparative Phsyiology and Psychology, 43,* 482–489.

Tsakiris, M., & Haggard, P. (2003). Awareness of somatic events following a voluntary action. *Experimental Brain Research, 149,* 439–446.

Tsakiris, M., Haggard, P., Franck, N., Mainy, N., & Sirigu, A. (in press). A specific role for efferent information in self-recognition. *Cognition.*

Van den Bos, E., & Jeannerod, M. (2002). Sense of body and sense of action both contribute to self-recognition. *Cognition, 85,* 177–187.

Varela, F. (1999). *Ethical know-how: Action, wisdom and cognition.* Stanford, CA: Stanford University Press.

Von Holst, E., & Mittelstaedt, H. (1950). Das Reaffernzprinzip wechselwirkungen zwichen zentrainervensystem und peripherie. *Naturwissenschalten, 37,* 464–476.

Wegner, D. M. (2003). The mind's best trick: How we experience conscious will. *Trends in Cognitive Sciences, 7,* 65–69.

Weiskrantz, L., Elliot, J., & Darlington, C. (1971). Preliminary observations of tickling oneself. *Nature, 230,* 598–599.

Wolpert, D. M. (1997). Computational approaches to motor control. *Trends in Cognitive Sciences, 1,* 209–216.

Zahavi, D. (2002). First-person thoughts and embodied self-awareness. *Phenomenology and Cognitive Sciences, 1,* 7–26.

COGNITIVE NEUROPSYCHOLOGY, 2005, 22 (3/4), 408–418

THE ROLE PLAYED BY TOOL-USE AND TOOL-LENGTH ON THE PLASTIC ELONGATION OF PERI-HAND SPACE: A SINGLE CASE STUDY

Alessandro Farnè
Università degli Studi di Bologna and Centro Neuroscienze Cognitive, Cesena, Italy
Silvia Bonifazi
Istituto S. Stefano, Villa Adria, Ancona, Italy
Elisabetta Làdavas
Università degli Studi di Bologna and Centro Neuroscienze Cognitive, Cesena, Italy

Consistent with neurophysiological findings showing expansion of the visual RF of visuo-tactile neurons along the rake used by monkeys to retrieve out-of-hand-reach objects (Iriki, Tanaka, & Iwamura, 1996), we have previously shown that also in humans the use of a tool can increase the spatial extent of the representation of peri-hand space, as revealed by an increase in the severity of cross-modal extinction after tool use (Farnè & Làdavas, 2000). Here we further explored the characteristics of such a transient elongation of the multisensory peri-hand space representation in a patient with visual-tactile extinction. By investigating the variation of cross-modal extinction following different types of tool-related experience, we found that passive exposure to the tool is not sufficient per se to induce peri-hand space extension, which instead requires that the tool is used. This increase of peri-hand extension might be related to the physical length of the tool.

INTRODUCTION

The space that closely surrounds our body parts has been referred to as peripersonal space which, in the case of the hand, is almost coincident with the reaching space. Several studies have now shown that human and nonhuman primates share similar multisensory systems coding for tactile and visual inputs within the peripersonal space of the hand, which can be functionally separated from those coding for visual information in the farther space (Làdavas, 2002; Rizzolatti, Matelli, & Pavesi, 1983). Peri-hand space representation in the monkey appears to be implemented by multisensory neurons within the putamen, parietal, and premotor areas (Bremmer, Schlack, Duhamel, Graf, & Fink, 2001a; Duhamel, Colby, & Goldberg, 1991, 1998; Graziano & Gross, 1995, 1998; Rizzolatti, Luppino, & Matelli, 1998; Rizzolatti, Scandolara, Matelli, & Gentilucci, 1981) that respond both to touches delivered within the hand somatotopic receptive field (RF) and to visual stimuli presented close to the same RF. Most important, the neuronal response to visual stimuli is spatially tuned, being stronger at shorter distances between the hand and the visual source, and vice versa (Duhamel et al., 1998; Fogassi, Gallese, Fadiga,

Correspondence should be addressed to Dr Alessandro Farnè, Department of Psychology, University of Bologna, Viale Berti Pichat, 5 - 40127 Bologna, Italy (Email: alessandro.farne@unibo.it).

We wish to thank LE for his willingness to collaborate. We thank Francesca Frassinetti for CT scan reading and lesion reconstruction. This work was supported by grants from MUIR and RFO.

Luppino, Matelli, & Rizzolatti, 1996; Fogassi, Raos, Franchi, Gallese, Luppino, & Matelli, 1999).

Similar multimodal structures have been identified in possibly homologous cerebral areas in humans by functional imaging studies (Bremmer et al., 2001b; Culham & Kanwisher, 2001; Grefkes, Weiss, Zilles, & Fink, 2002; Macaluso & Driver, 2001; Weiss et al., 2000), although comparative evidence of functional similarities in representing peripersonal space mainly stems from neuropsychological studies (di Pellegrino, Làdavas, & Farnè, 1997; Làdavas, di Pellegrino, Farnè, & Zeloni, 1998a; Làdavas, Zeloni, & Farnè, 1998b). Indeed, when simultaneously presented with bilateral cross-modal stimuli, some right brain-damaged (RBD) patients fail to report the leftward stimulus (e.g., tactile), which would be detected if presented in isolation, and only report the concurrent ipsilesional stimulus (e.g., visual). This cross-modal phenomenon is referred to as visuotactile extinction (Bender, 1952; Mattingley, Driver, Beschin, & Robertson, 1997). Similar to the neuronal response of bimodal visuotactile cells in the monkey, the strength of visuotactile extinction may vary as a function of the distance between the visual stimulus and the patient's ipsilesional hand. Typically, proximal visual stimuli (~5 cm from the hand) interfere with left tactile perception more severely than distant ones (~35 cm from the hand). The near–far modulation of cross-modal extinction has been interpreted as the behavioural hallmark of multisensory (visual-tactile) processing systems representing near peripersonal space in humans (di Pellegrino et al., 1997; Farnè & Làdavas, 2002; Làdavas et al., 1998a, 1998b).

The analogies between primate species in the coding of peripersonal space not only concern relatively static aspects as spatial tuning effects, but also dynamic aspects (for review, see Làdavas, 2002; Làdavas & Farnè, in press) such as those involved in the transient re-sizing of the peri-hand space representation, which can be produced by the use of a tool as a physical extension of the hand-grasping space (Farnè & Làdavas, 2000; Iriki, Tanaka, & Iwamura, 1996). The use of a rake to retrieve distant food pellets enlarges the visual RFs of bimodal neurons of the monkey's parietal cortex along the rake axis, showing a re-mapping of relatively far visual objects as nearer ones. The expansion is strictly dependent upon the active use of the rake, since no modification is manifest when monkeys passively hold the tool; passive tool-wielding actually brings about a contraction of visual RFs back to pre-tool-use size (Iriki et al., 1996).

We have recently provided behavioural evidence for similar tool incorporation into peri-hand space representation in right brain-damaged patients with visuotactile extinction (Farnè & Làdavas, 2000), by presenting visual stimuli at the distal edge of a 38 cm long rake held statically in the patients' ipsilesional hand. Patients' accuracy in detecting concurrent touches on their left hand was evaluated before and immediately after a 5 min period of tool use (retrieving distant objects with the rake), and showed that cross-modal extinction was more severe *after* than before tool use. This evidence of an expansion of peri-hand space was short-lasting, since after 5–10 min. of rest, during which the patient passively held the rake, the amount of cross-modal extinction had regained a pre-tool-use level, suggesting a back-contraction of the elongated peri-hand space. In addition, similar movements performed without the rake (pointing distant objects) did not affect cross-modal extinction, showing that tool incorporation was not merely due to any kind of directional motor activity (Farnè & Làdavas, 2000).

Complementary evidence of peri-hand space expansion has been reported by others (Ackroyd, Riddoch, Humphreys, Nightingale, & Townsend, 2002; Berti & Frassinetti, 2000; Maravita, Husain, Clarke, & Driver, 2001b) yielding consistent results, although in different situations. In a single case study, Maravita and colleagues (2001b) found increased visuotactile extinction when visual stimuli were presented at the end of a 50 cm long stick the patient held in his ipsilesional hand, compared to control conditions in which the stick was absent, or lying on the table, but not grasped by the patient. This finding suggests the possibility that the expansion of peri-hand space representation can also be induced passively, without any activity aimed at physically interacting with objects by means of a tool, but just by modifying the visual/proprioceptive information concerning the body configuration. At odds with this observation, in a more recent report on the same patient, Maravita and colleagues (Maravita, Clarke, Husain, & Driver, 2002a) found that cross-modal extinction was reduced after active tool use with the contralesional hand, but not after a passive experience with the same tool. Since in our previous report (Farnè & Làdavas, 2000) the effects of passively wielding the rake were not examined, the possible differential role played by passive vs. active experience with tools in determining changes in peripersonal space representation still constitutes an unsolved issue.

Therefore, a first aim of the present study was to investigate directly whether or not a prolonged, but passive, exposure to a hand-held tool is sufficient to elongate the peri-hand space representation. In the light of the above-cited neurophysiological findings, we hypothesised that tool *use* would be crucial for the tool to be incorporated into an expanded peri-hand area, whereas a passive change in the physical appearance of the body configuration, appearing to be elongated by the hand-held tool, would not be sufficient.

As a second aim, we asked whether a linear relationships exists between the length of a tool and the amount of peri-hand space that is elongated by its use. In other words, we investigated whether using a long or a short tool would produce differential amounts of peri-hand space elongation, as assessed by cross-modal extinction at the same far location in the nonreachable space. The linear relationships hypothesis would predict that, with respect to a fixed far location (60 cm from the hand), the use of a 30 cm long tool would induce a smaller elongation, if any at all, than the use of a 60 cm long tool. In contrast, if peri-hand space is an all-or-none phenomenon, a comparable amount of elongation would be found independent of tool-length.

In order to verify these hypotheses, a right-brain-damaged patient with left tactile, as well as cross-modal, extinction was examined in a visuo-tactile paradigm involving different tool-related situations in which he was (a) exposed passively to the experience of holding a 60 cm long tool in his ipsilesional hand, and (b) required to actively use either the same or (c) a shorter 30 cm long tool to physically interact with out-of-reach objects. Following our hypotheses, the amount of cross-modal extinction, as assessed far from the patient's ipsilesional hand before tool use, should increase after active use of a tool, but not after an equally long period of passive exposure to the same tool; moreover, cross-modal extinction induced by equally *far* visual stimuli should increase after active use of the long, but not the short tool.

MATERIALS AND METHODS

Case report

Patient LE is an 69-year-old right-handed male (13 years of education) who gave his informed consent to participate in the study. He suffered an ischaemic stroke in the right hemisphere 17 months before the test, when he still presented with a mild left hemiparesis as assessed by a motricity index scale (Demeurisse, Demol, & Robaye, 1980). Some proprioceptive deficit was also present in the contralesional arm. A CT scan revealed a large lesion in the territory of the right middle cerebral artery damaging both cortical and subcortical structures (see Figure 1). On clinical examination he was alert and oriented in time and space. No visual field defects were evident when assessed by Goldman perimetry. At the time of testing, the initially severe neglect had recovered almost completely, as shown by a variety of tests included into the Behavioural Inattention Test (BIT) battery (Wilson, Cockburn, & Halligan, 1987). LE scored well above cut-off level on both BIT versions (135 on the conventional, 76 on the behavioural), presenting some slight, residual sign of ipsilesional bias on the bell cancellation test (Gauthier, Dehaut, & Joanette, 1989), in which he cancelled out 13 vs. 15 items on the left and right side of the sheet, respectively. No left–right bias was shown by LE on either line (Albert, 1973) or letter (Diller & Weinberg, 1977) cancellation tasks, nor was he affected by personal neglect (Cocchini, Beschin, & Jehkonen, 2001). In contrast, LE showed visual extinction on confrontation test (80% of accuracy on single left vs. 40% under double simultaneous stimulation).

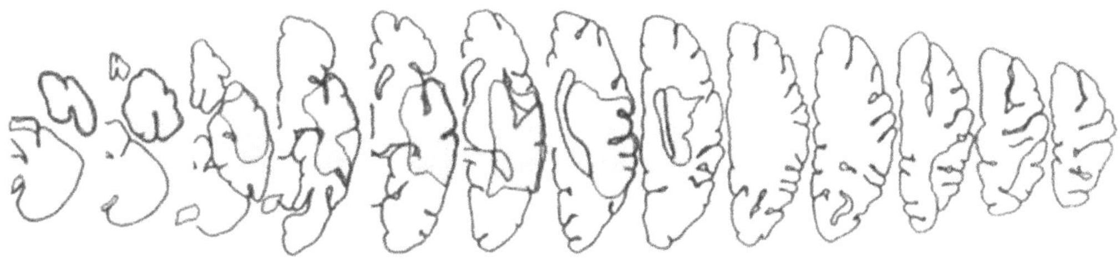

	F8	F9	T3	T5	T6	T7	T8	T9	T12	P1	P5	O6	BG1,2	BG3,4	IC	Th
L.E.	X	X	X	X	X	X	X	X	X	X	X	X	X	X	X	X

Figure 1. *Affected areas (grey shaded) of the right hemisphere are reconstructed according to Damasio and Damasio's (1989) method and reported on standard brain template. The same coding system has also been used to identify areas that were involved by the lesion (x), reported in the lower part. F: frontal; T: temporal; P: parietal; O: occipital; BG: basal ganglia; IC: internal capsule; Th: thalamus.*

Most relevant for the purposes of the present study, the presence of left tactile extinction emerged under conditions of simultaneous bilateral tactile stimulation. Tactile extinction was assessed by delivering light touches to the dorsal surface of the 2nd phalanx of the subject's index fingers. Light taps were manually given by the examiner's index fingers. Twenty unilateral left and right tactile stimuli and 20 bilateral simultaneous tactile stimuli were delivered in each session before experimental testing. LE's performance on single stimuli was well preserved, insofar as he reported almost all single left touches (95% of correct detection), and all right tactile stimulation (100% of correct detection). His accurate tactile sensitivity also proved to be stable across all the experimental testing (see below) in relation to both hands. In contrast, he showed clear signs of left tactile extinction when two stimuli were simultaneously applied to the hands (48% of correct detection).

In addition, LE showed cross-modal visuotactile extinction, i.e., he largely missed left tactile stimuli, which were otherwise well detected (93% correct), when simultaneously presented with ipsilesional visual stimuli (40% correct). Visual stimuli were brief movements of the left experimenter's index finger in the patient's ipsilesional visual field. Most interestingly, left tactile detection under bilateral cross-modal stimulation was modulated by the distance at which visual stimuli were presented from the patient's right hand. LE was less accurate when presented with visual stimuli close to the ipsilesional hand (~5 cm above the patient's right hand, 30% correct) than far from the same hand (~35 cm above it, 50% correct).

Apparatus and procedure

The patient sat in quiet room, hands resting on a table surface and separated by approximately 40 cm. A red dot, aligned with the subject's body midline, was marked on the table surface in front of the subject (60 cm from the proximal border of the table), and served as fixation point. At the beginning of each trial, the experimenter checked that the subject was gazing at the fixation dot. A green plastic shield (width 18 cm, height 18 cm, depth 40 cm) prevented the subject from viewing tactile stimuli delivered either to the left or right hand (unimodal tactile condition), or the left hand (cross-modal conditions). Tactile stimulation was silently applied by means of a pair of synthetic monofilaments analogous to Semmes-Weinstein probes, mounted on a plastic rod handled by the experimenter, that had been chosen to bring about the same amount of extinction obtained through manual palpation (45 gm required for the monofilament to buckle). The probes were used to deliver brief touches (< 1 s) on the dorsal aspect of the 2nd phalanx of the subject's index fingers. Visual stimuli consisted of a rapid flexion-extension of the examiner's left index finger (approximately 5 cm of excursion). Visual stimuli were always presented far from the patient's right hand (60 cm away in the radial plane) with the exception of one cross-modal condition, in which they were presented in the peri-hand space (~5 cm above the patient's right hand). Depending on the experimental condition (see below), cross-modal extinction was assessed while the patient statically held one of two possible tools in the ipsilesional hand. The tools were either a long (60 cm), or a short (30 cm) wooden rake, each attached to a wooden ergonomic handle (14 cm long), which was gently grasped by the patient, with the right hand passively laying on the table surface.

Four types of stimulation were delivered in each experimental condition: unilateral left or right stimulation, bilateral simultaneous stimulation, or no stimulation at all (catch trials). For each type of stimulation, 20 trials were presented according to a fixed pseudorandom sequence. The patient was informed that on some occasions he would not receive any stimulus (CT), and was instructed to report verbally the side of the stimulation with the words "left," "right," "both," or "none," independent of whether a stimulus was felt or seen. He was submitted twice to the following unimodal and cross-modal conditions.

In the unimodal tactile condition (T-T), somatosensory stimuli were delivered to either the right, left, or both (screened) hands.

In the first cross-modal condition (V-T Near), only the left hand was screened and visuotactile extinction was evaluated by delivering ipsilesional visual stimuli close to the patient's right hand (see Figure 2a).

Cross-modal condition 2 (V-T Far) was similar to the previous one, except that visuotactile extinction was evaluated by presenting the visual stimulus 60 cm away, on the radial plane, from the patient's right hand (Figure 2a). This condition provided a direct estimate of the amount of cross-modal extinction obtained by visually stimulating the far peripersonal space.

Cross-modal condition 3 (V-T Far long-tool-exposure) was identical to the previous one, except that the gap between the patient's hand and the far visual stimulus location was filled by the presence of a long rake (60 cm), statically held in the patient's right hand. The visual stimulus was equally far from the patient's hand (60 cm), being thus presented at the distal edge of the rake, without touching it (Figure 2b). Visuotactile extinction was assessed, as described above, immediately after a 5-min period during which the patient was passively exposed to the visual/somatosensory experience of having a long tool in his own hand. During this period the patient was instructed to look at the tool without moving it, and the experimenter verified the absence of hand movements.

Cross-modal condition 4 (V-T Far long-tool-use) was similar to condition 3, with the exception that cross-modal extinction was assessed after a 5-min period during which the patient was engaged in an active task involving the use of the hand-held rake to retrieve distant objects, located out of the hand-reaching space. Objects were plastic disks (3 cm in diameter, 1 cm thick) presented one at a time in a working area that was located out of the hand-reaching space, at the distal edge of the table. The patient was asked to reach and retrieve each object with the rake. Disks were randomly presented in correspondence with patients' mid-sagittal axis, or 10 and 20 degrees to the left and to the right of the central position. After 50 retrieval movements, lasting about 5 min, cross-modal extinction was reassessed as in condition 3 (see Figure 2b), while the patient was statically holding the rake.

Cross-modal condition 5 (V-T Far short-tool-use) was similar to condition 4, but the patient statically held the short (30 cm) rake in his right hand (see Figure 2c). The visual stimulus was always located at the same far position (60 cm away from the patient's hand) well beyond the distal edge of the rake, and visuotactile extinction was evaluated after 50 movements, lasting about 5 minutes, aimed at retrieving less distant objects from the work-area by actively using the short rake.

In each cross-modal condition, tactile stimuli were delivered to the patient's left screened hand

(Figure 2d). All conditions lasted about 5 min and were run in separate blocks following a randomised order that was inverted between sessions. An interval of 5–10 min was introduced at the end of each condition, during which the tool (if present) was removed and the patient was allowed to rest, and verbally interact with the experimenter.

RESULTS

Patient LE showed a highly reliable pattern of performance, producing only one false alarm (coded as "left") in response to catch trials across all conditions and sessions. Tactile sensitivity was well preserved and proved to be very stable throughout the testing. On average, tactile stimuli singly delivered to the left hand were correctly reported on 93% of trials, without varying significantly across conditions (range 90–98%). LE performed the task flawlessly when considering single tactile or visual stimuli presented in the right hemispace.

In contrast, LE showed left spatial extinction after both unimodal and cross-modal bilateral stimulation. Concerning unimodal extinction, left tactile stimuli were reported on 43% of trials when presented together with a simultaneous touch on the right, whereas they were detected on 93% of trials when presented alone ($p < .0001$ by Fisher Exact test). A substantial extinction phenomenon was also present when visual stimuli were concurrently presented on the ipsilesional side (V-T conditions 1 and 2 collapsed), whereby left touches were overall reported on a lesser proportion (49%) compared to single left stimulation (92%, $p < .0001$ by Fisher Exact test).

As expected, the amount of visuotactile extinction obtained when the tool was not present nor

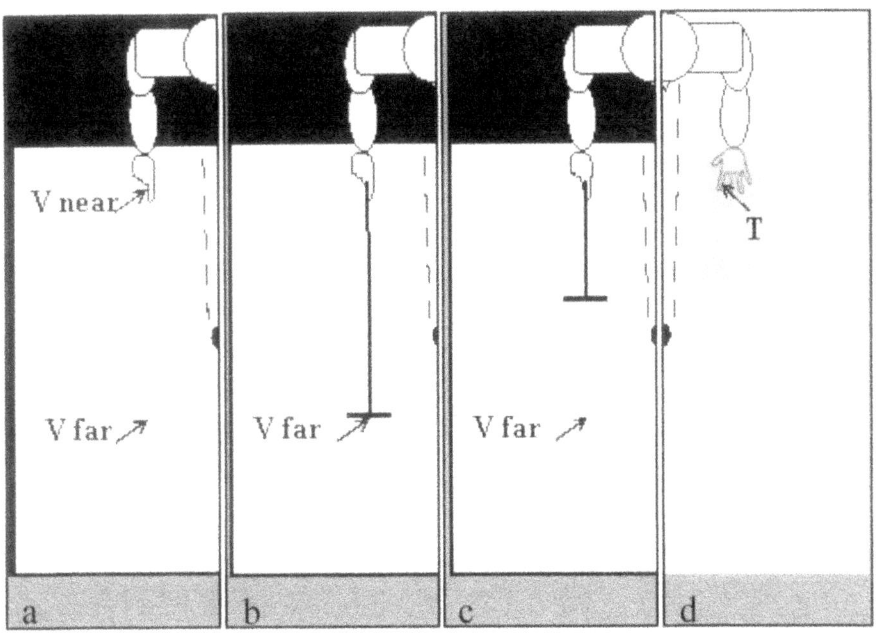

Figure 2. *Schematic illustration of the cross-modal visual-tactile conditions and experimental setting, viewed from above. The visual stimulus (V) could be located near or far from the patient's right hand in conditions not involving the tool (a), but only in the far position in those involving the tool (b, c). Tactile (T) stimuli were delivered to the patients' left hand (d) whose vision was prevented by a shield (grey rectangle). Note that the visual stimulus was presented always in the same distant position (60 cm from the hand) in all the far conditions: (a) without any tool, (b) after passive visual/proprioceptive exposure to the long tool and after active long tool use, (c) after active use of the short tool.*

used was significantly modulated by the distance of the visual stimulus from the patient's hand (see Figure 3). Cross-modal extinction was more severe in the V-T Near (38% of accuracy) than in the V-T Far condition (60% of accuracy; $p < .04$ by Fisher Exact test). In addition, the severity of cross-modal extinction produced by visual stimulation of the peri-hand space was comparable to that obtained by tactile stimulation of the ipsilesional hand (38% and 43% of accuracy, respectively).

To test whether and to what extent the passive exposure to the hand-held tool modified the patient's accuracy, cross-modal extinction obtained in condition 2 and 3 (V-T Far and V-T Far long-tool-exposure, respectively) was compared. As can be seen in Figure 3, no significant change was observed between the latter conditions, patient's accuracy showing a comparable amount of extinction when the tool was absent (60% of accuracy) or present after passive exposure (65% correct).

To verify whether and to what extent the active use of the hand-held tool influenced the patient's accuracy, cross-modal extinction obtained in condition 3 and 4 (V-T Far long-tool-exposure and V-T Far long-tool-use, respectively) was compared. As shown in Figure 3, cross-modal extinction obtained after active use of the long tool (43% of accuracy) was significantly more severe than that obtained after the passive exposure to the same tool (60% of accuracy, $p < .04$ by Fisher Exact test). Interestingly, the severity of visuotactile extinction observed after active long-tool-use (43% of accuracy) was comparable to that shown by the patient when the visual stimulus was presented close to his right hand (38% accuracy).

Finally, to test whether and to what extent the active use of a short tool modified the patient's accuracy, cross-modal extinction obtained in condition 3 and 5 (V-T Far long-tool-exposure and V-T Far short-tool-use, respectively) was compared. Figure 3 shows that patients' accuracy in the far space was somewhat reduced after the use of the short tool (55% of accuracy) compared to the condition in which the patient was passively exposed to the long tool (65% of accuracy), although this difference did not reach significance. Similarly, the amount of cross-modal extinction assessed in the far space after active short-tool-use (55% of accuracy) was less severe than that obtained after active use of the long tool (43% of accuracy), without reaching significance. No other significant difference were found.

DISCUSSION

Consistent with neurophysiological findings showing expansion of the visual RF of visuotactile neurons along the rake used by monkeys to retrieve out-of-hand-reach objects (Iriki et al., 1996; Obayashi et al., 2001), recent studies have shown fast and reversible elongation of the multisensory peripersonal space representation in humans (Farnè & Làdavas, 2000; Maravita et al., 2001b). The results of the present study clearly show that a relatively prolonged, but passive experience with a tool is not sufficient to induce such a dynamic remapping of far space as near space. Indeed, when cross-modal effects were assessed in the far space after a short period of passive exposure to the proprioceptive and visual experience of wielding a

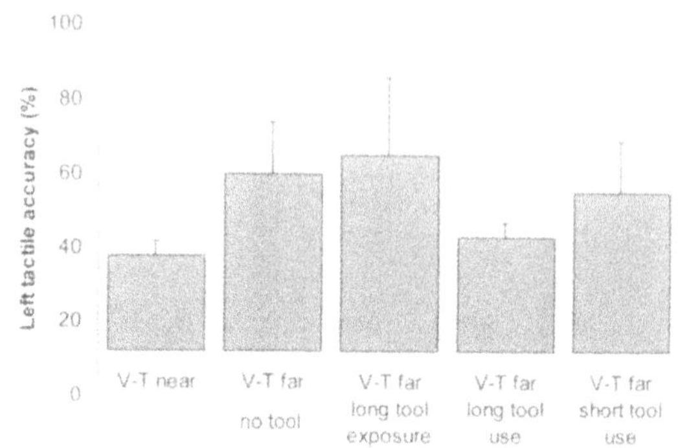

Figure 3. *The mean percentage of left contralesional tactile detection is reported as a function of bilateral stimulation in the cross-modal visual-tactile (V-T) conditions. From left to right, percentage accuracy is reported for conditions wherein visual stimuli were presented at a small (~5 cm, near) and large distance (~60 cm, far) from the patient's right hand, when the rake was absent (no tool), after the passive exposure to the long rake (long tool exposure), and after active use of either the long (long tool use) or short (short tool use) rake.*

rake, the severity of visual-tactile extinction was absolutely comparable to that obtained when the tool was actually absent. This favours the idea that plastic modifications of the body schema (Head & Holmes, 1911) are not the product of passive changes in proprioceptive/kinaesthesic or visual inputs per se.

Long-lasting experience with objects that have been in contact with the body is known to possibly give raise to their inclusion into the mental representation of someone's body, as has been reported by Aglioti and colleagues (Aglioti, Smania, Manfredi, & Berlucchi, 1996) in a right-brain-damaged patient. By investigating the delusional belief of disownership of her left hand, they elegantly demonstrated that the body schema can be extended to include paraphernalia, such as rings, whose ownership was also denied only when they were worn on the refuted left hand. While at first sight the incorporation of rings in the body schema might be thought as an example of passive tool embodiment, the aged experience with rings is most likely to be an active process, since a ring would mediate most of the hand-related multisensory information during daily activities.

Similarly, an artificial extension of our reachable space by a hand-held tool would not necessarily imply a tool incorporation phenomenon unless the tool is used in some active way. Indeed, when cross-modal extinction was assessed equally far in space, but immediately after the active use of a long tool, we observed in LE a significant increase of cross-modal extinction. Consistent with the results of our previous group study, the worsening of this visual-tactile phenomenon confirms the notion that the area surrounding the hand, within which visual and tactile information is processed by multisensory mechanisms, had expanded along the tool axis towards the distal edge of the rake (Farnè & Làdavas, 2000; Iriki et al., 1996). Most interestingly, this considerably extends our knowledge about dynamic tool incorporation in humans, by making it clear that the plastic modifications are tightly linked to the active, purposeful use of a tool as physical extension of the body, which allows interaction with otherwise nonreachable objects. Indeed, the results of the present study, whereby the cross-modal effects obtained after a protracted, passive tool exposure have been directly contrasted with those obtained after an equally long period of active tool use, strongly favour the idea that the key aspect of tool incorporation is the functional activity performed with the tool itself.

When considering closely related evidence, the fact that active use of a tool is necessary to obtain plastic elongation of peri-hand space is prima facie at variance with a previous single case study (Maravita et al., 2001), and in agreement with more recent findings reported on the same patient (Maravita, Spence, Kennett, & Driver, 2002). A protracted experience in using a tool with the contralesional hand may reduce extinction (see Maravita et al., 2002), whereas a passive experience with a tool held in the ipsilesional hand may increase extinction (Maravita et al., 2001). However, this inconsistency might be only apparent. In the latter case study, despite the lack of any training activity with the tool (a 50 cm long stick), the patient was *actively* wielding and orienting the stick to keep its distal end in contact with a small mark in the far space, and this active component of the task was reinforced (Maravita et al., 2001b, p. 582). In addition, no re-mapping effect on extinction was found when the stick was passively laying on the table and physically disconnected from the patient's hand. Therefore, it might be possible to consider that pointing with a stick and retrieving objects with a rake are similarly active processes, which can be equally efficient in widening the area of visual-tactile processing of the hand. This possibility is further strengthened by considering the different functional properties that characterise different tools, as well as the different goals the tools are used for. While a rake is most obviously related to the aim of reaching out-of-reach objects in order to grasp them, a stick is most likely to be useful for precisely indicating far positions in space, in a much more efficient way than the deictic pointing of a finger (Bates & Dick, 2002). Thus, both the previous reports may actually converge with the findings we reported here in showing the key role played by active tool use in dynamic size-change of peri-hand space.

On the basis of the present study, we further suggest not only that a mere directional motor activity cannot widen the peri-hand space (Farnè & Làdavas, 2000), but also that the appropriate tool-related action might be necessary to achieve such a widening.

It is noteworthy that the present findings are also consistent with neurophysiological studies showing that the effects on their visual RFs can be found immediately after tool use, but not passive tool wielding. In all the cases reported in animals, tool use involved rake-shaped tools and the associated retrieving actions (Iriki et al., 1996; Obayashi et al., 2001; Obayashi, Tanaka, & Iriki, 2000). Moreover, several other instances of near–far space re-mapping as a function of tool use have been reported so far in normal subjects (Maravita et al., 2002) and neglect patients (Ackroyd et al., 2002; Berti & Frassinetti, 2000). Further, the typical rightward bias of neglect on line cancellation tasks can be modulated by the use of different types of tools, both in the near and far space (Pegna et al., 2001). In all these neuropsychological cases, patients actively used sticks or rulers as tools, and neglect behaviour was altered in an almost on-line way, i.e., during the use of sticks either for bisecting lines or locating objects in space, without previous training. It is therefore possible that the elongation of the multisensory area surrounding the hand also depends upon the complexity of the action that is required for using a tool, and future studies will hopefully reveal whether the incorporation of different types of tools or paraphernalia might require differential amount of practice, as large and long-lasting effects may be obtained after an extensive training (see Maravita et al., 2002).

As a second aim of the present study, we asked whether the phenomenon of tool incorporation is linearly modulated by physical aspects of the tool, and in particular by its length. When compared with our previous results, the present findings show that peri-hand space elongation can be similarly induced, within the same paradigm, by using either a short tool (16% post-tool use increase in V-T extinction, in Farnè & Làdavas, 2000), or a much longer tool (22% post-tool use increase in V-T extinction, this study), provided that cross-modal extinction is assessed at the distal edge of each tool. This would imply that the multisensory integrative area elongates to include the space located (at least) at the distal edge of both tools. In addition, the present findings support the idea that this change is related to the length of the tool. Indeed, when cross-modal extinction was assessed after the use of a short tool at the same far location in space, and thus beyond the distal edge of the tool, no significant decrease in LE's performance was obtained. This finding strongly suggests that the spatial extent of the peri-hand space elongation induced by using a short rake is smaller compared to that induced by a long(er) rake. This, in turn, would favour the hypothesis of a linear relationship between tool-length and amount of peri-hand space elongation. However, the results also showed that cross-modal extinction after active use of a long tool did not differ significantly from that obtained, in the same far position, after the active use of the short tool. The latter finding might indicate that the degree of elongation produced by short tool use partly extended beyond its tip, although not sufficiently to reveal significant modifications of performance at the far distance. Therefore, it might be difficult to clearly disambiguate, on this single case basis, which kind of relationships exist between the length of a tool and peri-hand elongation induced by its use. The possibility that the border of this elongation does not sharply correspond to the distal edge of the tool, but rather extends beyond it, has been recently investigated, receiving support from the findings of a group study (Farnè, Iriki, & Làdavas, in press).

In summary, while it would be interesting to assess in the future whether peripersonal space size-changes following tool use take place only along the tool axis (i.e., elongation), or would actually spread in different directions from the hand (i.e., widening), the present study showed that functional motor activity performed with the tool is a crucial condition for tool embodiment to occur, the degree of this phenomenon being possibly related to the physical length of the tool.

PrEview proof published online 20 December 2004

REFERENCES

Ackroyd, K., Riddoch, M. J., Humphreys, G. W., Nightingale, S., & Townsend, S. (2002). Widening the sphere of influence: Using a tool to extend extrapersonal visual space in a patient with severe neglect. *Neurocase, 8*, 1–12.

Aglioti, S., Smania, N., Manfredi, M., & Berlucchi, G. (1996). Disownership of left hand and objects related to it in a patient with right brain damage. *NeuroReport, 8*, 293–296.

Albert, M. L. (1973). A simple test for visual neglect. *Neurology, 23*, 658–664.

Bates, E., & Dick, F. (2002). Language, gesture, and the developing brain. *Developmental Psychobiology, 40*, 293–310.

Bender, M. B. (1952). *Disorders in perception*. Springfield, IL: C.C. Thomas.

Berti, A., & Frassinetti, F. (2000). When far becomes near: Remapping of space by tool use. *Journal of Cognitive Neuroscience, 3*, 415–420.

Bremmer, F., Schlack, A., Duhamel, J. R., Graf, W., & Fink, G. R. (2001a). Space coding in primate posterior parietal cortex. *NeuroImage, 14*, S46–S51.

Bremmer, F., Schlack, A., Shah, N. J. Z. O., Kubischik, M., Hoffmann, K. P., Zilles, K., & Fink, G. R. (2001b). Polymodal motion processing in posterior parietal and premotor cortex: A human fMRI study strongly implies equivalencies between humans and monkeys. *Neuron, 29*, 287–296.

Cocchini, G., Beschin, N., & Jehkonen, M. (2001). The Fluff Test: A simple test to assess body representation neglect. *Neuropsychological Rehabilitation, 11*, 17–31.

Culham, J. C., & Kanwisher, N. G. (2001). Neuroimaging of cognitive functions in human parietal cortex. *Current Opinion in Neurobiology, 11*, 157–163.

Damasio, H., & Damasio, A. R. (1989). *Lesion analysis in neuropsychology*. New York: Oxford University Press.

Demeurisse, G., Demol, O., & Robaye, E. (1980). Motor evaluation in vascular hemiplegia. *European Neurology, 19*, 382–389.

Diller, L., & Weinberg, J. (1977). Hemi-inattention in rehabilitation: The evolution of a rational remediation program. *Advances in Neurology, 18*, 63–82.

di Pellegrino, G., Làdavas, E., & Farnè, A. (1997). Seeing where your hands are. *Nature, 338*, 730.

Duhamel, J. R., Colby, C. L., & Goldberg, M. E. (1991). Congruent representation of visual and somatosensory space in single neurons of monkey ventral intraparietal area (VIP). In J. Paillard (Ed.), *Brain and space* (pp. 223–236). New York: Oxford University Press.

Duhamel, J. R., Colby, C. L., & Goldberg, M. E. (1998). Ventral intraparietal area of the macaque: Congruent visual and somatic response properties. *Journal of Neurophysiology, 79*, 126–36.

Farnè, A., Demattè, M. L., & Làdavas, E. (2003). Beyond the window: Multisensory representation of peripersonal space across a transparent barrier. *International Journal of Psychophysiology, 50*, 51–61.

Farnè, A., Iriki, A., & Làdavas E. (in press). Shaping multisensory action-space with tools: Evidence from patients with cross-modal extinction. *Neuropsychologia*.

Farnè, A., & Làdavas, E. (2000). Dynamic size-change of hand peripersonal space following tool use. *NeuroReport, 85*, 1645–1649.

Farnè, A., & Làdavas, E. (2002). Auditory peripersonal space in humans. *Journal of Cognitive Neuroscience, 14*, 1030–1043.

Fogassi, L., Gallese, V., Fadiga, L., Luppino, G., Matelli, M., & Rizzolatti, G. (1996). Coding of peripersonal space in inferior premotor cortex (area F4). *Journal of Neurophysiology, 76*, 141–157.

Fogassi, L., Raos, V., Franchi, G., Gallese, V., Luppino, G., & Matelli, M. (1999). Visual responses in the dorsal premotor area F2 of the macaque monkey. *Experimental Brain Research, 128*, 194–199.

Gauthier, L., Dehaut, F., & Joanette, Y. (1989). The bells test: A quantitative and qualitative test for visual neglect. *International Journal of Clinical Neuropsychology, 11*, 49–54.

Graziano, M. S. A., & Gross, C. G. (1995). The representation of extrapersonal space: A possible role for bimodal, visuotactile neurons. In M. S. Gazzaniga (Ed.), *The cognitive neuroscience* (pp. 1021–1034). Cambridge, MA: MIT Press.

Graziano, M. S. A., & Gross, C. G. (1998). Visual responses with and without fixation: Neurons in premotor cortex encode spatial locations independently of eye position. *Experimental Brain Research, 118*, 373–380.

Grefkes, C., Weiss, P. H., Zilles, K., & Fink, G. R. (2002). Crossmodal processing of object features in human anterior intraparietal cortex: A fMRI study implies equivalencies between human and monkeys. *Neuron, 35*, 173–184.

Head, H., & Holmes, G. (1911). Sensory disturbances from cerebral lesion. *Brain, 34*, 102–254.

Iriki, A., Tanaka, M., & Iwamura, Y. (1996). Coding of modified body schema during tool use by macaque postcentral neurones. *NeuroReport, 7*, 2325–2330.

Làdavas, E. (2002). Functional and dynamic properties of visual peripersonal space in humans. *Trends in Cognitive Sciences, 6*, 17–22.

Làdavas, E., di Pellegrino, G., Farnè, A., & Zeloni, G. (1998a). Neuropsychological evidence of an integrated visuo-tactile representation of peripersonal space in humans. *Journal of Cognitive Neuroscience, 10,* 581–589.

Làdavas, E., & Farnè, A. (in press). Neuropsychological evidence for multimodal representations of space near specific body parts. In C. Spence & J. Driver (Eds.), *Crossmodal space and crossmodal attention.* Oxford: Oxford University Press.

Làdavas, E., Zeloni, G., & Farnè, A. (1998b). Visual peripersonal space centred on the face in humans. *Brain, 121,* 2317–2326.

Macaluso, E., & Driver, J. (2001). Spatial attention and crossmodal interactions between vision and touch. *Neuropsychologia, 39,* 1304–1316.

Maravita, A., Clarke, K., Husain, M., & Driver, J. (2001a). Active tool use with the contralesional hand can reduce cross-modal extinction of touch on that hand. *Neurocase, 8,* 411–416.

Maravita, A., Husain, M., Clarke, K., & Driver, J. (2001b). Reaching with the tool extends visual-tactile interactions into far space: Evidence from cross-modal extinction. *Neuropsychologia, 39,* 580–585.

Maravita, A., Spence, C., Kennett, S., & Driver, J. (2002). Tool-use changes multimodal spatial interactions between vision and touch in normal humans. *Cognition, 83,* B25–B34.

Mattingley, J. B., Driver, J., Beschin, N., & Robertson, I. H. (1997). Attentional competition between modalities: Extinction between touch and vision after right hemisphere damage. *Neuropsychologia, 35,* 867–880.

Obayashi, S., Suhara, T. Kawabe, K., Ochauki, T., Maeda, J., Akine, Y., Onoe, H., & Iriki, A. (2001). Functional brain mapping of monkey tool use. *NeuroImage, 14,* 853–861.

Obayashi, S., Tanaka, M., & Iriki, A. (2000). Subjective image of invisible hand coded by monkey intraparietal neurons. *NeuroReport, 11,* 3499–3505.

Pegna, A. J., Petit, L., Caldara-Schnetzer, A. S., Khateb, A., Annoni, J. M., Sztajzel, R., & Landis, T. (2001). So near yet so far: Neglect in far or near space depends on tool use. *Annals of Neurology, 50,* 820–822.

Rizzolatti, G., Luppino, G., & Matelli, M. (1998). The organization of the cortical motor system: New concepts. *Electroencephalography and Clincal Neurophysiology, 106,* 283–296.

Rizzolatti, G., Matelli, M., & Pavesi, G. (1983). Deficits in attention and movement following the removal of postarcuate (area 6) cortex in macaque monkeys. *Brain, 106,* 655–673.

Rizzolatti, G., Scandolara, C., Matelli, M., & Gentilucci, M. (1981). Afferent properties of periarcuate neurons in macaque monkeys. II Visual responses, *Behavioral Brain Research, 2,* 147–63.

Weiss, P., Marshall, J. C., Wunderlich, G., Tellmann, L., Halligan, P. W., Freund, H. J., Zilles, K., & Fink, G. R. (2000). Neural consequences of acting in near versus far space: A physiological basis for clinical dissociations. *Brain, 123,* 2531–2541.

Wilson, B., Cockburn, J., & Halligan, P. (1987). Development of a behavioral test of visuospatial neglect. *Archives of Physical and Medical Rehabilitation, 68,* 98–102.

COGNITIVE NEUROPSYCHOLOGY, 2005, 22 (3/4), 419–432

GOAL-DIRECTED IMITATION IN PATIENTS WITH IDEOMOTOR APRAXIA

Harold Bekkering

Max-Planck-Institute for Psychological Research, Cognition and Action, Munich, Germany, University of Groningen, and Radboud University Nijmegen, The Netherlands

Marcel Brass

Max-Planck-Institute for Psychological Research, Cognition and Action, Munich and Max-Planck-Institute of Cognitive Neuroscience, Leipzig, Germany

Susanne Woschina

Max-Planck-Institute for Psychological Research, Cognition and Action, Munich and University of Eichstätt, Germany

Arthur M. Jacobs

University of Eichstätt and Freie Universität Berlin, Germany

The present study compared imitation performance in patients with ideomotor apraxia (IMA), eight right hemispheric-damaged patients, and eight control participants without neurological damage in three experiments. Experiment 1 confirmed in the Goldenberg test that IMA patients were particularly impaired in hand gestures and combined finger and hand gestures, but not in the imitation of finger gestures, compared to the other two groups. Experiment 2, however, demonstrated that finger selection is not per se preserved in imitative behaviour in patients with IMA. Experiment 3 confirmed this finding in an experiment under visual control. Together, the results add evidence to the idea that imitation should be viewed from a goal-directed rather than a body-mapping perspective, and that highest priority is given to more distal aspects of imitation as reaching for the correct object, rather than the means used to achieve the goal of a modelled action.

INTRODUCTION

Imitation

Imitation, or performing an act after perceiving it (Thorndike, 1898), is currently in the focus of attention of researchers from many different disciplines like biology, neurology, artificial intelligence, and psychology. Regarding human beings, there is little doubt about the fact that to some extent we do learn to interact with the surrounding world by means of imitation. However, one question unresolved as yet is how the imitator can *execute* a similar action to a *perceived* action performed by a model. That this is not a trivial question becomes apparent in the case of patients with ideomotor apraxia (IMA). Ideomotor apraxia is characterised by the inability to imitate gestures, to pantomime tool use, or to perform gestures on verbal command

Correspondence should be addressed to Harold Bekkering, University of Nijmegen, NICI, PO Box 9104, 6500 HE Nijmegen, The Netherlands (Email: h.bekkering@nici.kun.nl).

The authors wish to thank all patients and staff of the clinics in Kipfenberg, Bad Aibling, and Bad Heilbrunn that participated in these studies. The authors would like to thank Georg Goldenberg for detailed information about the gestures used in Experiment 1. We also thank Rafaella Rumiati, Glyn Humphreys, and an anonymous reviewer for improving previous versions of the manuscript. IST-grant 2000-29689 supported the first author.

(e.g., De Renzi & Faglioni, 1999; Goldenberg, 1995; Liepmann, 1900), which is commonly observed after damage to the left parietal or frontal lobes. The disorder cannot be explained by weakness, deafferentation, abnormalities of posture or tone, involuntary movement disorder, or an inability to comprehend (Heilman & Rothi, 1993). The mechanisms underlying apraxia in general, and the inability to imitate gestures in specific, are poorly understood. It is the purpose of this paper to investigate the functional deficits in IMA patients in relation to current neuro-cognitive theories of imitation, and vice versa to investigate these theories in more detail in relation to the deficits observed in IMA patients.

Neurocognitive theories of imitation

It is likely that the most crucial mechanism that has to be explained to better understand the functioning of imitation is the transfer from perception of the model's movement into the action execution of the imitator (Bekkering, 2002). Neurocognitive theories about this transformation mechanism can be ordered on a continuum from concepts that advocate a direct route between the perception and the production of an act to concepts that interpret imitation as a goal-directed behaviour. Briefly, the direct mapping theories assume that a perception–production transduction transfers directly the perceptual information into innovatory motor patterns (e.g., Butterworth, 1990; Gray, Neisser, Shapiro, & Kouns, 1991; Vogt, 1995, 1996) and some neurophysiological evidence for this view has been reported (e.g., Baldissera, Cavallari, Craighero, & Fadiga, 2001; Fadiga, Fogassi, Gallese, & Rizzolatti, 1995).

In contrast, goal-directed theories of imitation postulate the presence of high-level information processing during imitation (e.g., Bekkering, Wohlschläger, & Gattis, 2000; Gleissner, Meltzoff, & Bekkering, 2000; Wohlschläger & Bekkering, 2002; see, for a review, Bekkering & Wohlschläger, 2002), a notion that also has recently found neurophysiological support (Aziz-Zadeh, Maeda, Zaidel, Mazziotta, & Iacoboni, 2002; Koski et al., 2002). The basic assumption here is that when we observe an action, we do not try so much to sequence the action elements observed into specific movements that have been made, rather we extract the perceivable action effects, typically called action goals. Consequently, the percepts of such action goals automatically activate the motor programme that is most strongly associated with this goal, and thus can result in imitative movements that strongly deviate from the movements observed from the model.

In between these poles are theories that negate a direct perceptuomotor transduction but state that the perceptual system and the action system are commensurable because they share equivalences such as the spatiotemporal structure or the metric used to equate acts seen and acts done in commensurable terms (e.g., the active intermodal mapping—AIM—theory of Meltzoff, 1993; Meltzoff & Moore, 1977). For instance, according to AIM, the observer codes the motor acts of another person in terms of "organ relations," that is, spatial arrangements between significant body parts such as hands, head, tongue, lips, etc. Importantly, the crucial difference between direct-mapping and body mapping theories on the one side and goal-directed theories of imitation on the other side is the issue of what gets activated when watching the model's act. Direct and body mapping theories presume that the equivalent body part of the imitator (effector) gets activated and, consequently, a motor programme that evokes a similar movement. The goal-directed theory, on the other hand, assumes that representations in the brain of the sensory consequences of the motor action rather than the effector involved gets activated and consequently a motor programme that evokes similar sensory consequences; see also Rumiati and Bekkering (2003) for an overview.

IMA

Research on ideomotor apraxia (IMA) has a long history and goes back to the beginnings of neuropsychology (Liepmann, 1900). Ideomotor apraxia must be distinguished from ideational apraxia (IA), which was introduced by Pick (1905). Ideational apraxia was assumed to be a sequencing disorder in the conceptual organisation of complex actions (Poeck, 1983). That is, patients with IA presumably have a more secondary motor deficit compared to patients with IMA (e.g., De Renzi & Lucchelli, 1988).

Theories about IMA also fall into two camps (Sunderland & Sluman, 2000). The dominant notion about IMA stays close to the concept of IMA as a disorder of action as proposed by Liepmann. From this perspective, the underlying deficit is hypothesised to be impaired storage, selection, or execution of the motor programme on which complex action depends (e.g., Rothi, Ochipa, & Heilman, 1991). The model of Rothi and colleagues, for example, defines a complex network of subsystems, which are involved in the production and imitation of actions, similar to the language domain. The central components of this system involve an action input lexicon and an action output lexicon, as well as an action semantic system. IMA in this model is attributed to various problems with the action output system.

A more recent view, on the other hand, questions whether IMA is a motor programming disorder in the first place, and instead suggests that the underlying problem is a deficit in a high-level representation of body postures that can then indirectly affect performance of certain actions (Goldenberg, 1995; Goldenberg & Hagmann, 1997; Goldenberg, Hermsdörfer, & Spatt, 1996; Hermsdörfer, Mai, Spatt, Marquardt, Veldkamp, & Goldenberg, 1996). Probably the most convincing evidence for the latter view was the finding that left-hemispheric patients who were apractic on direct imitation also showed a significant impairment when asked to replicate the model's posture by manipulating a life-size manikin (Goldenberg, 1995). Nonapractic left-hemisphere patients and those with right-hemispheric damage showed no such impairment. Goldenberg argued that this finding renders the classical view on IMA unlikely because the motor demands of direct gesture imitation vs. use of the manikin were completely different and yet showed defective imitation of meaningless gestures. Goldenberg and Hagmann (1997) provided further support for the high-level representation deficit view in IMA by reporting two patients who showed defective imitation of meaningless gestures (like hand-to-the-cheek) but normal imitation of meaningful gestures (like saluting). They argued that this preservation of one class of gestures but not the other was difficult to reconcile with an account of IMA that situates the problem at the level of motor programming or execution, as this would be necessary to achieve both types of gestures. Goldenberg therefore proposed that the problem lies at an earlier stage, when the patient has to translate the spatial relationships of the observed gesture into a mental representation of an equivalent spatial configuration of the own body. In addition, Goldenberg (1996) examined imitation of hand and finger postures in patients with unilateral brain damage. Imitation of finger postures was relatively defective in the right- brain-damaged patients and imitation of hand postures relatively defective in the left-brain-damaged patients. This finding again argues for a view that left brain damage confuses a more global body-schema and not so much the execution of finger movements, which are well-represented in the brain.

While disordered representation of the body might explain the difficulty in imitation in IMA patients, it is not obvious how it could also explain apractic difficulty in manipulating objects and tools (Goldenberg & Hagmann, 1998; Poizner, Clark, Merians, Macauley, Rothi, & Heilman, 1995). In addition, Sunderland, Bowers, Sluman, Wilcock, and Ardron (1999) reported that impaired gesture imitation was the strongest correlate of minor errors (but not slowing in motor execution) on tests of manual dexterity such as turning cards or spooning beans. Moreover, patients with IMA were found to be selectively impaired in reproducing a sequence of actions such as pressing a button, pulling a handle, and then pressing a bar, actions that do not rely heavily on a body schema representation (Harrington & Haarland, 1992; Kimura, 1977). However, it also has to be noted that some patients who fail to imitate actions are well able to manipulate objects and tools (e.g., De Renzi & Lucchelli, 1988).

Research hypothesis

In sum, recent findings of Goldenberg and colleagues challenge the more traditional view on

IMA as being a motor programming disorder. Rather, they suggest that the underlying problem is a conceptual deficit in a high-level representation of body posture, which can then indirectly affect performance of the action system in imitation of gestures. However, there is good evidence reported in the literature to assume that there is commonly a deficit in IMA that is evident not just on tasks directly involving the reproduction of seen gestures, but also on those having an effect on the manipulation of external objects and other actions (see, for a review, also Leiguarda & Marsden, 2000). Therefore, the present study was designed to investigate whether we could reconcile these findings with new insights derived from the goal-directed theory of imitation. First, we wanted to replicate the observation of Goldenberg that patients with IMA have less difficulty with the imitation of finger postures relative to that of hand postures (Experiment 1). This experiment is primarily carried out as a neuropsychological base line for our patient group. That is, we wanted to make sure that our group, known to be clinically diagnosed as IMA (and for instance lacking ideational apraxia), showed a similar imitation performance pattern as the patient groups used in the Goldenberg studies. Subsequently, we wanted to investigate if a conceptual deficit of body posture is the underlying problem in patients with IMA, or rather a more general conceptual problem as suggested by the goal-directed theory of imitation. Therefore, in the finger-to-ear experiment (Experiment 2), participants were asked to imitate a model that performed gestures that differed critically with respect to the ear (left or right), the distance (at or near), or the finger (little or index) to be used. The question addressed is whether patients with IMA are able to select and execute the proper finger (little or index), which is highly represented in the body-schema, and instead are confronted with impairments in the selection and or execution of the gesture to the correct side of the body (ipsi or contralateral) and the position (at or near the ear) as proposed by Goldenberg's and other body mapping theories of imitation. Alternatively, if the results would confirm the notion of the goal-directed theory of imitation (Bekkering et al., 2000) we expected that objects (such as an ear or a knee) that are high in the goal hierarchy are able to displace other goals, such as agent (finger) and position (at or near the ear). In addition, we wanted to broaden the scope of our research to transitive movements that involve non-body-related gestures. Therefore in the finger-to-object experiment (Experiment 3) the gestures were made to one of two objects frontoparallel to the model and imitator, and again finger (little or index), side of the object (ipsi or contralateral) and the position (at or near the object) was manipulated. Again, body-mapping theories of imitation would predict that finger selection should be preserved above object and position, whereas the goal-directed theory would predict that object-selection should be more accurate than finger-selection.

METHODS

Participants

All three experiments were performed with the same 24 participants; 8 of them were selected to have LH damage, 8 of them RH damage, and 8 participants were selected as control participants. The patients were selected from a large population of patients from three clinics in southern Germany (Clinic Kipfenberg, Bad Aibling, and Bad Heilbrunn, all in Bavaria, Germany), and were selected according to the following criteria. Only patients who had primary lesions within one hemisphere were taken into account. All patients were dominant right-handed. The LH patients had to have been diagnosed in the clinic as IMA. In addition each patient was tested on the Schnider, Hanlon, Alexander, and Benson test (1997) to confirm the presence of IMA at the moment of testing. Patients of different aetiologies, including traumatic brain injury, stroke, and tumour were included in the present study. Also, all patients with IMA were reported not to have major sensory or motor damage, and they were all able to understand verbally the instructions of the tasks. Nevertheless, four participants showed global aphasia and two showed Broca aphasia; see Table 1 for more details on the

Table 1. *Patient details*

Patient no.	*Age*	*Sex*	*Time since injury (mths)*	*Aetiology*	*Language comprehension*
			Left hemispheric patients		
1	36	f	2	CVA	intact
2	52	m	4	CVA	intact
3	52	m	4	CVA	intact
4	58	m	7	TBI	intact
5	62	m	3	CVA	reduced
6	63	m	4	CVA	intact
7	78	f	3	CVA	reduced
8	83	f	3	CVA	intact
			Right hemispheric patients		
1	18	f	6	TBI	
2	22	f	6	TBI	
3	48	m	6	CVA	
4	48	f	2	CVA	
5	65	f	3	T	
6	74	m	2	CVA	
7	77	f	3	CVA	
8	79	m	6	CVA	

TBI: traumatic brain injury; CVA: cerebro-vascular accident; T: tumour.

patients with LH damage (IMA). IMA patients were asked to imitate with their healthy left hand. See Table 1 for more details.

RH patients were selected according to the following criteria. None of them was diagnosed as IMA. None of them had major neglect deficits. RH patients were asked to imitate with their healthy right hand. The control group were all aged between 60 and 80 without a neurological history, seven of them were dominant right-handed, and one was dominant left-handed, but also performed the task with the right hand.

EXPERIMENT 1

Procedure

Experiment 1 was designed to be an exact replication of the Goldenberg test as described in his paper of 1996. The test items consisted of 10 finger, 10 hand, and 10 combined finger and hand gestures (see also Figure 1). Each participant received the same order of trials and the same order of blocks, namely finger, hand, and combined finger-hand gestures. This fixed order was chosen because the pilot phase showed that most IMA participants got demoralised after facing difficulties in the combined finger-hand gestures and sometimes even withdrew their participation on the other blocks of the experiment. All participants received the following instructions.

I would like you to model some simple, meaningless gestures with the right hand [with the left hand for RH patients]. Please try to imitate the movement with your healthy hand, [thus ipsilateral to the lesion, whereas control subjects always used their left hand] as if you were looking into a mirror. First I will show you the movement myself. Please look very carefully and watch every detail. Now it is your turn; try to imitate as precisely as possible. Good, now I will show you the next movement; please imitate carefully again. [Etc.]

Trials were repeated once if the patient did not imitate correctly.

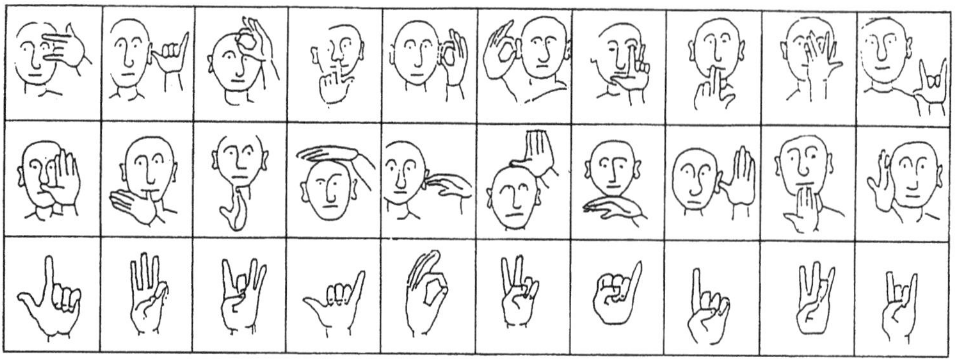

Figure 1. *In Experiment 1, the Goldenberg test was replicated as precisely as possible.*

Data analysis

All movements of both model and participants were videotaped and analysed off-line by independent paid students, who were not informed about the theoretical notion behind the experiments. Each student analysed one experiment. Correct imitation on the first trial scored 2 points and 1 point was given for correct imitation on a second attempt. As a result a maximum of 20 points could be earned for each block of trials. Finally, the combined finger-hand gesture was coded depending on whether the error was in the finger or in the hand part of the gesture.

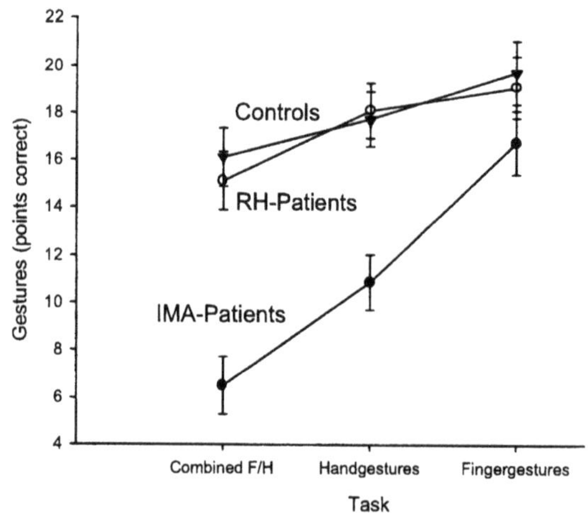

Figure 2. *The points obtained in the finger, hand, and combined gesture imitation of the Goldenberg test categories are depicted for IMA, RH patients, and control participants.*

Results

A two-way Analysis of Variance (ANOVA) showed a significant main effect between groups, $F(2, 21) = 16.4$, $p < .001$. An LSD (least significant difference corrected) post hoc comparison indicated that IMA patients scored significantly worse than the RH and control group (both $ps < .001$), who did not differ significantly from each other. Also, a main effect for conditions was found, $F(2, 21) = 38.9$, $p < .001$. Here, an LSD post hoc test indicated that combined finger-hand gestures were performed more poorly than hand gestures and finger gestures (all $ps < .001$). Importantly, an interaction effect between groups and condition was found, $F(4, 42) = 5.45$, $p < .001$. Separate LSD post hoc tests indicated that in the IMA group, the mean score on the combined finger-hand gestures (6.5) was lower than on the hand gestures (10.88), which again was significantly lower than performance on the finger gesture task (16.75), both $ps < .05$. The RH group and the healthy control group also showed lower mean values on the combined finger-hand gesture task (15.13 and 16.13, respectively) than on the hand gestures (18.15 and 17.75, respectively, although this value did not reach significance for the control group in a pairwise comparison, $p = .26$) and the finger gestures task

(19.16 and 19.76, respectively), all other $ps < .05$. However, for both the RH and the control group, hand and finger gestures did not significantly differ from each other, $ps > .05$, see also Figure 2.

EXPERIMENT 2

Procedure

In Experiment 2 a design with three factors (side of the ear, finger to use, movement end position, respectively), each with two levels (left or right ear, middle or index finger, and at the ear or 10 cm in front, respectively) was used. That is, the model performed eight different imitative movements either to the left or to the right ear, used either the index or the little finger (see also Figure 3), or ended the action either at the ear or 10 cm in front of the ear. Each trial was shown twice in a random order. All participants received the following instructions.

I would like you to model some simple, meaningless gestures with the right hand [with the left hand for RH patients]. Please try to imitate the movement with your left hand [with the right hand for RH patients] as if you were looking into a mirror. First I will show you the movement; they look all very similar. Please look very carefully and watch every detail. Now it is your turn; try to imitate as precisely as possible. Good, now I will show you the next movement, please imitate carefully again. [Etc.]

Data analysis

All movements of both model and participants were videotaped and analysed off-line by independent paid students. Each movement was judged on correctness of imitation of each of three manipulated variables (ear selection, finger selection, distance selection) and either got a 0 (correct imitation) or a 1 (wrong imitation). The scores reported are mean values of each scoring. Each variable also could return a maximum of 12 error points.

Results

A main effect between groups was found in a two-way ANOVA, $F(2, 21) = 21.91, p < .001$. An LSD post hoc test indicated that IMA patients scored significantly worse overall than the RH and control group (both $ps < .001$), who did not differ

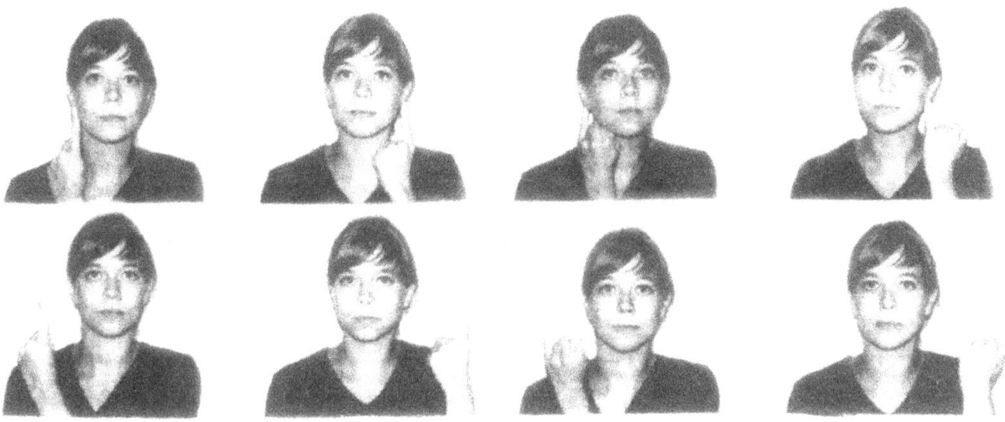

Figure 3. *In Experiment 2, IMA, RH patients, and control participants had to imitate ipsi and contralateral finger gestures to the ears that were modelled either with the little or index finger, directed either at the left or right ear, while the movement ended either at the ear or 10 cm away from it; see text for more details.*

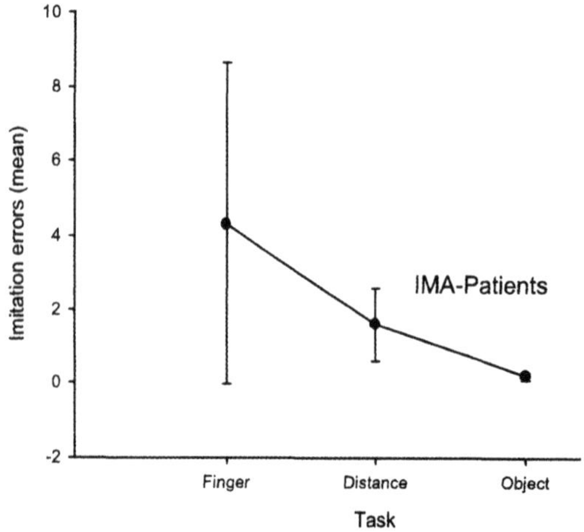

Figure 4. *The observed mean errors and standard errors of Experiment 2 are depicted for finger, object, and distance categories, respectively.*

significantly from each other. As described in the Method section, participants could make single, double, or triple errors. A significant interaction effect indicated that the IMA group produced both more single and double errors than the RH and control group, $F(4, 56) = 36.93$, $p < .01$. Importantly, a separate analysis was performed on the single errors within the IMA group; a paired sample t-test showed that significantly fewer errors were made for object selection than for finger selection, $t(7) = 2.58$, $p < .03$, and distance selection, $t(7) = 2.65$, $p < .03$. More finger selection errors were observed than distance selection errors, 4.63 and 1.13 per patient respectively, although this finding did not reach full significance, $t(7) = 1.8$, $p < .12$; see also Figure 4.

EXPERIMENT 3

Procedure

Experiment 3 was an exact replication of Experiment 2, except that here movements were not modelled to the ear. Instead, the same variables (left–right location, index–little finger, at or near end point) were now manipulated in relation to a wooden object located in the middle of the table between the model and the participants and, as a result, imitative gestures were under full visual control; see also Figure 5.

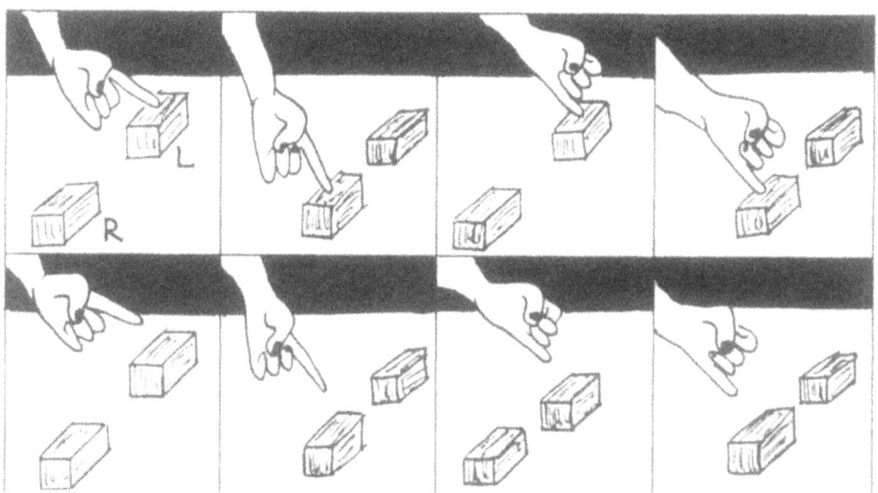

Figure 5. *In Experiment 3, IMA, RH patients, and control participants had to imitate ipsi and contralateral finger gestures to objects on the table in front of them. The gestures were modelled either with the little or index finger, directed either at the left or right object, while the movement ended either at the object or 10 cm away from it; see text for more details.*

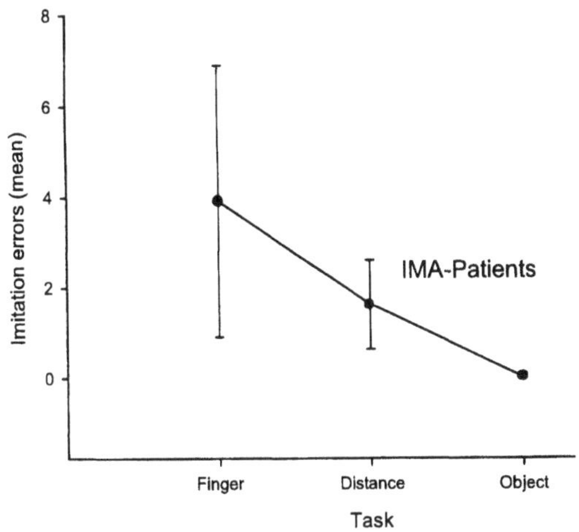

Figure 6. *The observed mean errors and standard errors of Experiment 3 are depicted for finger, object, and distance categories, respectively.*

Results

A main effect for groups was found in a two-way ANOVA, $F(2, 21) = 30.79, p < .001$. An LSD post hoc test indicated that IMA patients scored significantly worse than the RH and control groups (both $p < .001$), who did not differ significantly from each other. A significant interaction effect indicated that the IMA group produced both more single and double errors than the RH and control groups, $F(4, 56) = 33.63$, $p < .01$. A separate analysis was performed on the single errors within the IMA group; a paired sample t-test showed that significantly fewer errors were made for object selection than for finger selection, $t(7) = 2.72$, $p < .03$, and distance selection, $t(7) = 2.84$, $p < .03$. More finger selection errors were observed than distance selection errors, 3.88 and 1.88 respectively, although this finding did not reach full significance, $t(7) = 1.6$, $p < .13$, see also Figure 6.

GENERAL DISCUSSION

The main findings of the present study were the following:

1. We were able to replicate the observation in the Goldenberg test that our population of patients in the IMA group are worse at imitating hand (and combined hand-finger) gestures than finger gestures, whereas the RH and control group performed equally well on hand and finger gestures, although they also were impaired on imitation of the combined hand-finger gestures.

2. The results in the finger-to-ear experiment, however, demonstrated that finger selection is not per se preserved in imitative behaviour in apractic patients. While imitating hand gestures that differed in either the distance (at or near), the ear (left or right), or the finger (little or index), most errors were made in finger selection, some in distance, but no errors were observed in ear selection.

3. The finger-to-object experiment confirmed this finding in a setting in which the ear was replaced by an object. Again, most errors were made in finger selection even although the movements were now performed to objects that do not belong to the body schema and that were under visual control.

Consequences of this study for theories of IMA

Interestingly, patients with IMA neglected in a consistent way one or more aspects of a modelled action when asked to imitate it, whereas RH and control participants performed those actions almost perfectly. Nevertheless, patients with IMA always did perform a goal-directed action when asked to do so, and even more typically, they thought they had performed the correct imitative action. However, IMA patients quite frequently selected the wrong agent (finger) when performing the goal-directed action, while the more distal goals of the task (left or right ear or object to move to) and mostly also the location (at or near the object) were imitated correctly.

The finding of better performance on the finger gesture task compared to the hand gesture task in the Goldenberg test in Experiment 1 could also directly be reconciled in a goal-directed framework of imitation. Whereas some of the finger gestures as depicted in Figure 1 show meaningful signs as "ok" or "victory," respectively, the hand gestures all look very novel and meaningless. As we know from several recent studies, well-known actions are better imitated in healthy subjects (Rumiati & Tessari, 2002) as well as in patients with IMA (Goldenberg & Hagmann, 1997; Spatt, Bak, Patterson, & Hodges, 2002). In other words, finger movements typically elicit clear distal action effects (the ok sign) and therefore rely less on the activation of specific motor programmes at a means level.

These findings raise problems for theories that advocate a motor programming deficit as the mechanism underlying impaired (imitation) performance in patients with IMA. Clearly, these patients do not show problems in executing or programming the motor action per se, rather they seem to have difficulties in the selection of the different elements of a goal-directed action. Moreover, this selection deficit seems to follow the hierarchy described previously (Bekkering et al., 2000; Bekkering & Wohlschläger, 2002; Wohlschläger, Gattis, & Bekkering, 2003). That is, also in patients with IMA the more distal goals of an imitative action are at the top of the selection hierarchy and therefore preserved, while movement path and agent are lower in the hierarchy and sometimes mistaken.

An alternative account we like to address is the notion that patients with IMA might show a general resource reduction because of a poor ability in motor programming. Due to reduced resources the patients make errors, and these errors are for actions at the end of the motor hierarchy, which might be the actions that all participants find more difficult. Since the right-hemisphere patients and the control subjects are performing at a ceiling level, this alternative explanation cannot directly be excluded. In other words, the problems in imitation performance as found in patients with IMA might alternatively arise more from a quantitative deficit in motor programming, rather than a difficulty in reproducing motor actions low in a goal-based hierarchy of action. However, such a general resource reduction account cannot explain the specificity of other findings in the apractic literature like, for instance, the finding of failures in replicating the model's posture by manipulating a life-size manikin (Goldenberg, 1995). The present findings also raise problems for theories that propose an impaired body schema in IMA patients. The striking similarity between Experiment 2, where the movement is made to a body part, and Experiment 3, where the imitative movements are made to a distal object in visual space that is not a part of the body schema weakens such a notion. In addition, the finding that IMA patients are well able to select the correct ear, but not the correct finger—which presumably is better represented in the body schema in the brain—strongly argues against a body schema disorder as the primary source of impaired action control in patients with IMA.

In contrast, we tend to propose that impaired action control in IMA indeed takes place at a conceptual level before motor execution (Goldenberg, 1999; Goldenberg & Hagmann, 1997); however, it is not restricted to the construction of body movements. Rather, the present data strongly suggest that patients with IMA are limited in selecting (or binding) several separate action components from a movement observed into a new unified motor programme. Consequently, only the better-represented motor programmes are activated. Importantly, the present data stresses the point that motor programmes are not so well represented in body parts. Rather, as we have discussed extensively elsewhere (Bekkering & Wohlschläger, 2002; Wohlschläger et al., 2003), the selection of motor programmes might be directly coupled to the achievement of action goals. That is, the fingers that are topographically well represented in the brain are not primarily activated in imitation. Rather, highest priority is given to motor programme aspects that are related to more distal aspects of imitation such as reaching for the correct object of the modelled action.

Such a goal-directed account of motor programme selection could explain many of the findings in the literature about IMA that have been reported thus far. For instance, it could explain why meaningful gestures can be imitated better than more capacity-demanding meaningless gestures (Goldenberg, 1996; Goldenberg & Hagmann, 1997; Hermsdörfer et al., 2001). That is, meaningful gestures elicit clearer action effects and are therefore better represented in long-term memory in the brain, thus presumably needing less working memory capacity to be processed into an action plan (Rumiati & Tessari, 2002; Toraldo, Reverbi, & Rumiati, 2001). The present general view of action goal-dependent selection of motor programmes in IMA, rather then a deficient conceptual representation of the body (see also Sunderland & Sluman, 2000), can also explain why patients who are apractic on tests of gesture imitation also have great difficulties in mastering the three-stage action sequence of the Kimura box (Kimura, 1977, 1993), since in the Kimura box one needs to copy a sequence of three meaningless movements. Moreover, it can also explain why Harrington and Haarland (1992) found that the error rate for patients with IMA was only slightly elevated for repetition of one type of movement, but was dramatically increased when the apraxics had to produce long series with multiple changes of hand postures. In addition, an action goal-dependent selection of motor programmes in IMA can also explain why Goldenberg has reported similar deficits for patients with left brain damage when they need to imitate by means of a mannequin (Goldenberg, 1995), since the perception of action effects are model-independent. Finally, it also explains the finding that LH patients made more errors with hand than with finger postures not only in imitation, but also when judging pictures of actions among an array of four gestures (Goldenberg, 1999). This finding stresses the assumption that errors are caused by defective conceptual mediation in LBD at a higher, non-body-image related level. Clearly, defective motor execution does not appear to be a significant source of imitation errors in this finding. In other words, the limitation in patients with IMA is not specific for action planning of their own actions but also for the understanding of actions performed by a model (see the neurophysiological section for an elaboration of this topic).

Consequences of this study on theories of imitation

Interestingly, this study provides new support for the goal-directed theory of imitation. Previous criticism of the theory has been that whatever is not imitated is supposed to be a lower goal in the hierarchy. Here, we can show that patients with RH damage and control participants do imitate all three manipulated levels (object, location, and agent) while patients with IMS do not. However, patients with IMA also perform well above chance level, therefore it is likely that they did understand the purpose of the task, but unfortunately were not able to cope with all aspects of the task all the time. In other words, contrasting different subpopulations adds evidence to the view that imitation is a selective process where an observed action is represented as a set of goals (possible action effects) that activates the motor programmes that are most strongly associated with those goals. When processing capacity is limited (as in children, see Bekkering et al., 2000) so that multiple goals compete, goals higher in the hierarchy are reproduced at the expense of goals lower in the hierarchy. The results confirmed the proposal of Bekkering, Gattis, and Wohlschläger (Bekkering et al., 2000; Wohlschläger et al., 2003) that in imitation, objects (such as an ear or a knee) are high in the goal hierarchy, therefore likely to be imitated, and are able to displace other goals such as agent and movement. Whether the imitative gesture was visible or not (the object versus the ear) did not significantly influence imitative behaviour, suggesting that visual feedback does not play an important role in specifying goals in gestural imitation. Presumably, patients with IMA follow the same hierarchy, however their impairment resulted in ignoring some of the lower goal aspects, where control participants were still able to accomplish all action goals.

Neurophysiological considerations

A specialised role for the left parietal lobe in the production of human postures has been assumed in the literature for a long time (see Denes, Mantovan, Gallana, & Cappelletti, 1998, for an overview). Recent neuroimaging evidence, for instance, stresses the importance of the left superior parietal lobe in the selection of different grasping types (e.g., precision or full, Grafton, Hazeltine, & Ivry, 1998). However, there is also some counterevidence against this idea. First of all, patients with IMA do not always show damage in the left superior parietal lobe. In contrast, IMA can occur after lesions anywhere in the left frontoparietal brain. In addition, a review of visuomotor control systems primarily based on single cell studies did not find any evidence of a body schema representation and the ability to interrogate an explicit representation of posture in goal-directed action (Rizzolatti, Fogassi, & Gallese, 1997).

An alternative view is offered by the discovery of mirror neurons in monkey (Di Pellegrino, Fadiga, Fogassi, Gallese, & Rizzolatti, 1992; Gallese, Fadiga, Fogassi, & Rizzolatti, 1996), and in man (Baldissera et al., 2001; Fadiga et al., 1995; Iacoboni, Woods, Brass, Bekkering, Mazziotta, & Rizzolatti, 1999). The single cell studies, above all, show that mirror neurons react strongly when the monkey sees someone else perform a goal-directed hand movement with an object, but not when it sees the same movement performed without the object. Thus, they react to the hand–object interaction instead of to the hand movement in itself. This finding supports the view that action control takes place in distal codes that specify actions in external space and passes to lower levels of motor control the task of implementing body movements necessary for performing a comparable action to that observed. Consequently, the motor organisation required to implement such a comparable action can be expected to rely on a much broader network of brain activity. Recent neuroimaging data (Iacoboni et al., 1999, 2001; Nishitani & Hari, 2000) indeed suggest the involvement of predominantly Brodmann's areas 44 and 45 (Broca's areas), 40 (parietal lobe) and 21 (superior temporal sulcus), even in the case of simple finger movement imitation. In addition, in a recent study of Koski et al. (2002) using the paradigm developed by Wohlschläger and Bekkering (2002), participants imitated index finger movements in the absence and presence of visible goals (red dots that were reached for by the finger movement). Finger movements were either ipsilateral or contralateral. The pars opercularis of the inferior frontal gyrus (Broca's areas) showed increased blood oxygen level-dependent fMRI signal bilaterally for imitation of goal-oriented actions, compared with imitation of actions with no explicit goal. In addition, bilateral dorsal premotor areas demonstrated greater activity for goal-oriented actions and for contralateral movements, and an interaction effect such that goal-oriented contralateral movements yielded the greatest activity. These results support the hypothesis that areas relevant to motor preparation and motor execution are tuned to coding goal-oriented actions and are in line with single-cell recordings revealing that neurons in area F5 of the monkey brain represent goal-directed aspects of actions.

PrEview proof published online 20 December 2004

REFERENCES

Aziz-Zadeh, L., Maeda, F., Zaidel, E., Mazziotta, J., & Iacoboni, M. (2002). Lateralization in motor facilitation during action observation: A TMS study. *Experimental Brain Research, 144,* 127–131.

Baldissera, F., Cavallari, P., Craighero, L., & Fadiga, L. (2001). Modulation of spinal excitability during observation of hand actions in humans. *European Journal of Neuroscience, 13,* 190–194.

Bekkering, H. (2002). Imitation and the mediation of action images. In A. Meltzoff & W. Prinz (Eds.), *The imitative mind: Development, evolution and brain bases* (pp. 163–182). Cambridge: Cambridge University Press.

Bekkering, H., & Wohlschläger, A. (2002). Action perception and imitation: A tutorial. In W. Prinz & B. Hommel, (Eds.), *Common mechanisms in perception and action. Attention & performance, Vol. XIX* (pp. 294–314). Oxford: Oxford University Press.

Bekkering, H., Wohlschläger, A., Gattis, M. (2000). Imitation of gestures in children in goal-directed. *Quarterly Journal of Experimental Psychology, 53A,* 153–164.

Butterworth, G. (1990). On reconceptualizing sensorimotor coordination in dynamic system terms. In H. Bloch & B. I. Bertenthal (Eds.), *Sensory motor organizations and development in infancy and early childhood* (pp. 57–73). Amsterdam: Kluwer Academic Press.

Denes, G., Mantovan, M. C., Gallana, A., & Cappelletti, Y. T. (1998). Limb-kinetic apraxia. *Movement Disorder, 13,* 468–476.

De Renzi, E., & Fagliono, P. (1999). Apraxia. In G. F. Denes & L. Pizzamiglio (Eds.), *Handbook of clinical and experimental neuropsychology* (pp. 421–441). Hove, UK: Psychology Press.

De Renzi, E., & Lucchelli, F. (1988). Ideational apraxia. *Brain, 111,* 1173–1185.

Di Pellegrino, G., Fadiga, L., Fogassi, L., Gallese, V., & Rizzolatti, G. (1992). Understanding motor events: A neurophysiological study. *Experimental Brain Research, 91,* 176–180.

Fadiga, L., Fogassi, L., Pavesi, G., & Rizzolatti, G. (1995). Motor facilitation during action observation: A magnetic stimulation study. *Journal of Neurophysiology, 73,* 2608–2611.

Gallese, V., Fadiga, L., Fogassi, L., & Rizzolatti, G. (1996). Action recognition in the premotor cortex. *Brain, 119,* 593–609.

Gleissner, B., Meltzoff, A. N., & Bekkering, H. (2000). Children's coding of human action: Cognitive factors influencing imitation in 3-year-olds. *Developmental Science, 3,* 405–414

Goldenberg, G. (1995). Imitating gestures and manipulating a mannikin-the representation of the human-body in ideomotor apraxia. *Neuropsychologia, 33,* 73–82.

Goldenberg, G. (1996). Defective imitation of gestures in patients with damage in the left or right hemispheres. *Journal of Neurology, 61,* 176–180.

Goldenberg, G. (1999). Matching and imitation of hand and finger postures in patients with damage in the left or right hemispheres. *Neuropsychologia, 37,* 559–566.

Goldenberg, G., & Hagmann, S. (1997). The meaning of meaningless gestures: A study of visuo-imitative apraxia. *Neuropsychologia, 35,* 333–341.

Goldenberg, G., & Hagmann, S. (1998). Tool use and mechanical problem solving in apraxia. *Neuropsychologia, 36,* 581–589.

Goldenberg, G., Hermsdörfer, J., & Spatt, J. (1996). Ideomotor apraxia and cerebral dominance for motor control. *Brain Research and Cognition, 3,* 95–100.

Grafton S. T., Hazeltine, E., & Ivry, R. B. (1998). Abstract and effector-specific representations of motor sequences identified with PET. *Journal of Neuroscience, 18,* 9420–9428.

Gray, J. T., Neisser, U., Shapiro, B. A., & Kouns, S. (1991). Observational learning of ballet sequences: The role of kinematic information. *Ecological Psychology, 3,* 121–134.

Harrington, D. L., & Haarland, K. Y. (1992). Motor sequencing with left hemisphere damage. Are some cognitive deficits specific to limb apraxia? *Brain, 115,* 857–874.

Heilman, K. M., & Rothi, L. J. (1993). Apraxia. In K. M. Heilman & E. Valenstein (Eds.), *Clinical neuropsychology* (3rd ed., pp. 141–160). New York: Oxford University Press.

Hermsdörfer, J., Mai, N., Spatt, J., Marquardt, C., Veldkamp, R., & Goldenberg, G. (1996). Kinematic analysis of movement imitation in apraxia. *Brain, 119,* 1575–1586.

Hermsdörfer, J., Goldenberg, G., Wachsmuth, C., Conrad, B., Ceballos-Baumann, A. O., Bartenstein, P., Schwaiger, M., & Boecker, H. (2001). Cortical correlates of gesture processing: Clues to the cerebral mechanisms underlying apraxis during the imitation of meaningless gestures. *Neuroimage, 14,* 149–161.

Iacoboni, M., Koski, L. M., Brass, M., Bekkering, H., Woods, R. P., Dubeau, M. C., Mazziotta, J. C., & Rizzolatti, G. (2001). Reafferent copies of imitated actions in the right superior temporal cortex. *Proceedings of the National Academia of Science, 20,* 13995–13999.

Iacoboni, M., Woods, R. P., Brass, M., Bekkering, H., Mazziotta, J. C., & Rizzolatti, G. (1999). Cortical mechanisms of human imitation *Science, 286,* 2526–2528.

Kimura, D. (1977). Acquisition of a motor skill after left hemisphere damage. *Brain, 100,* 527–542.

Kimura, D. (1993). *Neuromotor mechanisms in human communication.* New York: Oxford University Press.

Koski, L., Wohlschläger, A., Bekkering, H., Woods, R. P., Dubeau, M. C., Mazziotta, J. C., & Iacoboni, M. (2002). Modulation of motor and premotor activity during imitation of target-directed actions. *Cerebal Cortex, 12,* 847–855.

Leiguarda, R. C., & Marsden, C. D. (2000). Limb apraxias: Higher-order disorders of sensorimotor integration. *Brain, 123,* 860–879.

Liepmann, H. (1900). Das Krankheitsbild der Apraxie (motorischen Asymbolie). *Montschrift fur Psychiatrie und Neurologie, 8,* 182–197.

Meltzoff, A. N. (1993). The centrality of motor coordination and proprioception in social and cognitive development: From shared actions to shared mind. In G. J. P. Savelsbergh (Ed.), *The development of coordination in infancy* (pp. 463–496). Amsterdam: Free University Press.

Meltzoff, A. N., & Moore, M. K. (1977). Imitation of facial and manual gestures by human neonates, *Science, 198,* 75–78.

Nishitani, N., & Hari, R. (2000). Temporal dynamics of cortical representation for action. *Proceedings of the National Academy of Science, 18,* 913–918.

Pick, A. (1905). *Studien zur motorischen Apraxie und ihr nahestendee Erscheinungen; ihre Bedeutung in der Symptomatologie psychopathischer Symptomenkomplexe.* Leipzig/Wien: Franz Deuticke.

Poeck, K. (1983). Ideational apraxia. *Journal of Neurology, 230,* 1–5.

Poizner, H., Clark, M. A., Merians, A. S., Macauley, B., Rothi, L. J., & Heilman, K. M. (1995). Joint coordination deficits in limb apraxia. *Brain, 118,* 227–242.

Rizzolatti, G., Fogassi, L., & Gallese, V. (1997). Parietal cortex: From sight to action. *Current Opinion in Neurobiology, 7,* 562–567.

Rothi, L. J. G., Ochipa, C., & Heilman, K. M. (1991). A cognitive neuropsychological model of limb apraxia. *Cognitive Neuropsychology, 8,* 443–458.

Rumiati, R. I., & Bekkering, H. (2003). To imitate or not to imitate: How the brain can do it, that is the question. *Brain and Cognition, 53,* 479–482.

Rumiati, R. I., & Tessari, A. (2002). Imitation of novel and well-known actions: The role of short-term memory. *Experimental Brain Research, 142,* 425–433.

Schnider, A., Hanlon, R. E., Alexander, D. N., & Benson, D. F. (1997). Ideomotor apraxia: Behavioral dimension and neuroanatomical basis. *Brain and Language, 58,* 125–136.

Spatt, J., Bak, T., Bozeat, S., Patterson, K., & Hodges, J. R. (2002). Apraxia, mechanical problem solving and semantic knowledge: Contributions to object usage in corticobasal degeneration. *Journal of Neurology, 249,* 601–608.

Sunderland, A., Bowers, M. P., Sluman, S. M., Wilcock, D. J., & Ardron, M. E. (1999). Impaired dexterity of the ipsilateral hand after stroke and the relationship to cognitive deficit. *Stroke, 30,* 949–955.

Sunderland, A., & Sluman, S. M. (2000). Ideomotor apraxia, visuomotor control and the explicit representation of posture. *Neuropsychologia, 38,* 923–934.

Thorndike, E. L. (1898). Animal intelligence: An experimental study of the associative process in animals. *Psychological Review Monograph, 2,* 551–553.

Toraldo, A., Reverbi, C., & Rumiati, R. I. (2001). Critical dimensions affecting imitation performance of patients with ideomotor apraxia. *Cortex, 37,* 737–740.

Vogt, S. (1995). On relations between perceiving, imagining and performing in the learning of cyclical movement sequences. *British Journal of Psychology, 86,* 191–216.

Vogt, S. (1996). Imagery and perception-action mediation in imitative actions. *Cognitive Brain Research, 3,* 79–86.

Wohlschläger, A., & Bekkering, H. (2002). Is human imitation based on a mirror-neuron system? Some behavioural evidence. *Experimental Brain Research, 143,* 335–341.

Wohlschläger, A., Gattis, M., & Bekkering, H. (2003). Action generation and action perception in imitation: An instance of the ideomotor principle. *Philosophical Transitions of the Royal Society of London: B Biological Science, 358,* 501–515.

COGNITIVE NEUROPSYCHOLOGY, 2005, 22 (3/4), 433–454

FAR FROM ACTION-BLIND: REPRESENTATION OF OTHERS' ACTIONS IN INDIVIDUALS WITH AUTISM

Natalie Sebanz and Günther Knoblich
Max Planck Institute for Psychological Research, Munich, Germany
Luitgard Stumpf
Integration Centre for Individuals with Autism, Munich, Germany
Wolfgang Prinz
Max Planck Institute for Psychological Research, Munich, Germany

It has been suggested that theory of mind may rely on several precursors including gaze processing, joint attention, the ability to distinguish between actions of oneself and others, and the ability to represent goal-directed actions. Some of these processes have been shown to be impaired in individuals with autism, who experience difficulties in theory of mind. However, little is known about action representation in autism. Using two variants of a spatial compatibility reaction time (RT) task, we addressed the question of whether high-functioning individuals with autism have difficulties in controlling their own actions and in representing those of others. Participants with autism showed automatic response activation and had no difficulties with response inhibition. When two action alternatives were distributed among pairs of participants, participants with autism represented a co-actor's task, showing the same pattern of results as the matched control group. We discuss the possibility that in high-functioning individuals with autism, the system matching observed actions onto representations of one's own actions is intact, whereas difficulties in higher-level processing of social information persist.

Recently, a number of authors have suggested that the ability to explain and predict other people's behaviour by attributing mental states to them—also known as having a "theory of mind" (ToM)—may be built on more basic processes of social cognition. Among these functions are the ability to distinguish between animate and inanimate entities (Frith & Frith, 1999), the ability to share attention (Baron-Cohen, 1994; Baron-Cohen & Cross, 1992; Leekam et al., 1997), the ability to distinguish between actions of oneself and others (Frith, 1996; Russel & Jarrold, 1999), and the ability to represent goal-directed actions (Blakemore & Decety, 2001; Frith & Frith, 1999; Frith, 2002; Leslie, 1994).

A large number of studies has shown that individuals with autism have impairments in ToM (for a review, see Baron-Cohen, 2000; Sodian, in press).

Correspondence should be addressed to Natalie Sebanz, Max Planck Institute for Psychological Research, Amalienstrasse 33, 80799 Munich, Germany (Email: sebanz@psy.mpg.de).

We thank Uta Frith for helpful suggestions during the planning phase of this study, Francesca Happé for sending us her advanced stories, Birte Kröger for her most valuable help in collecting the data, Beate Sodian for her advice and for establishing the contact to MAut, and all the staff members at MAut for their help in organising the test sessions.

These studies have mainly addressed the ability to understand that other people can have beliefs and desires different from one's own. Far fewer studies have addressed the question of whether autistic individuals also show deficits in the abilities thought to precede and underlie ToM. In particular, little is known about action representation in individuals with autism (cf. Moore, Hobson, & Lee, 1997).

In the present study, we addressed the question of whether autistic individuals have difficulties in controlling their own actions and in representing others' actions. With regard to action control, we investigated their ability to inhibit prepotent responses in a two-choice RT task, and their ability to inhibit responses in a go–nogo task. By distributing two action alternatives among pairs of participants, we investigated whether individuals with autism represent a co-actor's task and integrate it in their own action planning. To provide a theoretical context for our study, we first discuss recent findings that provide evidence for a link between ToM and more basic underlying processes of social cognition. We then derive predictions for action representation in autistic individuals, drawing on the three major theories developed to explain the cognitive characteristics observed in the autism spectrum disorders.

PRECURORS TO ToM

According to Tomasello, Kruger, and Ratner (1993), three levels of social understanding can be discerned. The first level is assumed to support the perception of the behaviour of animate beings and to allow one to predict the consequences of the observed behaviour. The second level entails the understanding that others' behaviour is goal-directed. Thus, on this level, other individuals are conceived of as intentional agents whose behaviour and attention are purposive. The third level of understanding corresponds to ToM, where other individuals are conceived of as agents whose thoughts and beliefs may differ from those directly inferred from their perceived behaviour. Neurophysiological and brain imaging results provide evidence that specific brain systems underlie the abilities at each of these levels, and may also support different abilities across levels. However, one must be cautious in drawing conclusions regarding the relationship between ToM and its putative precursors, as the data only provide indirect evidence for such a link.

Several studies have addressed the ability to distinguish between animate and inanimate entities (Blakemore & Decety, 2001; Frith, 1996). In order to be able to predict the behaviour of other individuals, it is crucial to identify the motion of animate beings from other forms of motion in the environment. Specific neural structures underlying this ability have been found in monkeys and humans. Single-cell studies have revealed cell populations in the monkey superior temporal polysensory area (STP) that respond selectively to biological motion (Oram & Perrett, 1994), and functional magnetic resonance imaging (fMRI) studies in humans have shown that a specific area, located in the superior temporal sulcus (STS), is specialised for processing biological motion (Grèzes & Decety, 2001; Grossmann et al., 2000).

A skill pertaining to the second level that has been proposed as a precursor to mentalising is the ability to infer others' intentions through gaze following and shared attention (Baron-Cohen, 1994; 1995; Baron-Cohen & Cross, 1992; Leekam et al., 1997). Evidence for this claim has recently been provided by neurophysiological studies. Using single cell recordings in macaque monkeys, Jellema et al. (2000) discovered a population of cells in the anterior part of the superior temporal sulcus (STSa), which responds selectively to the sight of reaching movements, but only when the agent performing the action is also seen to be attending to the target position of the reaching movement. Thus, these cells are at the same time sensitive to action and attention. The authors concluded that the combined analysis of direction of attention and body movements in STSa supports the detection of intentional actions. In line with this claim, fMRI studies in humans have shown that eye gaze processing and ToM tasks engage a similar region of the posterior STS (Calder et al., 2002; Frith & Frith, 1999; Gallagher et al., 2000). A second brain region associated with ToM, the medial prefrontal cortex, has recently also been shown to be activated during gaze processing (Calder et al., 2002).

A further mechanism assumed to underlie the understanding of others' intentions is the matching of an observed action onto a representation of one's own action. This mechanism relies on a close link between perception and action systems. According to the common coding theory (Hommel, Müsseler, Aschersleben, & Prinz, 2001; Prinz, 1997), actions are coded in terms of the perceivable effects they should generate. When an effect is intended, the movement that produces this effect as perceptual input is automatically activated, because actions and their effects are stored in a common representational domain. A further consequence of this match between perception and action is that observing actions or action effects produced by another individual may also activate a representation of one's own actions. Evidence from neurophysiological studies in monkeys suggests that common coding may occur at the level of single neurons. Mirror neurons in area F5 of the premotor cortex respond both when a monkey performs a certain action and when it observes another individual perform the same action (Gallese et al., 1996; Rizzolatti, Fogassi, & Gallese, 2001). Thus mirror neurons seem to form a system matching the observation and execution of goal-related actions.

Studies using Transcranic Magnetic Stimulation (TMS; Fadiga et al., 1995; Strafella & Paus, 2000), Positron Emission Tomography (PET; Decety et al., 1994; Grafton et al., 1996) and fMRI (Buccino et al., 2001) suggest that a mirror system also exists in humans, and that there is, to some degree, a functional equivalence between simulating, observing, and performing an action. Several areas, such as the supplementary motor area, the dorsal premotor cortex, the supramarginal gyrus, and the superior parietal lobe are activated when an action is imagined or carried out as well as when the same action is observed in others (Grèzes & Decety, 2001). It has been suggested that the function of this matching system may be to understand others' intentions through action simulation (Blakemore & Decety, 2001; Rizzolatti et al., 2001). Action simulation would allow one to infer what one's own intentions would be if one produced the observed action in the same context. This function could be a precursor to a more general mentalising ability (Gallese & Goldman, 1998).

Deficits in precursors to ToM in autism

A number of studies suggest that individuals with autism have difficulties with abilities assumed to underlie ToM. These include the ability to share attention with another person (Carpenter, Pennington, & Rogers, 2002; Leekam & Moore, 2001; Mundy & Stella, 2000), the ability to use and understand protodeclarative pointing (Baron-Cohen, 1989a), and the ability to infer mental states from gaze direction (Baron-Cohen, 1995; Baron-Cohen et al., 1995; Baron-Cohen & Cross, 1992; Leekam et al., 1997). Although action representation is also regarded as a precursor to ToM, little is known about deficits in action representation in individuals with autism, with the exception of imitation.

Clinical reports of autistic individuals' difficulties in imitation date back many years (e.g., Bosch, 1970; Kanner, 1943; Wing, 1969). Several studies reviewed by Meltzoff and Gopnik (1993) have shown that children with autism perform less well than controls on motor imitation of both pure body movements and actions on objects, and have particular problems imitating simple body movements (Curcio, 1978; Dawson & Adams, 1984; DeMyer et al., 1972; Jones & Prior, 1985; Sigman & Ungerer, 1984). A difficulty in copying body movements, gestures, single, and sequential actions has also been reported in older and high-functioning children with autism (Ohta, 1987; Rogers, 1998).

It has been suggested that the impairment in imitation may be due to deficits in the coordination of representations of self and other (Hobson & Lee, 1999; Rogers & Pennington, 1991). According to Williams et al. (2001), a delay or incomplete development of the mirror neuron system could lead to impaired formation and integration of self–other representations. They proposed that deficits in ToM, but also some of the other deficits observed in autism spectrum disorders, may be the result of a poorly functioning system of mirror neurons.

COGNITIVE THEORIES OF AUTISM

The three major theories developed to explain the cognitive deficits observed in individuals with autism (Sodian, in press) allow one, to some degree, to derive predictions about action representation. These theories conceptualise the cognitive deficits as a difficulty in ToM, an impairment in executive functioning, and an imbalance in the integration of information. They address different characteristics of cognitive processing and are not mutually exclusive. While the ToM approach focuses on the social difficulties observed in autism, the executive function theory and the theory of weak central coherence focus on the nonsocial deficits. In addition, the theory of weak central coherence aims to explain findings of superior performance.

The ToM deficit approach

Theories pertaining to this approach are based on the assumption that children with autism do not develop the ability to attribute mental states to themselves and to others as a way of explaining and predicting behaviour in the way that healthy children do. The performance of autistic children on false-belief tasks, which test the understanding that other people can have different beliefs from one's own in the same situation, supports this notion (for a review, see Baron-Cohen, 2000). It has repeatedly been shown that children with autism have difficulties in shifting their perspective to understand what another person thinks, instead of simply reporting what they themselves know (Baron-Cohen, Leslie, & Frith, 1985, 1986; Leekam & Perner, 1991; Perner et al., 1989).

Although some autistic children pass first-order tests, which require inferring another person's mental state, they do so at a much later age than healthy controls (Happé, 1995), and they often fail at second-order false belief tasks (Baron-Cohen, 1989b). Second-order tests involve considering embedded mental states; i.e., to solve these tasks, one needs to infer one person's beliefs about another person's beliefs. Some individuals with autism or Asperger Syndrome who are high functioning in terms of IQ and language (i.e., score at least average on corresponding tests) pass second-order tests (Bowler, 1992; Happé, 1993; Ozonoff, Pennington, & Rogers, 1991). However, they often show difficulties in advanced ToM tests, where one needs to infer complex mental states such as bluff and double-bluff in story characters (Happé, 1994), or where one needs to decode complex mental states from the expression in the eye region of the face (Baron-Cohen et al., 1997; Baron-Cohen, Wheelwright, & Joliffe, 1997).

Two different versions of the ToM deficit approach can be distinguished (cf. Russell & Hill, 2001). According to one view, the difficulty in understanding mental states is restricted to representational mental states such as beliefs (Leslie, 1987). According to the other view, all forms of mentalising are impaired, whether or not they take the form of beliefs (Baron-Cohen, 1989b, 1995; Baron-Cohen et al., 1997). What predictions about action representation in individuals with autism can be made on the basis of these views? Assuming that a more general deficit in mind-reading is present, one may predict that individuals with autism should also have difficulties in representing others' actions, and in integrating representations of their own and others' actions. This prediction is also supported by findings of deficits in more basic abilities, such as shared attention, gaze following, and, in particular, imitation. The representational view does not exclude the presence of other, non-ToM deficits. However, it is worth noting that the core assumption of this view does not imply that individuals with autism should show any impairments in controlling their own actions and in representing others' actions.

The executive deficit theory

Besides mentalising difficulties, individuals with autism also experience executive difficulties, that is, difficulties with action planning, action initiation, and action control. Whether and how the two difficulties are related is still controversial (Sodian, in press). Executive deficits have been found in individuals with autism of different ages and different IQ levels (e.g., Hughes & Russell, 1993; Hughes, Russell, & Robbins, 1994; for a review, see Ozonoff, 1997), among them also high-functioning adolescents and adults (Ozonoff et al., 1991; Rumsey, 1985). Several studies have tried to identify the specific executive function components that are impaired. In particular, two possibilities have been suggested: First, it could be that individuals with autism have an inhibitory deficit. This could apply to the inhibition of actions in general, or specifically to the inhibition of actions that have been pre-activated by the context and are thus prepotent (Hughes & Russell, 1993; Russell et al., 1991). Second, there could be difficulties with cognitive flexibility (Courchesne et al., 1994), e.g., the ability to switch between different tasks may be impaired.

Difficulties with the inhibition of prepotent responses have been reported (Hughes & Russell, 1993; Russell et al., 1991). For instance, in the "box" task (Hughes & Russell, 1993), children with autism showed difficulties inhibiting a direct reach for a desired object and throwing a switch before reaching instead. Furthermore, the empirical evidence suggests that individuals with autism have problems with cognitive flexibility (Courchesne et al., 1994). The evidence for impairments in action inhibition in response to neutral stimuli is mixed (Ozonoff & Strayer, 1997; Ozonoff, 2000). In a study by Ozonoff et al. (1994), the performance of autistic individuals in a go–nogo task was unimpaired. This task requires that one carries out a response to a neutral cue, the go stimulus (e.g., a circle), while simultaneously inhibiting responses to another neutral cue, the nogo stimulus (e.g., a square). In contrast, autistic individuals were clearly impaired in their performance when the mapping between the stimuli and the corresponding responses was frequently changed, placing demands on their ability for set-shifting.

Pacherie (1997) suggested that the executive difficulties of individuals with autism may originate from a specific impairment of their motor representations. According to her account, conscious access to motor representations gives individuals a basic form of awareness of the relationship between their representations and their actions, and of their status as agents and as the owners of representations. In particular, it allows one to experience a continuity between one's prior intentions and one's intentions-in-action (Searle, 1983). Pacherie assumes that individuals with autism have an impaired capacity for motor imagery and, hence, have difficulties in forming conscious motor representations. As a consequence, they have difficulties in simulating actions and in forming action plans, and they fail to experience themselves as the agents responsible for the continuity between their intentions and their actions. Pacherie points out that an impairment in the formation of motor representations could also lead to difficulties in mentalising. In order to attribute intentions to others, one must be able to construct motor representations when observing an action performed by someone else and match the observed action onto a representation of one's own (cf. Blakemore & Decety, 2001).

In a similar vein, Russell and Jarrold (1999) argued that individuals with autism fail to make an efference copy of their actions in a visual code. This may lead to deficits in self-monitoring, manifesting themselves as a difficulty with correcting errors and as a tendency to misdescribe intended actions. In a study on memory for actions, the authors showed that children with autism were impaired relative to normally developing children and children with mental handicap at remembering which actions had been performed by themselves and which had been performed by another person (but see Russell & Hill, 2001, for a study showing intact reporting of own intentions).

Taken together, the executive deficit account predicts deficits in action representation in individuals with autism that should affect the control of their own actions as well as the formation of representations of others' actions, and the integration of representations of self and other. In contrast, the deficits observed in precursors to ToM suggest a specific impairment of action representation in the social domain. Individuals with autism should have difficulties representing others' actions, but should be unimpaired in controlling their own actions.

The weak central coherence theory

Whereas the ToM approach and the executive deficit theory focus on the cognitive impairments observed in autistic individuals—the former addressing primarily social, the latter primarily nonsocial deficits—the theory of weak central coherence has been developed to explain findings of superior performance (e.g., Rimland & Hill, 1984) as well as nonsocial impairments. Assuming that the deficits and the assets in autism stem from a single cognitive characteristic, Frith (1989) proposed that individuals with autism are characterised by a specific imbalance in the integration of information at different levels. Central coherence, defined as the tendency to integrate diverse information to construct higher-level meaning in context, is assumed to be a characteristic of human information processing. According to Frith, this feature of information processing is disturbed in autism, leading to enhanced performance on tasks where attention to local information and piecemeal processing is advantageous, and to impaired performance on tasks requiring the recognition of global meaning or the integration of stimuli in context. Empirical evidence for this claim has been obtained at different levels of processing, ranging from low-level perceptual processes to higher levels involving the semantic system (for a review, see Happé, 2000).

A number of different studies suggests that weak central coherence is not related to ToM and may be present in all individuals with autism regardless of their ToM ability (Frith & Happé, 1994; Happé, 1996). According to Happé's view, there may, however, be a link between central coherence and general social understanding. She points out that in order to understand others' thoughts and feelings, one needs to take into account the context of a situation and integrate diverse information. It is likely that individuals with weak central coherence and detail-focused processing are at a disadvantage when it comes to integrating information necessary for social inference.

Following this notion, one may speculate that individuals with autism are also more likely than healthy controls to ignore others' actions in social context (cf. Baron-Cohen et al., 1999). This should especially be the case when others' actions have no direct bearing on their own, e.g., when there is no need for action coordination. Thus a deficit in action representation could be the consequence of a more general deficit in taking the social context of a situation, including other agents, into account. So far, weak central coherence has mainly been investigated with respect to nonsocial information processing. It remains to be examined whether this cognitive style also affects information processing within social context.

THE CURRENT STUDY

The aim of the present study was to investigate whether individuals with autism show impairments in action control and in representing others' actions. To exclude the possibility that any observed differences between autistic individuals and healthy control participants are attributable to a more general cognitive impairment, we decided to focus on high-functioning adolescents and adults with autism, who are normally intelligent and quite proficient in ToM tasks.

Action control

With regard to action control, we focused on two questions. First, do individuals with autism show difficulties inhibiting pre-activated and thus prepotent responses? Second, is the inhibition of responses to neutral cues impaired? To address the first question we devised a variant of a well-known spatial compatibility RT task, the Simon task (Craft & Simon, 1970; Simon, 1990). In a typical Simon task, one carries out a spatial two-choice response to a relevant stimulus feature (e.g., colour) that is presented along with an irrelevant spatial stimulus feature (e.g., location). In our version of the task, the stimuli were pictures of a hand pointing left or right. A red or green ring was attached

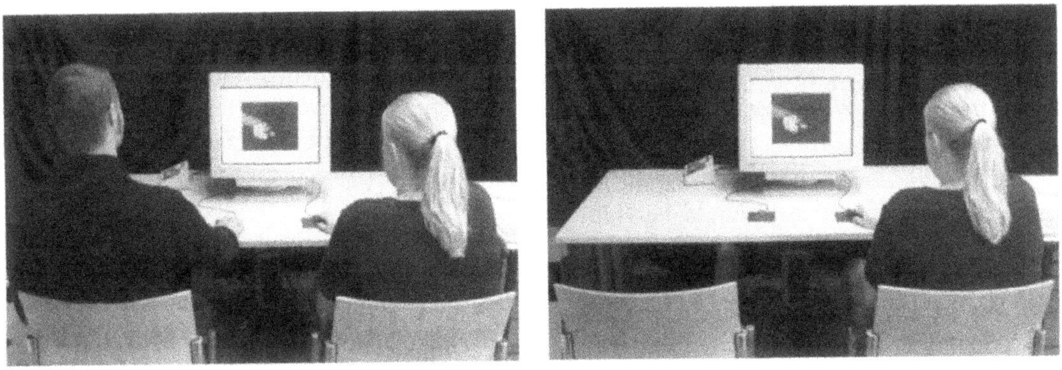

(a) Joint setting (b) Individual setting

Figure 1. *Setting (a) in the joint go–nogo task, and (b) in the individual go–nogo task.*

to the index finger of the hand. The ring colour was the relevant stimulus feature, and the pointing direction of the index finger was the irrelevant spatial stimulus feature. The standard finding in a Simon task is that responses are faster when there is an overlap between the irrelevant stimulus dimension and the response, and slower when the two conflict. For example, in our case, a person could be instructed to respond with a left key when the ring is red and to respond with a right key when the ring is green. On trials where the ring is red and the finger points left, and on trials where the ring is green and the finger points right, the irrelevant spatial dimension corresponds to the response to be given. Responses should be faster on these compatible trials compared to incompatible trials where the irrelevant spatial dimension and the response to be given do not correspond, i.e., where the ring is red and the finger points right, and where the ring is green and the finger points left.

According to Kornblum et al.'s dimensional overlap model (1990), this compatibility effect emerges because the irrelevant spatial dimension of the stimulus overlaps with the spatial dimension of the responses. Due to this overlap, the response corresponding to the spatial information provided by the stimulus will be automatically activated. For instance, when the finger points left, the left response is activated, and when it points right, the right response is activated. Responses are speeded when the response is the same as the one indicated by the relevant stimulus dimension, and slowed when the two conflict (see also Hommel & Prinz, 1997).

Predictions for the two-choice task: Control group. We expected a standard spatial compatibility effect for participants in the control group. Thus responses should be faster on compatible trials where the irrelevant spatial dimension and the response correspond, and slower on incompatible trials, where they conflict.

Predictions for the two-choice task: Autistic group. Different predictions can be derived from each of the three main theoretical approaches outlined above. Assuming that the cognitive deficits observed in autism are mainly due to a difficulty in ToM, there should be no difference in performance between the control group and the autistic group, because the task does not involve mentalising. Thus, like healthy controls, individuals with autism should show a compatibility effect. The executive deficit theory suggests that individuals with autism may have difficulties inhibiting prepotent responses. A response that has been preactivated by the irrelevant spatial dimension can be regarded as a prepotent response. Thus, on incompatible trials, where the pre-activated response must be inhibited, response conflict should be increased. This should result in a larger compatibility effect and/or a higher error rate on incompatible trials. Finally, from the findings of weak central coherence in visual processing (cf. Happé, 2000) one may infer that individuals with autism will be particularly good at focusing on the relevant stimulus feature and at ignoring the irrelevant dimension. Thus, they should be able to process the ring colour while ignoring the pointing stimulus. If the irrelevant spatial dimension is not consistently processed, there is less automatic response activation. Therefore weak central coherence predicts that individuals with autism should show a smaller compatibility effect than controls.

Our two-choice task can easily be transformed to a go–nogo task by assigning only one response alternative to a participant, so that he or she responds only to one color and not to the other (cf. Figure 1b). This allows one to further investigate whether autistic individuals have problems inhibiting responses to certain stimuli while responding to others.

Predictions for the go–nogo task: Control group. Usually, spatial compatibility effects are only observed in two-choice and not in go–nogo RT tasks (for an exception, see Hommel, 1996). Thus, no compatibility effect was expected. Responses should be equally fast no matter where the finger points, because there is no overlap between the spatial stimulus feature and the response, and hence, automatic response activation cannot occur.

Predictions for the go–nogo task: Autistic group. Assuming that a deficit in ToM is the central deficit of individuals with autism, no difficulties for this task are expected, because mentalising is not involved. The performance of participants with autism should not differ from the control group. However, results from studies on executive functioning suggest that individuals with autism might have difficulties inhibiting the response to certain stimuli while responding to others (Ozonoff, 1997). If weak central coherence affects visual processing of the stimuli in the way described above, no compatibility effect should occur.

Representation of others' actions

To investigate whether and how others' actions are represented we distributed the two-choice RT task among pairs of participants in two different ways (Experiment 1 and 2). In Experiment 1, each participant took care of one action alternative; each participant performed the go–nogo task in response to colour alongside another participant responding to the complementary colour (joint go–nogo condition; cf. Figure 1a). Performance in the group setting was compared to performance on exactly the same task in a setting in which the other participant was absent (individual go–nogo condition, as described above; cf. Figure 1b).

Predictions for the control group. For the joint and individual go–nogo condition, we expected to replicate findings from a previous study using the same paradigm (Sebanz, Knoblich, & Prinz, 2003a). Hence, we predicted that there would be a compatibility effect in the joint go–nogo condition, as opposed to the individual go–nogo condition. In the joint go–nogo condition, responses should be faster on trials where the finger points at the person to respond (compatible trials) and slower on trials where it points at the person not to respond (incompatible trials). Given that the task in the individual and the joint go–nogo condition is exactly the same, such a pattern of results can be interpreted as evidence that in the group, each participant represents not only his or her own task, but also the task at the other's disposal.

Predictions for the autistic group. To derive predictions for the autistic group, one must first consider what sort of demands on cognitive processing the task makes. Clearly, the optimal performance strategy for this task in the group condition is to ignore the other person and perform the task as if one were on one's own. However, previous results suggest that when two action alternatives are distributed among two participants, each participant represents the other's task (Sebanz et al., 2003a, 2003b). To form a representation of the other's task, only a very basic form of ToM is needed.

Given that our participants were high-functioning and able to solve first- and second-order ToM tasks, the representational view of a ToM deficit (Leslie, 1987) suggests they should behave like healthy controls, unless other nonmentalising deficits are present. Hence, a compatibility effect in the joint go-nogo condition should be observed. However, findings of action representation deficits in imitation (Meltzoff & Gopnik, 1993) and deficits in action monitoring (Russell & Jarrold, 1999) suggest that individuals with autism might not represent the other's actions, and hence, show no compatibility effect. Such a finding would be compatible with the assumption of a general mind-reading deficit (Baron-Cohen, 1995). This prediction also follows from the notion of an impaired mirror system (Williams et al., 2001), and the notion of an impairment in the formation of motor representations as suggested by Pacherie (1997). The theory of weak central coherence predicts no joint compatibility effect for two reasons: First, as for the two-choice condition and the individual go–nogo condition, it predicts that the irrelevant pointing direction is not processed. Hence, there should be no compatibility effect. Second, one could assume that weak central coherence also characterises the way the social context is processed (cf. Baron-Cohen et al., 1999). In this case, the other person should be ignored, and the task should be performed as if one were alone.

EXPERIMENT 1

Method

Participants

Thirteen high-functioning adults with autism or Asperger Syndrome (AS) and 13 healthy controls took part in Experiment 1. The participants with autism were recruited from MAut, a local care centre where they took part in a 2 year training programme aimed at vocational and social integration. The control group was recruited through advertisements in local newspapers. Eight of the autistic subjects had received a clinical diagnosis of Asperger Syndrome (AS), three of autism, and two of atypical autism.[1] None of the participants had a history of psychiatric disorder, neurological disorder, or a head injury. The control group was free of any family history of autism or AS. All participants had normal or corrected-to-normal vision. They received payment for their participation.

All participants were required to be of at least average intelligence (i.e., scoring >85) on the HAWIE-R (the German version of the WAIS-R; Tewes, 1994) on the full scale, performance, and verbal IQ. All except one participant from the autistic group and all participants from the control group passed first- and second-order ToM tasks. Each participant was given two first-order ToM tasks, two second-order ToM tasks, and two advanced stories (Happé, 1994). The first-order ToM tasks were the Smarties task (Perner et al., 1989) and a modified version of the Sally-Anne task (Wimmer & Perner, 1983). The second-order ToM tasks were Baron-Cohen's ice-cream van test (1989b), and the grandparents story (Hughes et al., 2000). The advanced stories comprised one double- bluff story and one persuasion story (Happé, 1994). Participants in the control group solved on average 5.7 of the 6 tests ($SD = 0.5$), whereas participants in the autistic group solved on average 4.7 of the 6 tests ($SD = 1.5$). Although all except one participant from the autistic group passed at least one of two tests in each category (first order, second order, and advanced), a two-tailed t-test showed that performance of the autistic group was clearly worse than performance of the control group, $t(12) = 2.45, p < .05$.

The control participants were chosen to match the clinical group as closely as possible with respect

[1] There has been a lot of controversy about whether there is as single condition of autism that varies in severity, or whether there are different types of autism (cf. Frith, 1989; Miller & Ozonoff, 1997; Happé, 1994). The most conspicuous difference between autism and AS is that in the former, there is often a delay in language development, whereas in the latter, language skills are unimpaired. Since we did not predict any differences in performance between individuals with autism and AS for our study, we included individuals with either diagnosis. By using the term "individuals with autism" we refer to both groups.

Table 1. *Experiment 1: Participant characteristics*

Group	*CA*	*VIQ*	*PIQ*	*FSIQ*
Control[a]				
Mean	19.85	113.69	118.46	117.85
SD	2.97	8.46	10.97	8.67
Range	(16–28)	(100–131)	(98–138)	(104–132)
Autism[a]				
Mean	20.92	105.38	109.46	109.00
SD	4.19	11.62	15.02	10.07
Range	(16–29)	(92–124)	(85–130)	(98–126)

[a] Both groups $n = 13$; 3 female.

to age, IQ, level of education, sex, and handedness. Table 1 gives the participant details of chronological age (CA), verbal IQ (VIQ), performance IQ (PIQ), and full scale IQ (FSIQ). Two-tailed *t*-tests showed no significant difference in chronological age, verbal IQ, and performance IQ between the two groups (all $p > .05$). However, there was a significant difference between the two groups with respect to full scale IQ, which was somewhat higher in the control group, $t(12) = 2.46$, $p < .05$. The IQ test and the ToM tests were carried out in a seperate session before the experiment. For the participants from the clinical group, this test session was performed at the integration centre.

Materials and procedure

Participants observed digital photographs of a right hand pointing to the left or to the right. On the index finger of the hand there was a ring coloured red or green (see Figure 2). The stimuli were presented centrally on a computer monitor, and the ring always appeared at the same location. Picture size was about 15 × 13 visual degree horizontally and vertically. The order of events in each trial was as follows: a fixation cross appeared for 100 ms, followed by a blank screen for 100 ms. Then a picture of the hand appeared. Three different stimulus onset asynchronies were used (cf. Figure 2b): The irrelevant pointing direction was either presented at the same time as the relevant ring colour (SOA 0), or it was presented some time in advance (100 ms or 300 ms). In the latter case, the ring on the index finger of the hand was initially grey and then turned red or green after 100 ms (SOA 100) or 300 ms (SOA 300), respectively. The SOA variation was introduced to prevent participants from developing response strategies and stable patterns of responding. The picture with the relevant colour cue remained on the screen for 500 ms. After a response time interval of 1000 ms, the next trial was initiated.

There were three different parts of the experiment. All participants performed the standard two-choice RT task, and the go–nogo task in an individual and a joint condition. In the two-choice task, they were instructed to respond to one ring colour with a left and to the other with a right button press. In the joint go–nogo condition, the original task was distributed among two individuals, so that each participant responded to only one of the two colours (see Figure 1a). Thus for each person, the task was a go–nogo task. In the individual go–nogo condition, the identical go–nogo task was performed alone (see Figure 1b). For the two-choice task, participants sat centrally in front of the screen. In the joint go–nogo condition, they sat side-by-side with a distance of about 40 cm between them. In the individual go–nogo condition, an empty chair remained beside each participant. In each of the three parts of the experiment, participants completed four blocks of 126 trials presented in random order. The order of conditions was counterbalanced across pairs of participants.

Stimulus presentation and data collection were controlled by an Apple Power PC. The pictures were presented on an Apple 21" monitor (resolution 1024 × 768 pixels). Button presses were recorded with a PsyScope button box (Cohen et al., 1993).

Results

Two-choice task

The error rate in the control group was 2.7%, and in the autistic group 1.7%. This difference was marginally significant, $t(12) = 2.06$, $p = .06$. In both groups, there was a tendency towards more errors on incompatible trials ($p < .10$). Error trials and trials on which RTs exceeded 800 ms were excluded

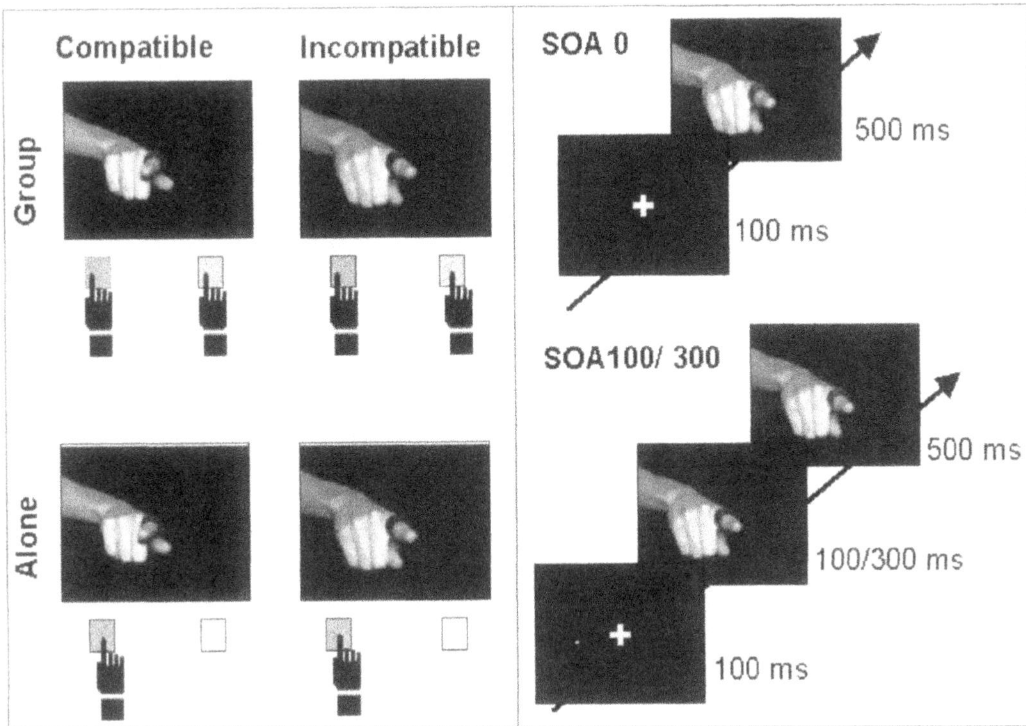

(a) Individual and joint go–nogo condition (b) Trial sequence

Figure 2. *(a) Graphic depiction of the task from the viewpoint of a participant sitting left and responding to red. Compatible trials are shown on the left, incompatible trials on the right. The upper panel shows the group setting, the lower panel the individual setting. (b) Sequence of events on each trial for SOA 0 (upper half) and SOA 100 and 300 (lower half).*

from the statistical analyses. These were approximately 5% of all trials in both groups. Figure 3a shows the results for the two-choice task. In both groups, mean RTs were faster on compatible than on incompatible trials. To analyse the observed RT differences, a 2×2 analysis of variance (ANOVA) with the between factor group (autistic vs. control) and the within factor compatibility (compatible and incompatible) was conducted. We do not report any SOA effects, because SOA did not interact with group. There was a significant main effect of compatibility, $F(1, 24) = 31.21$, $p < .001$. In both groups, RTs were faster on compatible than on incompatible trials. The general RT level in the two groups did not differ, $F(1, 24) = 1.66$, $p = .21$. The two-way interaction was not significant ($p > .05$).

Go–nogo task

The error rate for the control group was 1.2% in the joint go–nogo condition, and 2.8% in the individual go–nogo condition. For the autistic group, it was 1.8% in both conditions. There was no significant difference in error rate between the two groups, and between compatible and incompatible trials (all $p > .05$). Error trials and trials on which RTs exceeded 600 ms were excluded from the statistical analyses. Depending on the different groups and conditions, these were between 3.5% and 6.2%. Figures 3b and 3c show the results for the go–nogo conditions. In both groups, a compatibility effect was observed only in the joint go–nogo condition.

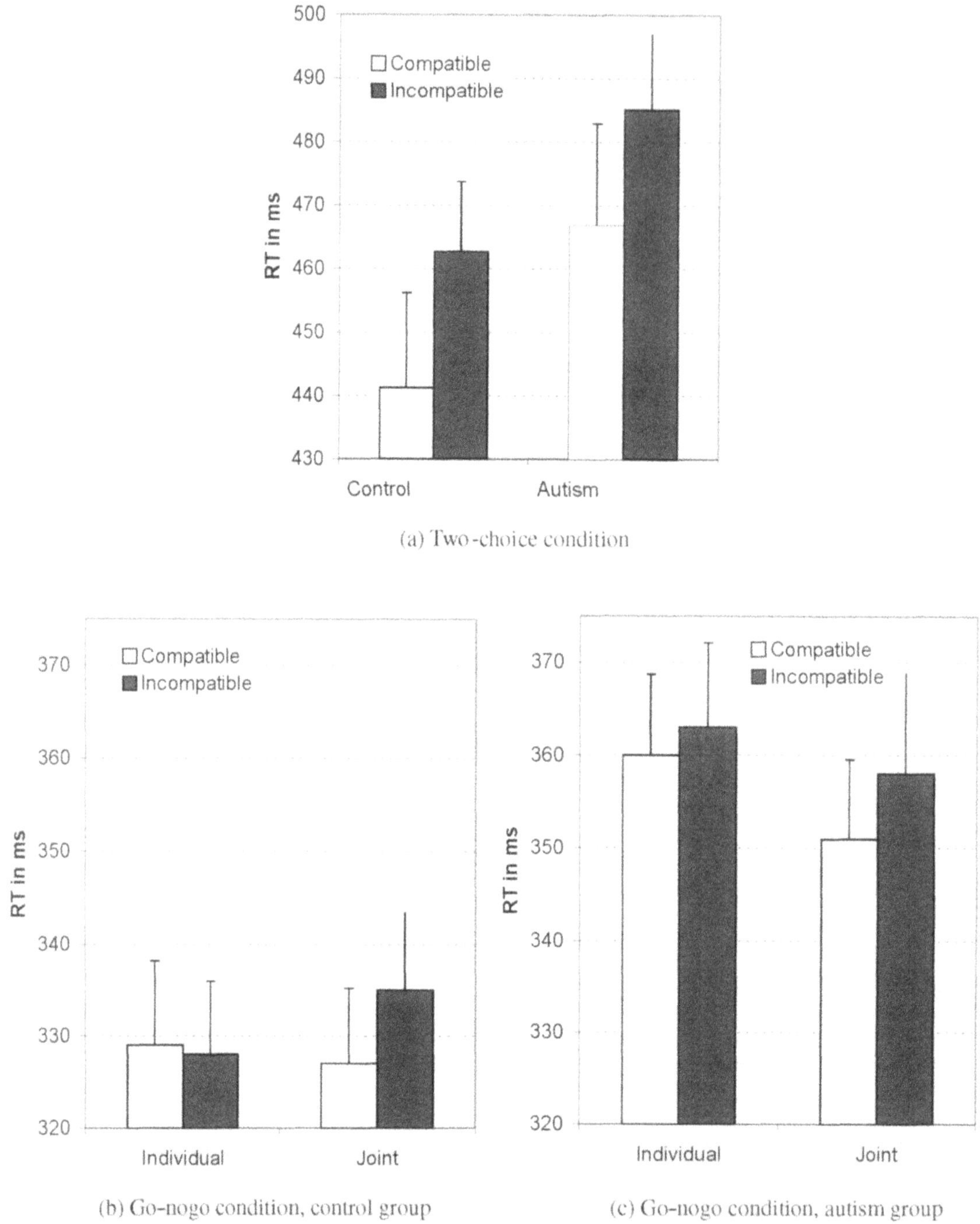

Figure 3. *Experiment 1: Mean RTs on compatible and incompatible trials in the two-choice condition (a), and in the individual and joint go–nogo condition for the control group (b), and the autism group (c).*

To analyse the observed RT differences, a $2 \times 2 \times 2$ ANOVA with the between factor group (control vs. autistic) and the within factors setting (individual and joint) and compatibility (compatible and incompatible) was conducted. SOA did not interact with group and is therefore not reported. There was a significant main effect of group, $F(1, 24) = 5.77$, $p < .05$. The general RT level in the control group was lower. There was no significant main effect of setting, $F(1, 24) = 0.26$, $p = .61$. The main effect of compatibility was significant, $F(1, 24) = 5.76$, $p < .05$. RTs were faster on compatible than on incompatible trials. Importantly, the interaction between setting and compatibility was significant, $F(1, 24) = 5.56$, $p < .05$. Post hoc tests (Newman-Keuls) confirmed that there was a significant difference between compatible and incompatible trials only in the joint setting ($p < .05$).

Finally, we analysed the RT differences in the autistic group seperately to determine whether the observed pattern of results, in particular the interaction between setting and compatibility, was present in this group. A within-subjects 2×2 ANOVA with the factors setting (individual and joint) and compatibility (compatible and incompatible) showed a significant main effect of compatibility, $F(1, 12) = 4.82$, $p < .05$, but the interaction between setting and compatibility did not reach significance, $F(1, 12) = 1.59$, $p = .23$. A Newman- Keuls post hoc test showed a significant difference between compatible and incompatible trials in the joint condition ($p < .01$), but not in the individual condition.

Discussion

The results for the two-choice RT task showed no difference between the autistic group and the control group. In both groups, a spatial compatibility effect was observed. This finding suggests that in both groups, the irrelevant spatial dimension was automatically processed and activated the corresponding response. Responses were faster when the irrelevant spatial dimension and the response indicated by the colour corresponded, and slower when the two conflicted. For the control group, this pattern of results had been expected. For the autistic group, these results had been predicted by the ToM deficit approach, suggesting that performance should not differ from the control group because mentalising is not involved. The prediction derived from weak central coherence theory, implying that autistic individuals would be able to focus only on the relevant colour stimulus and ignore the irrelevant pointing dimension, was not confirmed. Also, the prediction of deficits in the inhibition of prepotent responses derived from the executive deficit account was not confirmed. It must be noted, however, that previous findings of such deficits were obtained with more severely impaired autistic individuals, and with different tasks.

The results of the individual go–nogo condition provide further evidence that action control in the autistic group was intact. Participants with autism did not have specific problems inhibiting the response to certain stimuli and responding to others. This is in line with previous findings demonstrating that individuals with autism are unimpaired in their performance of go–nogo tasks (Ozonoff & Strayer, 1997; Ozonoff, 1997). This implies that the individual go–nogo condition can be regarded as a valid control condition for the joint go–nogo condition.

The results of the control group in the go–nogo conditions replicated previous findings. As expected, co-acting had an impact on the way a task was performed. Only in the group setting did the irrelevant spatial dimension affect RTs. Responses were faster on compatible trials, where the finger pointed at the person to respond, and slower on incompatible trials, where the finger pointed at the person not to respond. In previous experiments, we were able to show that this joint compatibility effect only appears when each participant is in charge of an action alternative. The effect does not appear in the mere presence of another person (Sebanz et al., 2003a). We interpret this finding as evidence that each participant represents not only his or her own action alternative, but also the action alternative at the other's disposal. When the finger points at oneself, this activates the representation of one's own action. When it points at the other agent, it activates the representation of the other's action alternative, creating response conflict. Thus, responses on compatible trials are facilitated, whereas responses on incompatible trials are impaired. In contrast, in the individual go–nogo condition, the other action alternative is not represented, and hence, there is no overlap between the irrelevant spatial dimension and the response. Thus no compatibility effect arises.

Surprisingly, the autistic group showed a similar pattern of results to the control group. A significant compatibility effect was present in the joint, but not in the individual, go–nogo condition. However, the interaction between setting and compatibility did not reach significance, so that the results must be interpreted with caution. At this point, it cannot be determined whether the co-actor was ignored or whether participants with autism represented the co-actor's task. On the one hand, a numerical difference between compatible and incompatible trials was also present in the individual go–nogo condition. It could be that this effect did not reach significance due to a problem of statistical power. This would imply that there was no difference between the two different settings and that the participants with autism ignored the co-actor. On the other hand, it could be that, again due to a problem of statistical power, the interaction between setting and compatibility did not reach significance, although the participants with autism represented the co-actor's task.

In the go–nogo conditions, the RT level was higher in the autistic group than in the control group. This difference between the two groups was also present in the two-choice task, but did not reach statistical significance, probably due to the large amount of variance in the autistic group. The slowing of participants with autism could be due to deficits in either central or more peripheral mechanisms of motor control. Another possibility is that it reflects more strategic processes. Behavioural observations during the testing session and the experimental session suggest that many of the participants with autism had a strong tendency to focus on accuracy rather than speed in their performance of different tasks. Thus the slowing in RTs could also reflect a speed–accuracy trade-off. As differences in the RT level do not affect our interpretation of the results, this issue is not discussed further.

EXPERIMENT 2

The results of Experiment 1 did not allow us to decide whether high-functioning individuals with autism ignore a co-actor, or integrate the other in their own action planning. In previous experiments, we showed that the joint compatibility effect increases in size in healthy adults when they perform the go–nogo task in response to colour alongside a co-actor responding to the pointing direction (Sebanz, Knoblich, & Prinz, 2003b). This result is best explained by the assumption that each co-actor represents the other's task. In Experiment 2, we thus asked the subjects who had participated in Experiment 1 to perform the joint go–nogo task alongside a confederate responding to the pointing direction. Again, the individual go–nogo condition served as a control.

Predictions for the control group. The predictions for the control group were the same as for Experiment 1, with the addition that we expected a larger compatibility effect in the joint go–nogo condition. In particular, RTs of the participant should be slower on trials where the finger points at the confederate (incompatible trials), because response conflict arises on these trials. The representation of the other's task and the corresponding action is activated, but the participant needs to respond him- or herself.

Predictions for the autistic group. For the autistic group, three different predictions can be made. First, it could be that the participants with autism represent the co-actor as an agent, but do not represent his or her specific task and the actions that are part of it. In this case, they should show a joint compatibility effect of similar size to that in Experiment 1. This prediction is supported by previous findings of deficits in action representation. Second, assuming that the participants with autism do represent the other's task, according to the executive deficit account, this may lead to difficulties in the coordination of the representation of their own and the other's actions. In contrast to Experiment 1, where on each trial only one of the two participants responded, the situation is more complex in Experiment 2, where in addition to trials where one participant responds, there are also trials on which both or neither respond. Therefore, one may expect an increase in the RT level and/or error rate due to the increased complexity of the task, or it could even be that participants are not able to perform the task adequately at all. Third, there may be no impairment in action representation. In this case, participants with autism should show a joint compatibility effect similar in size to the control group.

Method

Participants

Twelve adults with autism and 12 healthy controls took part in Experiment 2. All participants received payment for their participation. Twelve of the 13 participants with autism who had participated in Experiment 1 agreed to participate in Experiment 2. From the control group, eight of the participants from Experiment 1 were recruited again, and four additional participants were recruited through advertisements in local newspapers. They fulfilled the requirements described in Experiment 1. Again, the control group was matched as closely as possible in terms of age, IQ, level of education, sex, and handedness. Table 2 gives the participant details of chronological age (CA), verbal IQ (VIQ), performance IQ (PIQ), and full scale IQ (FSIQ).

Table 2. *Experiment 2: Participant characteristics*

Group	*CA*	*VIQ*	*PIQ*	*FSIQ*
Control[a]				
Mean	21.42	119.25	115.00	119.92
SD	3.37	12.76	10.09	10.31
Range	(16–29)	(100–137)	(98–130)	(104–137)
Autism[a]				
Mean	21.42	104.83	111.50	109.67
SD	4.30	11.96	13.68	10.21
Range	(17–29)	(92–124)	(85–130)	(95–126)

[a] Both groups $n = 12$; 3 female.

Materials and procedure

These were the same as in Experiment 1 with the following exceptions: Each participant carried out the go–nogo task alone (individual go–nogo condition) and alongside a confederate who carried out a go–nogo task in response to the pointing direction (joint go–nogo condition). The confederate responded when the finger pointed at her and did not respond when the finger pointed at the participant. Thus, on some trials, both individuals responded (25%), on some, none of them responded (25%), and on some, only the participant or only the confederate responded (50%, 25% each). The irrelevant pointing direction and the relevant colour cue always appeared at the same time (SOA 0). In both conditions (individual and joint), four blocks of 100 trials were presented. The order of conditions was balanced across participants. The order of events in each trial was as follows: A fixation cross appeared for 100 ms, followed by a blank screen for 100 ms. Then one of the four pictures appeared for 500 ms. After a response time interval of 1000 ms the next trial was initiated.

Results

The error rate for the control group was 1.3% in the joint go–nogo condition, and 2.6% in the individual go–nogo condition. For the autistic group, it was 1.7% in the joint and 1.2% in the individual condition. There was no significant difference in error rate between the two groups. In both groups, there were significantly more errors on incompatible trials in the joint go–nogo condition ($p < .001$). Error trials and trials on which RTs exceeded 600 ms were excluded from the statistical analyses. Depending on the different groups and conditions, these were between 3.0% and 3.3%. Figure 4 shows the results for the go–nogo conditions. In both groups, a large compatibility effect in the joint go–nogo condition was present.

To analyse the observed RT differences, a $2 \times 2 \times 2$ ANOVA with the between factor group (control vs. autistic) and the within factors setting (individual and joint) and compatibility (compatible and incompatible) was conducted. There was a

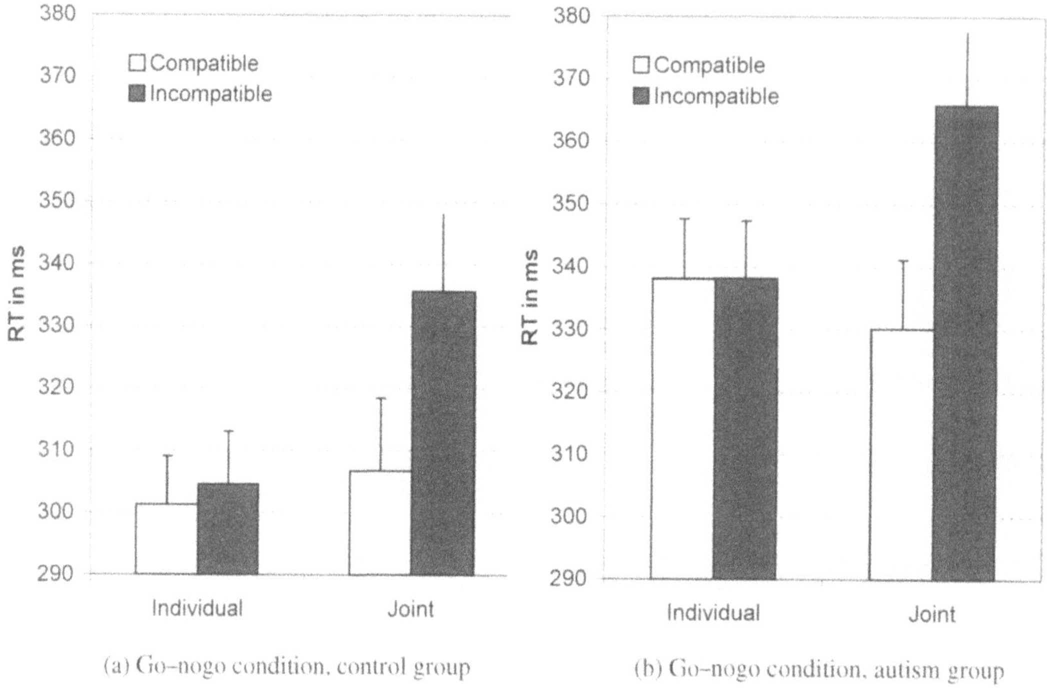

Figure 4. *Experiment 2: Mean RTs on compatible and incompatible trials in the individual and joint go–nogo condition for (a) the control group, and (b) the autism group.*

significant main effect for group, $F(1, 18) = 8.88$, $p < .01$. As in Experiment 1, the general RT level in the control group was lower. There was also a significant main effect for setting, $F(1, 18) = 7.93$, $p < .05$. RTs were slower in the joint go–nogo condition than in the individual go–nogo condition. The main effect for compatibility was significant, $F(1, 18) = 71.29$, $p < .001$; RTs were faster on compatible trials. Importantly, the interaction between setting and compatibility was again significant, $F(1, 18) = 109.41$, $p < .001$. In addition, the three-way interaction between group, setting, and compatibility was significant, $F(1, 18) = 4.46$, $p < .05$. Post hoc tests (Newman-Keuls) showed that in the control group, RTs on incompatible trials were significantly slower in the joint condition compared to the individual condition, whereas there was no difference between the two conditions with regard to RTs on compatible trials. However, in the autistic group, not only were RTs in the joint condition slower on incompatible trials, but RTs on compatible trials were faster compared to the individual condition (all $p < .05$). A two-tailed t-test comparing the size of the compatibility effect (difference between mean RTs on compatible and incompatible trials) in Experiments 1 and 2 within subjects showed that the compatibility effect was significantly larger in Experiment 2, $t(19) = 7.75, p < .001$.

Discussion

The results of Experiment 2 extend the findings of Experiment 1. A significant joint compatibility effect was observed in both groups. Numerically, it was about four times larger in size than in Experiment 1, suggesting that the nature of the co-actor's task had a specific impact on individual action planning. The pointing stimulus that was irrelevant for the participants' task, but relevant for the confederate, had a strong impact on the participants' actions. Participants responded faster when the finger pointed at themselves, requiring only their own response, and slower when it pointed at the confederate, requiring not only their own, but also the other's response. This provides evidence for the claim that participants represented the co-actor's task and integrated it in their action planning.

These findings are in accordance with the assumption that high-functioning individuals with autism have specific difficulties attributing representational states such as beliefs to others, but are unimpaired in more basic forms of mentalising, including action representation. The predictions derived from the executive deficit account were not confirmed, because difficulties in the coordination of the representation of their own and the other's actions were not observed.

Like in Experiment 1, the general RT level in the autistic group was higher than in the control group. As suggested before, this could reflect either central or more peripheral deficits in motor control, or a particular performance strategy. The RT level also differed between the two settings, RTs being slower in the group setting. This finding could reflect the increased difficulty of the task in the joint condition, where one represented not only one's own, but also the other's task.

The three-way interaction between group, setting, and compatibility suggests that in the group setting, individuals from the control group experienced interference on incompatible trials, whereas individuals from the autistic group also experienced facilitation on compatible trials. One possible post hoc explanation for this finding could be the following: On compatible trials, control subjects are already at ceiling, giving the response as fast as they can, and thus are not influenced by the spatial cue. Participants with autism may have a tendency to focus on accuracy and thus slow their responses to avoid errors. Given that their responses are not already as fast as possible, the cue can speed them up. A reason why this kind of facilitation did not appear in the joint go–nogo condition in Experiment 1 could be that the irrelevant dimension generally had less of an impact on actions.

Just as in Experiment 1, the amount of errors was so small that it is difficult to determine whether a group difference was present. Taking together the error results from Experiment 1 and 2, it seems that in the individual go–nogo condition, participants from the control group made more errors than participants from the autistic group, whereas there was no such difference in the joint go–nogo condition. Further investigation would be needed to find out whether this is a reliable pattern worth interpreting.

GENERAL DISCUSSION

Using a two-choice RT task, we demonstrated that high-functioning individuals with autism show the usual spatial compatibility effect, suggesting that they automatically process an irrelevant spatial cue that activates a spatial response. There was no evidence for a deficit in action control. Distributing the two-choice RT task among two persons allowed us to investigate whether a co-actor's task is represented. Our results suggest that when co-acting with another person, both individuals with autism and healthy controls represent the other's task.

These findings seem quite surprising given that impairments in action representation have been claimed by a number of authors, and have been shown in imitation and action monitoring. Furthermore, impairments in several other functions assumed to be pre-cursors to ToM have been reported, suggesting that there may be a link between mentalizing and more basic processes. The most surprising fact about our results is probably that individuals with autism represented another person's task despite the fact that their task did not require them to take the other person into account at all. We conclude from this finding that high-functioning individuals with autism may be mind-blind to some degree (Baron-Cohen, 1995), but they are far from action-blind.

It can be assumed that the joint compatibility effect observed in our experiments arises on a level at which one's own actions and others' actions are represented in a functionally equivalent way (cf. Sebanz et al., 2003a). As suggested by the common coding theory (Hommel et al., 2001; Prinz, 1997), observing actions performed by another person may activate the structures that are also involved in one's own control of these actions. Our findings suggest that in high-functioning individuals with autism, the system matching observed actions onto representations of one's own actions is unimpaired, contrary to Williams et al.'s (2001) proposal of an impairment of the mirror system.

This may lead one to speculate that high-functioning individuals with autism have a specific deficit in attributing representational states to others, whereas lower-level processing of social information is intact. Such a view has been propagated by Fodor (1992), Leslie and Thaiss (1992), and Scholl and Leslie (1999) who, among others, have proposed that the mentalising ability is based on a dedicated, domain-specific, and modular cognitive mechanism. We believe, however, that to interpret our findings in this way, additional evidence would be needed. First, the actions to be represented in our experiments were very simple. It is possible that our participants with autism would have had difficulties representing several different action alternatives, or complex action sequences. Hence, an impairment in the representation of more complex actions cannot be excluded. Second, it would be interesting to find out whether more severely impaired autistic individuals tested with the go–nogo condition would also show a joint compatibility effect, suggesting that they represent the other's task.[2] If this were the case, this would be strong evidence for a specific deficit in the processing of high-level social information. Finally, it would be important to determine whether our participants show deficits in other precursors to ToM, such as gaze processing.

One interesting possibility is that different precursors will be impaired to different degrees depending on the extent to which they rely on the neural networks involved in ToM. For instance, gaze processing activates some of the brain regions also activated in ToM tasks. Action representation, however, may engage mainly different brain areas to ToM, such as those pertaining to the mirror system (Grèzes & Decety, 2001). For this reason, it is conceivable that gaze processing may be impaired in individuals with difficulties in ToM, whereas action representation could be spared. However, a recent study investigating the neural correlates of action prediction (Ramnani & Miall, 2004) showed that predicting somebody else's actions activates paracingulate cortex and STS, which are areas typically activated during mentalising. This suggests that the brain areas involved in ToM may have multiple functions ranging from the attribution of complex mental states to the representation of simple actions (Frith & Frith, 1999; Frith & Frith, 2001; Gallagher & Frith, 2003; Sebanz & Frith, 2004). fMRI studies in individuals with autism may prove useful to find out more about the link beween ToM and its putative precursors (cf. Cody, Pelphrey, & Piven, 2002).

The participants with autism in our study did not show any executive deficits with respect to response inhibition. They were able to inhibit responses to neutral cues in the go–nogo task, and to inhibit prepotent responses in the two-choice RT task. The performance in the go–nogo task replicates previous results obtained with the go–nogo paradigm. It is somewhat more surprising that the inhibition of prepotent responses was unimpaired. This may be due to the fact that the participants were very high functioning, but could also be related to the nature of the task. It could be that other types of prepotent responses, such as responses that are of a more affective nature, e.g., grasping something one really wants to have, may be more difficult to inhibit (Russell et al., 1991). Our results do not allow us to draw any conclusions about cognitive flexibility. Further testing would be needed to gain a more complete picture of the participants' executive functioning abilities.

Contrary to previous findings, we could not find any evidence for weak central coherence. A processing style characterised by weak central coherence could have manifested itself in two ways: On the one hand, the visual stimuli could have been processed locally rather than globally. On the other hand, the other person could have been ignored rather than integrated in action planning. Neither of the two were observed. This finding is also supported by the fact that performance on the Block Design Subtest of the HAWIE-R did not differ from the control group (Shah & Frith, 1993). Thus,

[2] As mentioned before, there was one participant in our study who was not able to solve any ToM tasks. This participant did not show a significant joint compatibility effect in Experiment 1, but showed a rather large compatibility effect in Experiment 2.

we conclude that in our sample of individuals with autism, cognitive processing was not characterised by weak central coherence. It is tempting to speculate that the participants with autism were not action-blind because they were not context-blind. This applies to the visual processing level, where the processing of the irrelevant spatial dimension caused automatic response activation, and to the level of social information processing, where processing of the social context induced them to form a representation of the co-actor's task.

Additional direct testing of weak central coherence in our participants would be needed to evaluate this assumption in more depth. Also, we cannot fully exclude the possibility that deficits in central coherence and executive functioning were both present to some degree and obscured each other by yielding opposite effects. However, this possibility does not affect our conclusion that the other's task was represented. It is hard to see how the differential effect of the co-actor's task on individual action could be explained in terms of interference between weak central coherence and a deficit in executive functioning. Rather, it seems likely that high-functioning individuals with autism are surprisingly tuned in to others' actions.

PrEview proof published online 10 January 2005

REFERENCES

Baron-Cohen, S. (2000). Theory of mind and autism: A fifteen year review. In S. Baron-Cohen, H. Tager-Flusberg, & D. J. Cohen (Eds.), *Understanding other minds. Perspectives from developmental cognitive neuroscience* (pp. 3–20). Oxford: Oxford University Press.

Baron-Cohen, S. (1995). *Mindblindness: An essay on autism and theory of mind.* Cambridge, MA: MIT Press.

Baron-Cohen, S. (1994). How to build a baby that can read minds: Cognitive mechanisms in mindreading. *Cahiers de Psychologie Cognitive, 13,* 513–552.

Baron-Cohen, S. (1989a). Perceptual role taking and protodeclarative pointing in autism. *British Journal of Developmental Psychology, 7,* 113–127.

Baron-Cohen, S. (1989b). The autistic child's theory of mind: A case of specific developmental delay. *Journal of Child Psychology and Psychiatry, 30,* 285–297.

Baron-Cohen, S., Campbell, R., Karmiloff-Smith, A., Grant, J., & Walker, J. (1995). Are children with autism blind to the mentalistic significance of the eyes? *British Journal of Developmental Psychology, 13,* 370–389.

Baron-Cohen, S., & Cross, P. (1992). Reading the eyes: Evidence for the role of perception in the development of a theory of mind. *Mind and Language, 6,* 173–186.

Baron-Cohen, S., Joliffe, T., Mortimore, C., & Robertson, M. (1997). Another advanced test of theory of mind: Evidence from very high functioning adults with autism or Asperger Syndrome. *Journal of Child Psychology and Psychiatry, 38,* 813–822.

Baron-Cohen, S., Leslie, A. M., & Frith, U. (1986). Mechanical, behavioural and intentional understanding of picture stories in autistic children. *British Journal of Developmental Psychology, 4,* 113–125.

Baron-Cohen, S., Leslie, A. M., & Frith, U. (1985). Does the autistic child have a "theory of mind"? *Cognition, 21,* 37–46.

Baron-Cohen, S., O'Riordan, M., Stone, V., Jones, R., Plaisted, K. (1999). Recognition of faux pas by normally developing children and children with Asperger Syndrome or high-functioning autism. *Journal of Autism and Developmental Disorders, 29,* 407–418.

Baron-Cohen, S., Wheelwright, S., & Joliffe, T. (1997). Is there a "language of the eyes"? Evidence from normal adults and adults with autism or Asperger syndrome. *Visual Cognition, 4,* 311–331.

Blakemore, S.-J., & Decety, J. (2001). From the perception of action to the understanding of intention. *Nature Reviews Neuroscience, 2,* 561–567.

Bosch, G. (1970). *Infantile autism: A clinical and phenomenological-anthropological investigation taking language as the guide.* New York: Springer.

Bowler, D. M. (1992). "Theory of mind" in Asperger syndrome. *Journal of Child Psychology and Psychiatry, 33,* 877–895.

Buccino, G., Binkofski, F., Fink, G. R., Fadiga, L., Fogassi, L., Gallese, V., Seitz, R. J., Zilles, K., Rizzolatti, G., & Freund, H.-J. (2001). Action observation activates premotor and parietal areas in a somatotopic manner: An fMRI study. *European Journal of Neuroscience, 13,* 400–404.

Calder, A. J., Lawrence, A. D., Keane, J., Scott, S. K., Owen, A. M., Christoffels, I., & Young, A. W. (2002). Reading the mind from eye gaze. *Neuropsychologia, 40,* 1129–1138.

Carpenter, M., Pennington, B. E., & Rogers, S. J. (2002). Interrelations among social-cognitive skills

in young children with autism. *Journal of Autism and Developmental Disorders, 32,* 91–106.
Cody, H., Pelphrey, K., & Piven, J. (2002). Structural and functional magnetic resonance imaging of autism. *International Journal of Developmental Neuroscience, 20,* 421–438.
Cohen, J., MacWhinney, B., Flatt, M., & Provost, J. (1993). PsyScope: An interactive graphic system for designing and controlling experiments in the psychology laboratory using Macintosh computers. *Behavior Research Methods, Instruments, and Computers, 25,* 257–271.
Courchesne, E., Townsend, J., Akshoomoff, N. A., Saitoh, O., Yeung-Courchesne, R., Lincoln, A. J., James, H. E., Haas, R. H., Schreibman, L., & Lau, L. (1994). Impairment in shifting attention in autistic and cerebellar patients. *Behavioral Neuroscience, 108,* 848–865.
Craft, J., & Simon, J. (1970). Processing symbolic information from a visual display: Interference from an irrelevant directional cue. *Journal of Experimental Psychology, 83,* 415–420.
Curcio, F. (1978). Sensorimotor functioning and communication in mute autistic children. *Journal of Autism and Childhood Schizophrenia, 8,* 281–292.
Dawson, G., & Adams, A. (1984). Imitation and social responsiveness in autistic children. *Journal of Abnormal Child Psychology, 12,* 209–225.
Decety, J., Perani, D., Jeannerod, M., Bettinardi, V., Tadary, B., Woods, R., Mazziotta, J. C., & Fazio, F. (1994). Mapping motor representations with positron emission tomography. *Nature, 371,* 600–602.
DeMyer, M. K., Alpern, D. G., Barton, S., DeMyer, W. E., Churchill, D. W., Hingtgen, J. N., Bryson, C. Q., Pontius, W., & Kimberlin, C. (1972). Imitation in autistic, early schizophrenic, and nonpsychotic subnormal children. *Journal of Autism and Childhood Schizophrenia, 2,* 264–287.
Fadiga, L., Fogassi, G., Pavesi, G., & Rizolatti, G. (1995). Motor faciliation during action observation: A magnetic stimulation study. *Journal of Neurophysiology, 73,* 2608–2611.
Fodor, J. A. (1992). A theory of the child's theory of mind. *Cognition, 44,* 283–296.
Frith, C. D. (2002). Attention to action and awareness of other minds. *Consciousness and Cognition, 11,* 481–487.
Frith, U. (1996). Social communication and its disorder in autism and Asperger syndrome. *Journal of Psychopharmacology, 10,* 48–53.
Frith, U. (1989). *Autism: Explaining the enigma.* Oxford: Blackwell.
Frith, C. D., & Frith, U. (2001). The biological basis of social interaction. *Current Directions in Psychological Science, 10,* 151–155.
Frith, C. D., & Frith, U. (1999). Interacting minds: A biological basis. *Science, 286,* 1692–1695.
Frith, U., & Happé, F. (1994). Autism: Beyond "theory of mind." *Cognition, 50,* 115–132.
Gallagher, H. L., & Frith, C. D. (2003). Functional imaging of "theory of mind." *Trends in Cognitive Sciences, 7,* 77–83.
Gallagher, H. L., Happé, F., Brunswick, N., Fletcher, P. C., Frith, U., & Frith, C. D. (2000). Reading the mind in cartoons and stories: An fMRI study of "theory of the mind" in verbal and nonverbal tasks. *Neuropsychologia, 38,* 11–21.
Gallese, V., Fadiga, L., Fogassi, L., & Rizzolatti, G. (1996). Action recognition in the premotor cortex. *Brain, 119,* 593–609.
Gallese, V., & Goldman, A. (1998). Mirror neurons and the simulation theory of mind-reading. *Trends in Cognitive Sciences, 2,* 493–501.
Grafton, S. T., Arbib, M. A., Fadiga, L., & Rizzolatti, G. (1996). Localization of grasp representations in humans by positron emission tomography 2. Observation compared with imagination. *Experimental Brain Research, 112,* 103–111.
Grèzes, J., & Decety, J. (2001). Functional anatomy of execution, mental simulation, observation, and verb generation of actions: A meta-analysis. *Human Brain Mapping, 12,* 1–19.
Grossman, E., Donnelly, M., Price, R., Pickens, D., Morgan, V., Neighbor, G., & Blake, R. (2000). Brain areas involved in perception of biological motion. *Journal of Cognitive Neuroscience, 12,* 711–720.
Happé, F. (2000). Parts and wholes, meaning and minds: Central coherence and its relation to theory of mind. In S. Baron-Cohen, H. Tager-Flusberg, & D. J. Cohen (Eds.), *Understanding other minds. Perspectives from developmental cognitive neuroscience* (2nd ed., pp. 150–181). Oxford: Oxford University Press.
Happé, F. (1996). Studying weak central coherence at low levels: Children with autism do not succumb to visual illusions: A research note. *Journal of Child Psychology and Psychiatry, 37,* 873–877.
Happé, F. (1995). The role of age and verbal ability in the theory of mind task performance of subjects with autism. *Child Development, 66,* 843–855.
Happé, F. (1994). An advanced test of theory of mind: Understanding of story characters' thoughts and feelings by able autistic, mentally handicapped, and

normal children and adults. *Journal of Autism and Developmental Disorders, 24,* 129–154.

Happé, F. (1993). Communicative competence and theory of mind in autism: A test of relevance theory. *Cognition, 48,* 101–119.

Hobson, R. P., & Lee, A. (1999). Imitation and identification in autism. *Journal of Child Psychology and Psychiatry, 40,* 649–659.

Hommel, B. (1996). S–R compatibility effects without response uncertainty. *Quarterly Journal of Experimental Psychology, 49A,* 546–571.

Hommel, B., Muesseler, J., Aschersleben, G., & Prinz, W. (2001). The Theory of Event Coding (TEC): A framework for perception and action planning. *Behavioral and Brain Sciences, 24,* 849–937.

Hommel, B., & Prinz, W. (1997). Theoretical issues in stimulus-response compatibility: An editor's introduction. In B. Hommel & W. Prinz (Eds.), *Theoretical issues in stimulus–response compatibility* (pp. 3–8). Amsterdam: North-Holland.

Hughes, C., Happé, F., Jackson, J., Taylor, A., & Caspi, A. (2000). Good test–retest reliability for standard and advanced false-belief tasks across a wide range of abilities. *Journal of Child Psychology and Psychiatry, 41,* 483–490.

Hughes, C., & Russell, J. (1993). Autistic children's difficulty with mental disengagement from an object: Its implications for theories of autism. *Developmental Psychology, 29,* 498–510.

Hughes, C., Russell, J., & Robbins, T. (1994). Evidence for executive dysfunction in autism. *Neuropsychologia, 32,* 477–492.

Jellema, T., Baker, C. I., Wicker, B., & Perrett, D. I. (2000). Neural representation for the perception of the intentionality of actions. *Brain and Cognition, 44,* 280–302.

Jones, V., & Prior, M. R. (1985). Motor imitation abilities and neurological signs in autistic children. *Journal of Autism and Developmental Disorders, 15,* 37–46.

Kanner, L. (1943). Autistic disturbances of affective contact. *Nervous Child, 2,* 217–250.

Kornblum, S., Hasbroucq, T., & Osman, A. (1990). Dimensional overlap: Cognitive basis for stimulus–response compatibility: A model and taxonomy. *Psychological Review, 97,* 253–270.

Leekam, S., Baron-Cohen, S., Perrett, D., Milders, M., & Brown, S. (1997). Eye-direction detection: A dissociation between geometric and joint attention skills in autism. *British Journal of Developmental Psychology, 15,* 77–95.

Leekam, S., & Moore, C. (2001). The development of attention and joint attention in children with autism. In J. A. Burack, T. Charman, N. Yirmya, & P. R. Zelazo (Eds.), *The development of autism: Perspectives from theory and research* (pp. 105–129). Mahwah, NJ: Lawrence Erlbaum Associates, Inc.

Leekam, S., & Perner, J. (1991). Does the autistic child have a metarepresentational deficit? *Cognition, 40,* 203–218.

Leslie, A. M. (1994). Pretending and believing: Issues in the theory of ToM. *Cognition, 50,* 211–238.

Leslie, A. M. (1987). Pretense and representation: The origins of "theory of mind." *Psychological Review, 94,* 412–426.

Leslie, A. M., & Thaiss, L. (1992). Domain specifity in conceptual development: Neuropsychological evidence from autism. *Cognition, 43,* 225–251.

Meltzoff, A. N., & Gopnik, A. (1993). The role of imitation in understanding persons and developing theories of mind. In S. Baron-Cohen, H. Tager-Flusberg, & D. J. Cohen (Eds.), *Understanding other minds: Perspectives from autism* (pp. 335–366). Oxford: Oxford University Press.

Miller, J., & Ozonoff, S. (1997). Did Asperger's cases have Asperger disorder? A research note. *Journal of Child Psychology and Psychiatry, 38,* 247–251.

Moore, D. G., Hobson, R. P., & Lee, A. (1997). Components of person perception: An investigation with autistic, nonautistic retarded and typically developing children and adolescents. *British Journal of Developmental Psychology, 15,* 401–423.

Mundy, P., & Stella, J. (2000). Joint attention, social orienting, and nonverbal communication in autism. In A. M. Wetherby & B. M. Prizant (Eds.), *Autism spectrum disorders: A transactional developmental perspective. Communication and language intervention series* (pp. 55–77). Baltimore, MD: Brookes.

Ohta, A. (1987). Cognitive disorders of infantile autism: A study employing the WISC, spatial relationship conceptualization, and gesture imitations. *Journal of Autism and Developmental Disorders, 17,* 45–62.

Oram, M., & Perrett, D. (1994). Modeling visual recognition from neurobiological constraints. *Neural Networks, 7,* 945–972.

Ozonoff, S. (1997). Components of executive function in autism and other disorders. In J. Russell (Ed.), *Autism as an executive disorder* (pp. 179–211). Oxford: Oxford University Press.

Ozonoff, S., Pennington, B. F., & Rogers, S. J. (1991). Executive function deficits in high-functioning autistic children: Relationship to theory of mind. *Journal of Child Psychology and Psychiatry, 32,* 1081–1106.

Ozonoff, S., & Strayer, D. L. (1997). Inhibitory function in nonretarded children with autism. *Journal of Autism and Developmental Disorders, 27,* 59–77.

Ozonoff, S., Strayer, D. L., McMahon, W. M., & Filloux, F. (1994). Excecutive function abilities in autism: An information processing approach. *Journal of Child Psychology and Psychiatry, 35,* 1015–1031.

Pacherie, E. (1997). Motor-images, self-consciousness, and autism. In J. Russell (Ed.), *Autism as an executive disorder* (pp. 215–255). Oxford: Oxford University Press.

Perner, J., Frith, U., Leslie, A. M., & Leekam, S. (1989). Exploration of the autistic child's theory of mind: Knowledge, belief, and communication. *Child Development, 60,* 689–700.

Prinz, W. (1997). Perception and action planning. *European Journal of Cognitive Psychology, 9,* 129–154.

Ramnani, N., & Miall, R. C. (2004). A system in the human brain for predicting the actions of others. *Nature Neuroscience, 7,* 85–90.

Rimland, B., & Hill, A. L. (1984). Idiot savants. In J. Wortis (Ed.), *Mental retardation and developmental disabilities* (pp. 155–169). New York: Plenum Press.

Rizzolatti, G., Fogassi, L., & Gallese, V. (2001). Neurophysiological mechanisms underlying the understanding and imitation of action. *Nature Reviews Neuroscience, 2,* 661–670.

Rogers, S. J. (1998). An examination of the imitation deficit in autism. In J. Nadel & G. Butterworth (Eds.), *Imitation in infancy.* Cambridge: Cambridge University Press.

Rogers, S., & Pennington, B. F. (1991). A theoretical approach to the deficits in infantile autism. *Development and Psychopathology, 3,* 137–162.

Rumsey, J. M. (1985). Conceptual problem-solving in highly verbal, nonretarded autistic men. *Journal of Autism and Developmental Disorders, 15,* 23–36.

Russell, J., & Hill, E. L. (2001). Action-monitoring and intention reporting in children with autism. *Journal of Child Psychology and Psychiatry, 42,* 317–328.

Russell, J., & Jarrold, C. (1999). Memory for actions in children with autism: Self versus other. *Cognitive Neuropsychiatry, 4,* 303–331.

Russell, J., Mauthner, N., Sharpe, S., & Tidswell, T. (1991). The "windows task" as a measure of strategic deception in preschoolers and autistic subjects. *British Journal of Developmental Psychology, 9,* 331–349.

Scholl, B. J., & Leslie, A. M. (1999). Modularity, development, and "theory of mind." *Mind and Language, 14,* 131–153.

Searle, J. (1983). *Intentionality.* Cambridge: Cambridge University Press.

Sebanz, N., & Frith, C. (2004). Beyond simulation? Neural mechanisms for predicting the actions of others. *Nature Neuroscience, 7,* 5–6.

Sebanz, N., Knoblich, G., & Prinz, W. (2003a). Representing others' actions: Just like one's own? *Cognition, 8,* 11–21.

Sebanz, N., Knoblich, G., & Prinz, W. (2003b). Your task is my task. Shared task representations in dydic interactions. In R. Alterman & D. Kirsh (Eds.), *Proceedings of the 25th Annual Meeting of the Cognitive Science Society* (pp. 1–8). Mahwah, NJ: Lawrence Erlbaum Associates Inc.

Shah, A., & Frith, U. (1993). Why do autistic individuals show superior performance on the Block Design Task?. *Journal of Child Psychology and Psychiatry, 34,* 1351–1364.

Sigman, M., & Ungerer, J. A. (1984). Cognitive and language skills in autistic, mentally retarded, and normal children. *Developmental Psychology, 20,* 293–302.

Simon, J. (1990). The effects of an irrelevant directional cue on human information processing. In R. W. Proctor & T. G. Reeve (Eds.), *Stimulus–response compatibility: An integrated perspective* (pp. 31–86). Amsterdam: North-Holland.

Sodian, B. (in press). Tiefgreifende Entwicklungsstörungen: Autismus. In P. F. Schlottke, R. K. Silbereisen, S. Schneider, & G. W. Lauth (Eds.), *Enzyklopädie der Psychologie: Störungen im Kindes- und Jugendalter.* Göttingen, Germany: Hogrefe.

Strafella, A. P., & Paus, T. (2000). Modulation of cortical excitability during action observation: A transcranial magnetic stimulation study. *NeuroReport, 11,* 2289–2292.

Tewes, U. (1994). *Hamburg-Wechlser Intelligenztest für Erwachsene. 2., korrigierte Auflage.* Bern: Hans Huber.

Tomasello, M., Kruger, A., & Ratner, H. H. (1993). Cultural learning. *Behavioral and Brain Sciences, 16,* 495–552.

Williams, J. H. G., Whiten, A., Suddendorf, T., & Perrett, D. (2001). Imitation, mirror neurons and autism. *Neuroscience and Biobehavioral Reviews, 25,* 287–295.

Wimmer, H., & Perner, J. (1983). Beliefs about beliefs: Representation and constraining function of wrong beliefs in young children's understanding of deception. *Cognition, 13,* 103–128.

Wing, L. (1969). The handicaps of autistic children: A comparative study. *Journal of Child Psychology and Psychiatry, 10,* 1–40.

COGNITIVE NEUROPSYCHOLOGY, 2005, 22 (3/4), 455–479

THE BRAIN'S CONCEPTS: THE ROLE OF THE SENSORY-MOTOR SYSTEM IN CONCEPTUAL KNOWLEDGE

Vittorio Gallese
Università di Parma, Italy

George Lakoff
University of California, Berkeley, USA

Concepts are the elementary units of reason and linguistic meaning. They are conventional and relatively stable. As such, they must somehow be the result of neural activity in the brain. The questions are: Where? and How? A common philosophical position is that all concepts—even concepts about action and perception—are symbolic and abstract, and therefore must be implemented *outside* the brain's sensory-motor system. We will argue against this position using (1) neuroscientific evidence; (2) results from neural computation; and (3) results about the nature of concepts from cognitive linguistics. We will propose that the sensory-motor system has the right kind of structure to characterise both sensory-motor and more abstract concepts. Central to this picture are the neural theory of language and the theory of cogs, according to which, brain structures in the sensory-motor regions are exploited to characterise the so-called "abstract" concepts that constitute the meanings of grammatical constructions and general inference patterns.

INTRODUCTION

Concepts are the elementary units of reason and linguistic meaning. They are conventional and relatively stable. As such, they must somehow be the result of neural activity in the brain. The questions are: Where? and How?

First-generation cognitive science was strongly influenced by the analytic tradition of philosophy of language, from which it inherited the propensity to analyse concepts on the basis of formal abstract models, totally unrelated to the life of the body, and of the brain regions governing the body's functioning in the world.

Correspondence should be addressed to Vittorio Gallese, Dipartimento di Neuroscienze, Sezione di Fisiologia, Università di Parma, Via Volturno 39, 43100 Parma, Italy (Email: vittorio.gallese@unipr.it).

For many of the ideas put forward in the present paper the authors are indebted to, and would like to thank, the following members of the NTL Project at the International Computer Science Institute of the University of California at Berkeley: Jerome Feldman, Srini Narayanan, Lokendra Shastri, Eve Sweetser, Nancy Chang, Shweta Narayan, Ellen Dodge, Keith Sanders, and Ben Bergen. Many thanks also to Giacomo Rizzolatti and Maria Alessandra Umiltà, for their most valuable comments on an earlier version of this paper.

Vittorio Gallese, who was George Miller Visiting Professor at the University of California at Berkeley, would like to thank the Miller Institute for awarding him the fellowship that made this work possible. He was also supported by the EU Mirrorbot Project, and by the Eurocores Project "The Origin of Man, Language, and Languages."

Concepts, from this perspective, were conceived of as abstract, amodal, and arbitrary, represented in some "language of thought" (Fodor, 1975, 1987), made up of symbols and having the properties of productivity and compositionality, among others. In Fodor's theory (see Fodor, 1975), the purported amodal nature of concepts draws a sharp dividing line between the modular input/output brain structures and a generalised cognitive system (unanalysed at the level of the brain), whose functioning rules are totally independent from those governing the input/output modules. The propositional picture of the mind conveyed by early cognitivism is that of a functional system whose processes can be described in terms of manipulations of abstract symbols according to a set of formal syntactic rules (see Fodor, 1983; Pylyshyn, 1984). Knowledge is therefore represented in amodal symbolic form. Meaning is referential, in that it derives from a posited correspondence between the system of abstract symbols and their corresponding extensions, the objects and events in the world. Thus, following the line of arguments of early cognitivism, concepts are symbolic representations by nature, and as thinking, they can be reduced to symbolic (not neural) computation.

We will propose a radically different view. We will argue that conceptual knowledge is embodied, that is, it is mapped within our sensory-motor system. We will argue that the sensory-motor system not only provides structure to conceptual content, but also characterises the semantic content of concepts in terms of the way that we function with our bodies in the world. Before delving deeply into the argument, we should discuss a major finding in neuroscience that we will be assuming throughout: *Imagining and doing use a shared neural substrate.*

When one imagines seeing something, some of the same part of the brain is used as when one actually sees. When we imagine moving, some of the same part of the brain is used as when we actually move. Note that these facts undermine the traditional rationale given above. We can imagine grasping an object without actually grasping it. From this, it does not follow that actual grasping and imaginary grasping do not use a common neural substrate. One can reason about grasping without grasping; yet one may still use the same neural substrate in the sensory-motor system. Indeed, that is just what we shall argue. In doing so, we will extend what we know about doing and imagining sharing a common substrate via the following hypothesis: *The same neural substrate used in imagining is used in understanding.*

Consider a simple sentence, like "Harry picked up the glass." If you can't imagine picking up a glass or seeing someone picking up a glass, then you can't understand that sentence. Our hypothesis develops this fact one step further. It says that *understanding is imagination*, and that *what you understand of a sentence in a context is the meaning of that sentence in that context.*

Our proposal is not an internalist theory of meaning. The reason is that imagination, like perceiving and doing, is *embodied*, that is, structured by our constant encounter and interaction with the world via our bodies and brains. The result is an *interactionist* theory of meaning.

Accordingly, we will argue that a key aspect of human cognition is *neural exploitation*—the adaptation of sensory-motor brain mechanisms to serve new roles in reason and language, while retaining their original functions as well. We will discuss two cases: conceptual metaphor and cogs.

As we shall see, circuitry across brain regions links modalities, infusing each with properties of others. The sensory-motor system of the brain is thus "multimodal" rather than modular. Accordingly, language is inherently multimodal in this sense, that is, it uses many modalities linked together—sight, hearing, touch, motor actions, and so on. Language exploits the pre-existing multimodal character of the sensory-motor system. If this is true, it follows that there is no single "module" for language—and that human language makes use of mechanisms also present in nonhuman primates.

According to our proposal, the concept *grasp*, from which we will start, gets its meaning via our ability to imagine, perform, and perceive *grasping*. Our ability to imagine grasping makes use of the same neural substrate as performing and perceiving *grasping*. According to our proposal, imagining is a form of *simulation*—a mental simulation of action or perception, using many of the same neurons as actually acting or perceiving (Gallese, 2003a).

Before developing our arguments, we would like to conclude this introductory part by framing our proposal within the extant and copious literature on the neural underpinnings of conceptual knowledge. Any serious attempt to provide a neuroscientific account of conceptual content as nested in the activity of the brain faces the challenge of explaining how the localised patterns of activation of different neural cortical networks can enable the capacity to distinguish, recognise, categorise, and ultimately conceptualise objects, events, and the state of affairs in the world.

Two main approaches have so far challenged the view held by first-generation cognitive science on the nature of conceptual knowledge: clinical neuropsychology and cognitive neuroscience. Clinical neuropsychology has established a relationship between given patterns of localised brain damage and corresponding deficits in conceptual knowledge. Cognitive neuroscience has more recently tried to establish, mainly by means of brain imaging experiments, which brain regions are activated by different conceptual categories.

During the last two decades, an impressive amount of clinical data has accumulated, describing patients whose peculiarly localised brain lesions have determined selective impairments of their conceptual knowledge. Basically, most of these deficits encompass the loss of *some specific categories of conceptual knowledge*, such as living things, or nonliving objects (mainly tools and artifacts). An excellent and thorough survey of this literature can be found in the recent special issue of *Cognitive Neuropsychology* (Vol. 20, no. 3–6, 2003).

A parallel conspicuous brain imaging literature has accumulated on the neural correlates of distinct conceptual categories (for recent review, see Gainotti, 2004; Malach, Levy, & Hasson, 2002). The discussion of this vast literature is beyond the scope of the present article. What we would like to highlight here is that both the clinical and brain imaging literature have not to date provided a unified explanatory framework. Basically, three theories of conceptual deficit dominate the literature: sensory-functional theory, correlated structure theory, and domain-specific theory (see Martin & Caramazza, 2003; Simmons & Barsalou, 2003). These theories differ along many dimensions, the principal one being the extent to which conceptual knowledge is structured—and henceforth selectively affected by localised brain damage, by property or by category.

Similarly, it has recently been argued (Gainotti, 2004) that the overall picture provided by functional brain imaging studies is by no means consistent and clear-cut (see also Gallese, 2003b). It should be added that even if one could provide unambiguous evidence for the neural correlates of specific object concepts, the general principle defining the topology of such neural representation would need to be convincingly demonstrated. Unfortunately, as argued by Malach et al. (2002), to date no such convincing solution has been proposed.

Our present proposal does not aim to settle the clinical issues, and so we will not deal with clinical cases. Our goal is to follow an alternative route, that is, to provide a testable embodied theory of concepts, based on the results of research in neuroscience, neural computation, and cognitive linguistics, capable of reconciling both concrete and abstract concepts within a unified framework. The structure of our argument is delineated in the next section.

THE STRUCTURE OF THE ARGUMENT

We will begin with the action concept *grasp*. The argument will take the following form.

1. *Information structure*. We will show that the information structure needed to characterise the conceptual structure of *grasp* is available at the neural level in the sensory-motor system. That includes the semantic role structure, the aspectual structure, and certain hierarchical category structures.

2. *Multimodality*. Mirror neurons and other classes of premotor and parietal neurons are

inherently "multimodal" in that they respond to more than one modality. Thus, the firing of a single neuron may correlate with both *seeing* and *performing* grasping. Such multimodality, we will argue, meets the condition that an action-concept must fit both the performance and perception of the action.

3. *Functional clusters.* Multimodality is realised in the brain through *functional clusters*, that is, among others, parallel parietal-premotor networks. These functional clusters form *high-level units*—characterising the discreteness, high-level structure, and internal relational structure required by concepts.[1]

4. *Simulation.* To understand the meaning of the concept *grasp*, one must at least be able to imagine oneself or someone else grasping an object. *Imagination is mental simulation* (see Gallese, 2003a), carried out by the same functional clusters used in acting and perceiving. Any conceptualisation of grasping via simulation therefore requires the use of the same functional clusters used in the action and perception of grasping.

5. *Parameters.* All actions, perceptions, and simulations make use of neural parameters and their values. For example, the action of *reaching* for an object makes use of the neural parameter of direction; the action of *grasping* an object makes use of the neural parameter of force. So do the concepts of *reaching* and *grasping*. Such neural parameterisation is pervasive and imposes a *hierarchical structure* on the brain: The same parameter values that characterise the *internal structure* of actions and simulations of actions also characterise the *internal structure* of action concepts.

6. *Structured neural computation.* The neural theory of language (see Feldman & Narayanan, in press; Lakoff & Johnson, 1999) provides a theory of neural computation in which the same neural structures that allow for movement and perception in real time and in real sensory-motor contexts also permit real-time context-based inferences in reasoning. The same neural structures that carry out action and perception carry out inference.

These six points will allow us to characterise an *embodied* theory of concepts, grounded in the sensory-motor system. At first we will limit ourselves to the case of action-concepts like *grasp*. After that, we will suggest how this theory, with a couple of additions, will extend to concepts more generally.

There are several points to be borne in mind: First, the neuroscientific research we will cite is partly done on monkeys and partly on humans. We will use the results on monkeys as applying to humans for the simple reason that there is enough evidence to support the notion of an analogy—when not a homology—between the monkey and human brain regions we will be discussing (see Rizzolatti, Fogassi, & Gallese, 2002).

Second, there is far more to the sensory-motor system than we will be discussing, and much of it is relevant. For example, we will not be discussing the roles of basal ganglia, cerebellum, thalamus, and somato-sensory cortices. Though they would add to the argument, they would also add greatly to the length of this study, and we believe we can make our point without them.

Third, as we stated at the outset, any theory of concepts must account for how concepts are implemented in the brain and must provide empirical evidence for such a theory. Let us now turn to the results from neuroscience.

MULTIMODAL FUNCTIONAL CLUSTERS AND EMBODIED SIMULATION

Before we look at the multimodality of action concepts, we need to look at the multimodality of actions themselves. The action of *grasping* has both a motor component (what you do in grasping) and various perceptual components (what it looks like for someone to grasp and what a graspable object looks like). Although we won't discuss them here, there are other modalities involved as

[1] Our theory assumes that concepts do have internal structure. This notion, however, is controversial. For an alternative account, see Fodor (1998).

well, such as the somato-sensory component (what it feels like to grasp something).

It is important to distinguish multimodality from what has been called "supramodality." The term "supramodality" is generally (though not always) used in the following way: It is assumed that there are distinct modalities characterised separately in different parts of the brain and that these can only be brought together via "association areas" that somehow integrate the information from the distinct modalities. To claim that an action like grasping is "supramodal" is to say that it is characterised in an association area, distinct and different from the sensory-motor system, which integrates information from the motor system with information from sensory modalities. The point is that anything supramodal uses information coming from areas specialised for individual distinct modalities, but is not itself involved in the individual distinct modalities.

To claim, as we do, that an action like *grasping* is multimodal is to say that (1) it is neurally enacted using neural substrates used for both action and perception, and (2) that the modalities of action and perception are integrated at the level of the sensory-motor system itself and not via higher association areas.

To see the difference, consider the following example. Premotor area F4 (a sector of area 6 in the macaque monkey brain) was once conceived of as a relatively uninteresting extension of the primary motor cortex, whose only role was to control axial and proximal movements of the upper limbs. However, it has been shown that F4 contains neurons that integrate motor, visual, and somatosensory modalities for the purpose of controlling actions in space and perceiving peri-personal space, that is, the area of space reachable by body parts (Fogassi et al., 1992, 1996a; Gentilucci et al., 1988; Gentilucci, Scandolara, Pigarev, & Rizzolatti, 1983; Rizzolatti, Camarda, Fogassi, Gentilucci, Luppino, & Matelli, 1988; Rizzolatti, Fogassi, & Gallese, 2000b; Rizzolatti, Fadiga, Fogassi, & Gallese, 1997; Rizzolatti & Gallese, 2004; Rizzolatti, Matelli, & Pavesi, 1983; Rizzolatti, Scandolara, Matelli, & Gentilucci, 1981b). Similar results about multimodal integration in area F4 were independently obtained by Michael Graziano, Charlie Gross, and their co-workers (Graziano, Hu, & Gross, 1997a, 1997b; Graziano, Yap, & Gross, 1994; Gross & Graziano, 1995). More recently, Graziano, Reiss, and Gross (1999) showed that F4 neurons integrate not only visual but also auditory information about the location of objects within peripersonal space.

The point here is that the very same neurons that control purposeful actions also respond to visual, auditory, and somato-sensory information about the objects the actions are directed to. They do so because they are part of a parietal-premotor circuit (F4-VIP, see below) in charge of overall control of purposeful bodily actions in peri-personal space. This contrasts with the old notion that sensory-motor integration is achieved at a "higher" level at which separate neural systems for motor control and sensory processing are brought together in a putative "association area."

This is important theoretically because supramodality is consistent with the idea of strict modularity, while multimodality is not. Supramodality accords with a picture of the brain containing separate modules for action and for perception that need to be somehow "associated." *Multimodality denies the existence of such separate modules.*

Multimodality does everything that supramodality has been hypothesised to do, and more. Multimodal integration has been found in many different locations in the brain, and we believe that it is the norm (for a review, see Fogassi & Gallese, 2004). That is, sensory modalities like vision, touch, hearing, and so on are actually integrated with each other *and* with motor control and planning. This suggests that there are no pure "association areas" whose only job is to link supposedly separate brain areas (or "modules") for distinct sensory modalities.

The neuroscientific evidence accumulated during the last two decades shows the following. Cortical premotor areas are endowed with sensory properties. They contain neurons that respond to visual, somatosensory, and auditory stimuli. Posterior parietal areas, traditionally considered to process and associate purely sensory information, in fact play a major role in motor control. The premotor and parietal areas, rather than having separate and independent functions, are neurally integrated not only to control action, but also to serve the function of *constructing* an integrated representation of (1) actions together with (2) objects acted on and (3) locations toward which actions are directed.

In particular, these multimodal functions have been described within three parallel parietal-premotor cortical networks: F4-VIP, F5ab-AIP, and F5c-PF, which we will characterise as "functional clusters." By a "cluster" we do not just mean a bunch of individual neurons in the same place. A *functional cluster* is a cortical network that functions as a unit with respect to relevant neural computations.

1. The F4-VIP cluster functions to transform the spatial position of objects in peri-personal space into the most suitable motor programmes for successfully interacting with the objects in those spatial positions—reaching for them or moving away from them with various parts of your body such as the arm or head. The properties of the object are far less important than their spatial position. Damage to this cluster will result in the inability to be consciously aware of, and interact with, objects within the contralateral peri-personal space (see Rizzolatti, Berti, & Gallese, 2000a).
2. The F5ab-AIP cluster contains "canonical neurons," which transform the intrinsic physical features of objects (e.g., shape, size) into the most suitable hand motor programmes required to act on them—manipulate them, grasp them, hold them, tear them apart. In this cluster, the properties of the objects are far more important than their spatial location. Accordingly, damage to this functional cluster will induce visuo-motor grasping deficits, that is, the inability to grasp an object, despite having the motor capacity for grasping (see Fogassi et al., 2001; Gallese, Murata, Kaseda, Niki, & Sakata, 1994).
3. The F5c-PF cluster contains mirror neurons that discharge when the subject (a monkey in the classical experiments) performs various types of hand actions that are goal-related and also when the subject observes another individual performing similar kinds of actions (see Rizzolatti, Fogassi, & Gallese, 2001).

In the next three sections we will review some of the crucial properties of these three functional clusters, and discuss their functional mechanisms in terms of simulation.

Actions and their locations

The F4-VIP cluster: Simulation in action-location neurons

Actions occur at locations. Natural language codes the location where a given action occurs via locative adverbs, as in *He grasped the cup in front of him*. The semantic relation between an action and its location is part of conceptual structure. We submit that this semantic relation be characterised neurally by the following means.

Within the F4-VIP cluster, there are neurons that discharge when a subject (a monkey) turns its head toward a given location in peri-personal space. The same neurons also discharge when an object is presented, or a sound occurs, at the very same location toward which the head would be turned, if it were actually turned. Peri-personal space is by definition a *motor space*, its outer limits defined by the action space of the various body effectors—hands and arms, feet, head. In these cases, a position in peri-personal space can be specified in a number of ways: sound, sight, and touch (Duhamel, Colby, & Goldberg, 1998; Fogassi et al., 1996a; Gentilucci et al., 1988; Graziano & Gross, 1995; Graziano et al., 1994; Rizzolatti et al., 1997).

We maintain that what integrates these sensory modalities is *action simulation*. Because sound and action are parts of an integrated system, the sight of an object at a given location, or the sound it produces, automatically triggers a "plan" for a specific action directed toward that location. What is a "plan" to act? We claim that it is a simulated potential action.

These neurons control the execution of a specific real action (turning the head, say, 15 degrees to the right). When they fire without any action in presence of a possible target of action seen or heard at the same location (say, 15 degrees to the right), we hypothesise that they are *simulating* the action. This is explanatory for the following reason. In simulation the same neural substrate is used as in action. If simulation is being carried out here, this would explain why just those neurons are firing that otherwise could act on the same object in the same location.

Action, patients, and purposes

The F5ab-AIP cluster: Simulation in canonical neurons

Let us now turn to how various conceptual relations are realised neurally: The relation between an action and something acted on (a patient), as well as relations like manner and purpose. The same multimodal cluster characterises the relation between a general action and a specific type of action, as well as aspectual phases of an action. For the sake of brevity, we will focus only on the properties of the premotor pole of this cluster, that is, area F5 (for a description of AIP, see Murata, Gallese, Luppino, Kaseda, & Sakata, 2000; Rizzolatti, Fogassi, & Gallese, 2000a; Sakata & Taira, 1994).

In premotor area F5 (Matelli, Luppino, & Rizzolatti, 1985), there are action-only neurons, so-called because they only fire during real actions (Gentilucci et al., 1988; Hepp-Reymond, Hüsler, Maier, & Qi, 1994; Kurata & Tanji, 1986; Rizzolatti et al., 1988; Rizzolatti, Scandolara, Gentilucci, & Camarda, 1981a). These neurons discharge any time the subject (a monkey) performs hand or mouth movements directed to an object (Rizzolatti et al., 1988). Several aspects of these neurons are important. First, what correlates to their discharge is not simply a *movement* (e.g., flexing the fingers, or opening the mouth), but an *action*, that is, *a movement executed to achieve a purpose* (grasp, hold, tear apart an object, bring it to the mouth). Second, what matters is the *purpose of the action*, and not some dynamic details defining it, like force, or movement direction (see Rizzolatti et al., 2000b).

For any particular type of purposeful action, there are a number of kinds of subclusters.

1. *The general-purpose subclusters:* The neurons of these subclusters indicate the general goal of the action (e.g., grasp, hold, tear an object). They are not concerned with either the details of how the action is carried out, nor the effector used (e.g., hand, mouth), nor how the effector achieves the purpose of the action (e.g., grasping with the index and the thumb, or with the whole hand).
2. *The manner subclusters:* The neurons of these subclusters concern the various ways in which a particular action can be executed (e.g., grasping an object with the index finger and the thumb, but not with the whole hand).
3. *The phase subclusters:* The neurons of these subclusters deal with the temporal phases purposeful actions are segmented (e.g., hand/mouth opening phase, or hand/mouth closure phase).

Thus, there is a general grasping-purpose subcluster that is active whenever grasping of any kind is carried out. Consider a particular case: What is firing during the closure phase of a precision-grip grasp? Three subclusters. (1) The subcluster for general-purpose grasping. (2) The subcluster for precision-grip grasping (a particular manner). (3) The subcluster for closure phase grasping.

Of course, the general-purpose subcluster for grasping can never function alone in action, since all actions are carried out in some manner and are in one phase or another at some time. However, it is at least in principle possible for the general-purpose subcluster for grasping to fire without a manner subcluster firing, *in simulation*. That is, you should be able to simulate something in imagination that you cannot do—carry out a *general* action without specifying manner. This is important for the theory of concepts. We can conceptualise a generalised grasping without any particular manner being specified.

The action-only neurons fire only when actions are carried out. But premotor area F5 also contains what are called "canonical neurons"—grasping-related neurons that fire not only when a grasping action is carried out, but also when the subject (a monkey) sees an object that it could grasp, but doesn't (see Rizzolatti et al., 2000b). These canonical neurons have both a general-purpose subcluster and a manner subcluster for cases where the grasping action is carried out. No experiments have yet been done to determine in detail the phases of firing in such subclusters, though it is surmised that they will have phase subclusters as well.

There is a simulation explanation for the behavior of canonical neurons: If the sight of a graspable object triggers the simulation of grasping, we would expect there to be firing by at least some of the neurons that fire during actual grasping. This indeed is what happens with canonical neurons.

Strong evidence for the simulation hypothesis comes from the following data. In most canonical grasping-manner neurons, there is a strict correlation: The same neurons fire for a given manner of grasping as for merely observing an object that, if grasped, would require the same manner of grasping. For example, if a small object is presented, no matter what its shape is, then the same neurons fire as would fire if that small object were being picked up with a precision grip (as afforded by a small object of any shape). This is strong prima facie evidence that simulation is taking place: When you observe a graspable object, only the neurons with the right manner of grasping for that object fire (see Gallese, 2003b).

Observing the actions of others

The F5c-PF cluster: Simulation in mirror neurons

Within the F5c-PF cluster, there are individual neurons that are activated both during the execution of purposeful, goal-related hand actions, such as grasping, holding, or manipulating objects, and during the observation of similar actions performed by another individual. These neurons are called "mirror neurons" (Gallese, 1999, 2000a, 2001, 2003a, 2003b; Gallese, Fadiga, Fogassi, & Rizzolatti, 1996; Gallese, Fogassi, Fadiga, & Rizzolatti, 2002; Rizzolatti, Fadiga, Gallese, & Fogassi, 1996; Rizzolatti et al., 2000b, 2001). Mirror neurons, unlike canonical neurons, do not fire when just presented with an object one can act upon. They also do not fire when the observed action is performed with a tool, such as pliers or pincers.

Some mirror neurons (roughly 30%) are "strictly congruent." They fire when the action seen is exactly the same as the action performed. Others (roughly 70%) show hierarchical relations: They fire when either (1) the monkey grasps with a pincer grip, or (2) the monkey sees someone perform *any* type of grasping. (1) is a special case of (2), and hence the relationship between the special case and the general case is there in the neural structure.

Certain mirror neurons show aspectual phases such as the aspectual phases of an action, e.g., they fire during the central part of this action and the concluding part.

Here too, there is a general explanation in terms of simulation: When the subject (a monkey) observes another individual (monkey or human) doing an action, the subject is automatically simulating the same action. Since action and simulation use some of the same neural substrate, that would explain why the same neurons are firing during action-observation as during action-execution.

An even stronger argument in favour of the simulation interpretation comes from the following experiments. In the first series of experiments, F5 mirror neurons were tested in two conditions: (1) a condition in which the subject (a monkey) could see the entire action (e.g., a grasping-action with the hand), and (2) a condition in which the same action was presented, but its final critical part—that is, the hand–object interaction—was hidden. In the hidden condition the monkey only "knew" that the target object was present behind the occluder. The results showed that more than half of the recorded neurons responded in the hidden condition (Umiltà et al., 2001). These data indicate that, like humans, monkeys can also infer the goal of an action, even when the visual information about it is incomplete. This inference can be explained as the result of a simulation of that action by a group of mirror neurons (see also Gallese, 2003a).

A second series of experiments investigated what could possibly be the neural mechanism underpinning the capacity to understand the meaning of an action on the basis of its sound alone. F5 mirror neurons were tested in four conditions: When the monkey (1) executed noisy actions (e.g., breaking peanuts, tearing sheets of paper apart, and the like); and (2) just saw, (3) saw and heard, and (4) just heard the same actions performed by another individual. The results showed that a consistent percentage of the tested mirror neurons fired under all four conditions (Kohler et al., 2001, 2002). These neurons not only responded to the sound of actions, but also discriminated between the sounds of different actions: Each sound matched the appropriate action, whether observed or executed.

The hypothesis again is simulation: When the subject (a monkey) hears another individual performing an action with a distinctive sound, the subject is simulating the same action. Since action and simulation use some of the same neural substrate, that would explain why the same neurons are firing during observing, hearing, and executing the same action.

EVIDENCE FAVOURING THE HYPOTHESIS OF EMBODIED SIMULATION IN HUMANS

All of the cases cited above come from studies of monkeys. There are also correlates of the same results for humans. To the extent that the monkey studies constitute evidence for simulation, so do the studies on humans. This evidence for simulation makes even stronger the case for simulation made by the evidence given from the studies of visual and motor imagery (see below).

First, the action-location neurons: Recent brain-imaging experiments probed a cluster in humans located in the ventral premotor cortex and in the depth of the intraparietal sulcus, homologous to F4-VIP in monkeys. Neurons in this cluster were activated when subjects heard or saw stimuli being moved in their peri-personal space (Bremmer et al., 2001). The significance of this is that one of the areas activated during such perception is a premotor area, the area that would most likely control movements aimed at objects in peri-personal space.

Second, the canonical neurons: In several recent brain-imaging experiments, subjects were asked to (1) observe, (2) name silently, and (3) imagine using various man-made objects (e.g., hammers, screwdrivers, and so on). In all these cases, there was activation of the ventral premotor cortex, that is, the brain region activated when using those same tools to perform actions (Chao & Martin, 2000; Grafton, Arbib, Fadiga, & Rizzolatti, 1996; Martin et al., 1996; Perani et al., 1995).

Third, the mirror neurons: Several studies using different experimental methodologies and techniques have demonstrated in humans the existence of a mirror system, similar to that observed in monkeys, matching action observation and execution (see Buccino et al., 2001; Cochin, Barthelemy, Lejeune, Roux, & Martineau, 1998; Decety et al., 1997; Fadiga, Fogassi, Pavesi, & Rizzolatti, 1995; Grafton et al., 1996; Hari et al., 1998; Iacoboni et al., 1999; Rizzolatti et al., 1996). In particular, brain-imaging experiments in humans have shown that, during action observation, there is a strong activation of premotor and parietal areas, which are very likely to be the human homologue of the monkey areas in which mirror neurons were found (Buccino et al., 2001; Decety & Grèzes, 1999; Decety et al., 1997; Grafton et al., 1996; Iacoboni et al., 1999; Rizzolatti et al., 1996).

MENTAL IMAGERY: EMBODIED SIMULATION

All human beings entertain the capacity to imagine worlds that they have or have not seen before, to imagine doing things that they have or have not done before. The power of our imagination is seemingly infinite. Indeed, mental imagery has been considered for ages as one of the most characteristic aspects of the human mind, as it has been taken to epitomise its disembodied nature. Mental imagery used to be thought of as "abstract" and "fanciful", far from, and independent of, the perception of real objects and actions. In the light of neuroscientific research, though, things look quite different: We now know that visual and motor imagery *are embodied*.

1. Embodied visual imagery: *Some of the same parts of the brain used in seeing are used in visual imagination* (imagining that you are seeing). (For a comprehensive review, see Farah, 2000; Kosslyn & Thompson, 2000.)

2. Embodied motor imagery: *Some of the same parts of the brain used in action are used in motor imagination* (imagining that you are acting). Thus, imagination is not separate in the brain from perception and action (see Jeannerod, 1994).

The evidence comes from a variety of studies. For example, the time it takes to scan a visual scene is virtually identical to the time employed to scan the same scene when it is only imagined (Kosslyn, Ball, & Reiser, 1978). Furthermore, and more importantly, brain-imaging studies show that when we engage in imagining a visual scene, we activate regions in the brain that are normally active when we actually perceive the same visual scene (Farah, 1989; Kosslyn, 1994; Kosslyn et al., 1993). This includes areas, such as the primary visual cortex, involved in mapping low-level visual features (Le Bihan et al., 1993).

Motor imagery shows the same embodied nature as visual imagery. Mentally rehearsing a physical exercise has been shown to induce an increase of muscle strength comparable to that attained by a real exercise (Yue & Cole, 1992). When we engage in imagining the performance of a given action, several bodily parameters behave similarly to when we actually carry out the same actions. Decety (1991) has shown that heartbeat and breathing frequency increase during motor imagery of physical exercise. As in real physical exercise, they increase linearly with the increase of the imagined effort.

Finally, brain-imaging experiments have shown that motor imagery and real action both activate a common network of brain motor centres, such as the premotor cortex, the supplementary motor area (SMA), the basal ganglia, and the cerebellum (Decety, Sjoholm, Ryding, Stenberg, & Ingvar, 1990; Fox, Pardo, Petersen, & Raichle, 1987; Parsons et al., 1995; Roland, Larsen, Lassen, & Skinhoj, 1980; see also Jeannerod, 1994).

These data all together show that typical human cognitive activities such as visual and motor imagery, far from being of a disembodied, modality-free, and symbolic nature, make use of the activation of sensory-motor brain regions.

Let us conclude this section with a note on multimodality. In natural language, the same verbs refer to actions performed and the corresponding actions seen or heard. The verbs are not limited by a particular modality. There are two possible accounts of the neural underpinnings of this aspect of language. (1) Modality-neutrality—a neural system outside the sensory-motor system altogether, with verbs expressing modality-neutral concepts. (2) Multimodality of the sort we have just seen: Connections across brain areas result in coordinated multimodal neural firing, and verbs express such multimodal concepts. We have just seen evidence for the existence of the appropriate multi-modality. Before we go on to the implications of all this for concepts, we will take up the topic of parameters.

PARAMETERS

A cat has three gaits—strutting, trotting, and galloping. Each gait requires a distinct motor programme. In galloping, for example, the front legs move together and the back legs move together. Strutting and trotting involve very different motor control of the legs. In short, the cat has three very different motor circuits to control its gait.

What is remarkable is that it has been discovered that there is a single cluster of neurons, a central pattern generator, that controls which gait is chosen. When those neurons are firing at low frequency, the cat struts; when the firing is at intermediate frequency, the cat trots; and at high frequency, the cat gallops (for review, see Grillner & Wallen, 2002; Yamaguchi, 2004). In other words, there are three values of firing frequency over a single collection of neurons—low, medium, and high—that result in the activation of either the strutting, trotting, or galloping gait. The firing frequency over that collection of neurons is a *neural parameter* and the mutually exclusive low, medium, and high firing frequencies are *values* of that neural parameter.

Parameters can be seen as "higher-level" features of neural organisation, while the neural firings in particular motor circuits for various gaits can be seen as being at a "lower level" of organisation. Given the higher-level firing, all the lower-level firings are automatically driven as part of an encapsulated routine. To the higher-level parameters, the lower-level structure is "invisible." Parameterisation thus imposes a hierarchical structure on the neural system.

Parameterisation is a pervasive feature of the brain. Here are some further examples:

1. In any given motor task, a certain level of force is appropriate. Level of force is a parameter for each motor task, and degrees of force are its values. The degree of force is controlled in the brain in one of two ways: either the *level* of activation of some cluster of motor neurons, or the *number* of motor neurons activated (see Porter & Lemon, 1993).

2. Direction of motion is also a parameter for actions. Two mechanisms have been proposed for determining values of the direction of movement parameter: (a) groups of neurons are selectively tuned to control a movement in a particular direction (see Gentilucci et al., 1988); (b) direction is determined by a "vector sum" over a whole population of neurons, each of which is only broadly tuned, that is, tuned to a range of directions (see Georgeopoulos, Schwartz, & Kettner, 1986). In either case, there is a direction parameter and a neural mechanism for determining specific values of that parameter.

3. In any given action description, role parameters play a major role. Mirror neurons map different actions (e.g., grasping, holding, tearing, placing, kicking an object) by specifying the agentive relation, while being neutral about the specific quality or identity of the agentive/subjective parameter. Other clusters map this information. For example, the activation of pre-SMA or the primary motor cortex is present only when one executes the action, but not when one is observing it being performed by someone else (Buccino et al., 2001; Ehrrsson et al., 2000; for a recent review of the neural correlates of the *who* parameter, see Jackson & Decety, 2004).

The parameter–simulation link

In the enactment of any particular movement, say, pushing an object in a direction with a given force, the parameter values chosen determine where and how hard one pushes. Moreover, if the force required is very high, what is required is *shoving* rather than mere *pushing*. Shoving requires a different motor programme: setting the weight on the back foot, and so on. Thus, the choice of parameter values also determines motor programmes for humans as well as for cats. Moreover, parameter values govern simulations as well. Imagining pushing is different from imagining shoving.

The parameterisation hierarchy and the capacity to set parameter values are basic features of the brain. The parameters used in everyday perception and action are stable—built into our neural structure. In order to carry out any action or simulation, suitable parameter values must be activated. But there is a difference between parameter structures, on the one hand, and the actions and simulations they control. Both simulations and actions are *dynamic* and *contextually adapted*. Parameters are *fixed*. Whenever you act, there is always a neurally determined action, force, direction, amplitude, and so on. But the situation you are in affects the ultimate *values* of the parameters—exactly when, where, and how the action is carried out. Similarly, all simulation occurs via choice of the values of fixed parameters, which are determined dynamically in the context of the simulation.

The accessibility of parameters

Parameters and their values impose a hierarchical structure on the brain in the following sense. Once a value for a parameter is chosen, lower-level automatic neural mechanisms take over, say, to apply a force of a given magnitude or move in a given direction. Parameters and the kinds of values they have may be brought to consciousness. For example, all of us know we can press our palms forward with high degree of force. But we do not know how that is carried out neurally. Thus, parameters and their values are accessible to consciousness, while anything below the parameter value level is inaccessible.

Similarly, language may express parameters and their values, but language cannot express anything below the level of parameter values. Parameters and their values are thus also accessible to language, while lower-level neural structures are not.

After having discussed the relevance of parameters, there are more results from cognitive science that need to be mentioned before we move on. They concern basic-level categories.

BASIC-LEVEL CATEGORIES

The classic, and long taken for granted theory of categorisation assumed that categories formed a hierarchy—bottom to top—and that there was nothing special about those categories in the middle. This view was challenged by the research by Berlin, Rosch, and their co-workers in the 1970s (Berlin, Breedlove, & Raven, 1974; Berlin & Kay, 1969; Rosch, 1977, 1978, 1981, 1994; Rosch & Lloyd, 1978; Rosch, Mervis, Gray, Johnson, & Boyes-Braem, 1976). Take hierarchies like *furniture/chair/rocking chair* or *vehicle/car/ sports car*. The categories in the middle—*chair* and *car*—are special; what Rosch called "basic-level" categories. One can get a mental image of a chair or a car, but not of a piece of furniture in general or a vehicle in general. We have motor programmes for interacting with chairs and cars, but not with furniture in general or vehicles in general. The basic level is the highest level at which this is true. Moreover, words for basic-level categories tend to be recognisable via gestalt perception, be learned earlier, to be shorter (e.g., *car* vs. *vehicle*), to be more frequent, to be remembered more easily, and so on.

Rosch observed that the basic level is the level at which we interact optimally in the world with our bodies. The consequence is that categorisation is embodied—given by our interactions, not just by objective properties of objects in the world, as a long philosophical tradition had assumed. Without us—without the way we sit and the way we form images—the wide range of objects we have called "chairs" do not form a category. A simple sentence like *Some chairs are green* is not true of the world independent of us, since there are neither chairs nor green things independent of us. It is, of course, true relative to *our body-based understanding* of the world. Our concepts must also be characterised relative to such a body-based understanding.

AN EMBODIED NEURAL THEORY OF CONCEPTS

We are now in a position to propose how these basic results from neuroscience and cognitive science allow us to characterise in neural terms not just actions, but *action concepts*. We have chosen to start with the concept of *grasping* for two reasons. First, we know quite a lot about the neuroscience of grasping; enough, we believe, to get fairly far. Second, the traditional theory requires *all* concepts to be disembodied, that is, above the level of everything we have talked about so far and not making use of any of it. This includes action concepts like *grasping*. The usual assumption is that a *concept* is disembodied, that is, modality-neutral and symbolic, while the *action that the concept designates* is of course embodied. Proponents of the traditional view would therefore maintain that any attempt to say that concepts are embodied would amount to confusing the *concept* with *what the concept designates*.

Our response will have two parts: First, we will argue that parameters and simulations can do the jobs that everyone agrees that concepts must do. Second, we will argue that the traditional theory does not accord with the results of neuroscience that we have just given.

What is an embodied concept?

Here is our central claim on embodied concepts: *The job done by what have been called "concepts" can be accomplished by schemas characterised by parameters and their values.* Such a schema, from a neural perspective, consists of a network of functional clusters. The network constituting a schema contains:

1. One cluster for each *parameter*—a cluster that characterises that parameter.
2. One cluster for each *parameter value*, or range of values.
3. One "controller" cluster, whose activation is liked to the activation of the parameters and their values in the following way: If the controller is active, each of its parameters and the accompanying

values are active. If a sufficient number of parameters and their values are active (this may be as few as one), the controller is active.

These are neural computational conditions on the networks we call "schemas."

We have hesitated to call schemas "concepts," simply because concepts have long been traditionally thought of as being direct reflections or representations of external reality. Schemas are clearly not that at all. Schemas are *interactional*, arising from (1) the nature of our bodies, (2) the nature of our brains, and (3) the nature of our social and physical *interactions* in the world. Schemas are therefore not purely internal, nor are they purely representations of external reality. We will, for the moment, think of concepts as schemas, though that idea will be extended below when we discuss abstractions.

The example of grasp

The example we have been using all the way through is the concept *grasp*. Here is what a schema for *grasp* might look like in this theory. The parameters divide up in the following ways:

The grasp schema.

1. The role parameters: agent, object, object location, and the action itself.
2. The phase parameters: initial condition, starting phase, central phase, purpose condition, ending phase, final state.
3. The manner parameter.
4. The parameter values (and constraints on them).

The various parameters can be described as follows.

Agent: An individual.
Object: A physical entity with parameters: size, shape, mass, degree of fragility, and so on.
Initial condition::[2] Object Location: Within peri-personal space.
Starting phase:: Reaching, with direction: Toward object location; opening effector.
Central phase:: Closing effector, with force: A function of fragility and mass.
Purpose condition:: Effector encloses object, with manner (a grip determined by parameter values and situational conditions).
Final state:: Agent in-control-of object.

This should give the reader a pretty clear idea of how a *grasp* schema is structured in terms of neural parameters and values of the sort we described in the sections above on neuroscience. Note that we have written down symbols (e.g., *final state*) as our notation for functional clusters. This does *not* mean that we take functional clusters themselves to be symbolic. The symbols are only *our names* for functional clusters, which, as we have seen, function from a computational point of view as neurally realised units.

A note about schemas

Traditionally, concepts were seen as a set of necessary and sufficient conditions operating in a system of logic. Indeed, for many philosophers, that was a defining characteristic of what a concept was to be.

It might look from the notation as though the grasp schema is indeed defined by such a set of necessary and sufficient conditions. This is not the case. First, the activation of functional clusters is not all-or-none; there are degrees of activation. Such gradations are not part of the traditional notion of necessary and sufficient conditions. Second, there are variations on schemas, as when certain phases are optionally left out. Third, there are extensions of schemas; for example, we will discuss metaphorical extensions below. Fourth, and perhaps most important, schemas combine and operate dynamically, in context, by neural optimisation—that is, via best fit principles. For example, imagine that you intend to grasp, pick up, and throw what appears to be a ball. But the ball turns out to be made of iron and to have a slippery surface. You will grasp it as well as you can, though perhaps not

[2] The "::" notation indicates the content of a phase.

exactly fitting the schema (tightening your grip might be difficult). You may manage to pick it up, but hardly in the normal way. And being slippery and very heavy, your attempt to throw it may result in something closer to a shot-put motion.

In short, schemas are not like logical conditions. They run bodies—as well as they can.

The theory we are outlining uses the computational modelling mechanisms of the neural theory of language (NTL) developed in Berkeley by the groups of Jerome Feldman and George Lakoff (see Feldman & Narayanan, in press; Lakoff & Johnson, 1999). NTL makes use of a *structured connectionist* version of neural computation (see Feldman, 1982), which, though "localist," has units that are not just individual neurons, but rather *functional clusters* as we have discussed them throughout this paper. In such a structured connectionist model operating on functional clusters, the death or plasticity of individual neurons has virtually no effect, so long as the connectivity of the rest of the cluster remains intact.

NTL is therefore not subject to the "grandmother cell" objection, which assumes the following caricature of localist computation. In the caricature, each concept—say, the concept of your grandmother—is represented by one and only one neuron. If that neuron dies, then you lose the concept of your grandmother. No localist ever proposed such a theory, and nor do we.

From the structured connectionism perspective, *the inferential structure of concepts is a consequence of the network structure of the brain and its organisation in terms of functional clusters.* This brain organisation is, in turn, a consequence of our evolutionary history—of the way in which our brains, and the brains of our evolutionary ancestors, have been shaped by bodily interactions in the world.

WHAT WE HAVE SHOWN SO FAR

We have provided a reasonably detailed neural theory for one action concept—*grasping*. We have shown how the *sensory-motor* system can characterise a sensory-motor *concept*, not just an action or a perception, but a *concept* with all that that requires.

But we think we have shown something more powerful than that. According to our hypothesis, understanding requires simulation. The understanding of concrete concepts—physical actions, physical objects, and so on—requires sensory-motor simulation. But sensory-motor simulation, as suggested by contemporary neuroscience, is carried out by the sensory-motor system of the brain. It follows that the sensory-motor system *is required for understanding at least concrete concepts.* We see this as an insurmountable difficulty for any traditional theory that claims that concrete concepts are modality-neutral and disembodied.

There is a further argument against the traditional modality-neutral, disembodied account of concepts. In order to have a neural account of such a theory of action concepts, action *concepts*, like all other concepts, would have to be represented neurally *outside the sensory-motor system altogether.* That, in turn, would require complete duplication of the structure-characterising concepts that neuroscience has found *in the sensory-motor system*, namely, all the structure we have just outlined: *the manner subcases, the agent-object-location structure, the purpose structure, and the phase structure.*

The reason is this: All of that sensory-motor structure (agent-object-location, manner, purpose, and phases) has to be there, in anyone's account. Any neural theory of modality-neutral concepts must claim that such structure is located in the brain *outside the sensory-motor system*. But we know, from independent evidence that we have cited, that all that structure is indeed *inside the sensory-motor system*. The only way it could also be outside is if it were duplicated. Not just for one concept, but for *every action concept.* And it would not just have to be duplicated. There would have to be one-to-one connections to just the right parts of the premotor-parietal system in order for the concept to apply to real cases that are performed, observed, and simulated.

In short, we think there is an Occam's Razor argument here. The modality-neutral structure is just not needed.

We think we can safely say that something like the proposal we have made would have to work for the action concept of grasping, and probably for every other action concept as well. We believe that the same basic structures—schemas structuring sensory-motor parameterisations—can be used to characterise all concrete concepts. Take, for example, the basic-level concepts that we described above—chair, car, etc. As we saw, basic-level concepts are defined by the convergence of (1) gestalt object perception (observed or imaged) and (2) motor programmes that define the prototypical interaction with the object (again, performed or imaged). Thus, a chair looks a certain way (and we can imagine how it looks) and it is used for sitting in a certain position (and we can imaging sitting that way). What brings together the perceptual and motor properties are, we believe, functional neural clusters showing the analogous characteristics in humans that have been found for *canonical neurons* thus far in the brains of monkeys. Indeed, evidence suggesting the presence of the equivalent of canonical neurons in humans does exist, as we mentioned above (Chao & Martin, 2000; Grafton et al., 1996; Martin, Wiggs, Ungerleider, & Haxby, 1996; Perani, Cappa, Bettinardi, Bressi, Gorno-Tempini, & Fazio, 1995). The existence of canonical neurons and their putative equivalent in humans could underpin basic-level categories of objects. Subordinate-level categories, which *have more perceptual and motor details filled in*, would be accounted for by functional clusters of the type described before, with the values of more parameters specified. Schemas structuring the parameters over functional clusters would have the properties of basic-level and subordinate concrete object concepts.

We believe that *all* concrete concepts—concepts of things we can see, touch, and manipulate—can be addressed by the strategy outlined so far. Indeed, our proposal for object schemas is very close to the "sensory/motor model of semantic representations of objects" of Martin, Ungerleider, and Haxby (2000), which is based on a thorough survey of neuroscientific evidence.

THE LARGER CONTEXT

Neuroscience does not exist in a vacuum; it is part of the larger field of cognitive science, which has branches like neural computation and cognitive linguistics. The results we have just summarised fit into the larger context. Within the field of structured connectionist neural modelling, Srini Narayanan (1997, 1999) has constructed computational neural models of motor actions, including the tripartite breakdown: premotor, motor, and premotor–motor connections. The premotor model functioned dynamically to "choreograph" and carry out in proper sequence the simple movements of the motor cortex.

These premotor models turned out to have a uniform structure: (1) initial state, (2) starting phase transition, (3) precentral state, (4) central phase transition (either instantaneous, prolonged, or ongoing), (5) postcentral state, (6) ending phase transition, (7) final state. At the postcentral state, there are the following options: (a) a check to see if a goal state has been achieved, (b) an option to iterate or continue the main process, (c) an option to stop, and (d) an option to resume. Each complex motor programme is a complex combination of structures of this form, either in sequence, in parallel, or embedded one in another. What distinguishes actions from one another is (1) the version of this premotor structure and (2) bindings to the motor cortex and other sensory areas (for perceptual and somatosensory feedback). These premotor structures are called "executing schemas," or X-schemas for short. Naranayan (1997) noted that premotor structures also fit the perceptual structure of the motor actions modelled. In short, he modelled the structures described above for mirror neurons, canonical neurons, and action-location neurons.

Dynamic X-schemas can be seen as linking the functional clusters we have just discussed to characterise their temporal activation in either action or perception—or in imagination. In short, they are capable of carrying out imaginative simulations. Furthermore, those imaginative simulations can carry out *abstract conceptual reasoning* as well as actions and perceptions. The result is a neural theory of conceptual metaphor. We know from cognitive semantics that conceptual metaphors are one of the basic mechanisms of mind. Each conceptual metaphor is a mapping across conceptual domains, from a (typically) sensory-motor source domain to a (typically) non-sensory-motor target domain.

For example, the conceptual metaphor *love is a journey* maps travelers to lovers, vehicles to relationships, destinations to common life goals, and impediments to relationship difficulties, as shown by English expressions about love like *It's been a long bumpy road, The marriage is on the rocks, We're spinning our wheels, We're going in different directions, We're at a crossroads in the relationship*, and so on. The concept of love has a minimal nonmetaphorical structure with a lover, a beloved, a love relationship, and not much more. More than a dozen conceptual metaphors of this sort add to that minimal structure a very rich conceptual structure. Henceforth love can be conceptualised and reasoned about in terms not only of a journey, but also of a partnership, a joining-together, magic, heat, and so on. Most (not all) of the richness of the concept comes from these metaphors. (For detailed discussions of such metaphors and the evidence for them, see Kövecses, 2002; Lakoff & Johnson, 1980, 1999; and the references discussed in these works.)

What Narayanan (1997) did was to construct a computational neural model of such metaphorical mappings, in which each mapping is carried out by neural circuitry of certain regular structures. He then chose an abstract domain—international economics—and worked out the conceptual metaphors mapping physical actions to economics. He constructed computational neural models of both target and source domains and took sentences from such sources as the *NY Times Business Section* and the *Wall Street Journal*—sentences like *France fell into a recession; Pulled out by Germany*; and *India is stumbling toward economic liberalisation*, in which there are physical sensory-motor expressions like *fall into, pull out, and stumble toward.* He then showed that by using the mappings to combine source (sensory-motor) and target (economic) inferences, he could get the correct inferences in a neural computational simulation.

The same computational models of neural circuitry that can direct action and perceptions of actions can also simulate actions with the right structures to get all the conceptual inferences right. The sensory-motor system can characterise action concepts and, in simulation, characterise conceptual inferences. And the concepts characterised in the sensory-motor system are of the right form to characterise the source domains of conceptual metaphors.

THE THEORY OF COGS

Narayanan (1997) made another discovery. His premotor X-schemas have exactly the right structure to characterise the collection of concepts that linguists refer to as "aspect"—concepts that characterise the structure of events and our reasoning about events. Every language has a way of indicating aspect. English has terms like *about to, start to, be + Verb + ing, and have + Verb + Past Participle.* Thus, *he is about to run, he is starting to run, he is running, he has run.*

In actions, the premotor cortex is neurally connected to the motor cortex, choreographing simple movements into complex actions. But those premotor-to-motor connections can be inhibited, and the X-schemas of the premotor system can function independently, characterising the logic of aspect in the abstract. Thus, a sentence like *he is doing something stupid* doesn't tell what action he is carrying out, but does specify the ongoing aspectual structure, with the inferences that *he has already started doing something stupid* and *he hasn't finished doing something stupid.* These inferences are being computed via neural simulation by X-schema structure circuitry in the premotor cortex—with no active connections to the motor cortex. In short, a portion of the sensory-motor system (the premotor cortex) is being used to do abstract reasoning, reasoning that is not about any particular sensory-motor activity. Indeed, *the stupid thing he is doing* need not be physical at all.

Let us call the premotor cortex a "secondary" area—an area not directly connected to sensors or effectors, but which provides structure to information going to effectors or coming from sensors. On Narayanan's hypothesis, abstract aspectual concepts have the following properties:

- They are neurally simulated in a secondary area with no active connections to a primary area. For example, all such connections may be inhibited.

- Their inferences are computed via that simulation.
- They characterise concepts in the grammar of a natural language.
- As such, these concepts are general, and can apply to any special-case concepts when there are active connections to primary areas.
- When there are such active connections, the general concepts are an inseparable part of the structure of the special case concepts.

Lakoff (personal communication) has proposed a generalisation of Narayanan's account of aspect to include all concepts with such properties. Any concept that has the properties given in the above list is called a *cog*. In the theory of cogs, all concepts in the grammars (as opposed to the lexicons) of natural languages should have the properties given in the list above. That is, they should be computed in secondary areas. This could include all the primitive image-schemas, such as containment, source-path-goal, force dynamics, orientation schemas, etc. (see Casad & Langacker, 1985; Johnson, 1987; Lakoff, 1987; Langacker, 1986, 1990, 1991; Lindner, 1981; Talmy, 1983, 1988, 1996, 1999).

For example, according to Regier's (1996) neural computational theory of container schemas, containment is computed via a complex of topographical maps of the visual field. The computation is general; it can take any size or shape of container—a bottle, a cup, a room, a castle, a triangle—as input and characterise its interior, boundary, and exterior. But that input information (including shape) is not computed in topographic map areas. It is computed elsewhere, with input presumably coming via the parietal cortex. The complex of topographic maps computing containment constitutes a "secondary" area, while the input to it would come via an area that is more "primary."

What we know about image-schemas is that they characterise a wide range of general inference patterns, characterising all forms of causal, spatial, and event-based reasoning. They are universal, general, and appear in the semantics of grammar around the world. If they are all computed in secondary regions, that would explain why there is a limited range of them (there is a relatively small number of such regions), why they are universal (we all have the same basic brain structure), and why they are general (they provide structure to primary regions with specific information).

The theory of cogs is at present still vague. It does not specify exactly which areas compute which cogs using which circuitry. Its utility, however, lies in that: (1) it gives neuroscientists something to look for that they might not have thought to look for; (2) it provides a possible explanation for why image-schemas exist and why there is such a thing as the semantics of grammar; (3) it posits an interesting theory of the learning of general linguistic structures. Briefly, here is what the theory says:

- Because neural structures in secondary areas are inseparable in behaviour from the primary structures that they are connected to, they characterise generalisations that are inherent in and inseparable from special cases.
- The "learning" of general cases is not the acquisition of new structures, but rather the inhibition of the connections between secondary and primary areas.
- In other words, the generalisations are inherent in the special cases that are learned first. What is learned is the control of inhibitory connections.

EMPIRICAL VALIDATION OF OUR THEORY: FUTURE EXPERIMENTS

The theory of concepts that we have outlined here has empirical consequences that can be tested. In this theory, the same circuitry that can move the body and structure perceptions, also structures abstract thought. Of course, this does not imply that a paresis or sensory loss due to a localised brain damage affecting selected regions within the sensory-motor system should *necessarily* produce a deficit in the capacity to entertain abstract conceptual knowledge. This possibility is not, in principle, precluded, but is unlikely to arise. The reason is this: The distributed nature of the sensory-motor neural clusters responsible for structuring conceptual knowledge spans from frontal to parieto-temporal cortices. Because the operative neural clusters are distributed in this way, it is unlikely that a restricted brain lesion would be sufficient to impair their ability to function.

It should be added that standard neuropsychological testing for conceptual knowledge does not routinely investigate metaphorical conceptualisation in brain-lesioned patients. A systematic study of patients along these lines should be encouraged. If, however, a hypothetical brain lesion would prevent a patient from grasping objects, recognising other people doing it, or even imagining himself or others grasping objects, then our theory predicts that the same patient should also be impaired in metaphorically conceptualising grasping as understanding. We are not aware of any clinical report of specific and localised brain lesions (within or outside the sensory-motor system) causing the selective loss of *specific abstract concepts* such as causation, identity, love, and the like. In fact, at the core of our theory is the claim that there are no dedicated and specialised brain circuits for concepts in general, or for abstract concepts in particular.

The difficulty in relying on clinical cases, though, does not mean that our theory cannot generate empirically testable predictions. We know, for example, that the motor cortex is topographically organised, with the movements of effectors like the mouth, hands, and feet controlled in different sectors. These sectors are separated far enough from each other in the motor cortex so that they are clearly distinguishable in fMRI studies. The same holds for the premotor cortex, though with more overlap between regions. Moreover, premotor activations are clearly distinguishable from motor activations and from activations in other regions. We know that both premotor and motor cortices are both activated during mental motor imagery. According to our hypothesis, mental motor imagery is voluntary simulation of motor action (see Gallese, 2003a, 2003b).

In the theory we have outlined, the properties of action concepts are specified by parameter values and the simulations they govern. Such action simulations should be detectable through fMRI studies in the sensory-motor cortices that are responsible for controlling the corresponding actions. For example, in the case of the concept of *grasping*, one would expect the parietal-premotor circuits that form functional clusters for grasping to be active not only when actually grasping, but also when understanding sentences involving the concept of *grasping*. Moreover, when processing sentences describing actions performed by different effectors—the mouth in biting, the hands in holding, the feet in kicking—one would expect parietal-premotor regions for action by the mouth vs. hands vs. feet to be active not only when actually acting, but also when understanding the corresponding sentences. Preliminary evidence seems to confirm that this is the case (Tettamanti et al., in press)

A further prediction of our theory of concepts is that such results should be obtained in fMRI studies, not only with literal sentences, but also with the corresponding metaphorical sentences. Thus, the sentence *He grasped the idea* should activate the sensory-motor *grasping-related regions* of the brain. Similarly, a metaphorical sentence like *They kicked him out of class* should active the sensory-motor *kicking-related regions* of the brain. A series of brain-imaging experiments are currently being carried out to test this prediction.

Another series of experiments is being designed to test the parameters of force and direction in concepts. On the grounds of our proposal, we would predict that asking subjects to exert a force while reading sentences about force, or to move their hand along a given direction while reading sentences about directional actions, would either facilitate or interfere with the comprehension of such sentences. Indeed, Glenberg and Kaschak (2002) recently showed an action-sentence compatibility effect in normal subjects required to determine the correctness of read sentences describing concrete or abstract actions towards or away from the body, by moving their hand either towards or away from the body.

Such an experimental design could also be used to study metaphorical sentences, in which there is a metaphorical use of force or direction predicates (e.g., throw, bring, knock). The same logic should apply here as in the literal sentences. The application of force, or movement exerted along a given direction, should facilitate or interfere with the understanding of metaphorical sentences, depending on whether the force or direction in the source domain of the metaphor is or is not consistent with magnitude of the force applied or with the direction of movement.

CONCLUSIONS

We have argued that contemporary neuroscience seems to suggest that concepts of a wide variety make direct use of the sensory-motor circuitry of the brain. We began the argument with action concepts and with four central ideas triggered by neuroscience: multimodality, functional clusters, simulation, and parameters. We then turned to neuroscientific results: (1) visual and motor mental imagery, which, according to our hypothesis, imply sensory-motor simulation using the same brain resources as in observation and action; (2) detailed results concerning mirror neurons, canonical neurons, and action-location neurons. By applying the four ideas to these results, we proposed, for the action concept of *grasping*, that a directly embodied schema for grasping satisfies all principal criteria for concepts. We argued that a disembodied, symbolic account of the concept of *grasping* would have to duplicate elsewhere in the brain the complex neural machinery in three parietal-premotor circuits, which is implausible to say the least. We concluded that the action *concept* of *grasping* is embodied in the sensory-motor system.

We then went on to argue that arguments of the same form may apply to all other action concepts, to object concepts, and to abstract concepts with conceptual content that is metaphorical. Finally, we considered cogs, which we posit to be structuring circuits in the sensory-motor system, which normally function as part of sensory-motor operations, but whose neural connections to specific details can be inhibited, allowing them to provide inferential structure to "abstract" concepts. If all this is correct, then abstract reasoning in general *exploits* the sensory-motor system.

What is the import of our proposal on the nature of human cognition? We believe that it suggests that rational thought is not entirely separate from what animals can do, because it directly uses sensory-motor bodily mechanisms—the same ones used by nonhuman primates to function in their everyday environments. According to our hypothesis, rational thought is an exploitation of the normal operations of our bodies. As such, it is also largely unconscious.

Another major consequence concerns language. Language makes use of concepts. Concepts are what words, morphemes, and grammatical constructions express. Indeed, the expression of concepts is primarily what language is about. If we are right, then:

1. Language makes direct use of the same brain structures used in perception and action.
2. Language is not completely a human innovation.
3. There is no such thing as a "language module."
4. Grammar resides in the neural connections between concepts and their expression via phonology. That is, grammar is constituted by the connections between conceptual schemas and phonological schemas. Hierarchical grammatical structure is conceptual structure. Linear grammatical structure is phonological.
5. The semantics of grammar is constituted by cogs—structuring circuits used in the sensory motor system.
6. Neither semantics nor grammar is modality-neutral.
7. Neither semantics nor grammar is symbolic, in the sense of the theory of formal systems, which consists of rules for manipulating disembodied meaningless symbols.

Future empirical research will show whether and to what extent our hypotheses are correct.

PrEview proof published online 10 January 2005

REFERENCES

Albritton, D. (1992). *The use of metaphor to structure text representations: evidence for metaphor-based schemas.* PhD dissertation, Yale University, USA.

Bailey, D. (1997). *A computational model of embodiment in the acquisition of action verbs.* PhD dissertation. Computer Science Division, EECS Department, University of California, Berkeley, USA.

Berlin, B., Breedlove, D., & Raven, P. (1974). *Principles of Tzeltal plant classification.* New York: Academic Press.

Berlin, B., & Kay, P. (1969). *Basic color terms: Their universality and evolution.* Los Angeles: University of California Press.

Boroditsky, L. (1997). Evidence for metaphoric representation: Perspective in space and time. In M. G. Shafto & P. Langley (Eds.), *Proceedings of the Nineteeth Annual Conference of the Cognitive Science Society.* Mahwah, NJ: Lawrence Erlbaum Associates Inc.

Bremmer, F., Schlack, A., Jon Shah, N., Zafiris, O., Kubischik, M., Hoffmann, K. P., Zilles, K., & Fink, G. R. (2001). Polymodal motion processing in posterior parietal and premotor cortex: A human fMRI study strongly implies equivalences between humans and monkeys. *Neuron, 29,* 287–296.

Buccino, G., Binkofski, F., Fink, G. R., Fadiga, L., Fogassi, L., Gallese, V., Seitz, R. J., Zilles, K., Rizzolatti, G., & Freund, H.-J. (2001). Action observation activates premotor and parietal areas in a somatotopic manner: An fMRI study. *European Journal of Neuroscience, 13,* 400–404.

Carpenter, P. A., & Eisenberg, P. (1978). Mental rotation and the frame of reference in blind and sighted individuals. *Perception and Psychophysics, 23,* 117–124.

Casad, E., & Langacker, R. W. (1985). "Inside" and "outside" in Cora grammar. *International Journal of American Linguistics, 51,* 247–281.

Chao, L. L., & Martin, A. (2000). Representation of manipulable man-made objects in the dorsal stream. *Neuroimage, 12,* 478–484.

Cochin, S., Barthelemy, C., Lejeune, B., Roux, S., & Martineau, J. (1998). Perception of motion and qEEG activity in human adults. *Electroencephalography and Clinical Neurophysiology, 107,* 287–295.

Colby, C. L., Duhamel, J.-R., & Goldberg M. E. (1993). Ventral intraparietal area of the macaque: anatomic location and visual response properties. *Journal of Neurophysiology, 69,* 902–914.

Decety, J., & Grèzes, J. (1999). Neural mechanisms subserving the perception of human actions. *Trends in Cognitive Sciences, 3,* 172–178.

Decety, J., Grezes, J., Costes, N., Perani, D., Jeannerod, M., Procyk, E., Grassi, F., & Fazio, F. (1997). Brain activity during observation of actions. Influence of action content and subject's strategy. *Brain, 120,* 1763–1777.

Decety, J., Jeannerod, M., Germain, M., & Pastene, J. (1991). Vegetative response during imagined movement is proportional to mental effort. *Behavioral Brain Research, 34,* 35–42.

Decety, J., Jeannerod, M., Germain, M., & Pastene, J. (1999). Vegetative response during imagined movement is proportional to mental effort. *Behavioral and Brain Research, 31,* 1–5.

Decety, J., Jeannerod, M., & Prablanc, C. (1989). The timing of mentally represented actions. *Behavioral Brain Research, 34,* 35–42.

Decety, J., Sjoholm, H., Ryding, E., Stenberg, G., & Ingvar, D. (1990). The cerebellum participates in cognitive activity: Tomographic measurements of regional cerebral blood flow. *Brain Research, 535,* 313–317.

DeValois, R. L., & DeValois, K. (1975). Neural coding of color. In E. C. Careterette & M. P. Friedman (Eds.), *Handbook of perception, Vol. V, Seeing.* New York: Academic Press.

Duffy, J. R., & Watkins, L. B. (1984). The effect of response choice relatedness on pantomime and verbal recognition ability in aphasic patients. *Brain and Language, 21,* 291–306.

Duhamel, J.-R., Colby, C. L., & Goldberg, M. E. (1998). Ventral intraparietal area of the macaque: Congruent visual and somatic response properties. *Journal of Neurophysiology, 79,* 126–136.

Ehrsson, H. H., Fagergren, A., Jonsson, T., Westling, G., Johansson, R. S., & Forssberg H. (2000). Cortical activity in precision- versus power-grip tasks: An fMRI study. *Journal of Neurophysiology, 83,* 528–536.

Fadiga, L., Fogassi, L., Pavesi, G., & Rizzolatti, G. (1995). Motor facilitation during action observation: A magnetic stimulation study. *Journal of Neurophysiology, 73,* 2608–2611.

Farah, M. J. (1989). The neural basis of mental imagery. *Trends in Neuroscience, 12,* 395–399.

Farah, M. J. (2000). The neural bases of mental imagery. In M. S. Gazzaniga (Ed.), *The cognitive neurosciences* (2nd ed.). Cambridge, MA: MIT Press.

Feldman, J. (1982). Dynamic connections in neural networks. *Biological Cybernetics, 46,* 27–39.

Feldman, J., & Narayanan, S. (in press). Embodied meaning in a neural theory of language. *Brain and Language.*

Fillmore, C. (1982). Frame semantics. In Linguistic Society of Korea (Ed.), *Linguistics in the morning calm* (pp. 111–138). Seoul: Hanshin.

Fillmore, C. (1985). Frames and the semantics of understanding. *Quaderni di Semantica, 6,* 222–253.

Fodor, J. (1975). *The language of thought.* Cambridge, MA: Harvard University Press.

Fodor, J. (1983). *The modularity of mind: An essay on faculty psychology.* Cambridge, MA: MIT Press.

Fodor, J. (1987). *Psychosemantics: The problem of meaning in the philosophy of mind.* Cambridge, MA: MIT Press.

Fodor, J. (1998). *In critical condition.* Cambridge, MA: MIT Press.

Fogassi, L., & Gallese, V. (2004). Action as a binding key to multisensory integration. In G. Calvert, C. Spence, & B. E. Stein (Eds.), *Handbook of multisensory processes.* Cambridge, MA: MIT Press.

Fogassi, L., Gallese, V., Buccino, G., Craighero, L., Fadiga, L., & Rizzolatti, G. (2001). Cortical mechanism for the visual guidance of hand grasping movements in the monkey: A reversible inactivation study. *Brain, 124,* 571–586.

Fogassi, L., Gallese, V., di Pellegrino, G., Fadiga, L., Gentilucci, M., Luppino, G., Matelli, M., Pedotti, A., & Rizzolatti, G. (1992). Space coding by premotor cortex. *Experimental Brain Research, 89,* 686–690.

Fogassi, L., Gallese, V., Fadiga, L., Luppino, G., Matelli, M., & Rizzolatti, G. (1996a). Coding of peripersonal space in inferior premotor cortex (area F4). *Journal of Neurophysiology, 76,* 141–157.

Fogassi, L., Gallese, V., Fadiga, L., & Rizzolatti, G. (1996b). Space coding in inferior premotor cortex (area F4): Facts and speculations. In F. Laquaniti & P. Viviani (Eds.), *Neural basis of motor behavior* (pp. 99–120). *NATO ASI Series.* Dordrecht, The Netherlands: Kluwer Academic Publishers.

Fox, P., Pardo, J., Petersen, S., & Raichle, M. (1987). Supplementary motor and premotor responses to actual and imagined hand movements with Positron Emission Tomography. *Society for Neuroscience Abstracts, 13,* 1433.

Gainotti, G. (2004). A metanalysis of impaired and spared naming for different categories of knowledge in patients with a visuo-verbal disconnection. *Neuropsychologia, 42,* 299–319.

Gallese, V. (1999). From grasping to language: Mirror neurons and the origin of social communication. In S. Hameroff, A. Kazniak, & D. Chalmers (Eds.), *Towards a science of consciousness* (pp. 165–178). Cambridge, MA: MIT Press.

Gallese, V. (2000a). The acting subject: Towards the neural basis of social cognition. In T. Metzinger (Ed.), *Neural correlates of consciousness. Empirical and conceptual questions* (pp. 325–333). Cambridge, MA: MIT Press.

Gallese, V. (2000b). The inner sense of action: Agency and motor representations. *Journal of Consciousness Studies, 7,* 23–40.

Gallese, V. (2001). The "shared manifold" hypothesis: From mirror neurons to empathy. *Journal of Consciousness Studies, 8,* 33–50.

Gallese, V. (2003a). The manifold nature of interpersonal relations: The quest for a common mechanism. *Philosophical Transactions of the Royal Society of London, B, 358,* 517–528.

Gallese, V. (2003b). A neuroscientific grasp of concepts: From control to representation. *Philosophical Transactions of the Royal Society of London, B, 358,* 1231–1240.

Gallese, V., Fadiga, L., Fogassi, L., & Rizzolatti, G. (1996). Action recognition in the premotor cortex. *Brain, 119,* 593–609.

Gallese, V., Fogassi, L., Fadiga, L., & Rizzolatti, G. (2002). Action representation and the inferior parietal lobule. In W. Prinz & B. Hommel (Eds.), *Attention and performance XIX* (pp. 247–266). Oxford: Oxford University Press.

Gallese, V., & Goldman, A. (1998). Mirror neurons and the simulation theory of mind-reading. *Trends in Cognitive Sciences, 12,* 493–501.

Gallese, V., Murata, A., Kaseda, M., Niki, N., & Sakata, H. (1994). Deficit of hand preshaping after muscimol injection in monkey parietal cortex. *NeuroReport, 5,* 1525–1529.

Gentilucci, M., Fogassi, L., Luppino, G., Matelli, M., Camarda, R., & Rizzolatti, G. (1988). Functional organization of inferior area 6 in the macaque monkey: I. Somatotopy and the control of proximal movements. *Experimental Brain Research, 71,* 475–490.

Gentilucci, M., Scandolara, C., Pigarev, I. N., & Rizzolatti, G. (1983). Visual responses in the postarcuate cortex (area 6) of the monkey that are independent of eye position. *Experimental Brain Research, 50,* 464–468.

Gentner, D., & Gentner, D. R. (1982). Flowing waters or teeming crowds: Mental models of electricity. In D. Gentner & A. L. Stevens (Eds.), *Mental models.* Hillsdale, NJ: Lawrence Erlbaum Associates Inc.

Georgopoulos, A. P., Schwartz, A. B., & Kettner, R. E. (1986). Neuronal population coding of movement direction. *Science, 233,* 1416–1419.

Gibbs, R. (1994). *The poetics of mind: Figurative thought, language, and understanding.* Cambridge: Cambridge University Press.

Glenberg, A. M., & Kaschak, M. P. (2002). Grounding language in action. *Psychonomic Bulletin and Review, 9,* 558–565.

Grady, J. (1997). *Foundations of meaning: Primary metaphors and primary scenes.* PhD dissertation, University of California at Berkeley, USA.

Grafton, S. T., Arbib, M. A., Fadiga, L., & Rizzolatti, G. (1996). Localization of grasp representations in humans by PET: 2. Observation compared with imagination. *Experimental Brain Research, 112,* 103–111.

Grafton, S. T., Fadiga, L., Arbib, M. A., & Rizzolatti, G. (1997). Premotor cortex activation during observation and naming of familiar tools. *Neuroimage, 6,* 231–236.

Graziano, M. S. A., & Gross, C. G. (1995). The representation of extrapersonal space: A possible role for bimodal visual-tactile neurons. In M. S. Gazzaniga (Ed.), *The cognitive neurosciences* (pp. 1021–1034). Cambridge, MA: MIT Press.

Graziano, M. S. A., Hu, X., & Gross, C. G. (1997a). Visuo-spatial properties of ventral premotor cortex. *Journal of Neurophysiology, 77,* 2268–2292.

Graziano, M. S. A., Hu, X., & Gross, C. G. (1997b). Coding the locations of objects in the dark. *Science, 277,* 239–241.

Graziano, M. S. A., Reiss, L. A. J., & Gross, C. G. (1999). A neuronal representation of the location of nearby sounds. *Nature, 397,* 428–430.

Graziano, M. S. A., Yap, G. S., & Gross, C. G. (1994). Coding of visual space by premotor neurons. *Science, 266,* 1054–1057.

Grillner, S., & Wallen, P. (2002). Cellular bases of a vertebrate locomotor system-steering, intersegmental and segmental co-ordination and sensory control. *Brain Research Review, 40,* 92–106.

Hari, R., Forss, N., Avikainen, S., Kirveskari, S., Salenius, S., & Rizzolatti, G. (1998). Activation of human primary motor cortex during action observation: A neuromagnetic study. *Proceedings of the National Academy of Sciences USA, 95,* 15061–15065.

Heilman, K. M., & Rothi, L. J. (1993). Apraxia. In K. M. Heilman & E. Valenstein (Eds.), *Clinical neuropsychology* (pp. 141–163, 3rd ed.). New York: Oxford University Press.

Heilman, K. M., Rothi, L. J., & Valenstein, E. (1982). Two forms of ideomotor apraxia. *Neurology, 32,* 342–346.

Hepp-Reymond, M.-C., Hüsler, E. J., Maier, M. A., & Qi, H.-X. (1994). Force-related neuronal activity in two regions of the primate ventral premotor cortex. *Canadian Journal of Physiology and Pharmacology, 72,* 571–579.

Iacoboni, M., Woods, R. P., Brass, M., Bekkering, H., Mazziotta, J. C., & Rizzolatti, G. (1999). Cortical mechanisms of human imitation. *Science, 286,* 2526–2528.

Jackson, P. L., & Decety, J. (2004). Motor cognition: A new paradigm to study self-other interactions. *Current Opinions in Neurobiology, 14,* 259–263.

Jeannerod, M. (1994). The representing brain: Neural correlates of motor intention and imagery. *Behavioral Brain Science, 17,* 187–245.

Jeannerod, M., Arbib, M. A., Rizzolatti, G., & Sakata, H. (1995). Grasping objects: The cortical mechanisms of visuomotor transformation. *Trends in Neuroscience, 18,* 314–320.

Johnson, M. (1987). *The body in the mind: The bodily basis of meaning, imagination and reason.* Chicago: University of Chicago Press.

Kay, P., & McDaniel, C. (1978). The linguistic significance of the meanings of basic color terms. *Language, 54,* 610–646.

Kemper, S. (1989). Priming the comprehension of metaphors. *Metaphor and Symbolic Activity, 4,* 1–18.

Kerr, N. H. (1983). The role of vision in "visual imagery" experiments: Evidence from the congenitally blind. *Journal of Experimental Psychology: General, 112,* 265–277.

Kohler, E., Keysers, C., Umiltà, M. A., Fogassi, L., Gallese, V., & Rizzolatti, G. (2002). Hearing sounds, understanding actions: Action representation in mirror neurons. *Science, 297,* 846–848.

Kohler, E., Umiltà, M. A., Keysers, C., Gallese, V., Fogassi, L., & Rizzolatti, G. (2001). Auditory mirror neurons in the ventral premotor cortex of the monkey. *Society for Neuroscience Abstracts,* 27.

Kosslyn, S. M. (1994). *Image and brain: The resolution of the imagery debate.* Cambridge, MA: MIT Press.

Kosslyn, S. M., Alpert, N. M., Thompson, W. L., Maljkovic, V., Weise, S., Chabris, C., Hamilton, S. E., Rauch, S. L., & Buonanno, F. S. (1993). Visual mental imagery activates topographically organized visual cortex: PET investigations. *Journal of Cognitive Neuroscience, 5,* 263–287.

Kosslyn, S. M., Ball, T. M., & Reiser, B. J. (1978). Visual images preserve metric spatial information: Evidence from studies of image scanning. *Journal of Experimental*

Psychology: Human Perception and Performance, 4, 47–60.

Kosslyn, S. M., & Thompson, W. L. (2000). Shared mechanisms in visual imagery and visual perception: Insights from cognitive science. In M. S. Gazzaniga (Ed.), *The cognitive neurosciences* (2nd ed.). Cambridge, MA: MIT Press.

Kövecses, Z. (2002). *Metaphor: A practical introduction.* Oxford: Oxford University Press.

Kurata, K., & Tanji, J. (1986). Premotor cortex neurons in macaques: Activity before distal and proximal forelimb movements. *Journal of Neuroscience, 6,* 403–411.

Lakoff, G. (1987). *Women, fire, and dangerous things: What categories reveal about the mind.* Chicago: University of Chicago Press.

Lakoff, G., & Johnson, M. (1980). *Metaphors we live by.* Chicago: University of Chicago Press.

Lakoff, G., & Johnson, M. (1999). *Philosophy in the flesh.* New York: Basic Books.

Lakoff, G., & Turner, M. (1989). *More than cool reason: A field guide to poetic metaphor.* Chicago: University of Chicago Press.

Langacker, R. (1983). Remarks on English aspect. In P. Hopper (Ed.), *Tense and aspect: Between semantics and pragmatics* (pp. 265–304). Amsterdam: John Benjamins.

Langacker, R. W. (1986). *Foundations of cognitive grammar, vol. 1.* Stanford, CT: Stanford University Press.

Langacker, R. W. (1990). *Concept, image, and symbol: The cognitive basis of grammar.* Berlin: Mouton de Gruyter.

Langacker, R. W. (1991). *Foundations of cognitive grammar, vol. 2.* Stanford, CT: Stanford University Press.

Le Bihan, D., Turner, R., Zeffiro, T. A., Cuenod, C. A., Jezzard, P., & Bonnerot, V. (1993). Activation of human primary visual cortex during visual recall: A magnetic resonance imaging study. *Proceedings of the National Academy of Sciences, 90,* 11802–11805.

Lindner, S. (1981). *A lexico-semantic analysis of verb-particle constructions with* up *and* out. PhD dissertation, University of California at San Diego, USA.

Luppino, G., Murata, A., Govoni, P., & Matelli, M. (1999). Largely segregated parietofrontal connections linking rostral intraparietal cortex (areas AIP and VIP) and the ventral premotor cortex (areas F5 and F4). *Experimental Brain Research, 128,* 181–187.

Malach, R., Levy, I., & Hasson, U. (2002). The topography of high-order human object areas. *Trends in Cognitive Sciences, 6,* 176–184.

Marmor, G. S., & Zaback, L. A. (1976). Mental rotation by the blind: Does mental rotation depend on visual imagery? *Journal of Experimental Psychology: Human Perception and Performance, 2,* 515–521.

Martin, A., & Caramazza, A. (2003). Neuropsychological and neuroimaging perspectives on conceptual knowledge: An introduction. *Cognitive Neuropsychology, 20,* 195–212.

Martin, A., & Chao, L. L. (2001). Semantic memory and the brain: Structure and processes. *Current Opinion in Neurobiology, 11,* 194–201.

Martin, A., Ungerleider, L. G., & Haxby, J. V. (2000). Category specificity and the brain: The sensory/motor model of semantic representations of objects. In M. Gazzaniga (Ed.), *The new cognitive neurosciences* (pp. 1023–1036, 2nd ed.). Cambridge, MA: MIT Press.

Martin, A., Wiggs, C. L., Ungerleider, L. G., & Haxby, J. V. (1996). Neural correlates of category-specific knowledge. *Nature, 379,* 649–652.

Matelli, M., Camarda, R., Glickstein, M., & Rizzolatti, G. (1986). Afferent and efferent projections of the inferior area 6 in the macaque monkey. *Journal of Comparative Neurology, 251,* 281–298.

Matelli, M., & Luppino, G. (1997). Functional anatomy of human motor cortical areas. In F. Boller & J. Grafman (Eds.), *Handbook of neuropsychology, Vol. 11.* Amsterdam: Elsevier Science.

Matelli, M., Luppino, G., & Rizzolatti, G. (1985). Patterns of cytochrome oxidase activity in the frontal agranular cortex of the macaque monkey. *Behavioral Brain Research, 18,* 125–137.

Mervis, C. (1986). Child-basic object categories and early lexical development. In U. Neisser (Ed.), *Concepts and conceptual development: Ecological and intellectual factors in categorization* (pp. 201–233). Cambridge: Cambridge University Press.

Mervis, C., & Rosch, E. (1981). Categorization of natural objects. *Annual Review of Psychology, 32,* 89–115.

Mountcastle, V. B. (1995). The parietal system and some higher brain functions. *Cerebral Cortex, 5,* 377–390.

Murata, A., Fadiga, L., Fogassi, L., Gallese, V., Raos, V., & Rizzolatti, G. (1997). Object representation in the ventral premotor cortex (Area F5) of the monkey. *Journal of Neurophysiology, 78,* 2226–2230.

Murata, A., Gallese, V., Luppino, G., Kaseda, M., & Sakata, H. (2000). Selectivity for the shape, size and orientation of objects in the hand-manipulation-related neurons in the anterior intraparietal (AIP) area of the macaque. *Journal of Neurophysiology, 83,* 2580–2601.

Narayanan, S. (1997). *KARMA: Knowledge-based Active Representations for Metaphor and Aspect.* PhD dissertation, Computer Science Division, University of California, Berkeley, USA (http://www.icsi.berkeley.edu/snarayan/thesis.pdf).

Narayanan, S. (1999). Moving right along: A computational model of metaphoric reasoning about events. *Proceedings of the National Conference on Artificial Intelligence AAAI-99,* Orlando, FL, USA (http://www. icsi.berkeley.edu/~snarayan/met.ps).

Nishitani, N., & Hari, R. (2000). Temporal dynamics of cortical representation for action. *Proceedings of the National Academy of Sciences, 97,* 913–918.

Parsons, L., Fox, P., Downs, J., Glass, T., Hirsch, T., Martin, C., Jerabek, J., & Lancaster, J. (1995). Use of implicit motor imagery for visual shape discrimination as revealed by PET. *Nature, 375,* 54–58.

Perani, D., Cappa, S. F., Bettinardi, V., Bressi, S., Gorno-Tempini, M., & Fazio, F. (1995). Different neural systems for the recognition of animals and man-made tools. *Neuroreport, 21,* 1637–1641.

Perani, D., Schnur, T., Tettamanti, M., Gorno-Tempini, M., Cappa, S. F., & Fazio, F. (1999). Word and picture matching: A PET study of semantic category effects. *Neuropsychologia, 37,* 293–306.

Porro, C. A., Francescato, M. P., Cettolo, V., Diamond, M. E., Baraldi, P., Zuiani, C., Bazzocchi, M., & di Prampero, P. E. (1996). Primary motor and sensory cortex activation during motor performance and motor imagery. A functional magnetic resonance study. *Journal of Neuroscience, 16,* 7688–7698.

Porter, R., & Lemon, R. N. (1993). *Corticospinal function and volunatry movement.* Oxford: Clarendon Press.

Pylyshyn, Z. W. (1984). *Computation and cognition: Toward a foundation for cognitive science.* Cambridge, MA: MIT Press.

Regier, T. (1995). A model of the human capacity for categorizing spatial relations. *Cognitive Linguistics,* 6–1, 63–88.

Regier, T. (1996). *The human semantic potential: Spatial language and constrained connectionism.* Cambridge, MA: MIT Press.

Rizzolatti, G., Berti, A., & Gallese, V. (2000a). Spatial neglect: Neurophysiological bases, cortical circuits and theories. In F. Boller, J. Grafman, & G. Rizzolatti (Eds.), *Handbook of neuropsychology, Vol. I* (pp. 503–537, 2nd ed.) Amsterdam: Elsevier Science.

Rizzolatti, G., Camarda, R., Fogassi, M., Gentilucci, M., Luppino, G., & Matelli, M. (1988). Functional organization of inferior area 6 in the macaque monkey: II. Area F5 and the control of distal movements. *Experimental Brain Research, 71,* 491–507.

Rizzolatti, G., Fadiga, L., Fogassi, L., & Gallese, V. (1997). The space around us. *Science, 277,* 190–191.

Rizzolatti, G., Fadiga, L., Gallese, V., & Fogassi, L. (1996). Premotor cortex and the recognition of motor actions. *Cognitive Brain Research, 3,* 131–141.

Rizzolatti, G., Fogassi, L., & Gallese, V. (2000b). Cortical mechanisms subserving object grasping and action recognition: A new view on the cortical motor functions. In M. S. Gazzaniga (Ed.), *The cognitive neurosciences* (pp. 539–552, 2nd ed.). Cambridge, MA: MIT Press.

Rizzolatti, G., Fogassi, L., & Gallese, V. (2001). Neurophysiological mechanisms underlying the understanding and imitation of action. *Nature Neuroscience Reviews, 2,* 661–670.

Rizzolatti, G., Fogassi, L., & Gallese, V. (2002). Motor and cognitive functions of the ventral premotor cortex. *Current Opinion in Neurobiology, 12,* 149–154.

Rizzolatti, G., & Gallese, V. (2004). Do perception and action result from different brain circuits? The three visual systems hypothesis. In L. van Hemmen & T. Sejnowski (Eds.), *Problems in systems neuroscience.* Oxford: Oxford University Press.

Rizzolatti, G., & Gentilucci, M. (1988). Motor and visuomotor functions of the premotor cortex. In P. Rakic & W. Singer (Eds.), *Neurobiology of neocortex* (pp. 269–284). Chichester, UK: Wiley.

Rizzolatti, G., Luppino, G., & Matelli, M. (1998). The organization of the cortical motor system: New concepts. *Electroencephalography and Clinical Neurophysiology, 106,* 283–296.

Rizzolatti, G., Matelli, M., & Pavesi, G. (1983). Deficits in attention and movement following the removal of postarcuate (area 6) and prearcuate (area 8) cortex in macaque monkeys. *Brain, 106,* 655–673.

Rizzolatti, G., Scandolara, C., Gentilucci, M., & Camarda, R. (1981a). Response properties and behavioral modulation of "mouth" neurons of the postarcuate cortex (area 6) in macaque monkeys. *Brain Research, 255,* 421–424.

Rizzolatti, G., Scandolara, C., Matelli, M., & Gentilucci, M. (1981b). Afferent properties of periarcuate neurons in macaque monkeys. II. Visual responses. *Behavioral Brain Research, 2,* 147–163.

Roland, P., Larsen, B., Lassen, N., & Skinhoj, E. (1980). Supplementary motor area and other cortical areas in organization of voluntary movements in man. *Journal of Neurophysiology, 43,* 118–136.

Rosch, E. (1977). Human categorization. In N. Warren (Ed.), *Studies in cross-cultural psychology*. London: Academic Press.

Rosch, E. (1978). Principles of categorization. In E. Rosch & B. B. Lloyd (Eds.), *Cognition and categorization* (pp. 27–48). Hillsdale, NJ: Lawrence Erlbaum Associates Inc.

Rosch, E. (1981). Prototype classification and logical classification: The two systems. In E. Scholnick (Ed.), *New trends in cognitive representation: Challenges to Piaget's theory* (pp. 73–86). Hillsdale, NJ: Lawrence Erlbaum Associates Inc.

Rosch, E. (1994). Categorization. In V. S. Ramachandran (Ed.), *The encyclopedia of human behavior*. San Diego, CA: Academic Press.

Rosch, E., & Lloyd, B. B. (1978). *Cognition and categorization.* Hillsdale, NJ: Lawrence Erlbaum Associates Inc.

Rosch, E., Mervis, C., Gray, W., Johnson, D., & Boyes-Braem, P. (1976). Basic objects in natural categories. *Cognitive Psychology, 8,* 382–439.

Sakata, H., & Taira, M. (1994). Parietal control of hand action. *Current Opinion in Neurobiology, 4,* 847–856.

Shastri, L., & Ajjanagadde, V. (1993). From simple associations to systematic reasoning. *Behavioral and Brain Sciences, 16,* 417–494.

Simmons, K., & Barsalou, L. W. (2003). The similarity-in-topography principle: Reconciling theories of conceptual deficits. *Cognitive Neuropsychology, 20,* 451–486.

Talmy, L. (1983). How language structures space. In H. L. Pick & L. P. Acredolo (Eds.), *Spatial orientation: Theory, research, and application.* New York: Plenum Press.

Talmy, L. (1988). Force dynamics in language and cognition. *Cognitive Science, 12,* 49–100.

Talmy, L. (1996). Fictive motion in language and "ception." In P. Bloom, M. Peterson, L. Nadel, & M. Garrett (Eds.), *Language and space* (pp. 211–275). Cambridge, MA: MIT Press.

Talmy, L. (1999). *Toward a cognitive linguistics.* Cambridge, MA: MIT Press.

Tettamanti, M., Buccino, G., Saccuman, M. C., Gallese, V., Danna, M., Scifo, P., Fazio, F., Rizzolatti, G., Cappa, S. F., & Perani, D. (in press). Listening to action-related sentences activates fronto-parietal motor circuits. *Journal of Cognitive Neuroscience.*

Thompson, E. (1995). *Colour vision. A study in cognitive science and the philosophy of perception.* London: Routledge.

Umiltà, M. A., Kohler, E., Gallese, V., Fogassi, L., Fadiga, L., Keysers, C., & Rizzolatti, G. (2001). "I know what you are doing": A neurophysiological study. *Neuron, 32,* 91–101.

Varela, F., Thompson, E., & Rosch, E. (1991). *The embodied mind: Cognitive science and human experience.* Cambridge, MA: MIT Press.

Yamaguchi, T. (2004). The central pattern generator for forelimb locomotion in the cat. *Progress in Brain Research, 143,* 115–122.

Yue, G., & Cole, K. (1992). Strength increases from the motor program: Comparison of training with maximal voluntary and imagined muscle contractions. *Journal of Neurophysiology, 67,* 1114–1123.

Zeki, S. M. (1974). Functional organization of a visual area in the posterior bank of the superior temporal sulcus of the rhesus monkey. *Journal of Physiology, 236,* 549–573.

Zimler, J., & Keenan, J. M. (1983). Imagery in the congenitally blind: How visual are visual images? *Journal of Experimental Psychology: Learning, Memory, and Cognition, 9,* 269–282.

COGNITIVE NEUROPSYCHOLOGY, 2005, 22 (3/4), 480–494

THE ORCHESTRATION OF THE SENSORY-MOTOR SYSTEMS: CLUES FROM NEUROPSYCHOLOGY

Bradford Z. Mahon and Alfonso Caramazza
Harvard University, Cambridge, USA

Research over the last several decades has led to clear and empirically tractable proposals about the representation of conceptual knowledge in the brain. Here we argue that there are already sufficient data from neuropsychology to strongly constrain extant hypotheses about the representation of conceptual knowledge. One constraint imposed by these neuropsychological data is that recognition of actions and understanding of objects do not necessarily depend on the ability to produce object-associated actions. This conclusion compels a reconsideration of the role played by motor planning and/or execution processes in action and object recognition and understanding.

INTRODUCTION

As the articles in this Special Issue of *Cognitive Neuropsychology* attest, the role of the sensory-motor systems in higher cognitive functions is a hot topic in the cognitive brain sciences. Convergence of the methods of cognitive neuropsychology, functional imaging, and behavioural work with normal subjects has led to clear hypotheses about the roles of sensory-motor processes and structures in higher-order cognitive processes. Such roles range from inferring and/or understanding the intentions and emotions of conspecifics (Adolphs, 2003; Blakemore & Decety, 2001; Gallese & Goldman, 1998) to the principles that determine the organisation and representation of conceptual knowledge of concrete objects and actions (Allport, 1985; Barsalou, Simmons, Barbey, & Wilson, 2003; Gallese & Lakoff, 2005; Martin, Ungerleider, & Haxby, 2000; Warrington & McCarthy, 1983, 1987; Warrington & Shallice, 1984). In this article, we focus on the role of the sensory-motor systems in representing conceptual knowledge of concrete objects and actions.

One way to organise theories of the representation of conceptual knowledge is to distinguish so-called "embodied" from "disembodied" theories (e.g., Fadiga & Craighero, 2003; Feldman & Narayanan, 2003; Garbarini & Adenzato, 2004; Lakoff & Johnson, 1999). Embodied theories of conceptual representation argue that conceptual content is reducible (i.e., really *is*) sensory-motor content (e.g., Barsalou et al., 2003; Lakoff & Johnson, 1999; Pulvermuller, 2001); disembodied theories of conceptual representation argue that the information/processes internal to the sensory-motor system are not sufficient to exhaust what we know about concrete object and action concepts (e.g., Caramazza, Hillis, Rapp, & Romani, 1990; Humphreys & Forde, 2001; Plaut, 2002; Tyler & Moss, 2001; Warrington & McCarthy, 1987). The notion of simulation, or

---

Correspondence should be addressed to Alfonso Caramazza, Department of Psychology, William James Hall, Harvard University, 33 Kirkland Street, Cambridge, MA 02138, USA (Email: Caram@wjh.harvard.edu).

Preparation of this manuscript was supported in part by NIH grant DC04542 to AC, and by an NSF Graduate Research Fellowship to BZM. We are grateful to Jorge Almeida, Leslie Gonzalez-Rothi, Raffaella Rumiati, Kyle Simmons, and Naomi Zack for comments on an earlier version of this manuscript.

the reactivation of sensory-motor information in the course of conceptual processing, is required by embodied but not by disembodied theories of concept representation.

We discuss two aspects of the hypothesis of embodied conceptual knowledge: (1) the role of motor production processes in the recognition of visually presented actions; and (2) the role of motor production processes in the representation of conceptual knowledge of objects and actions. The discussion is organised in this way because there are varying degrees of strength at which the hypothesis of embodied conceptual knowledge may be developed. We take as the immediate stimulus for our discussion of these important issues the recent article by Gallese and Lakoff (2005 this issue), in which the authors defend a particularly strong version of the embodied hypothesis. For instance, while previous authors (e.g., Barsalou et al., 2003) have argued for a central role of sensory-motor content in representing conceptual knowledge of objects and actions, Gallese and Lakoff argue for the stronger position that integrative processes within the sensory-motor system obviate the need to postulate such processes outside the sensory-motor system.[1]

We undertake this project because we believe that there are already sufficient neuropsychological data to constrain hypotheses about the role of motor production processes in the recognition and understanding of objects and actions. At present, the available neuropsychological data may not be sufficiently rich as to adjudicate at a fine-grained level between specific implementations of the embodied and disembodied hypotheses. However, we believe that there is already sufficient neuropsychological evidence to define the boundaries of empirically viable theories of the representation of conceptual knowledge.

ACTION RECOGNITION

Research over the last several decades has produced a rich array of empirical demonstrations of neural activation of sensory-motor structures that is not specific to a given modality of input or output. Much of what is known comes from single-cell recordings in macque monkeys (for reviews, see, e.g., Fadiga & Craighero, 2003; Rizzolatti, Fogassi, & Gallese, 2001); more recently, functional imaging techniques have permitted analogous questions to be addressed to the human brain (e.g., Bremmer et al., 2001; Buccino et al., 2001; Hari, Forss, Avikainen, Kirveskari, Salenius, & Rizzolatti, 1998; Iacoboni, Woods, Brass, Bekkering, Mazziotta, & Rizzolatti, 1999; Martin, Wiggs, Ungerleider, & Haxby, 1996; Tettamanti et al., 2005; for reviews, see Grèzes, & Decety, 2001; Martin & Chao, 2001). Behavioural work with human subjects has also implicated motor planning and/or execution processes in the recognition of sensory input (e.g., Edwards, Humphreys, & Castiello, 2003; Shiffrar & Freyd, 1990; Viviani & Stucchi, 1989).

One phenomenon central to the hypothesis of embodied cognition is the behaviour of mirror neurons: neurons that are activated both during motor execution as well as during action observation (e.g., Gallese, Fadiga, Fogassi, & Rizzolatti, 1996). The types of visual input that are sufficient to activate mirror neurons are highly constrained, for instance by the types of motor movements for which the neurons also fire. Recent work has also shown that some mirror neurons in macaque premotor cortex are activated by both visual and auditory input (Kohler, Keysers, Umiltà, Fogassi, Gallese, & Rizzolatti, 2002).

[1] "To claim, as we do, that an action like *grasping* is multimodal is to say that (1) it is neurally enacted using neural substrates used for both action and perception, and (2) that the modalities of action and perception are integrated at the level of the sensory-motor system itself and not via higher association areas" (p. 459, emphasis original). Gallese and Lakoff (2005) situate these proposals in a broader theory of human cognition that treats a wide range of issues, from the principles that guide praxis, to the architecture of the sensory-motor system, to whether human cognition is mediated by symbols. We will not discuss the issues of imagination, parameters, metaphor, structured neural computation, nor the implications of their basic assumptions for a theory of language (for recent discussion of the available hypothesis space on the latter issue, see Fitch, Hauser, & Chomsky, in press; Pinker & Jackendoff, 2005).

One way in which such phenomena (e.g., mirror neuron activation) have been interpreted within the embodied cognition framework is that motor production processes and structures are necessarily involved in the recognition of visually presented actions. We will refer to this proposal as the "Motor Theory of Action Recognition," after a closely related theory of speech perception (Liberman, Cooper, Shankweiler, & Studdert-Kennedy, 1967): The claim made by the Motor Theory of Speech Perception was that in order to recognise speech sounds, it was necessary for the listener to run or simulate the corresponding motor programs that would result in the production of the same sounds.

Broadly speaking, there are two levels of strength at which the Motor Theory of Action Recognition can be formulated, roughly corresponding to two ways in which the behaviour of (e.g.) mirror neurons might be interpreted. The weaker interpretation is that motor processes/structures *respond* to visual or auditory input. In this sense, the process is multimodal not (necessarily) in terms of the perceptual content that is represented, but in terms of the types of perceptual content (perhaps represented elsewhere) that trigger the process. A stronger interpretation that may be given to the claim that a process is multimodal is that sensory content or sensory properties of a given type (e.g., auditory) are represented in motor cortex (or the cortex formerly known as motor). Recent discussion of these issues has emphasised that hypotheses about the nature of the mapping from perceptual input to motor output representations lie along a continuum (Rumiati & Bekkering, 2003).

Gallese and Lakoff (2005) advance a strong interpretation of the behaviour of mirror neurons, in proposing that "[c]ortical pre-motor areas are endowed with sensory properties" (p. 459), and that "... circuitry across brain regions links modalities, infusing each with properties of others" (p. 456). This strong interpretation is consistent with the authors' broader theoretical commitments about the structure of the mind/brain: namely, that all of the integration required by higher cognitive functions occurs inside the sensory-motor system.[2] Here we focus on one central empirical commitment of the Motor Theory of Action Recognition, which can be reduced to either of two hypotheses:

Hypothesis I: Recognition of action is mediated by processes required to produce action, and, at least at the level required for successful recognition of actions, recognition and production processes are not functionally separable.

Hypothesis II: At the levels of representation required for successful recognition and production of actions, recognition and production are functionally separable; however, evaluation of the perceptual input requires simulation of the corresponding motor output routines.[3]

One way to evaluate the Motor Theory of Action Recognition is to consider the performance of patients with apraxia, an impairment in using objects that cannot be attributed to aphasia, sensory impairment, or an impairment to basic motor responses. Both Hypotheses I and II generate the prediction that apraxia will necessarily be associated with an inability to correctly recognise visually presented actions. Contrary to this

[2] It is sometimes not clear if Gallese and Lakoff (2005) are arguing *for* multimodality or *against* modularity. These authors distinguish their use of the term "multimodality" from "supramodality": "This is important theoretically because supramodality is consistent with the idea of strict modularity, while multimodality is not. Supramodality accords with a picture of the brain containing separate modules for action and for perception that need to be somehow 'associated.' *Multimodality denies the existence of such separate modules*" (p. 459, emphasis original). The claim that "[m]ulti-modality denies the existence of... modules" (p. 459) does not accord with all construals of either multimodality or modularity. In the way modularity was originally proposed (Fodor, 1983), it was not a property of cognitive processes that distinguished (either empirically, or a priori) between modality-specific and multimodal systems. One could, by hypothesis, have modular multimodal processes; perhaps the process(es) underlying the McGurk effect illustrate(s) one such example (Fodor, 1983; Footnote 13 therein).

[3] For instance, it might be argued that selection of the "correct" interpretation of perceptual input is guided by motor planning and/or execution programs (e.g., Viviani & Stucchi, 1992).

prediction is the performance of a number of patients who are impaired at using objects but who are not impaired at distinguishing correct from incorrect object-associated actions (Bartolo, Cubelli, Della Sala, Drei, & Marchetti, 2001; Bergego, Pradat-Diehl, & Deloche, 1992; Dumont & Ska, 2000; Dumont, Ska, Schiavetto, 1999; Halsband, Schmitt, Weyers, Binkofski, Grützner, & Freund, 2001; Mozaz, Rothi, Anderson, Crucian, & Heilman, 2002; Ochipa, Rothi, & Heilman, 1989; Rapcsak, Ochipa, Anderson, & Poizner, 1995; Rumiati, Zanini, Vorano, & Shallice, 2001; Schwartz, Montgomery, Fitzpatrick-DeSalme, Ochipa, Coslett, & Mayer, 1995).

For instance, Rumiati and colleagues (2001) report two apraxic patients, DR and FG, neither of whom presented with visual agnosia for objects or for pantomimes.[4] Patients DR and FG were impaired at demonstrating the correct actions associated with the use of objects, both for single object use (DR: 16/28; FG: 18/28) and for multiple object use (DR: 4/10; FG: 2/10; data from session IV). However, the ability of both patients to sequence photographs of actions in the correct order (9/10 both patients; session IV) and to recognise the correct actions associated with objects (DR: 15/15; FG 14/15) was preserved. Of particular interest is the fact that patient FG was 95% correct (19/20) at discriminating correct from incorrect actions when the incorrect actions were reproductions of actual errors that FG had made in a previous testing session.

The majority of FG's errors were "conceptual errors," or movements that were kinematically fluent but were (for instance) not appropriate to the object at hand, or were applied to the incorrect part of the object. Thus, it might be argued that the impairment in FG is actually "more abstract" than the level at which action recognition processes are mediated by action production processes. However, the same pattern observed in FG is observed in patients who make predominantly kinematic (or production) errors. One clear and carefully studied case, GW (Rapcsak et al., 1995), was not able to produce any correct pantomimes of object use (to 15 stimuli) across a range of input modalities: visual presentation of objects, verbal command, and imitation. GW was also severely impaired at using actual objects correctly (1/15 right hand; 3/15 left hand). Spatio-temporal errors accounted for 90% of the patient's errors in action production, with the remaining 10% classified as body-part-as-object errors. Neither conceptually inappropriate actions nor perseverations were observed. Despite a prevalence of kinematic errors in action production, GW was flawless at naming object associated pantomimes (15/15), and was very good at discriminating correct from incorrect transitive pantomimes (14/15).

According to the Motor Theory of Action Recognition, the ability to recognise actions depends on the integrity of processes required to produce actions. The dissociation between action production and action recognition indicates that production processes are not required for correct recognition. Furthermore, it cannot be argued that recognition of actions is *merely* easier than production of actions, as the reverse impairment has also been observed. The pattern of impairment labelled "pantomime agnosia" (Rothi, Mack, & Heilman, 1986) consists of impaired recognition of the correct actions associated with the use of objects, but relatively unimpaired production of object-associated actions (Bell, 1994; Rothi et al., 1986, see Cubelli, Marchetti, Boscolo, & Della Salla, 2000, for a double dissociation between apraxia-without-pantomime-agnosia versus pantomime-agnosia-without-apraxia over the same materials).[5]

[4] Where clarity of exposition requires, we will distinguish "transitive" from "intransitive" pantomimes. Following conventions in the literature "transitive pantomimes" are mimed actions that are associated with objects (e.g., hammering), whereas "intransitive pantomimes" are mimed actions that do not involve an object (e.g., waving goodbye).

[5] Pantomime agnosia cannot be attributed to a "general" agnosia, for two reasons. First, patients with visual agnosia for objects do not necessarily present with pantomime agnosia (Schwartz, Barrett, Crucian, & Heilman, 1998); and second, the patient reported by Rothi and colleagues (1986) who was impaired at discriminating and identifying correct pantomimes, was not impaired at imitating pantomimes. The fact that the patient was not impaired at pantomime imitation indicates that the inability to identify actions cannot be due to a "general" visual impairment.

The observation of clear impairments to action production, but spared recognition of object-associated actions, is difficult to reconcile with certain construals of the Motor Theory of Action Recognition. Most obviously, it cannot be true that perception and production of actions are *completely* integrated at the level required for correct recognition. As discussed above, it is not entirely clear whether or not this was the intended claim of Gallese and Lakoff (2005).[6] Second, these data indicate that even if perceptual and production processes are assumed to be functionally separate at the level required for correct recognition, the ability to produce correct actions is not necessary for successful recognition.

We have interpreted the Motor Theory of Action Recognition as assuming that the ability to produce learned object-associated actions is what supports successful recognition of visually presented actions. However, another way in which this theory could be developed would be to assume that what supports correct recognition of actions is a more basic ability to translate visual input to motor output. In other words, it might be argued that it is the ability to imitate that is required in order to recognise actions. There are, however, findings contrary to this development of the Motor Theory of Action Recognition. In a group study, Halsband and colleagues (2001) found that while patients with lesions to parietal areas were impaired at imitating visually presented actions, they were relatively unimpaired at recognising visually presented actions; importantly, there was no correlation between the ability to imitate gestures and the ability to recognise gestures. The pattern of dissociation observed by Halsband and colleagues in their group study has been corroborated by single case studies as well. Recall that for both of the apraxic patients DR and FG (Rumiati et al., 2001) discussed above, recognition of actions was not impaired. However, while patient DR was classified as impaired for action imitation, FG was classified as performing within the normal range, indicating that the ability to imitate visually presented actions is not causally related to the ability to recognise actions. The same conclusion is compelled by the performance of patient BS (Bartolo et al., 2001; see also Goldenberg & Hagmann, 1997), who was in the normal range at recognising and identifying visually presented actions, pantomiming both transitive and intransitive actions to verbal, visual, and tactile input, as well as imitating both transitive and intransitive learned pantomimes. However, this patient was impaired (4/15) at imitating meaningless (i.e., unlearned) actions. It seems that what the patient has lost is the ability to translate arbitrary actions (presented visually) to motor output; such an ability would seem to be the most basic mechanism underlying simulation, and thus embodied recognition of actions. Given that recognition is not impaired in this patient, we can conclude that the ability to imitate actions is not required to successfully recognise actions.[7]

The empirical generalisations that emerge from this brief review of the neuropsychological evidence can be summarised as follows: (1) production of actions can be impaired while recognition of actions is spared; (2) recognition of actions can be impaired while production of actions is spared; and (3) imitation of meaningless actions can be impaired while recognition of actions is spared. These empirical facts have been summarised previously (Cubelli et al., 2000;

[6] For example: "Multimodality does everything that supramodality has been hypothesised to do, and more. Multimodal integration has been found in many different locations in the brain, and we believe that it is the norm..."(Gallese & Lakoff, 2005, p. 459).

[7] The fact that BS was unimpaired at imitating transitive and intransitive actions indicates that a general input deficit cannot explain the patient's inability to imitate meaningless gestures. Similarly, this deficit cannot be attributed to a production deficit, since the patient was not markedly impaired at producing transitive and intransitive gestures across a number of modalities of input. Following the model of praxis proposed by Rothi and colleagues (1991), the impairment in BS would be localised to the "sub-lexical" route for extracting motor information from visual input. This mechanism is similar to the orthography-phonology conversion mechanism postulated by many models of language processing, in that it is motivated by patients (e.g., BS) who are impaired at imitating meaningless gestures (cf. reading nonwords) but not meaningful or learned gestures (cf. reading real words).

Johnson-Frey, 2004; Rothi et al., 1991) and are consistent with models of praxis that draw a functional distinction between the representations that underlie perception and the representations that underlie production of actions (e.g., Cubelli et al., 2000; Rapcsak et al., 1995; Rothi et al., 1991; Rumiati et al., 2001).[8] Theories that assume that motor production processes are necessary to successfully recognise actions have difficulty accounting for these empirical facts.

UNDERSTANDING OBJECTS AND ACTIONS

A second aspect of the hypothesis of embodied cognition concerns the role of sensory-motor processes in higher cognitive functions such as language, theory of mind, and conceptual processing. Here we focus on the role of simulation over sensory-motor processes in the representation of object and action concepts, as we believe this issue is directly tractable from the perspective of extant neuropsychological data. The possible hypothesis space for the role of sensory-motor simulation in the representation of conceptual content spans a wide range: from no role at all to exhaustive, including a middle position in which simulation adds to, but does not exhaust, the content of concrete object concepts.[9] Again, we take as an impetus for our discussion the particularly strong hypothesis advanced by Gallese and Lakoff (2005, p. 456): "We will argue that conceptual knowledge is embodied, that is, it is mapped within our sensory-motor system. We will argue that the sensory-motor system not only provides structure to conceptual content, but also characterises the semantic content of concepts in terms of the way we function with our bodies in the world."

This proposal can be distinguished from the Sensory/Motor Theory of Martin and colleagues (2000; see also Allport, 1985). The Sensory/Motor Theory argues that the organisation of the sensory-motor system drives the *organisation*, and perhaps in part underlies the representation, of conceptual knowledge of concrete objects and actions. The Sensory/Motor Theory does not assume that sensory-motor information/processes are sufficient to represent *all* that we know about concrete object and action concepts.[10]

Consider some of the empirical findings Gallese and Lakoff (2005) cite in support of their proposal.[11] Of particular importance are data from what have been referred to as "canonical neurons." Single-cell recording studies in monkeys have revealed populations of neurons that fire

[8] Nontrivial predictions can be extrapolated from these generalisations. For instance, recall the study on mirror neurons by Kohler and colleagues (2002). In that study, it was observed that a population of neurons responded both to the auditory and to the visual presentation of actions. The position which holds that recognition of actions is independent of production processes at the level required for successful recognition predicts that it should be possible to observe apraxic patients who are not impaired at recognising the correct sounds associated with those actions that they are not able to correctly produce.

[9] This portrayal of the hypothesis space goes back to antiquity: "As to the nature and number of the first principles opinions differ. The difference is greatest between those who regard them as corporeal and those who regard them as incorporeal, and from both dissent those who make a blend and draw their principles from both sources. The number of principles is also in dispute; some admit one only, others assert several" (Aristotle, *De Anima*, 405a, 30–35).

[10] In fact, Gallese and Lakoff (2005) advance the even stronger claim that the "inferential structure" of abstract concepts can also be reductively traced back to sensory-motor information/processes. Here we restrict our discussion to the representation of concrete concepts, on the assumption that if [sensory-motor content + simulation] is not sufficient to represent concrete object concepts, then [sensory-motor content + simulation + metaphor] will not be sufficient to represent abstract concepts.

[11] The arguments developed by Gallese and Lakoff (2005) assume that evidence for the existence of simulative processes is ipso facto evidence for the claim that such simulation grounds conceptual content. For instance: "According to our hypothesis, understanding requires simulation. The understanding of concrete concepts—physical actions, physical objects, and so on—requires sensory-motor simulation. But sensory-motor simulation, as suggested by contemporary neuroscience, is carried out by the sensory-motor system of the brain. It follows that the sensory motor system *is required for understanding at least concrete concepts.* We see this as an insurmountable difficulty for any traditional theory that claims that concrete concepts are modality-neutral and disembodied" (p. 468, emphasis original). We will take up in the final section 'PULLING IT ALL TOGETHER' the issue of whether demonstrations of simulative processes present an insurmountable difficulty for disembodied theories.

both when the monkey performs a goal-directed action on an object, and when the monkey sees the object (e.g., for review, see Rizzolatti et al., 2001). In humans, arguably comparable findings consist of the observation that ventral premotor cortex is more activated when subjects are presented with familiar tools than with equally familiar but not graspable objects (for review, see Martin & Chao, 2001). Gallese and Lakoff contend that "[t]he existence of canonical neurons and their putative equivalent in humans could underpin basic-level categories of objects," and further, that "... *all* concrete concepts—concepts of things we can see, touch, and manipulate—can be addressed by [this] strategy ..." (p. 469; emphasis original).[12] This is a particularly strong claim, and it generates predictions of the following form. In order to name a picture of a pair of scissors it is necessary to retrieve the motor programs associated with the use of scissors. Or, in order to judge that a pair of scissors is more similar to a knife than to a mallet in terms of function (function understood as what the object is used for), again, it is necessary to retrieve the motor information that allows correct utilisation of scissors, knives, and mallets.

The view assumed by Gallese and Lakoff (2005) is committed to the claim that there can be no understanding of concrete object concepts if the sensory-motor content over which such concepts are distributed is not present. Contrary to this hypothesis is the performance of apraxic patients who are not impaired for conceptual knowledge of graspable objects. There are a number of such patients (Buxbaum & Saffran, 2002; Buxbaum, Sirigu, Schwartz, & Klatzky, 2003; Buxbaum, Veramonti, & Schwartz, 2000; Cubelli et al., 2000; Halsband et al., 2001; Hodges, Spatt, & Patterson, 1999; Montomura & Yamadori, 1994; Moreaud, Charnallet, & Pellat, 1998; Ochipa et al., 1989; Rapcsak et al., 1995; Rosci, Valentina, Laiacona, & Capitani, 2003; Rumiati et al., 2001; for review, see Johnson-Frey, 2004; for discussion, see Dumont, Ska, & Joanette, 2000; Hodges, Bozeat, Lambon Ralph, Patterson, & Spatt, 2000; Mahon & Caramazza, 2003). For instance, Rosci and colleagues (2003) designed a study to specifically investigate the issue of whether impairments for object use are related to deficits in conceptual knowledge of manipulable objects. A group of 15 apraxic patients were administered: (1) a picture-naming test, (2) an auditory word–picture matching test, and (3) two tests of praxis performance (pantomime of object use to visual presentation of the object, and pantomime imitation). The stimuli used in the picture naming and auditory picture–word matching test consisted of 20 manipulable objects, 15 manmade but nonmanipulable objects, and 15 animals; the same 20 manipulable objects were used in the picture naming and word–picture matching test as were used in the object use test. The authors divided the patients into two groups twice: either in terms of whether or not they were impaired at imitation or in terms of whether or not they were impaired at pantomiming the use of objects. There was no indication of worse performance for manipulable objects compared to nonmanipulable objects in either the picture naming or the picture–word matching tasks. This was the case for: (1) patients who were impaired at imitation, (2) patients who were impaired at pantomiming the use of objects, and (3) patients who were impaired both at imitation and pantomiming the use of objects. Thus, neither a deficit for imitating visually presented actions nor a deficit for producing learned object-associated actions is

[12] Two types of simulative processes that Gallese and Lakoff (2005) take to bear equally on their proposal must be distinguished. Some types of simulative processes may be understood as being voluntary and/or explicit (e.g., mental imagery, mental rotation, etc.), while some types of simulative processes may be understood as being automatic and/or implicit (e.g., the behaviour of mirror neurons and canonical neurons). It is not at all clear that the evidence for voluntary simulation is relevant to a theory of the representation of conceptual knowledge. The reason is that such evidence does not bear on either of two claims, one of which must be intrinsic to the content-reductive hypothesis: (1) simulation over sensory-motor content exhausts conceptual content; (2) simulation over sensory-motor content is necessary for understanding concrete concepts.

necessarily associated with a disproportionate conceptual impairment for manipulable objects.

Individual case studies have confirmed the observations made by Rosci and colleagues (2003). For instance, patients FG and DR (Rumiati et al., 2001), discussed above, were perfect at identifying objects based on descriptions of the objects' function. This was the case even for the same objects on which the patients made apraxic errors. Similarly, both patients were perfect at matching objects to descriptions of the purpose or function of their appropriate actions (e.g., bar soap: to wash hands, to wash dishes, to wash the car; see also patient JK, Schwartz et al., 1995). Similarly, the apraxic patient GW (Rapcsak et al., 1995), discussed above, who was unimpaired at recognising transitive gestures despite an inability to produce such gestures without movement errors, was at ceiling on several tasks investigating the integrity of conceptual knowledge. For instance, this patient was at ceiling on tasks requiring a tool to be: (1) matched to its correct function, (2) selected from a set of alternatives in order to complete an unfinished task, as well as (3) selected as an alternative (i.e., noncanonical tool) to complete an unfinished task. GW was also unimpaired at providing verbal descriptions of: (1) the actions associated with objects, and (2) the functions of tools.

The empirical generalisation that emerges is that impairments in using objects correctly are not associated with impairments to conceptual knowledge of either objects or the functions of the actions associated with those objects.[13] Previous reviews have arrived at this empirical generalisation (Cubelli et al., 2000; Hodges et al., 2000; Johnson-Frey, 2004; Rothi et al., 1991; Rumiati et al., 2001; for further discussion, see Mahon & Caramazza, 2003). From this fact, it follows that conceptual knowledge of concrete object and action concepts is not exhausted by simulation over sensory-motor content.

PULLING IT ALL TOGETHER

We have focused on two central aspects of the proposal that cognition is embodied. First, we discussed what we referred to as the Motor Theory of Action Recognition; this hypothesis holds that motor production processes and structures are necessarily implicated in the successful recognition of visually presented actions. Neuropsychological data were reviewed indicating that recognition of visually presented actions does not depend on either, (1) the ability to imitate visually presented actions, or (2) the ability to produce the correct actions associated with objects. Second, we discussed the hypothesis that the content of concrete object and action concepts can be reductively traced back through simulation to sensory-motor content. Neuropsychological data were reviewed, indicating that motor production processes are not required to support intact conceptual knowledge of manipulable objects or their associated actions.

We have chosen to focus on a rather narrow range of neuropsychological data in our review, but there are other neuropsychological phenomena that would also potentially bear on the embodied cognition hypothesis. For instance, similar to the double dissociation between apraxia-without-pantomime-agnosia versus pantomime-agnosia-without-apraxia is the dissociation between optic-ataxia-without-visual-form-agnosia versus visual-form-agnosia-without-optic-ataxia. Patients with optic ataxia are impaired at making visually guided prehension movements, but are spared for the motor movements involved in prehension as well as visually discriminating the relevant perceptual aspects of objects required for visually guided prehension (e.g., Jeannerod, Decety, & Michel, 1994; Milner et al., 2001). In contrast, visual form agnosics, such as patient DF, extensively studied by Goodale, Milner, and colleagues (e.g., Goodale, Milner, Jakobson, & Carey, 1991; Milner et al.,

[13] This pattern constitutes one side of a double dissociation: The other side concerns patients who are impaired for conceptual knowledge of objects but relatively unimpaired at using objects correctly (e.g., Negri, Lunardelli, Gigli, & Rumiati, in press; Sirigu, Duhamel, & Poncet, 1991).

1991) are impaired at visually discriminating objects, but unimpaired at making visually guided prehension movements.

As outlined in the Introduction, strong versions of the embodied cognition hypothesis (e.g., Gallese & Lakoff, 2005) assume that all "higher-order cognitive processes" (e.g., conceptual processing, syntactic processing) reduce to sensory-motor processes. In other words, on the strong version of the embodied cognition hypothesis, simulation over sensory-motor content obviates the need to postulate "higher-order cognitive systems' in the first place (e.g., a conceptual system, a narrow language faculty). In contrast, disembodied theories assume that the information/processes internal to sensory-motor systems are not sufficient to represent such higher-order processes.

The evidence that is cited for the embodied hypothesis is not inconsistent with the disembodied hypothesis. For instance, Baldissera, Cavallari, Craighero, and Fadiga (2001) demonstrated modulation of spinal excitability during observation of hand actions in humans. Equally striking, Fadiga, Fogassi, Pavesi, and Rizzolatti (1995) observed modulation of responses in hand muscles when subjects observed an agent grasping an object. In one sense, these data demonstrate that recognition and understanding really *are* embodied: The effects of observing grasping behaviour promulgates all the way to the hand. But this does not mean that the muscles in the hand play any role in recognition and/or understanding; these findings do not embarrass a view that holds that conceptual knowledge is functionally distinct from the processes subserved by spinal neurons and/or hand muscles. In other words, these data could just as readily be used to ground a *reductio* argument against strong versions of the embodied cognition hypothesis (for discussion, see Oliveri, Finocchiaro, Shapiro, Gangitano, Caramazza, & Pascual-Leone, 2004). To the degree that one is not compelled to infer the necessity of muscle activation for conceptual understanding, why then make the inference that the activation of motor cortices is necessary for understanding? Or similarly, to the degree that one is not compelled to assume that muscle/spinal activation is sufficient to ground conceptual understanding, why then make the inference that motor information is sufficient to ground conceptual knowledge?

In contrast, the neuropsychological evidence we have reviewed is inconsistent with the embodied hypothesis but not with the disembodied hypothesis. The fact that apraxic patients are not necessarily impaired for conceptual knowledge of the same objects that they cannot correctly manipulate indicates that conceptual knowledge is not exhausted by motor information corresponding to the ways in which objects are manipulated (for further discussion, see Mahon & Caramazza, 2003). We believe that the neuropsychological approach is extremely useful in this regard, as it permits causal inferences to be drawn about the organisation and representation of cognitive processes.

The neuropsychological phenomena that we have reviewed compel a model that assumes the orchestration of "independent" perceptual and motor processes.[14] By "independent", we mean that at the relevant level of analysis, perceptual and motor processes are functionally separable. The "relevant level of analysis" is determined by the minimal computations that would be necessary in order to succeed in a given task, for instance

[14] On the terminology of some authors (e.g., Gallese & Lakoff, 2005) any systems/processes that "orchestrate" sensory-motor systems are, by definition, "disembodied." Furthermore, there seems to be some antipathy toward postulating cognitive processes that are in this sense disembodied, presumably because it is believed that disembodied cognitive processes are not tractable constructs from a biologically/neurologically oriented account of behaviour. It is not obvious what the weight of this charge might be; this use of the term "disembodied" seems to suggest cognitive processes that could not (in principle) be described as neural processes, or could not (in principle) exist "in the brain." Another way to view these relations is that *no* cognitive processes are "in the brain" or "in the body," in the way that, for instance, coffee is "in the cup" or the car is "in the garage." Rather, mental processes *are* the functioning of the brain, in the sense that digestive processes *are* the functioning of the digestive system. We have adopted the embodied–disembodied terminology in order to facilitate connection of the issues discussed herein with those discussed by other authors.

recognition of pantomimes or production of pantomimes. In other words, we have argued that the assumption is compelled that perceptual and motor processes are "independent" *to the degree warranted* by the double dissociation between pantomime-agnosia-without-apraxia and apraxia-without-pantomime-agnosia. This does not imply, however, that multimodal integrative processes are not involved in, or do not affect, recognition of sensory input.

The situation is similar in regard to the inference that conceptual knowledge is not exhausted by information internal to the sensory-motor systems: This inference does not commit one to the assumption that simulation over sensory-motor content does not make important contributions to our conceptual knowledge of objects and actions (for discussion, see Caramazza & Mahon, in press). Consider, for instance, the recent and elegant study by Tettamanti and colleagues (2005), in which it was demonstrated that even just listening to simple sentences describing actions involving parts of the human body leads to activation of body-specific areas of motor planning structures. One way to interpret these data would be to assume that the activation of motor structures is necessary in order to understand verbs describing bodily actions. However, the data do not sanction this inference; much stronger data would be required in order to argue for the necessity of motor structures in conceptual understanding. Namely, it would have to be shown that, effectively removing such structures impairs the ability to understand verbs describing bodily actions. The data reported by Tettamanti and colleagues sanction the inference that such activation is an automatic consequence of exposure to the semantic content of actions describing bodily actions. This inference then opens up the issue of what the consequences of this automatic activation are, if any, for how we understand such verbs.

Even before the advent of technologies that permitted cognitive scientists to address questions to the brain, similar theoretical issues have been raised by behavioural work demonstrating interactions between distinct modalities. For instance, Seidenberg and Tanenhaus (1979; Donnenwerth-Nolan, Tanenhaus, & Seidenberg, 1981) demonstrated an influence of orthographic similarity on rhyme judgments for auditorily presented words (see also Tanenhaus, Flanigan, & Seidenberg, 1980 for an analogous effect between visually presented primes and targets that are phonologically but not orthographically related; for recent review, see Muneaux & Ziegler, 2004). The basic finding reported by Seidenberg and Tanenhaus (1979) was that subjects are faster to decide that two words rhyme when they are orthographically similar (e.g., pie–tie) than when they are orthographically dissimilar (e.g., rye–tie). What is surprising about these data is that orthography has an influence *at all* on the decision process of whether two auditorily presented words rhyme. In this case, however, the implication is not that there is a representation in common between phonology and orthography; the reason why is that there is nothing in common between the motor movements involved in producing phonology and the motor movements involved in writing. Even if one were to ascend, as it were, to a more abstract level, it is not likely to be the case that a common, motor-relevant representation underlies phonological and orthographic information. Instead, one inference to be extracted from these data is that the auditory presentation of a word automatically leads to activation of its orthography, and that the *decision* process in a given task uses any information that is available for the execution of that task. In other words, the lack of a motor-relevant isomorphism between phonology and orthography blocks, as it were, the inference that simulation over orthographic representations is required in order to make rhyme judgments on auditory input.

In the case of human action recognition, however, there is a clearer isomorphism between the visual input and the motor output. As we have argued, the fact that motor production systems are engaged during recognition of actions does not imply that simulation is required for successful recognition and understanding. The neuropsychological evidence from apraxia substantiates this argument. Thus, an isomorphism between perception and action *may* implicate a mechanism or representation common to perception and action, but it need not. Furthermore, even if it were assumed that the presence of an isomorphism between perception and action does implicate a common mechanism, it is an independent issue as to where in the cognitive architecture that shared representation is to be located.

One case of a clear isomorphism across perception and action is demonstrated by an elegant series of studies by Viviani and his collaborators. Lacquaniti, Terzuolo, and Viviani (1983) observed that the velocity of extemporaneous (i.e., unconstrained) hand movements at any point in a curvilinear planar trajectory is proportional to the cubic root of the instantaneous radius of curvature: as the radius of curvature decreases (i.e., the trajectory becomes more curved) the velocity decreases (this relation is referred to as the Two-Thirds Power Law). Thus, if, subjects are asked to move their hand in a circle, the velocity of the movement is constant; if however, subjects are asked to move their hand in an elliptical path, the velocity of the movement is lowest at the poles and greatest in the flatter parts. Interestingly, if subjects are presented with a visual stimulus of a dot moving in the geometric trajectory of a circle, but following the velocity profile natural to manual elliptical motion, the stimulus is perceived to be flatter (i.e., more like an ellipse) than it actually is. Similarly, the perceived path of a dot moving in the geometric trajectory of a horizontal ellipse but following the velocity profile that would be natural to an ellipse rotated 90 degrees (i.e., a vertical ellipse) is rounder (i.e., more like a circle) than it actually is (Viviani & Stucchi, 1989, 1992). Subsequent work (Viviani, Baud-Bovy, & Redolfi, 1997) demonstrated that the identical illusion observed in the visual modality is also observed kinaesthetically when the hand is passively moved and subjects are blindfolded.

The work of Viviani and colleagues elegantly portrays a clear isomorphism; the Two-Thirds Power Law is observed to constrain in qualitatively the same way both the interpretation of visual and kinaesthetic input as well as overt movements of the hands. This isomorphism between perception and action would seem, if anything would, to warrant an interpretation in terms of simulation. A simulationist perspective would place the Two-Thirds Power Law constraint internal to the motor system; for instance, it could be assumed that automatic activation of motor engrams constrains selection of perceptual input (e.g., Viviani & Stucchi, 1992). However, it is also clear that it is at least logically possible that the shared mechanism could be either (1) internal to the visual system, or (2) an amodal representation accessed by both the visual and the motor systems.

In a study of smooth pursuit eye movements, de'Sperati and Viviani (1997) demonstrated that, as is the case for hand movements, smooth pursuit eye movements are also constrained by the Two-Thirds Power Law. Given that movements of the hands and smooth pursuit movements of the eyes are subserved by separate neural and muscular systems, it becomes perhaps less likely that simulation over motor production processes are responsible for the perceptual illusions. Which motor production processes are simulated: those subserving smooth pursuit movements of the eyes or those subserving movements of the hands? As argued by Viviani and colleagues (de'Sperati & Viviani, 1997; Viviani et al., 1997) these data may suggest that the Two-Thirds Power Law exerts its influence on motor output, kinaesthetic input, and visual input at a more central, amodal level of representation.

Our intention here is not to argue for any specific locus in the cognitive architecture of the Two-Thirds Power Law constraint, but merely to make the following point: The presence of a strict isomorphism between perception and action does not, in and of itself, sanction the inference that simulation of motor processes underlies the perceptual phenomenon. To the degree that it is assumed that an isomorphism implies a shared mechanism, it remains an independent issue as to where in the cognitive architecture that shared mechanism is to be located.

Alternatively, there is the possibility that at the level(s) of representation sufficient to process the perceptual input and motor output correctly, perceptual and motor processes are functionally distinct. In other words, it could be the case that visual perception and motor production are subject to analytically identical, but functionally distinct, constraints.

Neuropsychological data play an important role in constraining embodied and disembodied theories of cognition. The neuropsychological approach is powerful because it can be used to establish causal inferences regarding the organisation and representation of cognitive processes. Of course, however, the neuropsychological approach, as all approaches, is not without its limitations. One potential limitation relevant to the issues discussed herein concerns the possibility that the ways in which the mind/brain successfully completes a given task under conditions of damage may involve processing steps that are not implicated as necessary processing steps under normal (i.e., undamaged) conditions. This possibility has important implications for determining the minimal computations (i.e., the relevant level(s) of analysis) that are necessarily required in order to successfully complete a given task. Notwithstanding such potential limitations (see Caramazza, 1992, for discussion), the neuropsychological approach, in concert with functional neuroimaging and neurophysiological methodologies, can support strong inferences about the principles that govern the organisation and representation of cognitive processes.

It has also been our intention to highlight the importance of the embodied cognition hypothesis and, in particular, the notion that simulation may play an important role in many cognitive processes. In one sense, perception must ultimately be *for* action, in that it is only action that allows an organism to interact, and ultimately survive and reproduce. The simulation hypothesis is a very important proposal, and is fruitfully pursued at first in its strongest form. Careful consideration of the strong version of the embodied cognition hypothesis opens up important questions. For instance, it is an open issue as to what the role of simulation is in a theory of action recognition and understanding. Clearly, there is rich evidence from functional neuroimaging and neurophysiology suggesting that simulation plays an important role. Balancing the neuroimaging and neurophysiology data against the patterns of dissociation observed with the neuropsychological approach is, we believe, a profitable strategy towards understanding the role of simulation in the representation of conceptual knowledge.

PrEview proof published online 16 March 2005

REFERENCES

Adolphs, R. (2003). Cognitive neuroscience of human social behaviour. *Nature Reviews Neuroscience*, *4*, 165–178.

Allport, D. A. (1985). Distributed memory, modular subsystems and dysphasia. In S.K. Newman & R. Epstein (Eds.), *Current perspectives in dysphasia*. New York: Churchill Livingstone.

Aristotle. (1992). *Introduction to Aristotle* (Ed. by Richard McKeon). New York: The Modern Library.

Baldissera, F., Cavallari, P., Craighero, L., & Fadiga, L. (2001). Modulation of spinal excitability during observation of hand actions in humans. *European Journal of Neuroscience*, *13*, 190–194.

Barsalou, L. W., Simmons, W. K., Barbey, A. K., & Wilson, C. D. (2003). Grounding conceptual knowledge in the modality-specific systems. *Trends in Cognitive Sciences*, *7*, 84–91.

Bartolo, A., Cubelli, R., Della Sala, S., Drei, S., & Marchetti, C. (2001). Double dissociation between meaningful and meaningless gesture reproduction in apraxia. *Cortex*, *37*, 696–699.

Bell, B. D. (1994). Pantomime recognition impairment in aphasia: An analysis of error types. *Brain and Language*, *47*, 269–278.

Bergego, C., Pradat-Diehl, P., & Deloche, G. (1992). Apraxie idéatorie et reconnaissance de l'utilisation des objets. *Revue de Neuropschologie*, *2*, 193–206.

Blakemore, S. J., & Decety, J. (2001). From the perception of action to the understanding of intention. *Nature Reviews Neuroscience*, *2*, 561–567.

Bremmer, F., Schlack, A., Shah, N. J., Zafiris, O., Kubischik, M., Hoffmann, K.-P., Zilles, K., & Fink, G. R. (2001). Polymodal motion processing in posterior parietal and premotor cortex. A human fMRI study strongly implies equivalencies between humans and monkeys. *Neuron*, *29*, 287–296.

Buccino, G., Binkofski, F., Fink, G. R., Fadiga, L., Fogassi, L., Gallese, V., Seitz, R. J., Zilles, K., Rizzolatti, G., & Freund, H. J. (2001). Action observation activates premotor and parietal areas in a somatotopic manner: An fMRI study. *European Journal of Neuroscience*, *13*, 400–404.

Buxbaum, L. J., & Saffran, E. M. (2002). Knowledge of object manipulation and object function: Dissociations in apraxic and non-apraxic subjects. *Brain and Language*, *82*, 179–199.

Buxbaum, L. J., Sirigu, A., Schwartz, M. F., & Klatzky, R. (2003). Cognitive representations of hand posture in ideomotor apraxia. *Neuropsychologia*, *41*, 1091–1113.

Buxbaum, L. J., Veramonti, T., & Schwartz, M. F. (2000). Function and manipulation tool knowledge in apraxia: Knowing "what for" but not "how." *Neurocase*, *6*, 83–97.

Caramazza, A. (1992). Is cognitive neuropsychology possible? *Journal of Cognitive Neuroscience*, *4*, 80–95.

Caramazza, A., Hillis, A. E., Rapp, B. C., & Romani, C. (1990). The multiple semantics hypothesis: Multiple confusions? *Cognitive Neuropsychology*, *7*, 161–189.

Caramazza, A., & Mahon, B. Z. (in press). The organization of conceptual knowledge in the brain: The future's past and some future directions. *Cognitive Neuropsychology.*

Cubelli, R., Marchetti, C., Boscolo, G., & Della Sala, S. (2000). Cognition in action: Testing a model of limb apraxia. *Brain and Cognition*, *44*, 144–165.

de'Sperati, C., & Viviani, P. (1997). The relationship between curvature and velocity in two-dimensional smooth pursuit eye movements. *Journal of Neuroscience*, *17*, 3932–3945.

Donnenwerth-Nolan, S., Tanenhaus, M. K., & Seidenberg, M. S. (1981). Multiple code activation in word recognition: Evidence from rhyme monitoring. *Journal of Experimental Psychology: Human Learning and Memory*, *7*, 170–180.

Dumont, C., & Ska, B. (2000). Pantomime recognition impairment in Alzheimer's Disease. *Brain and Cognition*, *43*, 177–181.

Dumont, C., Ska, B., & Joanette, Y. (2000). Conceptual apraxia and semantic memory deficit in Alzheimer's disease: Two sides of the same coin? *Journal of International Neuropsychological Society*, *6*, 693–703.

Dumont, C., Ska, B., & Schiavetto, A. (1999). Selective impairment of transitive gestures: An unusual case of apraxia. *Neurocase*, *5*, 447–458.

Edwards, M. G., Humphreys, G. W., & Castiello, U. (2003). Motor facilitation following action observation: A behavioural study in prehensile action. *Brain and Cognition*, *53*, 495–502.

Fadiga L., & Craighero L., (2003). New insights on sensorimotor integration: From hand action to speech perception *Brain and Cognition*, *53*, 514–524.

Fadiga, L., Fogassi, L., Pavesi, G., & Rizzolatti, G. (1995). Motor facilitation during action observation: A magnetic stimulation study. *Journal of Neurophysiology*, *73*, 2608–2611.

Feldman, J., & Narayanan, S. (2003). Embodied meaning in a neural theory of language. *Brain and Language*, *89*, 385–392.

Fitch, W. T., Hauser, M. D., & Chomsky, N. (in press). Evolution of the language faculty: Clarifications and implications. *Cognition.*

Fodor, J. A. (1983). *The modularity of mind.* Cambridge MA: MIT Press.

Gallese, V., Fadiga, L., Fogassi, L., & Rizzolatti, G. (1996). Action recognition in the premotor cortex. *Brain*, *119*, 593–609.

Gallese, V., & Goldman, A. (1998). Mirror neurons and the simulation theory of mind reading. *Trends in Cognitive Sciences*, *2*, 493–501.

Gallese, V., & Lakoff, G. (2005). The brain's concepts: The role of the sensory-motor system in conceptual knowledge. *Cognitive Neuropsychology*, *22*, 455–479.

Garbarini, F., & Adenzato, M. (2004). At the root of embodied cognition: Cognitive science meets neurophysiology. *Brain and Cognition*, *56*, 100–106.

Goldenberg, G., & Hagmann, S. (1997). The meaning of meaningless gestures: A study of visuo-imitative apraxia. *Neuropsychologia*, *35*, 333–341.

Goodale, M. A., Milner, A. D., Jakobson, L. S., & Carey, D. P. (1991). A neurological dissociation between perceiving objects and grasping them. *Nature*, *349*, 154–156.

Grèzes, J., & Decety, J. (2001). Functional anatomy of execution, mental simulation, observation, and verb generation of actions: A meta-analysis. *Human Brain Mapping*, *12*, 1–19.

Halsband, U., Schmitt, J., Weyers, M., Binkofski, F., Grützner, G., & Freund, H. J. (2001). Recognition and imitation of pantomimed motor acts after unilateral parietal and premotor lesions: A perspective on apraxia. *Neuropsychologia*, *39*, 200–216.

Hari, R., Forss, N., Avikainen, S., Kirveskari, E., Salenius, S., & Rizzolatti, G. (1998). Activation of human primary motor cortex during action observation: A neuromagnetic study. *Proceedings of the National Academy of Sciences*, *95*, 15061–15065.

Hodges, J. R., Bozeat, S., Lambon Ralph, M. A., Patterson, K., & Spatt, J. (2000). The role of conceptual knowledge in object use. Evidence from semantic dementia. *Brain*, *123*, 1913–1925.

Hodges, J. R., Spatt, J., & Patterson, K. (1999). "What" and "how": Evidence for the dissociation of object knowledge and mechanical problem-solving skills in the human brain. *Proceedings of the National Academy of Sciences, USA*, *96*, 9444–9448.

Humphreys, G. W., & Forde, E. M. (2001). Hierarchies, similarity, and interactivity in object recognition: "Category-specific" neuropsychological deficits. *Behavioural and Brain Sciences*, *24*, 453–509.

Iacoboni, M., Woods, R. P., Brass, M., Bekkering, H., Mazziotta, J. C., & Rizzolatti, G. (1999). Cortical mechanisms of human imitation. *Science*, *286*, 2526–2528.

Jeannerod, M., Decety, J., & Michel, F. (1994). Impairment of grasping movements following bilateral posterior parietal lesion. *Neuropsychologia*, *32*, 369–380.

Johnson-Frey, S.H. (2004). The neural basis of complex tool use in humans. *Trends in Cognitive Sciences*, *8*, 71–78.

Kohler, E., Keysers, C., Umiltà, M. A., Fogassi, L., Gallese, V., & Rizolatti, G. (2002). Hearing sounds, understanding actions: Action representation in mirror neurons. *Science*, *297*, 846–848.

Lacquaniti, F., Terzuolo, C., & Viviani, P. (1983). The law relating the kinematic and figural aspects of drawing movements. *Acta Psychologica*, *54*, 115–130.

Lakoff, G., & Johnson, M. (1999). *Philosophy in the flesh*. New York: Basic Books.

Liberman, A. M., Cooper, F. S., Shankweiler, D. P., & Studdert-Kennedy, M. (1967). Perception of the speech code. *Psychological Review*, *74*, 431–461.

Mahon, B. Z., & Caramazza, A. (2003). Constraining questions about the organization and representation of conceptual knowledge. *Cognitive Neuropsychology*, *20*, 433–450.

Martin, A., & Chao, L. L. (2001). Semantic memory and the brain: Structure and processes. *Current Opinion in Neurobiology*, *11*, 194–201.

Martin, A., Ungerleider, L. G., & Haxby, J. V. (2000). Category specificity and the brain: The Sensory/Motor Model of Semantic Representations of Objects. In M. S. Gazzaniga (Ed.), *The new cognitive neurosciences*. Cambridge, MA: MIT Press.

Martin, A., Wiggs, C. L., Ungerleider, L. G., & Haxby, J. V. (1996). Neural correlates of category-specific knowledge. *Nature*, *379*, 649–652.

Milner, A. D., Dijkerman, H. C., Pisella, L. McIntosh, R. D., Tilikete, C., Vighetto, A., & Rossetti, Y. (2001). Grasping the past: Delay can improve visuomotor performance. *Current Biology*, *11*, 1896–1901.

Milner, A. D., Perrett, D. I., Johnson, R. S., Benson, O. J., Jordan, T. R., Heeley, D. W., Bettucci, D., Mortara, F., Mutani, R., Terazzi, E., & Davidson, D. L. W. (1991). Perception and action "visual form agnosia." *Brain*, *114*, 405–428.

Montomura, N., & Yamadori, A. (1994). A case of ideational apraxia with impairment of object use and preservation of object pantomime. *Cortex*, *30*, 167–170.

Moreaud, O., Charnallet, A., & Pellat, J. (1998). Identification without manipulation: A study of the relations between object use and semantic memory. *Neuropsychologia*, *36*, 1295–1301.

Mozaz, M., Rothi, L. J. G., Anderson, J. M., Crucian, G. P., & Heilman, K. M. (2002). Postural knowledge of transitive and pantomimes and intransitive gestures. *Journal of the International Neuropsychological Society*, *8*, 958–962.

Muneaux, M., & Ziegler, J. C. (2004). Locus of orthographic effects in spoken word recognition: Novel insights from the neighborhood generation task. *Language and Cognitive Processes*, *19*, 641–660.

Negri, G. A. L., Lunardelli, A., Gigli, G. L., & Rumiati, R. I. (in press). Degraded semantic knowledge and accurate object use in semantic dementia. *Cortex*.

Ochipa, C., Rothi, L. J. G., & Heilman, K. M. (1989). Ideational apraxia: A deficit in tool selection and use. *Annals of Neurology*, *25*, 190–193.

Oliveri, M., Finocchiaro, C., Shapiro, K., Gangitano, M., Caramazza, A., & Pascual-Leone, A. (2004). All talk and no action: A transcranial magnetic stimulation study of motor cortex activation during action word production. *Journal of Cognitive Neuroscience*, *16*, 374–381.

Pinker, S., & Jackendoff, R. (2005). The faculty of language: What's special about it? *Cognition*, *95*, 201–236.

Plaut, D. C. (2002). Granted modality-specific specialization in semantics: A computational account of optic aphasia. *Congnitive Neuropsychology*, *19*, 603–639.

Pulvermuller, F. (2001). Brain reflections of words and their meaning. *Trends in Cognitive Sciences*, *5*, 517–524.

Rapcsak, S. Z., Ochipa, C., Anderson, K. C., & Poizner, H. (1995). Progressive ideomotor apraxia: Evidence for a selective impairment of the action production system. *Brain and Cognition*, *27*, 213–236.

Rizzolatti, G., Fogassi, L., & Gallese, V. (2001). Neurophysiological mechanisms underlying the understanding and imitation of action. *Nature Review Neuroscience*, *2*, 661–670.

Rosci, C., Valentina, C., Laiacona, M., & Capitani, E. (2003). Apraxia is not associated to a disproportionate naming impairment for manipulable objects. *Brain and Cognition*, *53*, 412–415.

Rothi, L. J. G., Mack, L., & Heilman, K. M. (1986). Pantomime agnosia. *Journal of Neurology, Neurosurgery, and Psychiatry*, *49*, 451–454.

Rothi, L. J. G., Ochipa, C., & Heilman, K. M. (1991). A cognitive neuropsychological model of limb praxis. *Cognitive Neuropsychology*, *8*, 443–458.

Rumiati, R. I., & Bekkering, H. (2003). To imitate or not to imitate? How the brain can do it, that is the question! *Brain and Cognition*, *53*, 479–482.

Rumiati, R. I., Zanini, S., Vorano, L., & Shallice, T. (2001). A form of ideational apraxia as a selective deficit of contention scheduling. *Cognitive Neuropsychology*, *18*, 617–642.

Schwartz, R. I., Barrett, A. M., Crucian, G. P., & Heilman, K. M. (1998). Dissociation of gesture and object recognition. *Neurology*, *50*, 1186–1188.

Schwartz, M. F., Montgomery, M. W., Fitzpatrick-DeSalme, E. J., Ochipa, C., Coslett, H. B., & Mayer, N. H. (1995). Analysis of a disorder of everyday action. *Cognitive Neuropsychology*, *12*, 863–892.

Seidenberg, M. S., & Tanenhaus, M. K. (1979). Orthographic effects on rhyme monitoring. *Journal of Experimental Psychology: Human Learning and Memory*, *5*, 546–554.

Shiffrar, M., & Freyd, J. J. (1990). Apparent motion of the human body. *Psychological Science*, *1*, 257–264.

Sirigu, A., Duhamel, J., & Poncet, M. (1991). The role of sensorimotor experience in object recognition. *Brain*, *114*, 2555–2573.

Tanenhaus, M. K., Flanigan, H. P., & Seidenberg, M. S. (1980). Orthographic and phonological activation in auditory and visual word recognition. *Memory and Cognition*, *8*, 513–520.

Tettamanti, M., Buccino, G., Saccuman, M. C., Gallese, V., Danna, M., Scifo, P., Fazio, F., Rizzolatti, G., Cappa, S. F., & Perani, D. (2005). Listening to action-related sentences activates fronto-parietal motor circuits. *Journal of Cognitive Neuroscience*, *17*, 273–281.

Tyler, L. K., & Moss, H. E. (2001). Towards a distributed account of conceptual knowledge. *Trends in Cognitive Science*, *5*, 244–252.

Viviani, P., Baud-Bovy, G., & Redolfi, M. (1997). Perceiving and tracking kinesthetic stimuli: Further evidence of motor-perceptual interactions. *Journal of Experimental Psychology: Human Perception and Performance*, *23*, 1232–1252.

Viviani, P., & Stucchi, N. (1989). The effect of movement velocity on form perception: Geometric illusions in dynamic displays. *Perception and Psychophysics*, *46*, 266–274.

Viviani, P., & Stucchi, N. (1992). Biological movements look uniform: Evidence of motor-perceptual interactions. *Journal of Experimental Psychology: Human Perception and Performance*, *18*, 603–623.

Warrington, E. K., & McCarthy, R. (1983). Category specific access dysphasia. *Brain*, *106*, 859–878.

Warrington, E. K., & McCarthy, R. (1987) Categories of knowledge: Further fractionations and an attempted integration. *Brain*, *110*, 1273–1296.

Warrington, E. K., & Shallice, T. (1984). Category-specific semantic impairment. *Brain*, *107*, 829–854.

COGNITIVE NEUROPSYCHOLOGY, 2005, 22 (3/4), 495–496

SUBJECT INDEX

For Product Safety Concerns and Information please contact our EU
representative GPSR@taylorandfrancis.com
Taylor & Francis Verlag GmbH, Kaufingerstraße 24, 80331 München, Germany

www.ingramcontent.com/pod-product-compliance
Ingram Content Group UK Ltd.
Pitfield, Milton Keynes, MK11 3LW, UK
UKHW050755180926
475701UK00007B/1068
9781138878013